EXCEL

Work like a pro with Excel 5

For Windows

Anne Prince

Mike Murach & Associates

4697 West Jacquelyn Avenue, Fresno, California 93722-6427
(209) 275-3335

Managing editor:	Mike Murach
Graphics designer:	Steve Ehlers
Other books for Excel users:	Excel 5: Lists, Pivot Tables & External Databases
	The Essential Guide: Excel 5.0 for Windows
Other books for Windows users:	Work Like a Pro with Word 6 for Windows
	Word 6 for Windows: How to use the Mail Merge Feature
	The Essential Guide: Word 6.0 for Windows
	The Essential Guide: WordPerfect 6.0 for Windows
	The Essential Guide: 1-2-3 for Windows Release 4
	The Least You Need to Know about Windows 3.1

© 1995, Mike Murach & Associates, Inc.

All rights reserved.

Printed in the United States of America.

10 9 8 7 6 5 4 3 2 1

ISBN: 0-911625-89-5

Library of Congress Cataloging-in-Publication Data

Prince, Anne.
    Work like a pro with Excel 5 / Anne Prince.
      p.   cm.
    "Excel 5 for Windows."
    Includes index.
    ISBN 0-911625-89-5 (alk. paper)
    1. Microsoft Excel for Windows. 2. Business--Computer programs.
3. Electronic spreadsheets.   I. Title.
HF5548.4.M523P757   1995
005.369--dc20
                                          95-19201
                                             CIP

Contents

Introduction		V
Prerequisites	The essential Windows skills	1
Section 1	**The essential worksheet skills**	**29**
Chapter 1	How to create, print, and save a worksheet	31
Chapter 2	How to edit a worksheet	63
Chapter 3	How to format a worksheet	87
Chapter 4	Commands and features for working with larger worksheets	115
Section 2	**The commands and features that help you work like a pro**	**141**
Chapter 5	How to work with more than one worksheet at a time	143
Chapter 6	How to create charts	169
Chapter 7	Advanced skills for working with formulas and functions	193
Chapter 8	How to set defaults, protect data, convert files, and use online Help	215
Appendix	The Excel features and commands that aren't presented in this book	235

Introduction

Ever notice how easy the best PC professionals make it look? Ask them to show you how to do something, and they do it so quickly and easily that you can't follow it. Ask them to slow down and do it again, and you wonder how they can remember all the details.

The good news is that it's surprisingly easy to become a skilled PC user. In just 240 pages, for example, this book shows you how to use Excel the way the best professionals use it. It even includes exercises that help you get started the right way. All you have to add is some practice.

5 ways this book differs from other Excel books

- Instead of showing you how to use all of the Excel commands and techniques, this book shows you how to use the 20 to 30 percent that the best professionals use all the time. That's why this book is 240 pages long instead of 1200.

- Each Excel function is presented in a single figure (illustration) that shows and summarizes everything you need to know to do that function. That's why we say that you can learn more just by paging through this book than by studying other books.

- The procedures in the figures can easily be applied to any situation you run into. In contrast, many books present procedures that apply only to specific situations. Those work fine until you want to do something a little more advanced or until Excel displays a screen that's not shown in the procedure. At that point, you'll appreciate that the procedures in this book tell you what you need to know.

- Excel often gives you several options for doing the same function. So besides showing you *how* to do each Excel function, this book also shows you the fastest way to do it. You'll soon find yourself taking just 5 minutes to do jobs that take other Excel users much longer.

- Each chapter includes practice exercises that get you started right. These exercises have you use the most efficient methods for doing each function; they encourage you to experiment with new functions; they require nothing but this book and your PC; and they are an essential part of the learning process.

Who this book is for

Because of the way the content is organized and presented, this book works for beginners as well as for experienced spreadsheet users who are upgrading or converting to Excel 5. From the start, you learn the skills of the best professionals, and that's what you need to learn whether Excel 5 is your first spreadsheet program or your fifth.

If you're a beginner, of course, it's going to take you longer to go through this book than if you have some experience. Not only will it take you longer to read the text and figures, but you should also make a point of doing all the exercises. As you will see, they often show you how easy it is to use a function or feature that may seem difficult when you first read about it.

In contrast, if you're an experienced spreadsheet user, you should be able to go through this book quite rapidly. For most functions, you'll be able to get the information you need from the figures alone. You'll also be able to do the exercises more quickly. Please don't skip the exercises, though, because they force you to use some efficient new techniques that you might otherwise overlook.

What are the prerequisites for this book? The basic Windows skills that you probably have if you've used another Windows program or if you've taken a Windows course: opening, closing, and sizing windows, moving between windows, switching between applications, and working with menus, commands, dialog boxes, directories, and files. If you don't have these skills, or you're not sure that you have them, the prerequisites chapter that follows is a crash course in Windows that presents everything you need to know.

Let us know how this book works for you

It's clear by now that Windows is here to stay, and Excel is here to stay too. In fact, with just some trivial changes, you can expect to use your Excel 5 skills for years to come. Yes, there will be new and improved versions of Excel, but they're going to work the way Excel 5 does. As a result, you may want to learn some of the new features that become available, but you won't have to re-learn your Excel 5 skills.

That's why it makes sense to master Excel 5 now, and that's why this book does everything possible to help you master it. If this book helps you work just 20 percent faster and better than you would otherwise, you'll save dozens and even hundreds of hours of Excel time during the next five years. But the best PC professionals work 100 or 150 percent faster than their peers, and this book tells you everything you need to know to become one of the best.

If you have any comments about this book, we would enjoy hearing from you. That's why there's a postage-paid comment form at the back. In particular, we'd like to know whether the methods we've used to present the material help you learn faster than others you've used. As always, our goal is not only to help you get the most from your software, but to help you do that as quickly and easily as possible.

Mike Murach
Editor

Anne Prince
Author

Prerequisites

The essential Windows skills

This chapter presents the skills that are the same for all Windows programs. That includes working with windows, starting and ending programs, using menus and commands, and opening and saving files. So if you already have experience with one or more Windows programs, you can probably skip this chapter.

If you're new to PCs or to Windows, though, you need to study this chapter carefully and do all of its exercises. Once you master the skills of this chapter, you will have the background that you need for working with any Windows program. That will make it easier for you to master Excel 5 as you learn about it in the other chapters of this book.

Throughout this book, all the examples are for Windows release 3.1. So if you're still using Windows 3.0, the screens will look somewhat different on your PC. Keep in mind, though, that the skills are the same for both releases.

If you eventually convert to the next Windows release (Windows 95), you'll see that Excel 5 still works the same with some minor differences in appearance. You will, however, start programs like Excel in a new way. These changes are summarized in the last two figures in this chapter.

An introduction to Windows 3.1 and its Program Manager
   Application and document windows
   How to perform the four basic mouse actions
   How to minimize, maximize, or restore a window
   How to move or size a window
   How to scroll through a window
   How to exit from Windows

How to start, switch between, and end applications
   How to start an application from the Program Manager
   How to switch from one application window to another
   How to exit from an application

How to work with menus and commands
   How to issue a command
   How to work with a dialog box
   Keyboard techniques for working with dialog boxes
   How to work with a dialog box that contains tabs
   How to use the Exit command

How to work with directories and files
   Paths, file names, and wildcard specifications
   An introduction to the functions of the File Manager
   How to use the standard Open command
   How to select a drive and directory in a dialog box
   How to select a file in a dialog box
   How to use the standard Save As command

How to use Windows 95 with your applications
   How to start an application
   Differences in the application window

Perspective

Summary

An introduction to Windows 3.1 and its Program Manager

When you start your PC, Windows will probably start automatically. As it starts, a logo screen is displayed followed by an hourglass that indicates that the start-up procedure is in progress. When this procedure is finished, a screen that looks something like the one in figure P-1 is displayed.

During the start-up procedure, Windows always starts at least one program called the *shell program*. On almost all Windows systems and in figure P-1, this shell program is the Program Manager. You use this program for starting your other Windows programs.

The first time you start Windows after you install it, the starting display looks like the one in figure P-1. But the starting display usually changes after that. As a result, the starting display on a PC in school or business may look quite different. On some PCs, for example, more than one program is started when you turn the PC on, so the starting display has several windows.

If Windows doesn't start automatically when you turn your PC on, you have to start it from DOS. To do that, just type *win* and press the Enter key as shown in figure P-1. Note, however, that the DOS prompt may not look exactly like the one in this figure.

If you're completely new to PCs, you may not know that DOS is the Disk Operating System that has been used to run most PCs since the early 1980s. Once you start Windows, though, you can forget about DOS.

How to start Windows from the DOS prompt

Type *win* and press the Enter key.

```
C:\>win
```

The starting Windows display right after installation

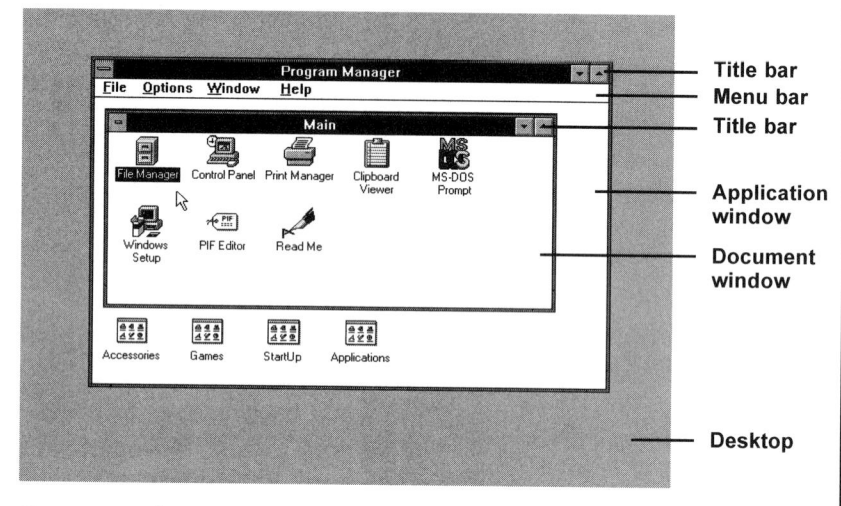

[Screenshot of Program Manager with labels: Title bar, Menu bar, Title bar, Application window, Document window, Desktop]

Concepts and terms

- On many PCs, Windows is started when you start the PC so you don't have to start it from the DOS prompt.

- A program runs in an *application window*. A *document window* provides a workspace for the program that's in the application window, and it's always within an application window.

- When you use the Program Manager, a document window is usually called a *group window* because it contains groups of programs.

- The *title bar* of an application window gives the program name. The title bar of a document window usually gives the document name.

- A *menu bar* appears only in an application window. It provides the menus that list the commands you can use with a program.

- The program that is running when you start Windows is called the *shell program*. This is usually the Program Manager as shown above.

Figure P-1 Windows concepts and terms

The essential Windows skills

Application and document windows

In figure P-1, you can see three Windows components: the *desktop*, an *application window*, and a *document window*. The desktop is just the background that the windows are displayed on. An application window contains a program (in this case, the Program Manager). And a document window provides a workspace that's used by the program.

It's easy to tell the difference between an application window and a document window because a document window is always within an application window. In addition, application windows have menu bars, but document windows don't.

When you use the Program Manager, the document windows are generally referred to as *group windows* because they contain groups of programs. When you use other programs, the document windows may be referred to by other names. When you use Excel, for example, the document windows are known as *workbook windows*.

How to perform the four basic mouse actions

Windows was designed for use with a mouse. That's why you can perform many functions more quickly with a mouse than you can with the keyboard.

To use a mouse with Windows, you need to master the four mouse actions that are summarized in figure P-2. Although these actions may seem difficult if you haven't used a mouse before, you'll quickly become adept at using them.

Action	How to do it
Point	Move the mouse so the mouse pointer is positioned on the object that you're interested in.
Click	Without moving the mouse pointer off the object you're pointing to, press and release the left mouse button so it clicks.
Double-click	Without moving the mouse pointer off the object you're pointing to, press and release the left mouse button twice in succession. Do this quickly, in less than a second.
Drag	After you point to an object, press and hold down the left mouse button, move the mouse pointer to a new location, then release the left mouse button.

Notes

- You use the left mouse button for all of the actions above. In the other chapters of this book, you'll learn some uses for the right mouse button, but there are only a few.
- If you're left-handed, you can use one of the Windows programs to change the functions of the mouse buttons so you can click the right mouse button to perform the above actions. Because you won't learn how to do that in this book, you'll need to get technical help to make this change.

Figure P-2 The four basic mouse actions

How to minimize, maximize, or restore a window

Figure P-3 shows how to *minimize*, *maximize*, or *restore* either an application or a document window. To maximize the application window in figure P-1, for example, you just click on its maximize button. Then, the window covers the entire desktop as shown in the first part of figure P-3. When you use a program like Excel, you'll work with a maximized application window most of the time. You'll also work with maximized document windows most of the time so you can see more of your work at one time.

From a maximized window, you can click on the restore button to return it to its previous size. Or, you can click on the minimize button to reduce the window to an *icon*. An icon for a minimized application window is displayed on the desktop as shown in the second part of figure P-3. In this example, four application programs have been minimized so four icons are shown on the desktop. In contrast, an icon for a minimized document window is displayed in the application window, but you'll probably never need to minimize a document window.

If you minimize a window by accident, it can be quite surprising, and novices often fear that they've lost their work when this happens. To restore the window to its previous state, however, you just need to double-click on its icon. Or, you can use the icon's *control menu* to restore or maximize the window.

The Windows display when the Program Manager is maximized and all group windows except the Main group are minimized

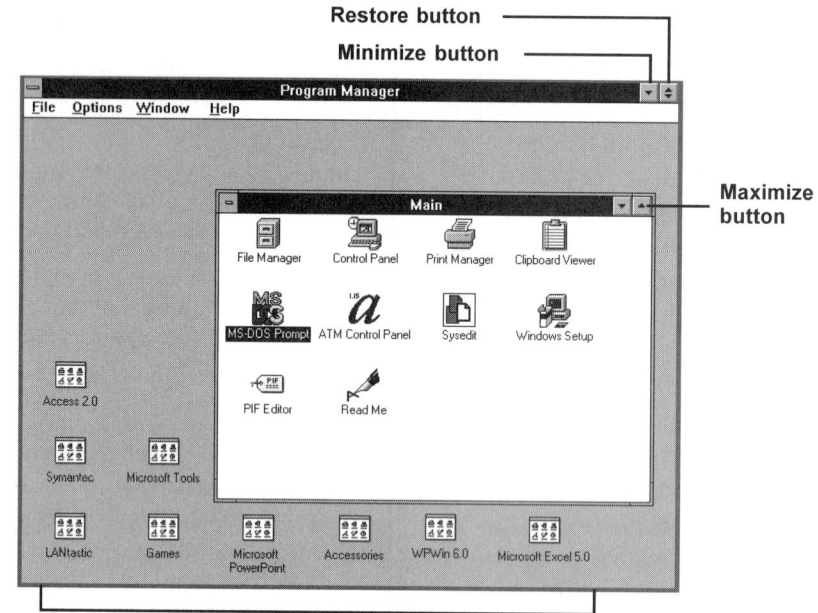

The Windows display when all application windows are minimized

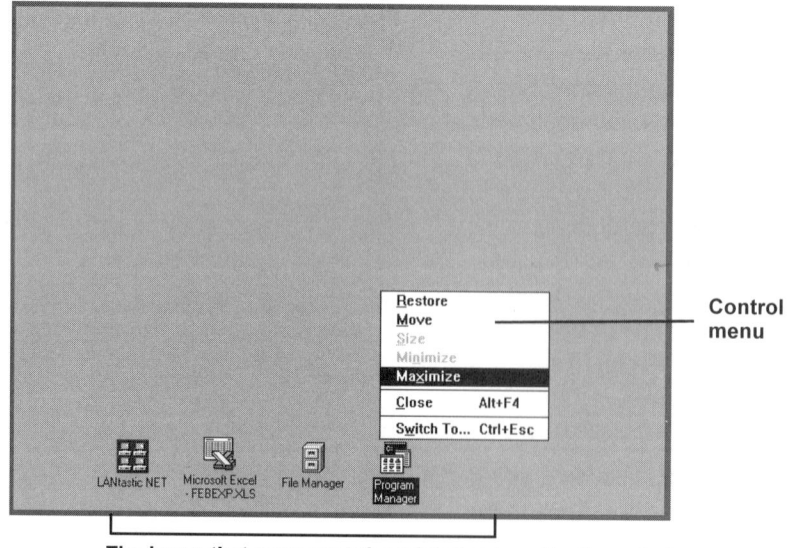

Operation

- Double-click on an icon to restore the size of a minimized window. Or, single-click on an icon to display its control menu. Then, click on Restore or Maximize in the menu.
- Click on the maximize button in a window to maximize it.
- Click on the restore button in a maximized window to return it to its previous size.

Figure P-3 How to minimize, maximize, or restore a window

How to move or size a window

When a window isn't maximized or minimized, you can move or size it as shown in figure P-4. To move a window, you just drag its title bar with the mouse. To size a window, you move the mouse pointer over a border or corner until its normal arrow shape changes to a double-headed arrow. Then, you drag the border or corner until the window is the size you want.

When will you want to move or size a window? Only for special circumstances. Sometimes, for example, you will want to move a window so you can see what's behind it. Sometimes, you will want to size and move windows so you can arrange two or more on the screen at the same time.

How to move a window

1. Place the mouse pointer over the window's title bar and drag it. As you drag, an outline appears to let you know where the window will be moved to:

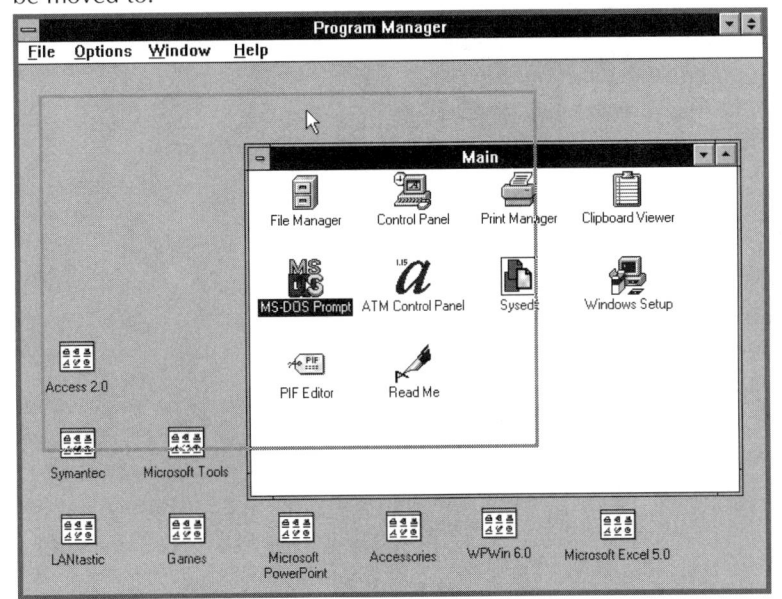

2. Release the mouse button and the window is moved to the new location.

How to size a window

1. Move the mouse pointer over the side or corner of a window until it changes to a double headed arrow. Then, drag the side or corner to increase or decrease the size of the window. As you drag, an outline appears to show you what the new size will be:

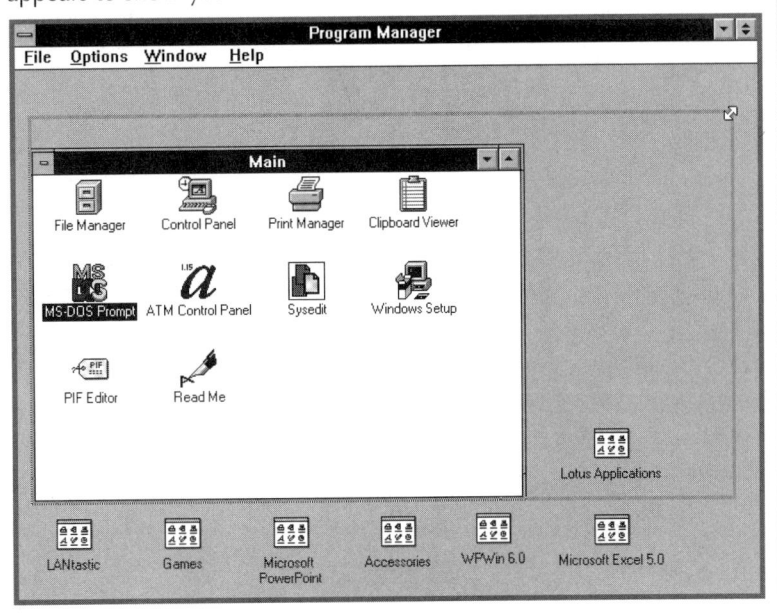

2. Release the mouse button and the window is changed to the new size.

Figure P-4 How to move or size a window

How to scroll through a window

If a window is too small to show all of its contents, *scroll bars* are automatically added to it. Then, you can use the mouse to scroll through the contents of the window as summarized in figure P-5. By clicking on the *scroll arrows* or scroll bar, you can scroll in small or large increments. By dragging the *scroll box* a distance that's relative to the entire scroll bar, you can scroll the contents of the window a proportional amount. If you experiment with these controls, you'll quickly see how easy they are to use.

A window with a vertical scroll bar

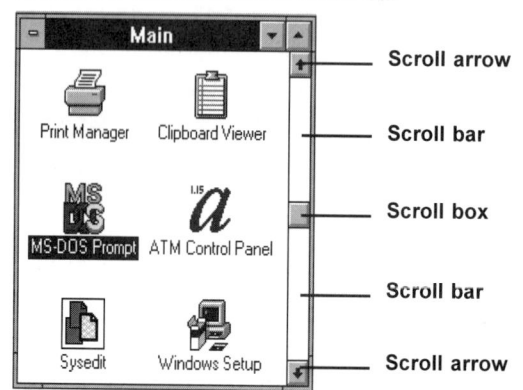

— Scroll arrow
— Scroll bar
— Scroll box
— Scroll bar
— Scroll arrow

How to use the vertical scroll bar

- Click on the up or down scroll arrow to scroll up or down in small increments. Press and hold the left mouse button on the up or down scroll arrow to scroll up or down continuously.

- Click on the scroll bar above or below the scroll box to scroll up or down in larger increments.

- Drag the scroll box up or down in the scroll bar to move to that relative position in the window's contents. If, for example, you drag the scroll box halfway down the scroll bar, the contents of the window are scrolled to their halfway point.

How to use a horizontal scroll bar

- When a horizontal scroll bar is displayed, you can scroll left or right to review the contents of a window. The horizontal scroll bar has the same components as the vertical scroll bar, and you use them the same way. The only difference is that the movement is left and right instead of up and down.

Figure P-5   How to scroll through a document window

How to exit from Windows

To exit from Windows and return to DOS, you can use the control menu for the Program Manager's window as shown in figure P-6. Since the Program Manager is the shell program, closing its window also closes the windows for all other programs. If any of your work hasn't been saved, however, Windows displays a dialog box that gives you a chance to save it.

Although you shouldn't really have to exit from Windows before you turn your PC off, it's still a recommended practice. That way, you can be sure that you've saved all your work. You can also be sure that Windows does whatever housekeeping it needs to do at the end of a work session.

The Program Manager with its control menu displayed

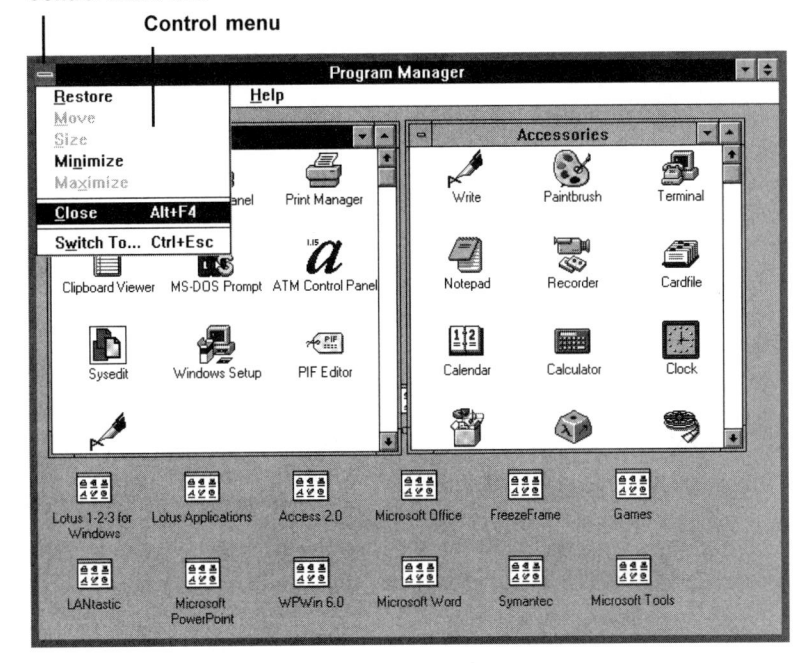

Two ways to exit from Windows

- Double-click on the control-menu box for the Program Manager's window.

- Single-click on the control-menu box for the Program Manager's window to display the control menu. Then, click on Close in the menu.

Notes

- Technically, a control menu applies to a window, not to the program or document in the window. When you close any application window, though, its program ends.

- When you close the application window for the Windows Program Manager, all programs are ended and you are returned to the DOS prompt. Before this happens, though, Windows displays a dialog box that gives you a chance to cancel the operation. Also, if you haven't saved all of the work that you did with other programs, dialog boxes are displayed that give you a chance to save the work.

- You can also use a control menu to restore, move, size, minimize, and maximize a window (see the options in the menu above). However, you can do these functions more quickly by using the mouse techniques that you've already learned.

Figure P-6 How to exit from Windows

Exercise set P-1

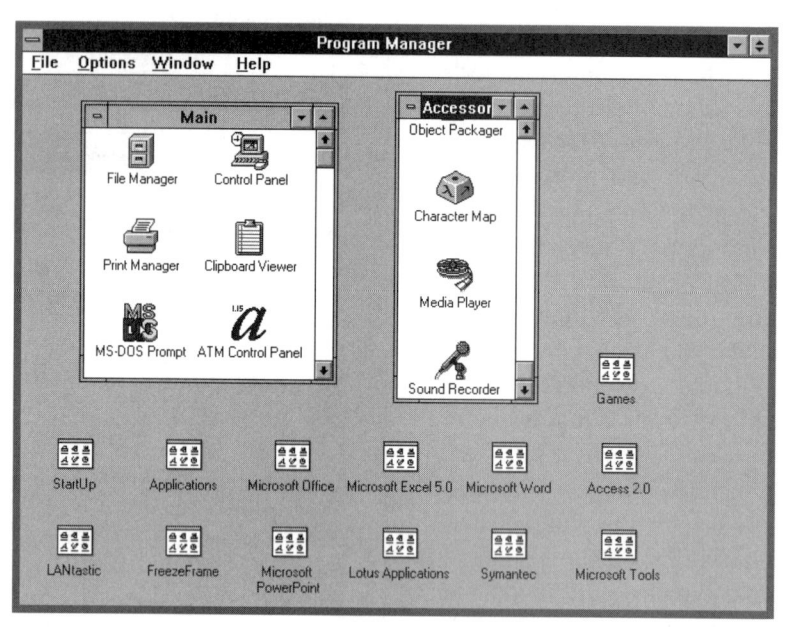

How the Program Manager window should look after exercise 5

The exercises that follow are designed to get you started with Windows and give you some practice with the four basic mouse actions.

1. Start your PC. Does Windows start automatically? If not, start Windows from DOS as shown in figure P-1. Is the Program Manager displayed when the start-up procedure finishes?

2. Minimize all of the application windows as shown in figure P-3. How many programs are running besides the Program Manager (if any)? Then, restore the window for the Program Manager, and maximize it if it isn't maximized already.

3. Minimize all of the group windows that are open (if any). Then, restore the Main group window, maximize it, and restore it again.

4. Move the Main group window to the upper left corner of the Program Manager window as shown in figure P-4. Next, enlarge it as shown in this figure by dragging the lower right corner of the window. Then, decrease the width of the window to two icons by dragging its right edge, and decrease the height of the window to three icons by dragging its top or bottom. Last, maximize the window, and restore it again. Note that the window gets restored to its new size and location.

5. Open the Accessories window, size it so it's one icon wide and three deep, and move it so it doesn't overlap the Main group window. Then, use the scroll bar to scroll through it's contents: click on the down arrow until you reach the last icon in the window; drag the scroll box to the top of the scroll bar so the first icon is displayed; and click on the scroll bar until you reach the last icon again.

6. Click on the control-menu box for the Accessories group window. Next, click on Close to close the window. This is the same as minimizing the window. Then, double-click on the Accessories icon to restore the window. Is it restored to the same size and location that it was last in?

7. Click on the control-menu box for the Program Manager's application window so the window's control menu is displayed. Note that the next to last command is Close. Don't issue that command now, or the Program Manager will end and you'll be returned to DOS. Instead, click outside the menu to remove it from the screen.

How to start, switch between, and end applications

One of the benefits that you get from using Windows is that you can run more than one program at the same time. This is referred to as *multitasking*. After you use the Program Manager to start the programs that you want to use, you can use Windows techniques to switch from one to the other.

How to start an application from the Program Manager

When you use Windows, your programs are referred to as *applications*. To start any Windows application, you can use the Program Manager as shown in figure P-7. In step 1, you double-click on a *program group icon* to open a group window. In step 2, you double-click on the *program icon* for the program you want to start.

When you use an application like Excel, the program icon is likely to be in the *program group* for Microsoft Office as shown in figure P-7. If it's not there, it will probably be in a group that contains other programs that are related to it. Once you find the group icon, open its window, and double-click on the program icon, the application is started in a new application window and you are switched to that window.

The Program Manager with three group windows open

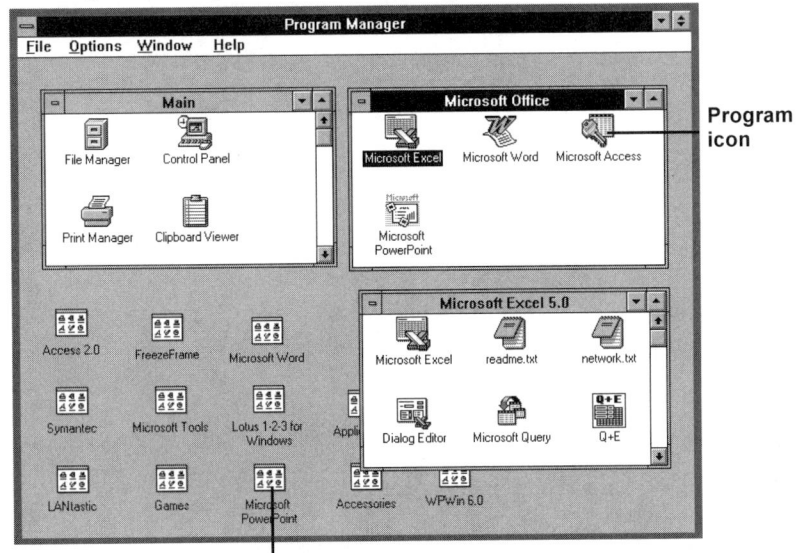

Procedure

1. Double-click on the program group icon for the program group that contains the icon for the program you want to start. This opens a group window.
2. Double-click on the program icon for the program that you want to start. Or, click on the icon to highlight it, and press the Enter key.

Notes

- When you use Windows, a program is usually referred to as an *application*.
- When an application starts, an application window is opened for it, and you are switched to that window.
- It's possible that the icon for an application will be in two or more group windows. In the example above, the Microsoft Excel icon is in both the Microsoft Office and the Microsoft Excel 5.0 windows.

Figure P-7 How to start an application

How to switch from one application window to another

Although several applications can be running at one time when you use Windows, you can only work with one program at a time. That program is called the *active program*, and it runs in the *active application window*. If several application windows are displayed at the same time because the windows aren't maximized, the active window is always the one on top, and the title bar of the active program is always highlighted.

To switch from one application to another, you can use the techniques in figure P-8. Of these, Alt+Tab switching is probably easiest to use, so it's the technique that we recommend. If you're interested, though, you can experiment with the other techniques to see whether you prefer one of them.

How to exit from an application

One way to exit from an application is to close its window, just as you close the window for the Program Manager when you want to exit from Windows. To close a window, you can double-click on the control-menu box for the window or choose Close in the control menu itself. In the next topic, you'll learn another way to exit from an application.

The application window for Microsoft Excel with the Alt+Tab panel displayed over it

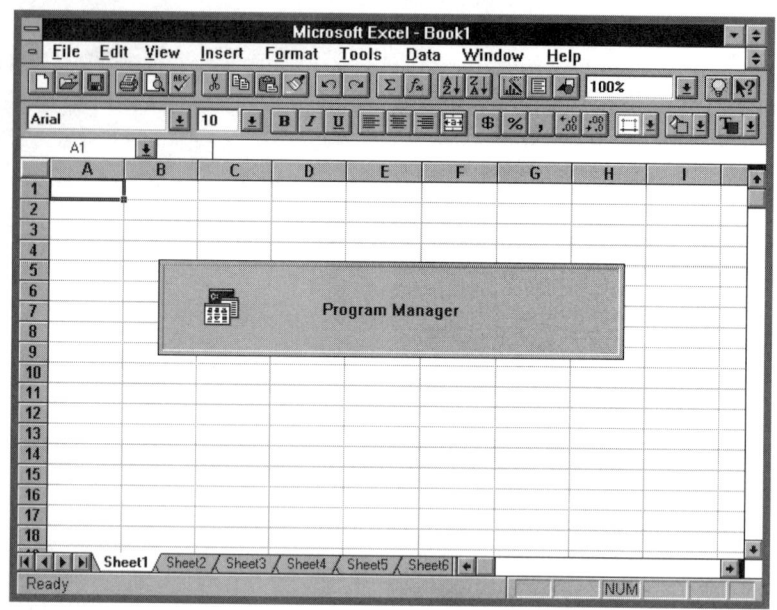

How to use Alt+Tab switching

1. Hold down the Alt key and press the Tab key to display a panel that indicates the next application in sequence.

2. If that isn't the application that you want to switch to, press the Tab key again while you continue to hold down the Alt key. When the box displays the name of the application that you want to switch to, release the Alt key.

Four more ways to switch from one application to another

- If two or more application windows are displayed at the same time, click on any part of the window you want to switch to.
- Press Alt+Esc to move to the next application in sequence.
- Minimize all application windows. Then, double-click on the icon for the application that you want to switch to.
- Use the Switch To command in the control menu for the application window or press Ctrl+Esc to display a Task List. Then, double-click on the name of the program that you want to switch to.

Note

- It's possible (but unlikely) that someone has turned the option for Alt+Tab switching off on your PC. Then, you can use one of the other methods to switch from one program to another. Later, when you learn more about Windows, you can turn the option back on.

Figure P-8   How to switch from one application to another

Exercise set P-2

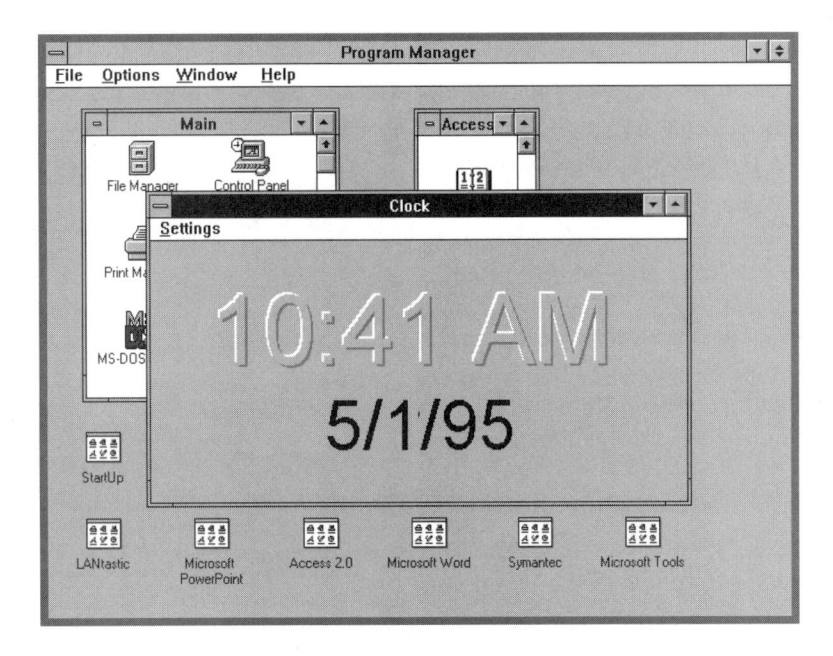

How your screen should look after you start the clock in exercise 4

This exercise set is designed to give you some experience with starting programs, switching between them, and ending them. For the time being, don't worry about what the programs do. Just concentrate on the starting, switching, and ending techniques.

1. If your PC is the way you left it at the end of the last exercise set, the Program Manager is the active application window and the Main and Accessories windows are open. If that's not the case, minimize all application windows, maximize the Program Manager window, minimize all group windows, and restore the Main and Accessories windows.

2. Use the technique shown in figure P-7 to start Excel, and maximize its window if it's not already maximized. At least two applications are now running at the same time.

3. Use Alt+Tab switching to switch to the Program Manager as shown in figure P-8. Use it again to switch to Excel. Then, use Alt+Esc to switch to the Program Manager.

4. Start the File Manager, which is one of the applications in the Main group. Switch back to the Program Manager, and start the Clock, which is one of the applications in the Accessories group. Next, use Alt+Tab switching to switch to Excel, and use it again to switch to the File Manager. Then, use Alt+Esc to switch back to Excel.

5. Minimize all of the application windows. Next, switch to Excel by restoring its window. Then, minimize its application window, and switch to the Clock by restoring its window.

6. Exit from the Clock program by double-clicking on the control-menu box for its application window. Next, exit from the File Manager and Excel by popping up their control menus from their minimized application windows and clicking on Close. Then, double-click on the Program Manager icon to restore it to its previous size.

How to work with menus and commands

Another benefit that you get from using Windows is that all Windows applications use a standard interface. In particular, the techniques that you use for accessing menus and issuing commands are the same in all Windows applications. So if you know how to use menus, commands, and dialog boxes in one Windows application, you know how to use them in all applications. These standard techniques are presented next.

How to issue a command

Figure P-9 shows how to issue a *command* from one of the *menus* that you can pull down from the menu bar for an application. These menus are sometimes called *program menus* or *application menus* to distinguish them from control menus, but that usually isn't necessary. As you can see, you can use either mouse or keyboard techniques to issue a command, and both are efficient. You can also combine mouse and keyboard techniques as you issue commands.

When you use Excel, you'll see that some menu choices lead to other menus, called *submenus*. If, for example, you choose Column in the Format menu, a submenu is displayed. To issue a command from a submenu, just continue the techniques that got you to the submenu.

Two ways to issue a command with the mouse

- Click on the menu name in the menu bar to pull the menu down, then click on the command name:

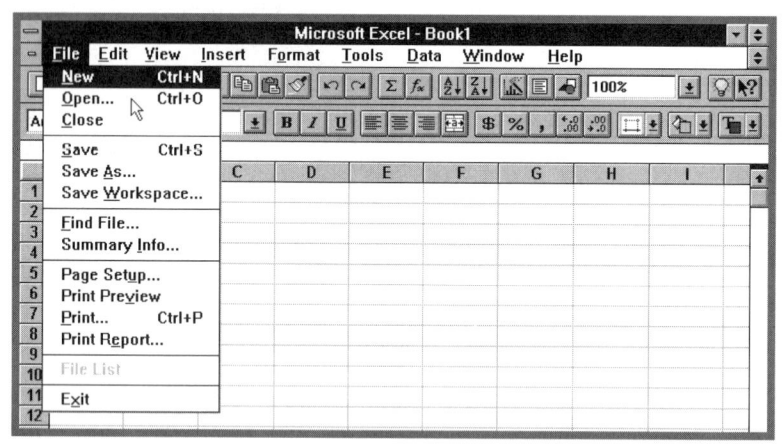

- Press and hold the mouse button on the menu name in the menu bar to pull the menu down. Then, drag the highlight from the menu name to the command you want to issue and release the mouse button.

Two ways to issue a command from the keyboard

- Press Alt to activate the menu bar; press the underlined letter in the menu that you want to pull down; and press the underlined letter in the command that you want to issue.

- Press Alt to activate the menu bar; press the right arrow key to highlight the menu you want and press the Enter key; press the down arrow key to highlight the command you want and press the Enter key.

How to close a menu without issuing a command

- With the mouse, click anywhere outside the menu, or drag the highlight off the menu. With the keyboard, press the Esc key twice.

How to issue a command from a submenu

- Click on the command, continue to drag from the menu to the submenu command before releasing the mouse button, or use keyboard techniques:

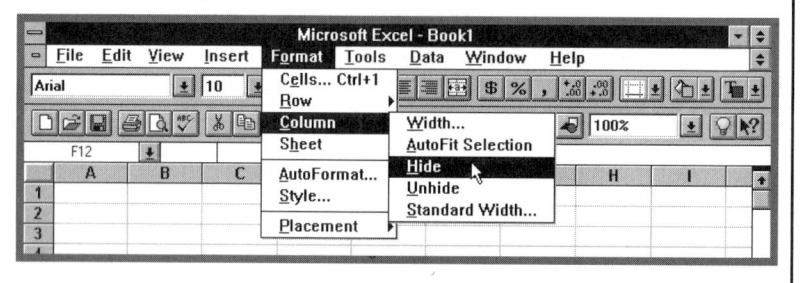

Figure P-9   How to issue a command from a pull-down menu

How to work with a dialog box

If you look at the menus in figure P-9, you can see that some menu items are followed by three dots (...). This means that a *dialog box* is displayed by the command before the command is run. Then, to complete the command, you must fill in the dialog box.

Figure P-10 summarizes the basic techniques for working with dialog box controls. If you use a mouse, you'll find that it's easy to change controls like *option buttons*, *spin boxes*, and *check boxes*. You'll also find that it's easy to choose an item from a *list box*, drop down a list from a *text box* and choose an item from the list, and to start the command that's represented by a *command button*. When you've got everything in a dialog box set the way you want it, you can start the command by clicking on the OK button. The dialog box in figure P-10 illustrates all of these controls except for a list box. You'll see a list box later in this chapter when you learn how to use the Open command.

Often, a dialog box is set the way you want it when it's first displayed. For instance, the Print dialog box in figure P-10 is ready for use if you want to print all the pages in a Word document. Then, if the OK button has a dark outline as it does in this example, you can start the command by pressing the Enter key.

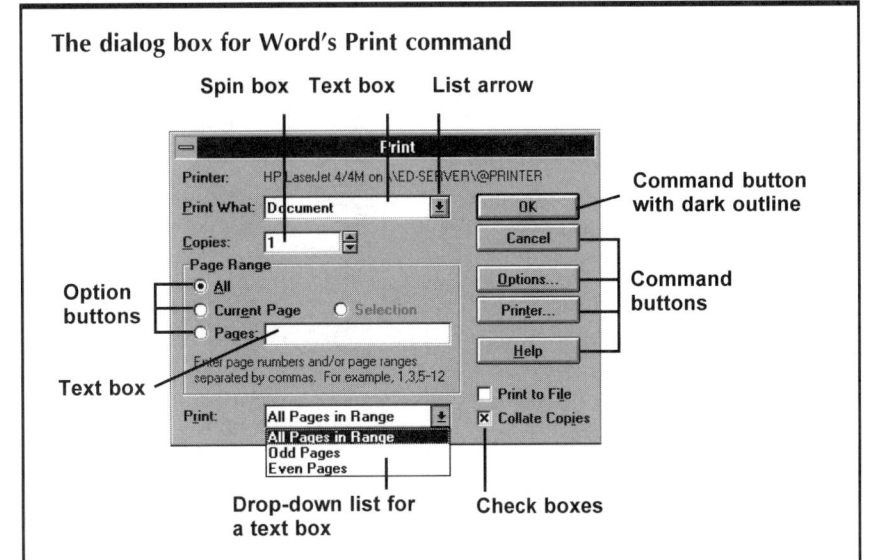

The dialog box for Word's Print command

Control	Operation
Command button	Click on the button to issue the command. Or, press the Enter key to issue the command for the button that has the focus on it.
Text box	To move the highlight to a text box, click in it; then, type an entry in the box. Or, if there's a list arrow to the right of the box, click on it to drop down a list of options; then, click on the option that you want.
List box	Click on the option that you want.
Check box	Click on a box to check it (turn an option on) or uncheck it (turn an option off).
Spin box	To move the highlight to a spin box, click in it; then, type a value in the box. Or, click on the up or down arrow to the right of the box to increase or decrease the value that's displayed in the box.
Option button	Click on the button for the option you want. This turns off the other buttons in the group.

How to start a command when all the controls are set up right

Click on the OK button. Or, if the OK button has a dark outline as it does in the example above, press the Enter key.

How to cancel a command and remove the dialog box from the screen

Press the Esc key or click on the Cancel button.

Figure P-10 How to work with a dialog box

Keyboard techniques for working with dialog boxes

For most people, using the mouse is the most efficient way to work with dialog boxes. If you prefer to use the keyboard, though, you can use the techniques presented in figure P-11.

Before you can use the keyboard to change a control setting, you have to move the *focus* to it. To do that, you can use the techniques shown at the start of figure P-11. Then, you can use the remaining techniques to change the setting.

Sometimes, it's difficult to tell which control has the focus on it so you have to look closely for it. If, for example, an option button or check box has the focus, that's indicated by a light dotted line around the option or box name. In contrast, the focus on a text box is indicated by the insertion point or highlighting, and the focus on a command button is indicated by a dark outline.

The Print dialog box with the focus on a check box

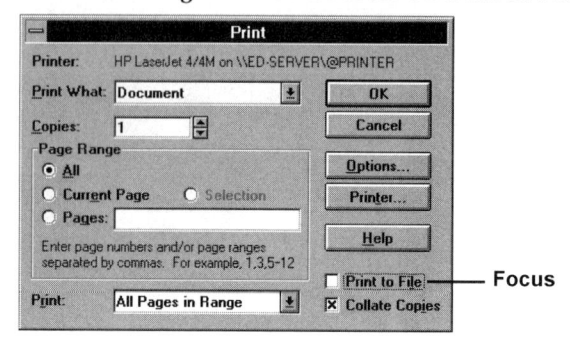

Keys for moving the focus

Key	Function
Tab	Moves the focus forward from one control to the next.
Shift+Tab	Moves the focus backward from one control to the next.
Alt+Underlined-letter	Moves the focus to the control with the underlined letter in its name. If the control is a command button, this also activates the button. If the control is a text box that has a list arrow to its right, this also drops down the list.

Keyboard techniques for working with controls

Control	Operation
Command button	Press the Enter key to activate the button.
Text box	Type the new value. Or, if the text box has a list arrow to its right, press Alt+Down-arrow to drop down the list; then, use the Down-arrow or Up-arrow key to highlight the option that you want.
List box	Use the Down-arrow or Up-arrow key to highlight the option that you want.
Check box	Press the Spacebar to turn the option on or off.
Option button	Press the arrow keys to move to another option in the group.
Spin box	Type the new value. Or press the Up-arrow or Down-arrow key to increase or decrease the value.

Figure P-11   Keyboard techniques for working with a dialog box

How to work with a dialog box that contains tabs

When you use Excel, some of the dialog boxes have *tabs* as shown in figure P-12. These tabs are often used to organize a series of options. To switch from one tab to another, just click on the tab. When you complete the command, any changes that you've made to any of the tabs are put into effect.

How to use the Exit command

To exit from a program, you can use the Exit command in the File menu. This has the same effect as double-clicking on the control-menu box for the application window.

A dialog box that contains 10 tabs with the View tab displayed

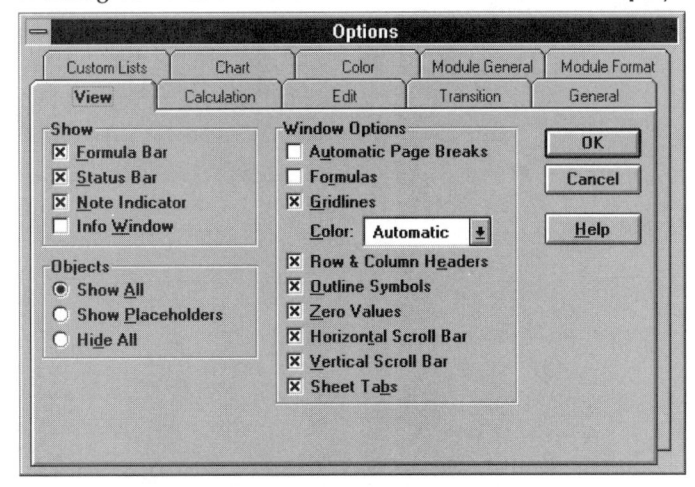

The same dialog box with the Edit tab displayed

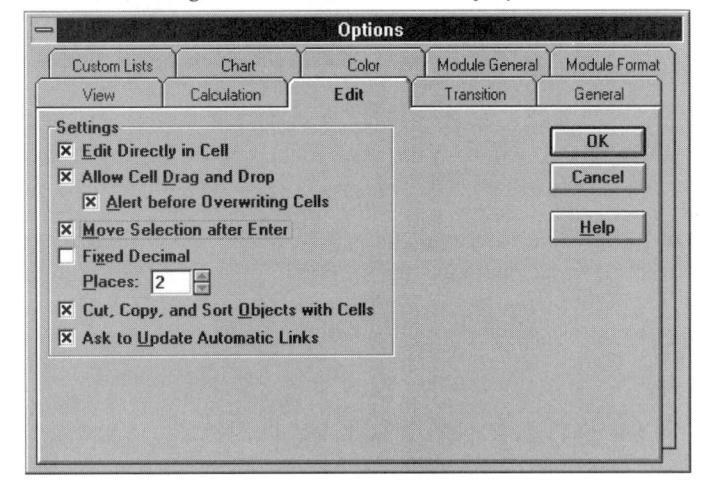

Operation

- To switch from one tab to another, click on a tab name. You can also press Ctrl+Tab to switch to the next tab or Shift+Ctrl+Tab to switch to the previous tab.

- When you click on the OK button in a tab to close the dialog box, all changes that you made to any of the tabs go into effect.

Figure P-12   How to work with dialog boxes that contain tabs

Exercise set P-3

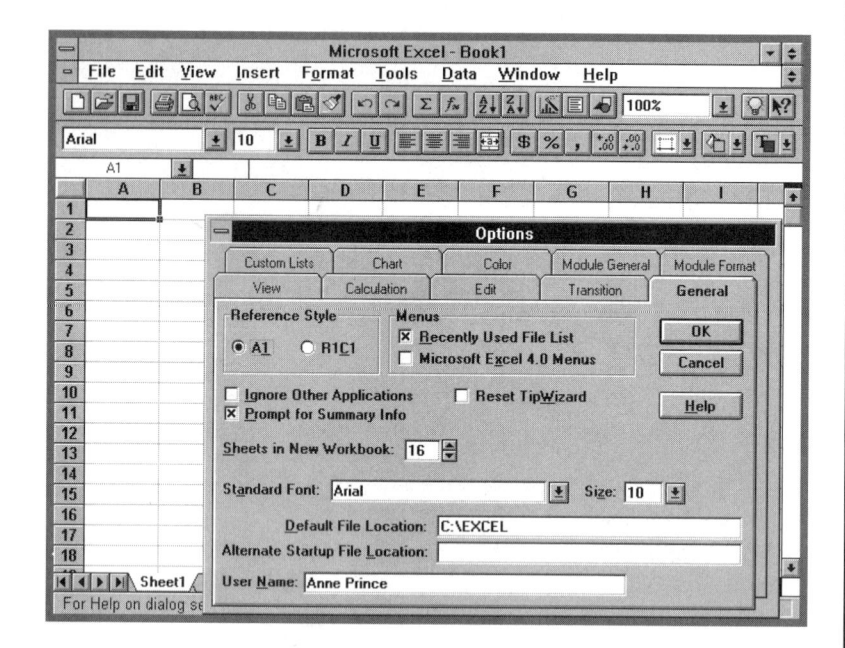

How the Options dialog box should look when you access it in exercise 3

1. Activate the Program Manager if it's not already the active program, and open the Main and Accessories group windows if they're not already open. Next, use the first mouse method in figure P-9 to issue the Tile command from the Windows menu. Then, use the second mouse method to issue the Cascade command from the Windows menu. Note that neither command requires a dialog box.

2. Use the first keyboard method in figure P-9 to issue the Tile command again. Note that you can access any command with just three keystrokes. Then, use the second keyboard method to issue the Cascade command again. This isn't as efficient, but it lets you review the menus and commands at a leisurely pace.

3. Start Excel and issue the Options command from the Tools menu. Then, click on the General tab in the dialog box that's displayed. Use the mouse techniques of figure P-10 to drop the list for the Standard Font and Size boxes, to change the Reference Style from A1 to R1C1, to change the Sheets in New Workbook count to 1, and to check the Reset TipWizard box. Then, click on the Cancel button to cancel the command.

4. Issue Excel's Options command again and the General tab should be displayed automatically. This time, use the keyboard techniques of figure P-11 to change the Sheets in New Workbook count to 1, change the Reference Style option to R1C1, drop the list for the Standard Font box, and check the Reset TipWizard box. Then, press the Esc key to cancel the command.

5. Issue the Options command one more time. Then, switch from the General tab to the View tab using the Ctrl+Tab key combination. Next, switch to the Edit tab using the mouse. Finally, click on the Cancel button to cancel the command, and issue the Exit command to end Excel.

How to work with directories and files

When you use any PC program, you save your work in *files* that are stored on *disk drives*. To help keep these files organized, they are kept in *directories*. If you've been using DOS programs, you may have had trouble working with directories and files because some of the required notation was so difficult.

When you use Windows programs, though, standard dialog boxes let you select the directories and files that you want to work with. In addition, Windows provides a program called the File Manager that makes it easier to create directories, copy and move files, and so on. As a result, you shouldn't have any trouble with files and directories, but you need to get started right.

Figure P-13 presents the concepts and terms that you need for working with directories and files. It also illustrates the application window for the File Manager. By experimenting with this program, you can better understand the directories and files that are part of a Windows system.

When you use the File Manager, its document window is normally referred to as a *directory window*. Within this window, the *tree pane* shows the structure of the directories that are stored on a disk. The *directory pane* shows the files that are stored in the directory that's highlighted in the tree pane.

In figure P-13, the highlighted directory is the one that's set up when you install Excel 5. If you study the directory pane, you can see that this directory contains six subdirectories (see the folder icon in front of the first six entries) and

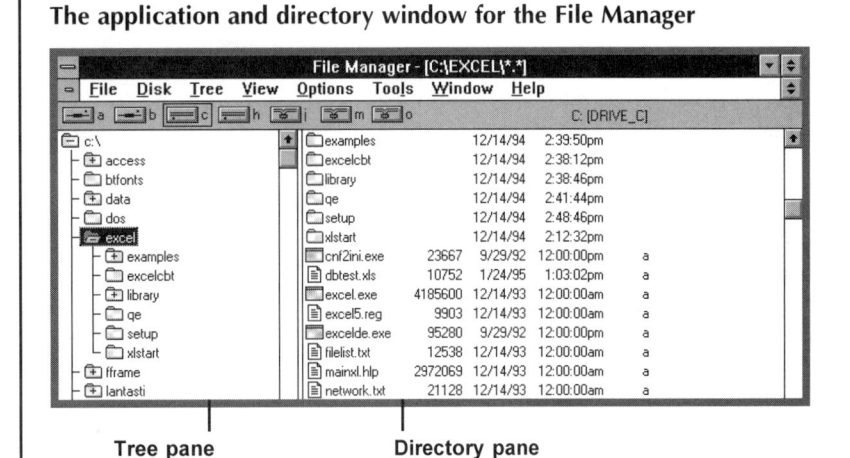

The application and directory window for the File Manager

Tree pane   Directory pane

General

- When you use any Windows program, you save your work in *files* that are stored on *hard disks* or *diskettes*. The devices that save files on a disk or retrieve files from a disk are called *disk drives*.

- When you use Windows, a file is always stored in a *directory*. A hard disk is likely to contain dozens of directories that help organize hundreds of files. A diskette is likely to contain only one directory.

- The File Manager is a Windows program that can be found in the Main program group. It can help you manage the files and directories on your disk drives. Its document windows are usually called *directory windows*, and each one contains two *panes* by default.

Disk drives

- The icons that are shown below the menu bar of the File Manager represent the disk drives that are available to your PC. Drives A and B are the *diskette drives* on your PC (if you have two of them). Drive C is the primary *hard disk drive* on your PC, but there may be others like drive H in the example above. Note the differences in the icons for diskette and hard disk drives.

- If your PC is attached to a network, a third type of disk icon represents a hard disk drive on the network. In the example above, drives J, M, and O are *network disk drives*.

Directories and files

- The File Manager's *tree pane* shows the structure of the directories on a disk. This structure starts at the top with the *root directory*. On a hard disk, the root directory always contains other directories, which can be called *subdirectories*. These directories in turn can contain other directories, so this structure is usually several levels deep.

- The File Manager's *directory pane* lists the directories, programs, and files that are stored in the directory that's highlighted in the tree pane. The icons before the entries indicate the type of entry.

Figure P-13   Concepts and terms for working with files

four programs (see the program icon in front of the seventh entry). This directory also contains 20 data files (note the icons). (Your Excel directory may look different depending on what components were installed.) If you check the directories for other programs like Word 6 (WINWORD) or Windows, you'll see that what we often think of as one program is actually one or more directories that contain dozens of program and data files.

Paths, file names, and wildcard specifications

Figure P-14 presents other information that you need for working with files and directories. This time, the directory pane of the File Manager shows the files that are stored in a data directory for Excel documents.

In the title bar for the application window, you can see the *path* of the highlighted directory. With DOS programs, you often had to type paths like that. With Windows programs, you never need to type them, but you occasionally need to interpret them.

When you create a new file, you need to know how to create valid *file names* so figure P-14 gives the rules for forming them. Most of the time, you can omit the *extension* of the file because the application you're working with will add it automatically.

Last, figure P-14 presents what you need to know about *wildcard specifications*. You need to know what these specifications mean because they are used by the File Manager and by applications like Excel. You'll see an example in just a moment.

A File Manager window for another directory on the C drive

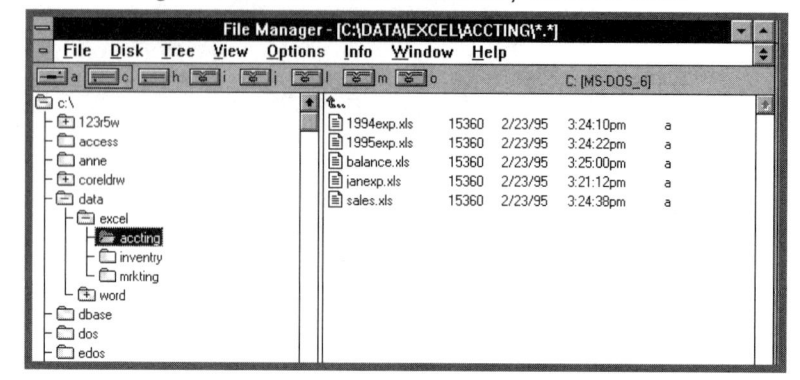

Paths

- In the title bar of the application window shown above, you can see the notation for the directory that's highlighted in the tree pane:

    `C:\DATA\EXCEL\ACCTING\*.*`

- The letter and colon at the start of this notation indicate the disk drive that the directory is on. After that, you can see the *path* of the directory. Starting with the root directory, the path gives the sequence of directories that you have to go through to reach the highlighted directory. The directory names in the path are separated by backslashes.

File names

- A *file name* consists of a name that is 1 to 8 characters long, a dot (or period), and an *extension* that is from 1 to 3 characters long. If the extension is omitted, the dot can be omitted too.

- A file name must start with a letter or number. After that, the characters in the name or the extension can be letters (either uppercase or lowercase), numbers, or any of these special characters:
  ! @ # $ % ^ & ( ) _ + - { } < > ' ~

Wildcard specifications

- After the path in the title bar above, you can see this *wildcard specification*: *.*

- Since the * *wildcard* means "any characters," this specification means that file names with any characters before the dot and any characters after the dot should be listed in the directory pane (all files). In contrast, a specification like *.XLS means that only files with XLS as the extension should be listed.

Figure P-14   Paths, file names, and wildcard specifications

An introduction to the functions of the File Manager

When you use a Windows application like Excel, you use the Windows File Manager to manage the directories and files that you use. To give you some idea of how easy the File Manager is to use, figure P-15 summarizes some of its basic functions.

Note that you can even start an application from the File Manager. To do that, you just double-click on a file name that has an icon like the ones in figure P-14 or P-15 before it. This icon indicates that the file is associated with a program. If, for example, you double-click on a file that has XLS as the extension, Excel is started. When the application starts, it also retrieves the data file that you double-clicked on.

This summary, however, doesn't begin to indicate the power of the File Manager. To move or copy several files at a time, for example, you can highlight the files before you drag them to a new directory. And to move or copy files from one disk drive to another, you can open two directory windows at the same time and drag the files from one window to another. In short, if you frequently need to reorganize your files and directories, you should make a point of learning more about the File Manager.

A File Manager window for a diskette drive

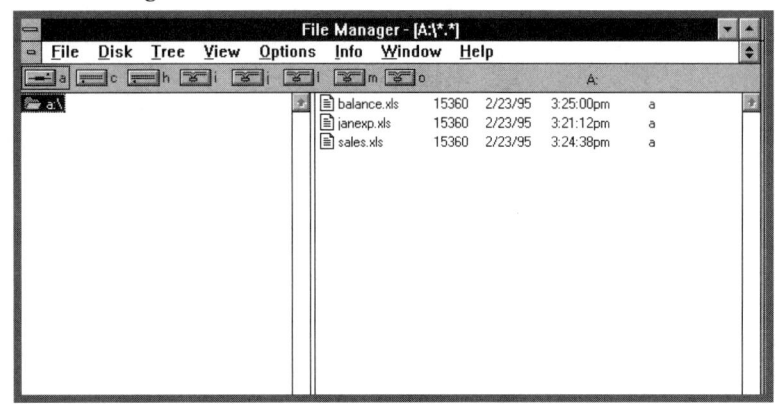

How to change the display in the tree and directory panes

- To change the drive that's displayed, click on one of the drive icons at the top of the window.
- To display the files for another directory in the directory pane, click on a directory in the tree pane.
- To hide subdirectories in the tree pane, double-click on the icon for the directory that they're subordinate to. To display the subdirectories for a directory that has an icon with a plus sign on it, double-click on the icon.

How to create a new directory

- Click on the directory in the tree pane that you want to create a subordinate directory for. Then, issue the Create Directory command from the File menu.

How to start an application that's associated with a file

- The icons before the files in the directory pane above indicate that the files are associated with an application. To start that program, just double-click on the file name. After the program starts, it retrieves that file.
- A file name is associated with an application through its extension. By default, XLS is associated with Excel 5.

How to delete or rename a file or directory

- To delete a file or directory, highlight it, press the Delete key, and respond to the dialog boxes that follow.
- To rename a file or directory, highlight it, issue the Rename command from the File menu, and respond to the dialog box that follows.

How to move or copy a file on the same disk

- To move the highlighted file, drag the file name to a directory in the tree pane and release the mouse button.
- To copy the highlighted file, hold down the Ctrl key while you drag the file name to the directory.

Figure P-15 An introduction to the functions of the File Manager

How to use the standard Open command

The Open command in any Windows application retrieves a file from disk, opens a document window for it, and displays the contents of the file in the window. To use this command, you need to know what disk drive the file is stored on, what directory the file is in, and what the name of the file is. This is true for all Windows applications, and the dialog box for the Open command works the same in all Windows applications.

Figure P-16 presents the dialog box that's displayed when you issue the Open command in Excel. Because identifying the drive, directory, and file can be confusing if you haven't used a dialog box like this before, you'll learn how to do that in the next two figures. Once you learn the techniques in those figures, you'll be able to identify files in other dialog boxes as well.

The Excel dialog box for the Open command

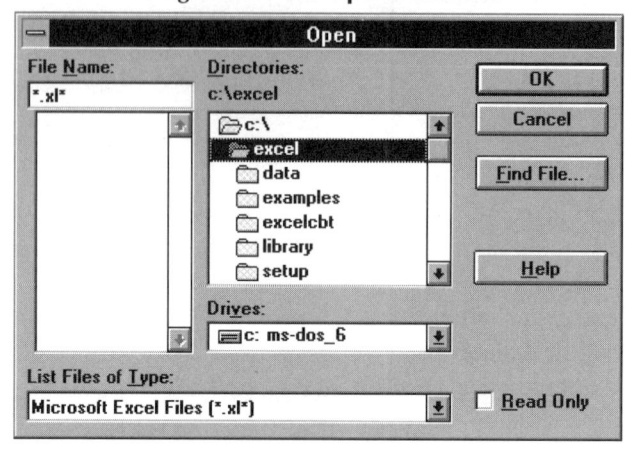

What the Open command does

- Retrieves a file from disk, opens a document window for it, and displays the file in the document window.
- The file can be stored on a diskette, a hard disk on your own PC, or a hard disk on the network.

What you have to know to use the Open command

- What disk drive the file is stored on
- What directory the file is stored in
- What the name of the file is

Figure P-16 An introduction to the standard Open command

The essential Windows skills

How to select a drive and directory in a dialog box

To identify the drive that contains the file you want to open, you select it from the list that drops down from the Drives box in the Open dialog box. This list is shown at the top of figure P-17. After you identify the drive, Excel displays the directory structure for that drive in the Directories list box. When this dialog box is first displayed as shown in figure P-16, only one directory at each level but the last is displayed, and the indentation shows the levels of directories.

To change to a different directory, you have to first find the directory using the techniques in figure P-17. These techniques are similar to the ones you use in the tree pane of the File Manager. To start, you usually scroll to the root directory at the top of the *directory tree*. When you double-click on the root directory, all the directories at the next level are displayed. You can then continue down the levels of directories until you find the one you want to use.

When you complete the procedure in figure P-17, the path of the directory that you selected is shown above the directory tree. Then, you can check to make sure that this is the directory that contains the file you want to retrieve. If you didn't double-click properly on the last directory in the path, the directory tree may appear to be correct, but the notation won't be.

How to select a disk drive

1. Click on the arrow to the right of the Drives box to drop down the drives list:

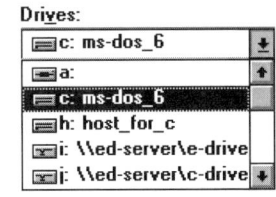

   Drives:
   - c: ms-dos_6
   - a:
   - c: ms-dos_6
   - h: host_for_c
   - i: \\ed-server\e-drive
   - j: \\ed-server\c-drive

2. Click on the letter of the drive you want to use.

How to select a directory

1. Double-click on the root directory at the top of the directory tree. This displays the first level of directories on the drive:

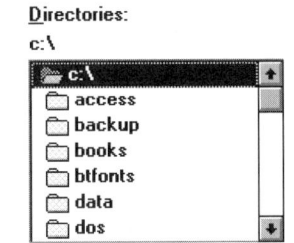

   Directories:
   c:\
   - c:\
   - access
   - backup
   - books
   - btfonts
   - data
   - dos

2. If necessary, scroll to the directory that you want to use at the next level. Then, double-click on it to display the next level of directories:

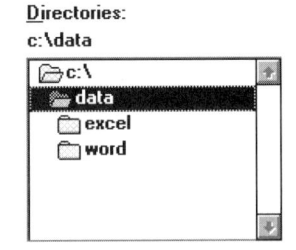

   Directories:
   c:\data
   - c:\
   - data
   - excel
   - word

3. Continue down the tree in this way until you double-click on the directory that you want. At this point, the path for the directory should be displayed above the Directories box:

   Directories:
   c:\data\excel\accting
   - c:\
   - data
   - excel
   - accting

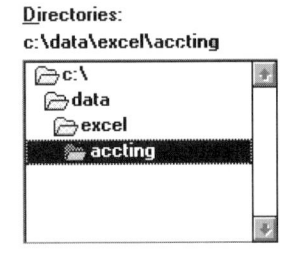

Figure P-17 How to select a drive and directory

How to select a file in a dialog box

Figure P-18 shows how the Open dialog box looks after you identify the drive and directory for a file. Since this is the Open dialog box for Excel 5, the wildcard specification in the File Name box is for files that have an extension that begins with XL. As a result, only files with a matching extension are listed in the File Name list box.

To open one of the files that are listed in the box, you can double-click on its file name. Or, you can move the highlight to the file name before choosing the OK button to start the command.

If all the file names in the directory don't fit in the list box, you can use the scroll bars to scroll through the list. Or, you can type one or more characters in the File Name text box to jump the highlight to the file name that begins with those characters.

Finally, if you want to open a file that doesn't have the extension given by the wildcard specification, you can select a different wildcard specification from the List Files of Type list. Or, you can type your own wildcard specification into the File Name text box. Although most Excel 5 files have XLS as the extension, that's not a requirement.

The Open dialog box after the drive and directory have been selected

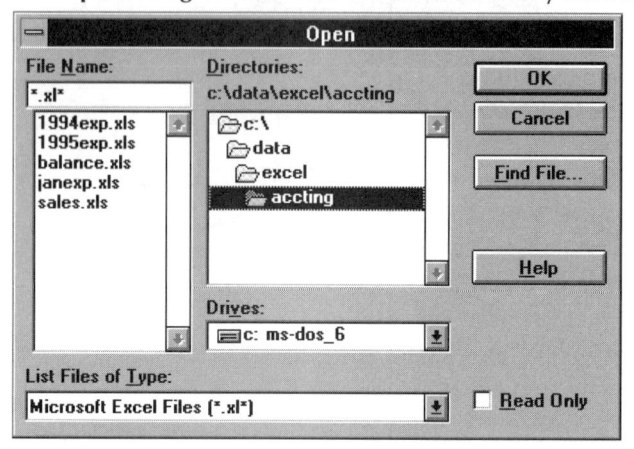

Two ways to select a file in the list box and start the command

- Double-click on the file name in the File Name list box.
- Move the highlight to the file name by using mouse or keyboard techniques. This moves the file name into the File Name text box. Then, choose the OK button by clicking on it or by pressing the Enter key (since the OK button has a dark outline).

How to change the types of files that are displayed

- By default, an application displays only those file names that have the extension that is related to it. For instance, Excel 5 displays only files that have an extension that begins with XL.
- To display files with another extension, drop down the list from the List Files of Type box and choose the file type. To display all files regardless of the extension, choose All Files.
- If you want to display files in the File Name list box that have an extension that isn't in the List Files of Type box, you can type your own wildcard specification in the File Name text box.

Notes

- Until Version 4.0 of Excel, the default extension for an Excel file was XLS. In Version 4.0, the concept of workbooks was introduced. With that version, a worksheet was saved in a file with the extension XLS, but a workbook, which contained two or more worksheets, was saved in a file with the extension XLW. In Version 5.0, all worksheets are saved in workbooks, and the extension XLS is used by default.
- If the file you want doesn't appear in the File Name list, you can use the scroll bars or the Down-arrow key to scroll through the list. Or, you can type one or more characters into the File Name text box to move the highlight to the first file name that starts with those characters.

Figure P-18   How to select a file

The essential Windows skills

How to use the standard Save As command

Figure P-19 shows how to use the standard Save As command. This is the command that you use when you save your work on a diskette or hard disk. After you select the disk drive and directory that you want to store the file in, you type a valid file name in the File Name text box and complete the command.

The Excel dialog box for the Save As command

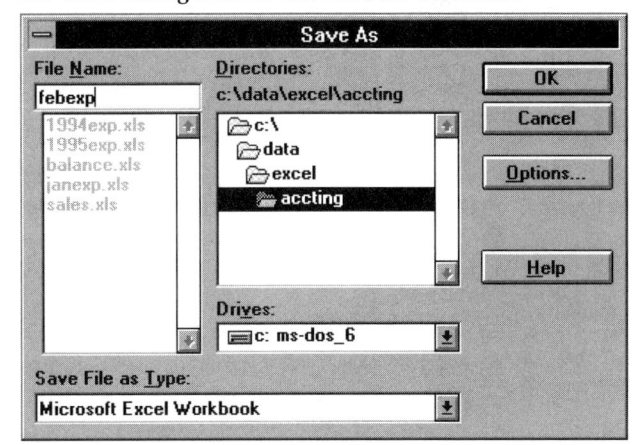

[Save As dialog box showing File Name: febexp; Directories: c:\data\excel\accting with folders c:\, data, excel, accting; file list: 1994exp.xls, 1995exp.xls, balance.xls, janexp.xls, sales.xls; Drives: c: ms-dos_6; Save File as Type: Microsoft Excel Workbook; buttons: OK, Cancel, Options..., Help]

What the command does

- Copies your work from the document window to a diskette, hard disk on your PC, or hard disk on the network.
- When you save a file, it remains in the document window.

The importance of this command

- If you don't save your work on a diskette or hard disk, it is lost when you turn off the PC.

How to use this command

- Select the drive and directory that you want to save the file in just as you do for an Open command.
- Enter a valid file name in the File Name text box and choose the OK button. If you omit the extension, the application program usually adds the extension that is related to it. For instance, Excel 5 adds XLS as the extension.
- To replace a file name in the File Name text box with a new name, just start typing when the name is highlighted. To highlight the name, you can drag the mouse across it, double-click on it, or press Alt+N (the keyboard method for moving the insertion point to the File Name box). These are standard Windows techniques for working with the text in text boxes.

Notes

- Before you start saving files on a PC at school or in business, you need to find out what disk drive and what directory your files should be saved in.
- Before you start saving files on your own PC, you should use the File Manager to create one or more directories for them.

Figure P-19 An introduction to the standard Save As command

Exercise set P-4

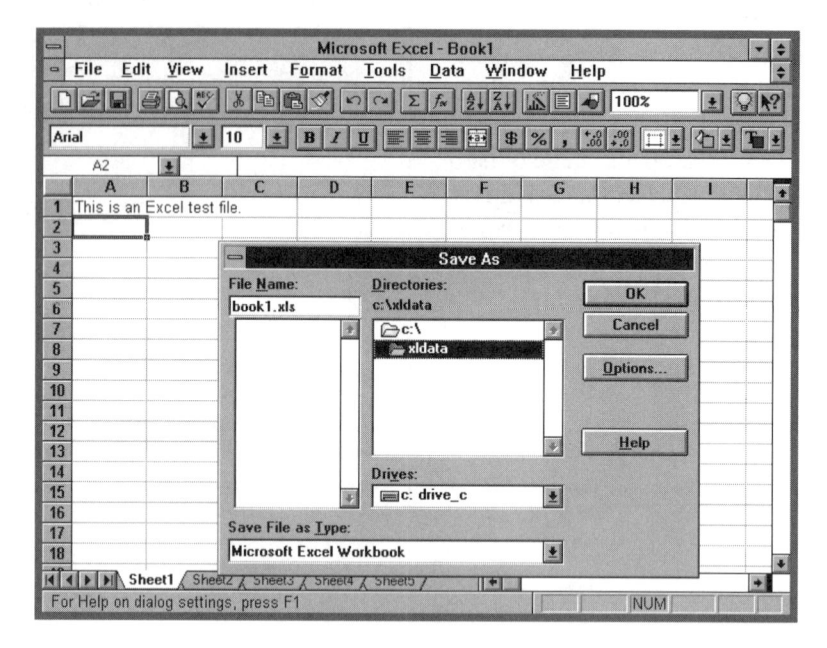

How the Save As dialog box should look after you change the directory in exercise 5

1. Start the File Manager from the Main group of the Program Manager. If the application and directory windows aren't maximized, maximize them. Then, study the disk drive icons at the top of the directory window. What diskette drives are available to your PC? What hard drives? What network drives?

2. If necessary, click on the icon for drive C so the hard disk on your PC is displayed in the directory window. Then, scroll down to the Windows directory in the tree pane and double-click on it to display its subdirectories in the tree pane and its files in the directory pane. How many subdirectories does this directory contain? How many files altogether are there in this directory? You can see a summary at the bottom of the directory window.

3. Highlight the root directory on the C drive. Then, access the Create Directory command in the File menu and create a directory named XLDATA. When that's done, scroll down the directory tree until you find this directory.

4. Switch to the Program Manager, and start Excel. Then, type "This is an Excel 5 test file" in the worksheet that's displayed, and press the Enter key.

5. Issue the Save As command from the File menu. What is the starting drive and directory? If necessary, use the technique in figure P-17 to change the drive to the C drive. Next, use the techniques in that figure to change the directory in the Directories box to the one you created in exercise 3. At this point, the Save As dialog box should look like the one above. Then, highlight the default file name (book1.xls) by dragging the mouse across it, double-clicking on it, or pressing Alt+N, and replace the default name by typing TESTFILE as the file name. Don't include an extension, though, because Excel will automatically add XLS. To complete the command, click on the OK button, and click again on the OK button if the Summary Info dialog box appears. Last, issue the Close command from the File menu.

6. Issue the Open command from the File menu, and open the file that you just saved. To do that, double-click on TESTFILE in the File Name list box. This should display the file that you created in its own window. Then, issue the Exit command in the File menu to end Excel.

7. Switch to the File Manager. Then, highlight the TESTFILE file in the Directory pane for the XLDATA directory, press the Delete key, and respond to the dialog boxes that follow until the file is deleted. Next, highlight the XLDATA directory in the tree pane, press the Delete key, and respond to the dialog boxes that follow until the directory is deleted.

8. Exit from Windows. This closes all applications and returns control of the PC to DOS.

How to use Windows 95 with your applications

Windows 95 is the name of the next release of Windows. If you're interested in how that release will affect the skills that are presented in this book, please read on. Otherwise, you can skip to the Perspective heading near the end of this chapter.

The good news is that Windows 95 will have little or no effect on applications like Excel 5, although there will be minor differences in the appearance of the application windows. Even the File Manager will work the same as it does with Windows 3.1. On the other hand, the Program Manager has been dropped from Windows 95 so you will have to use different techniques for starting your applications.

Of course, Windows 95 will come with many new functions and features that aren't available in Windows 3.1. I just want you to know that these functions and features will have little effect on what you learn in this book.

How to start an application

Figure P-20 shows how to start an application from Windows 95. Instead of using group windows and icons, you use menus with simplified mouse actions. To move from menu to menu, you just move the mouse pointer (no clicking). To start a program from a menu, you single click (no double-clicking).

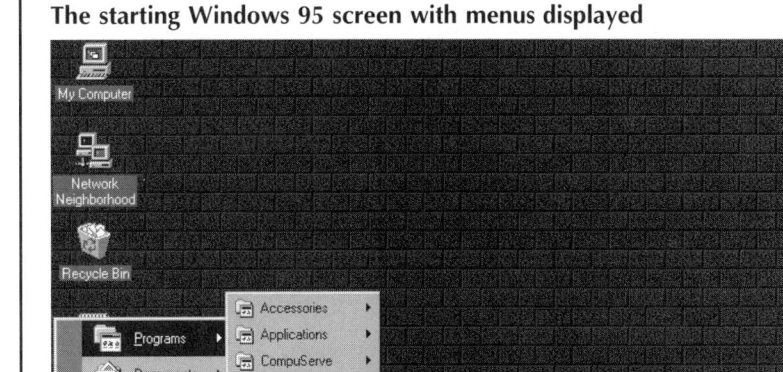

The starting Windows 95 screen with menus displayed

Procedure

1. Click on the Start button in the lower left corner to display the first menu on the left of the screen.
2. Move (don't drag) the mouse pointer to Programs in the first menu. That displays the next menu to the right.
3. Move the mouse pointer to the type of program you want to start. That displays the next menu to the right.
4. Click (don't double-click) on the name of the program that you want to start.

Figure P-20 How to start an application in Windows 95

Differences in the application window

Figure P-21 summarizes the differences you can expect in the application window for Excel 5. As you can see, the appearance of the bars above the document window has been changed slightly, and all of the window buttons are on the right side of the title bar.

At the bottom of the application window is a row of buttons that represent the applications that are running. To switch to one of these applications, you can just click on its button. However, you can still use Alt+Tab switching and most of other switching methods that work with Windows 3.1.

Everything else in your applications should work the same way it works in Windows 3.1. With some minor operational changes, that should also be true when upgraded versions of your applications become available for use with Windows 95. As a result, the skills that you learn in this book should serve you well for many years to come.

The Excel 5 window when displayed by Windows 95

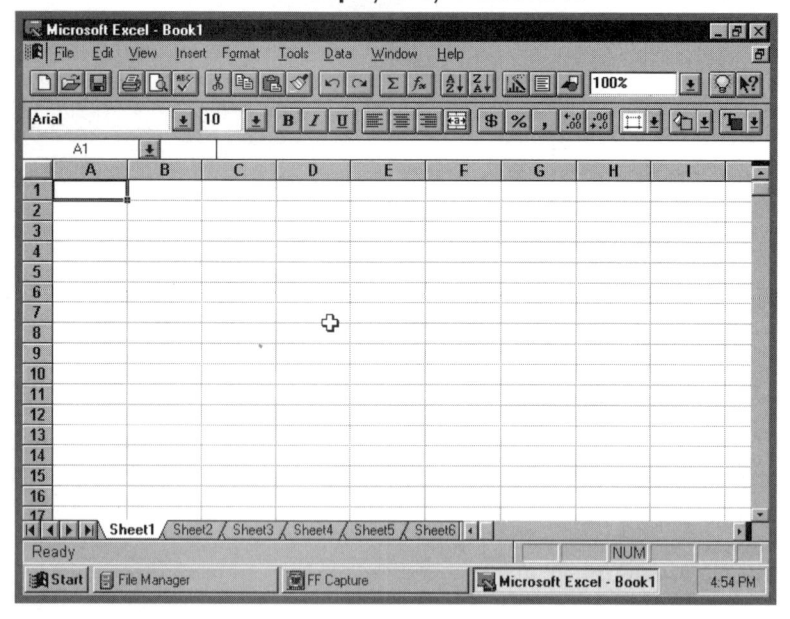

Primary differences in appearance

- The title bar has three buttons, all on the right side. The first is the minimize button; the second is the restore or maximize button; the third is the button for closing the window and exiting from the program. Just one click on any of these buttons starts the action.

- Below the status bar is a row of buttons that represent the programs that are in operation.

How to switch from one program to another

- Click on one of the buttons at the bottom of the window.

- You can also use Alt+Tab switching just as you can with Windows 3.1.

Figure P-21 Differences in the application window for Windows 95

The essential Windows skills

Perspective

You can think of this chapter as a crash course in Windows. It has presented the minimum set of skills that every Windows user should have. Because this chapter has presented so much information, though, you may be slightly overwhelmed by it. That's even more likely if you're new to PCs or Windows.

In practice, though, the skills that are presented in this chapter shouldn't give you much trouble. After a few trials, starting a program from the Program Manager becomes a trivial task, and switching from one program to another does too. Later, when you start using Excel, you'll find that issuing commands from menus and working with dialog boxes also becomes routine.

In fact, the only skills that continue to give people trouble are those for working with directories and files. So if you're at all uneasy about those skills, you may want to go through exercise set P-4 again. In particular, you should make sure that you know how to select a directory as you open or save a file. Once you're confident that you can do that, you're ready for Excel.

Summary

- When Windows starts, its *shell program* is started too. This program is usually the Program Manager. That's the program that you use to start your *applications*.

- When you start an application, an *application window* is opened for it. Within this application window, a program creates its own workspaces called *document windows*.

- To use the mouse, you need to know the four basic mouse actions: *point*, *click*, *double-click*, and *drag*.

- You can *maximize*, *restore*, or *minimize* an application or document window by clicking on its maximize, restore, or minimize button. When a window is minimized, it takes the form of an *icon* that you can restore or maximize with the mouse. You can also move or size a window with the mouse if it's not maximized.

- When a window is too small to show all of its contents, *scroll bars* are added to it. Then, you can use the mouse to scroll through the window by clicking on the scroll bar or *scroll arrows* or by dragging the *scroll box*.

- To close a window, you can double-click on the *control-menu box* or use the *control menu* for the window. If the window is an application window, this also ends the application. If the window contains the Program Manager, this ends all programs and returns you to DOS.

- The Program Manager organizes your applications in *program groups*. To open a *group window*, you double-click on a *program group icon*. To start a program, you double-click on its *program icon*.

- Windows provides several methods for switching from one application to another. One of the best is Alt+Tab switching.
- You can use either mouse or keyboard techniques to access *menus* from the *menu bar* and to issue *commands* from the menus. These techniques work the same in all Windows programs.
- When you issue some commands, a *dialog box* is displayed. To change the settings or supply the information that's required by the dialog box, you can use the mouse or the keyboard. Some of the common dialog box controls are *command buttons, option buttons, spin boxes, check boxes, tabs, list boxes,* and *text boxes*.
- When you use any Windows program, you save your work on a *hard disk* or *diskette* in *files* that are organized in *directories*. A *path* shows how to get to a directory from the *root directory*. A *file name* consists of a name and an optional *extension* that are separated by a dot (or period).
- The File Manager is a Windows program that helps you manage directories and files. The *tree pane* in one of its *directory windows* shows the directory structure for a disk drive; the *directory pane* shows the files that are in the highlighted directory in the tree pane.
- The Open command is the standard Windows command for opening a file. The Save As command is the standard Windows command for saving a file on a diskette or hard disk. To use these commands, you don't need to enter *path* specifications. Instead, you select the drive and directory that you want to use.
- Although Windows 95 will offer some important new functions and features, it should have only a trivial effect on how you start and use applications like Excel 5.

Section 1

The essential worksheet skills

The first three chapters in this section show you how to create, edit, and format an Excel worksheet. You need to master those skills for any worksheet you create. Then, the fourth chapter presents the extra commands and features that you need when you work with large worksheets.

Whether you're a spreadsheet novice or a person who's upgrading or converting to Excel 5, you should read all four chapters in sequence. From the start, you'll be learning the most useful and productive ways to work with Excel 5. When you complete this section, you will be able to use Excel 5 to create, edit, and format worksheets of all sizes the way the best professionals do.

Chapter 1

How to create, print, and save a worksheet

Excel 5 is a complex program that provides dozens of commands and features. To learn all of them would take many hours. To create, print, and save a simple worksheet, though, you only need to master a few of those commands and features. You can learn them in just an hour or two, and that's what this chapter is designed to teach you.

This chapter will get you started with Excel 5 whether you're a complete beginner or a person who is upgrading or converting to Excel 5 from another spreadsheet program. The intent is to teach you Excel 5 the way the best professionals use it right from the start. How much experience you have will of course determine how long it takes you to complete this chapter. But when you're done, you'll be well on your way to Excel competence.

If you haven't used a spreadsheet program before, it's especially important to do the exercises that are presented throughout this chapter. They are a critical part of the learning process because they force you to use the skills that are described in the text. As you will see, a skill that may seem difficult when you read about it is quite manageable when you actually try it.

An introduction to Excel for Windows
    How to interpret the Excel window
    How to move the cell pointer
    How to use the toolbar buttons

How to enter data into a worksheet
    How to enter text into a worksheet
    How to adjust the column width
    How to enter numbers into a worksheet
    How to use the range entry technique
    How to enter dates and times into a worksheet
    How to edit the contents of a cell

How to format the entries in a worksheet
    How to select two or more cells
    How to use toolbar buttons to align entries
    How to use toolbar buttons to format numbers

How to enter formulas and functions into a worksheet
    How to enter formulas into a worksheet
    How to copy formulas to adjacent cells
    How to enter functions into a worksheet
    How to use the AutoSum toolbar button
    How to align and format the result of a formula or function

How to use the commands in the File menu
    How to print a worksheet
    How to save a workbook
    How to close a workbook
    How to open a workbook
    How to start a new workbook
    How to exit from Excel

Perspective

Summary

An introduction to Excel for Windows

If you know how to start applications from the Program Manager, you shouldn't have any trouble starting Excel 5. Otherwise, you can read the prerequisites chapter to learn how to start Excel.

How to interpret the Excel window

When you start Excel, an *application window* like the one in figure 1-1 opens. Within the application window is a *document window* that is referred to as a *workbook window* when you use Excel because it contains a *workbook*. When you first start Excel, the workbook window is empty. In figure 1-1, the workbook window contains a workbook named FEBEXP.XLS.

Each Excel workbook can contain one or more *worksheets* identified by *sheet tabs* at the bottom of the workbook window. In chapter 5, you can learn how to work with more than one worksheet in a workbook. To start, though, you'll be working with a single worksheet.

The main portion of the worksheet consists of columns and rows. In figure 1-1, for example, you can see 8 columns and 16 rows. However, an Excel worksheet contains many more columns and rows than can be displayed at one time.

The intersection of a column and a row is called a *cell*. Each cell can be identified by a *cell reference* that consists of its column letter and row number. For

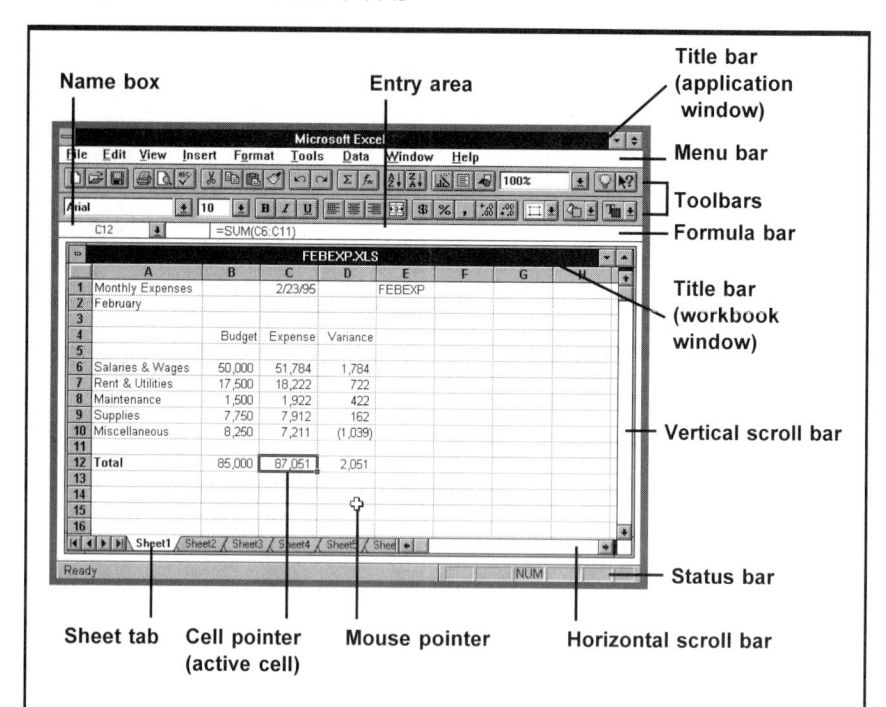

Concepts

- A *workbook* consists of one or more *worksheets*. The worksheets are identified by the *sheet tabs* at the bottom of the *workbook window*. By default, Excel creates each workbook with 16 worksheets.

- The name of the workbook is displayed in the title bar of the workbook window. Or, if the workbook window is maximized, the name is displayed along with the application name in the title bar of the application window.

- Each *cell* in a worksheet is identified by the column letter and row number found in the *worksheet frame* at the top and left side of the workbook window.

- The *title bar* at the top of the Excel window contains the name of the application. The *menu bar* contains the menus you can use to issue commands. The *toolbars* contain buttons and drop-down lists that let you perform pre-defined functions. The *formula bar* consists of the *Name box*, which displays the cell reference of the *active cell*, and the *entry area*, which displays the contents of the active cell.

- The left side of the *status bar* at the bottom of the application window shows the current operating mode of Excel. The right side of the status bar shows the current keyboard modes.

Figure 1-1 The Excel application window

example, the cell reference for the cell in the first column and first row is A1, and the cell reference for the cell in the third column and fourth row is C4.

The *active cell* is identified by the *cell pointer*. The cell pointer is indicated by a dark outline around the cell. In figure 1-1, the cell pointer is on cell C12.

Above the workbook window are five bars. These include the *menu bar*, two *toolbars*, and the *formula bar*. You'll learn how to use these bars in this chapter and throughout this book.

If you start Excel and its application window doesn't look like the one in figure 1-1, some of Excel's view options may have been changed. To change the view options back to the defaults, you can use the commands in the View menu. Exercise 2 in exercise set 1-1, gives you a chance to do that.

How to move the cell pointer

Before you can enter data into a cell, you have to move the cell pointer to the cell. Figure 1-2 shows how to do that. As you can see, you can use either the mouse or the keyboard to move the cell pointer.

Note in this figure how the Num Lock and Scroll Lock keys can affect the movement of the cell pointer. When you work with Excel, you usually want Num Lock on and Scroll Lock off. With Num Lock on, you can use the numeric keypad to enter numeric data, which is more efficient than entering it with the typewriter portion of the keyboard.

With the keyboard

Right-arrow or Tab	Moves the cell pointer right one cell.
Left-arrow or Shift+Tab	Moves the cell pointer left one cell.
Down-arrow or Enter	Moves the cell pointer down one cell.
Up-arrow or Shift+Enter	Moves the cell pointer up one cell.
Page-up	Moves the cell pointer up one screen.
Page-down	Moves the cell pointer down one screen.
Alt+Page-up	Moves the cell pointer left one screen.
Alt+Page-down	Moves the cell pointer right one screen.
Home	Moves the cell pointer to the first cell in the current row.
Ctrl+Home	Moves the cell pointer to cell A1.
Ctrl+End	Moves the cell pointer to the last row and column in the worksheet that contains data.

With the mouse

- Click on a cell to move the cell pointer to that cell. Use the scroll bars to scroll the workbook window if the cell you want to move to isn't visible.

How Num Lock and Scroll Lock affect cell pointer movement

- The Num Lock key in the upper left corner of the numeric keypad turns Num Lock mode off or on. When this mode is on, you can use the numeric keypad to enter numbers, and that's usually what you want when you work with Excel. When this mode is off, you can use the keys on this keypad to move the cell pointer. When this mode is on, the Num Lock light on the keyboard is lit and the NUM indicator is on in the status bar of the Excel window as shown in figure 1-1.

- The Scroll Lock key in the top row of the keyboard turns Scroll Lock mode on or off. When this mode is off, you can use the arrow keys to move the cell pointer and scroll through the worksheet. When this mode is on, the arrow keys still scroll the worksheet, but the cell pointer doesn't move. When this mode is on, the Scroll Lock light on the keyboard is lit and the SCRL indicator is on in the status bar of the Excel window.

Figure 1-2   How to move the cell pointer

How to use the toolbar buttons

The buttons in Excel's toolbars let you perform a variety of functions. Because Excel provides so many different toolbars and buttons, it can be hard to remember all of their functions. But you can easily determine the function of a button by placing the mouse pointer over it as illustrated in figure 1-3. Once you identify the button you want to use, just click on it to start its function.

The buttons in the Standard and Formatting toolbars let you access the functions that you're most likely to need. However, Excel has 11 other toolbars with buttons for special functions, such as working with charts. Excel automatically displays some of these toolbars when you issue an appropriate command.

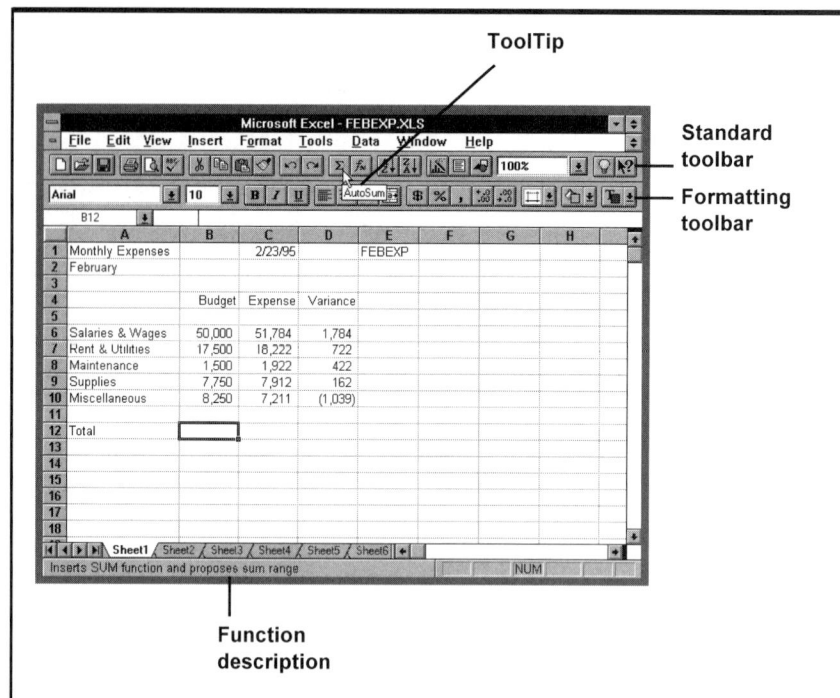

Operation

- When you point to a toolbar button with the mouse for a moment, the button name is displayed in the ToolTip and its function is described in the status bar.

- When you click on a button, its function is started.

Note

- ToolTips are displayed by default. If the ToolTips aren't displayed, choose the Toolbars command from the View menu and check the Show ToolTips option in the dialog box that's displayed.

Figure 1-3   How to use the toolbar buttons

Exercise set 1-1

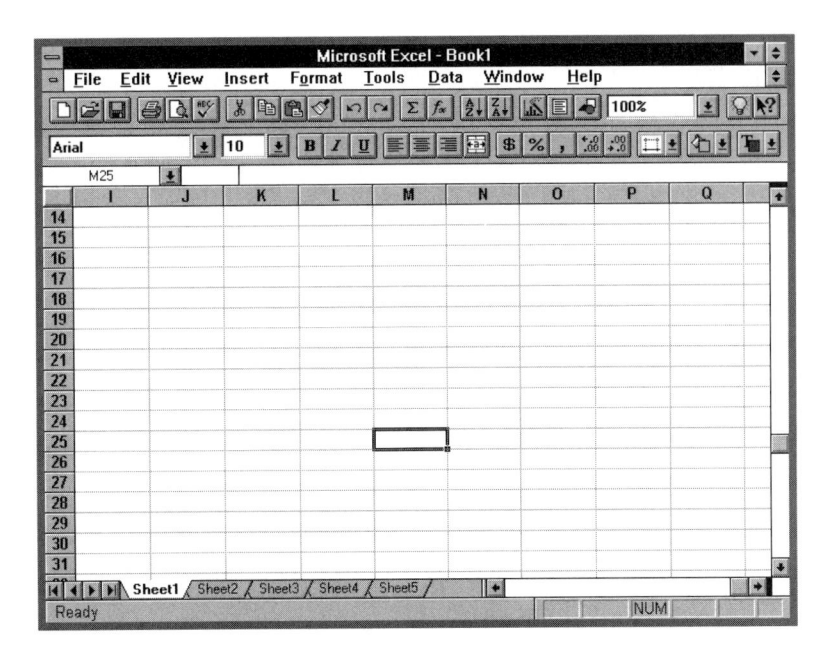

The workbook window in normal view with the pointer on cell M25

1. Start Excel from the Windows Program Manager. If the workbook window that opens up is non-maximized as in figure 1-1, click on the maximize button in the upper right corner of the window to maximize it. Because more rows and columns are displayed when the window is maximized, that's usually how you'll want to work in Excel.

2. If Excel's application window doesn't look like the one above, pull down the View menu. If the Full Screen option is checked, click on it to remove the check mark. Then, if the Formula bar isn't displayed, choose the Formula Bar command from the View menu. If the Status bar isn't displayed, choose the Status Bar command from the View menu. If the Standard and Formatting toolbars aren't displayed, choose the Toolbars command from the View menu, and check the Standard and Formatting boxes in the dialog box that appears. Finally, if the screen isn't displayed at 100%, choose the Zoom command from the View menu and choose the 100% option in the dialog box that appears. (The current magnification percent is displayed in a text box near the right side of the Standard toolbar.)

3. Turn Num Lock mode on and Scroll Lock mode off. Then, use the mouse techniques in figure 1-2 to move the cell pointer to cell M25. When you click on that cell, look in the Name box of the formula bar to confirm that it is M25.

4. Press Ctrl+Home to return to cell A1. Next, use keyboard techniques to move the cell pointer to cell M25, and to return to cell A1. Then, turn Scroll Lock mode on and try to repeat the cell pointer movements. Note that the cell pointer doesn't move when this mode is on. To move the cell pointer, you have to click on cell M25. Do that, then turn Scroll Lock off again.

5. Place the mouse pointer over any button in the Standard or Formatting toolbar. Note the description of the button's function in the status bar. Is the ToolTip displayed near the button? If not, choose the Toolbars command from the View menu, then check the Show ToolTips box.

6. Locate the TipWizard button near the right end of the Standard toolbar and click on it. What happens? Click on it again to see what happens. When the TipWizard is off and M25 is the active cell, your screen should look like the one above.

How to enter data into a worksheet

To create a worksheet, you usually begin by entering the data you want it to include. You may also have to adjust the widths of one or more columns so the data you entered is displayed properly. If you make errors during the entry process, you may also need to edit some of the entries.

How to enter text into a worksheet

In Excel terms, *text* is data that isn't going to be used in calculations. A text entry can consist of all alphabetic characters like the text entries shown in figure 1-4; it can be a combination of letters, numbers, and special characters; and it can be all numeric like a year.

Figure 1-4 summarizes what you need to know for entering text into a worksheet. In general, Excel assumes an entry is text if it contains at least one letter. But if you want Excel to interpret an entry as text even though it doesn't contain a letter, you can enter an apostrophe in front of the entry. This entry, for example, will be interpreted as a number: '1995. As a result, you won't be able to use the entry in a calculation.

When you begin typing, an *insertion point* appears inside the cell as shown in figure 1-4. This indicates where the next character you type will appear. If you press the Backspace key, the character to the left of the insertion point is deleted.

The text in a worksheet

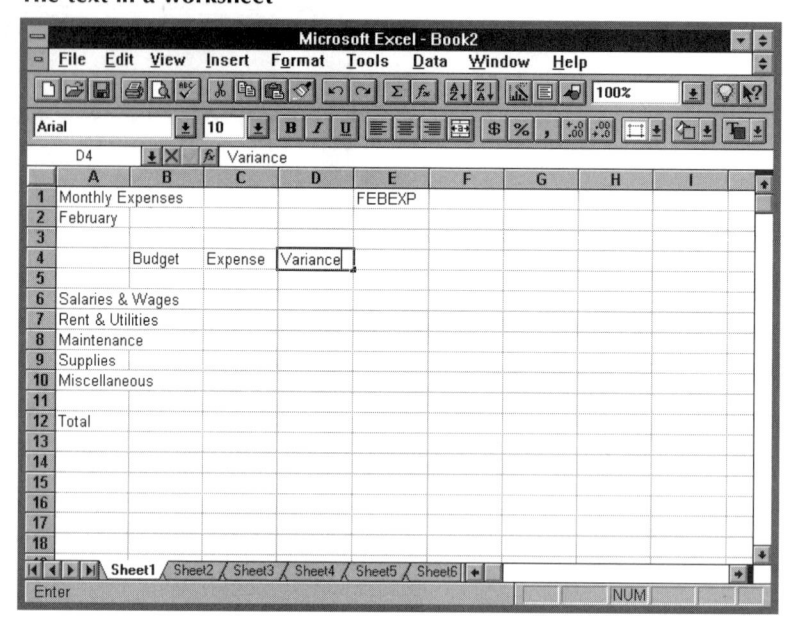

General procedure

1. Use the keyboard or the mouse to move the cell pointer to the cell where you want to enter the text.
2. Type the text.
3. Press the Enter key or an arrow key.

Notes

- To cancel an entry before you press the Enter key in step 3, press the Esc key.
- Excel assumes an entry is text if it contains a letter (it doesn't have to start with a letter) and doesn't match a standard pattern for a number, formula, date, or time. If you want Excel to treat a number, formula, date, or time as text, type an apostrophe as its first character.
- If the text is too long for the cell, the extra characters are displayed in the empty cells to the right. If the cells to the right aren't empty, the extra characters aren't displayed, although they are still stored in the active cell.
- If you need to change an entry, you can move the cell pointer back to the cell that contains the text and re-enter it. Or, you can use the techniques in figure 1-10 to edit the contents of the cell.
- By default, pressing the Enter key moves the cell pointer down one cell. If you don't want the cell pointer to move when you press the Enter key, choose the Options command from the Tools menu to display the Options dialog box. Then, click on the Edit tab and remove the check mark from the Move Selection after Enter option.

Figure 1-4 How to enter text into a worksheet

How to adjust the column width

When you enter text into a worksheet, the data is often too wide for the column. In figure 1-4, for example, many of the entries in column 1 are wider than the column. In this case, the text continues into the next column so that none of it is hidden, but that's not true if data is entered into the adjacent column. In that case, you'll want to widen the column.

Figure 1-5 shows two techniques for changing the width of a column using the mouse. When you use the first technique, the column width is changed so it accommodates the widest entry in the column. If the widest entry is smaller than the column width, Excel will reduce the column width. When you use the second technique in figure 1-5, the column width is changed to accommodate the number of characters you specify.

Additional information

✓ When you use the second technique, the width number in the Name box indicates the number of characters that can be displayed using the default font for the worksheet. If you use a smaller font, more characters will fit in the column than the number shown. If you use a larger font, fewer characters will fit.

How to change the width to accommodate the widest entry

1. Place the mouse pointer on the separator line to the right of the column letter for the column you want to adjust. When the pointer is in the correct position, it will change to a double-headed arrow:

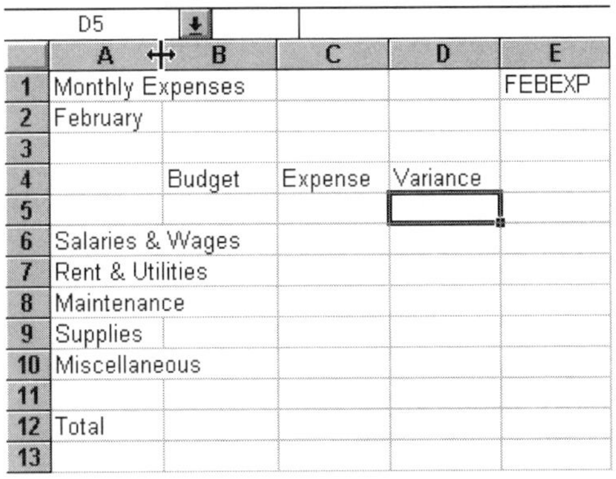

2. Double-click the left mouse button, and the column width is adjusted to accommodate the widest entry in the column:

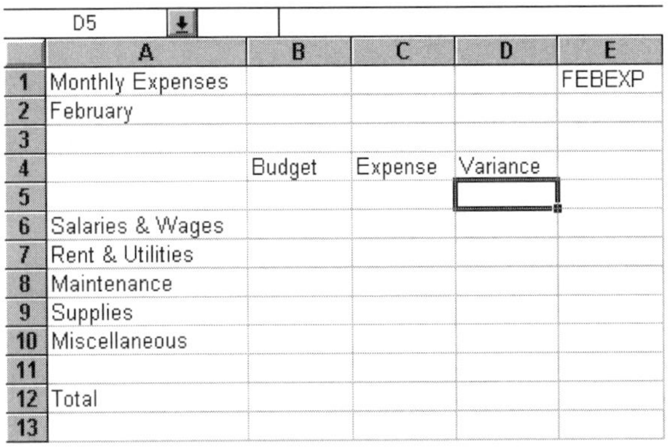

How to change the width to a specific number of characters

1. Position the mouse pointer as described above so it changes to a double-headed arrow.

2. Drag the double-headed arrow to the column width you want (the width in characters is displayed in the Name box):

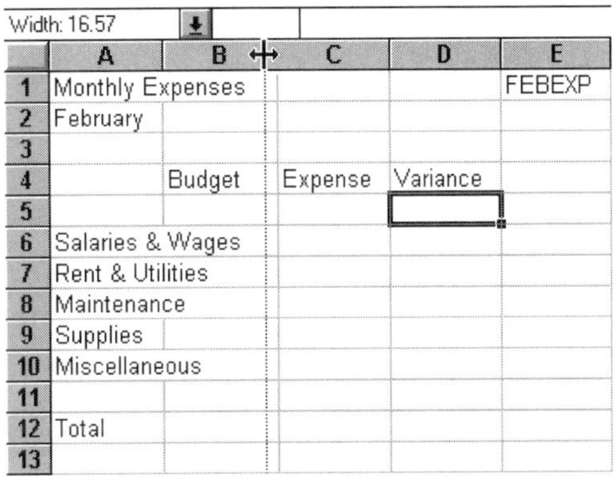

3. Release the mouse button and the column width is changed.

Figure 1-5   How to change the width of a column

How to enter numbers into a worksheet

Figure 1-6 shows how to enter *numbers* into a worksheet. As you can see, the general procedure is the same as the procedure for entering text. When you enter a number, however, you can also enter characters that tell Excel how you want the number formatted. To understand this, you need to understand the General format and how it works.

When you start a new worksheet, all of its cells are formatted with the General format. If you enter a number into a cell with the General format using only the digits 0 through 9, the format of the cell doesn't change. In figure 1-6, for example, all numbers are entered with digits only so the cells remain in the General format. In most cases, that's what you want. Then, when you finish entering a range of numbers, you can use the techniques you'll learn later in this chapter to format the numbers the way you want them.

The numbers in a worksheet

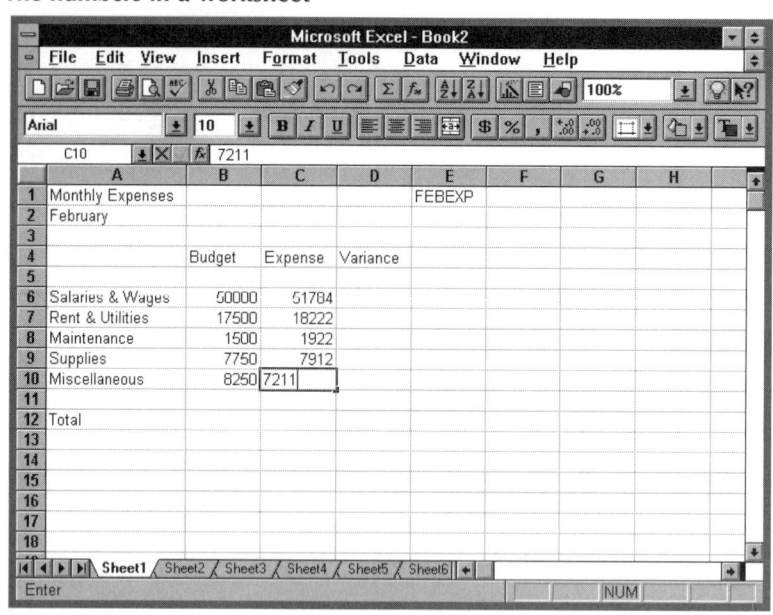

General procedure

1. Use the keyboard or the mouse to move the cell pointer to the cell where you want to enter the number.
2. Type the number using any of the valid characters listed below.
3. Press the Enter key or an arrow key.

Valid characters	Example
The digits zero through nine	189
Leading plus or minus sign	-97.5
One decimal point (period)	123.45
Leading dollar sign	$123.45
Comma	1,234.56
Trailing percent sign	45%

Notes

- By default, all of the cells in a new worksheet have the General format. When you enter a number with a dollar sign, comma, or percent sign in a cell with this format, its format is changed as summarized in figure 1-7.
- If a number is too wide to be displayed in its column, the cell is filled with pound signs (########).

Figure 1-6   How to enter a number into a worksheet

In contrast, if you enter numbers with dollar signs, commas, decimal points, or percent signs into cells that have the General format, the numbers are formatted as you enter them. Figure 1-7 shows how this works. This is useful when you want to enter and format just a few numbers. Note, however, that the format affects only how the number is displayed, not the value that's stored in the cell.

Entries in cells with General format

Entry	Value displayed	Value stored	New format category
12345	12345	12345	General (no change)
12,345	12,345	12345	Number
12,345.67	12,345.67	12345.67	Number (2 decimal places)
$12,345	$12,345	12345	Currency
$12,345.67	$12,345.67	12345.67	Currency (2 decimal places)
12%	12%	.12	Percentage (0 decimal places)
12.345%	12.35%	.12345	Percentage (2 decimal places)

Operation

- When you enter a number in a cell that has General format, the format of the cell changes if you enter a dollar sign, commas, a decimal point, or a percent sign. If you don't enter any of these characters, the General format remains.

Notes

- General is the default format for all the cells in a worksheet.

- When you enter a series of numbers like those in the example in figure 1-6, you shouldn't include dollar signs, commas, or percent signs. That way, you can use the numeric keypad to enter the numbers. When you're done, all of the cells will still have the General format. Then, you can use the techniques in figure 1-13 to format the numbers in those cells.

- When you want to enter a few numbers into a worksheet and format them at the same time, you can enter them with the appropriate dollar signs, commas, and percent signs. Then, you don't have to format them later on.

Figure 1-7   How the General format works

How to use the range entry technique

When you need to enter data into a series of cells in two or more columns, you may want to use the range entry technique presented in figure 1-8. To start, you identify the *range* of cells that you want to enter the data into. A range is just a rectangular group of cells. As you can see, you can use either the mouse or the keyboard to select the range.

Once you identify the range, you don't have to worry about moving the cell pointer from one column to the next as you type the entries. You just press the Enter key to end one entry and move to the next cell in the range. When you reach the bottom of one column, the Enter key automatically moves the cell pointer to the top of the next column. This means you can enter numbers from the numeric keypad without using the mouse or arrow keys to move the cell pointer. That's why this technique can often help you improve your entry efficiency.

How to enter data into a range of cells

1. Select the range of cells you want to enter data into using one of the techniques shown below. Then, type an entry into the first cell:

	A	B	C	D	E
1	Monthly Expenses		2/23/95		FEBEXP
2	February				
3					
4		Budget	Expense	Variance	
5					
6	Salaries & Wages	50000			
7	Rent & Utilities				
8	Maintenance				
9	Supplies				
10	Miscellaneous				
11					
12	Total				
13					

2. Press the Enter key and the cell pointer moves to the next cell in the column. Then, type an entry into the next cell:

	A	B	C	D	E
1	Monthly Expenses		2/23/95		FEBEXP
2	February				
3					
4		Budget	Expense	Variance	
5					
6	Salaries & Wages	50,000			
7	Rent & Utilities	17500			
8	Maintenance				
9	Supplies				
10	Miscellaneous				
11					
12	Total				
13					

3. Repeat step 2 until you've entered data into all of the cells. When you enter data into the last cell in a column, Excel advances the cell pointer to the first cell in the next column.

Two ways to select a range of cells

- Drag the mouse pointer over the cells that you want to enter data into.

- Use the keyboard to move the cell pointer to the first cell that you want to enter data into. Then, hold down the Shift key, move the cell pointer to the last cell that you want to enter data into, and release the Shift key.

How to move the cell pointer within the selected range

- To move the cell pointer to the previous cell in a column, use the Shift+Enter key combination. You can also use the Tab and Shift+Tab keys to move the cell pointer within the selected range.

Figure 1-8 How to use the range entry technique

How to enter dates and times into a worksheet

Figure 1-9 shows how to enter dates and times into a worksheet. Again, the general procedure is the same as for entering text or numbers. When you enter a date or time into a cell with General format, Excel recognizes a variety of formats for dates and times and formats the cell accordingly.

If you need to enter the current date or time into a worksheet, you probably won't use the procedure in figure 1-9. Instead, you'll use one of the functions that are provided by Excel. To enter the current date, for example, you can use the TODAY function. When you use this function, the date is automatically updated whenever Excel recalculates the worksheet.

The date in a worksheet (active cell)

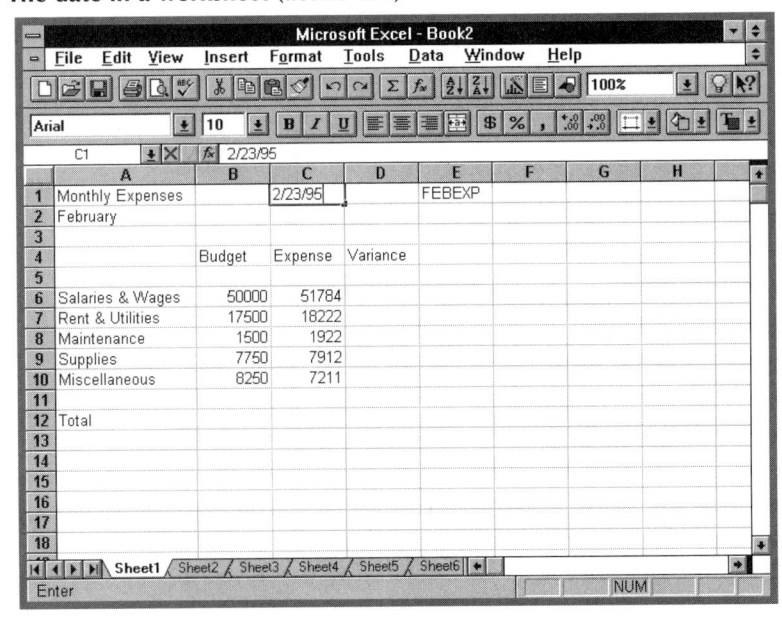

General procedure

1. Use the keyboard or the mouse to move the cell pointer to the cell where you want to enter the date or time.
2. Type the date or time using any of the valid formats listed below.
3. Press the Enter key or an arrow key.

Valid formats for date entries

3-Jul-95	July 3, 1995	7/3/95
3-Jul	July 3	7/95
Jul-95	7-3-95	

Valid formats for time entries

10:15	10:15 am	10:15 pm	22:15
10:15:30	10:15:30 am	10:15:30 pm	22:15:30

Notes

- You can type a date and a time in the same cell, separated by a space.
- When you enter a date or time in a cell that has General format, the format of the cell is changed to one of Excel's date or time formats.

Figure 1-9 How to enter a date or time into a worksheet

How to edit the contents of a cell

When you want to change the data you've entered into a cell, you can just re-enter it. Then, your new entry replaces the old entry.

Often, though, it's more efficient to *edit* the contents of the cell. This means that you change only those characters in the old entry that need to be changed.

Figure 1-10 presents the general procedure for editing the contents of a cell. Note that an *insertion point* is displayed in a cell as soon as you start to edit it. Then, you can move the insertion point to where you want to make a change. If you experiment with the control keys that are summarized in this figure, you shouldn't have any trouble figuring out how they work.

Additional information

✓ You can also edit the contents of a cell in the entry area of the formula bar. To do that, just click in the entry area after you move the cell pointer to the appropriate cell. This can be useful if you're editing a formula that's wider than the column that it's in, but it isn't needed for editing text or numbers.

✓ If the insertion point doesn't appear in the cell that you're editing, the option that lets you edit directly in a cell has been turned off. To turn it back on, choose the Options command in the Tools menu. Then, click on the Edit tab and check the Edit Directly in Cell option.

General procedure

1. Double-click on the cell you want to edit, or move the cell pointer to the cell you want to edit and press F2. Then, Excel places the insertion point inside the cell:

	A	B	C	D	E
1	Monthly Expenses		2/23/95		FEBEXP
2	February				
3					
4		Budget	Expense	Variance	
5					
6	Salaries & Wages	50000	51784		
7	Rent & Utilities	17500	18222		
8	Maintenance	1500	1922		
9	Supplies	7750	7912		
10	Miscellaneous	8250	7211		
11					
12	Total				
13					

2. Use the keyboard and the keys listed below to edit the cell contents.
3. Press the Enter key to accept the changes. To cancel the edit operation without accepting the changes, press the Esc key.

Keys you can use to edit the contents of a cell

Left-arrow	Moves the insertion point left one character.
Right-arrow	Moves the insertion point right one character.
Backspace	Erases the character to the left of the insertion point.
Delete	Erases the character to the right of the insertion point.
Home	Moves the insertion point before the first character.
End or Down-arrow	Moves the insertion point after the last character.
Ctrl+arrow	Moves the insertion point one word in the direction of the arrow.
Insert	Toggles between *insert* and *typeover mode*. When typeover mode is active, the insertion point changes to a block that marks the character that you're going to type over.

Figure 1-10 How to edit the contents of a cell

Exercise set 1-2

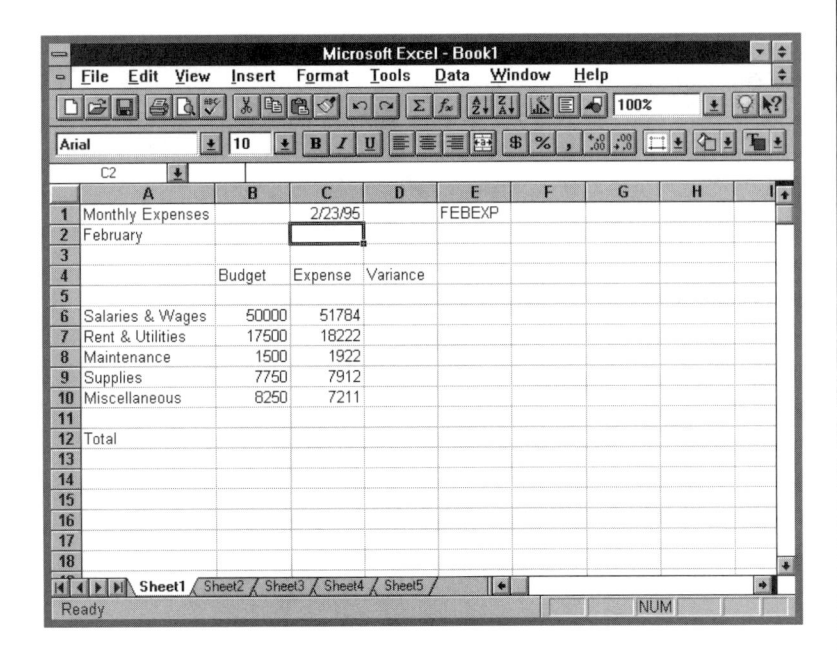

How your worksheet should look after exercise 5

[Screenshot of Microsoft Excel - Book1 showing worksheet with Monthly Expenses, February, date 2/23/95, FEBEXP, and columns Budget, Expense, Variance with rows: Salaries & Wages 50000 51784, Rent & Utilities 17500 18222, Maintenance 1500 1922, Supplies 7750 7912, Miscellaneous 8250 7211, Total]

1. Use the procedure in figure 1-4 to enter the text shown in that figure (and in the worksheet above).

2. Use the first technique in figure 1-5 to change the width of column A so the text in that column doesn't flow over into column B.

3. Use the procedure in figure 1-6 to enter the numbers shown in that figure (and above) into the appropriate cells. Make sure that Num Lock is on; use the numeric keypad on the right of the keyboard to type the numbers; don't use dollar signs or commas; and use the Enter key to complete each entry.

4. Drag the mouse over the numbers that you just entered to select them, and press the Delete key to delete them. Then, use the range entry technique presented in figure 1-8 to enter the numbers in figure 1-6 again. Use the numeric keypad, and don't use dollar signs or commas.

5. Use the procedure in figure 1-9 to enter the current date into your worksheet. Do this three times, one for each of the formats in the first row of the valid formats in this figure. For each format, note the value in the entry area of the formula bar. Is the value the same each time?

6. Use the procedure in figure 1-10 to edit cell A7 so it contains: Rent and Utilities. Then, edit it again to return it to the way it was.

7. Edit cell B6 so it contains 55000, but don't press the Enter key to complete the operation. Instead, press the Esc key. What happens?

8. Move the cell pointer to cell A14 and enter: $51,000. Next, move the cell pointer back to this cell, and look at the value in the entry area of the formula bar. Does it include the dollar sign and comma? Then, press the Delete key to delete the entry, enter 44000 into this cell, and move the cell pointer back to this cell. How is the value in the cell displayed and what is its value in the formula bar? This shows that the format of the cell has been changed from General to Currency format as summarized in figure 1-7. To finish this exercise, press the Delete key.

How to format the entries in a worksheet

After you enter data into a worksheet, you usually want to align the text in some cells and format the numbers in others. Now you'll learn the most efficient ways to do that. First, you'll learn how to select the cells you want to align or format. Then, you'll learn how to align or format them.

How to select two or more cells

Figure 1-11 shows you how to select two or more cells using the mouse or the keyboard. When you use either method, you can select a *range* of cells, one or more columns or rows, or the entire worksheet. As I mentioned earlier, a range is just a rectangular group of cells. After you select a range, you can align or format the cells in it.

When you select cells, you'll notice that the first cell in the range isn't selected, although it is enclosed in the selection border so you can tell that it's part of the range. The cell that isn't selected is the active cell in the range. In figure 1-11, for example, cell B6 is the active cell.

If you select a range that includes too few or too many cells, you can reduce or extend the range by using the second last technique in figure 1-11. Just hold the Shift key down and choose a new ending point for the range.

With Excel 5, you can select two or more ranges at the same time by using the last technique in figure 1-11. These selections are called *nonadjacent selections*. You'll see how this can be useful as you get more experience with Excel.

A range of ten cells (the highlighted cells)

	A	B	C	D	E
1	Monthly Expenses		2/23/95		FEBEXP
2	February				
3					
4		Budget	Expense	Variance	
5					
6	Salaries & Wages	50000	51784		
7	Rent & Utilities	17500	18222		
8	Maintenance	1500	1922		
9	Supplies	7750	7912		
10	Miscellaneous	8250	7211		
11					
12	Total				
13					

Select All button → (points to corner button)
Column portion of frame → (points to column headers)
Row portion of frame (points to row numbers)

How to select cells with the mouse

- Drag the mouse over the range of cells.
- Click or drag the mouse in the portion of the frame that contains column letters to select all the cells in one or more columns.
- Click or drag the mouse in the portion of the frame that contains row numbers to select all the cells in one or more rows.
- Click on the Select All button to select all the cells in the worksheet.

How to select a range of cells with the keyboard

1. Move the cell pointer to the first cell in the range.
2. Hold down the Shift key while you move the cell pointer to the last cell in the range.
3. Release the Shift key to complete the selection.

How to select cells with shortcut keys

Key	Function
Ctrl+Spacebar	Selects the entire column that the cell pointer is in.
Shift+Spacebar	Selects the entire row that the cell pointer is in.
Ctrl+A	Selects the entire worksheet.

How to reduce or extend a selection

- Hold down the Shift key. Then, click on a different ending point for the selection, or use the keyboard to move the highlight to a different ending point.

How to select two or more nonadjacent ranges at the same time

- Hold down the Ctrl key while you use the mouse to select two or more *nonadjacent selections*.

Figure 1-11   How to select cells

How to use toolbar buttons to align entries

By default, text is aligned on the left of a cell and numbers, dates, and times are aligned on the right. If you want to change the alignment of an entry, you can use the buttons in the Formatting toolbar presented in figure 1-12. These buttons let you align the entries on the left or right of the cells or in the center of the cells.

Three cells that have been right aligned

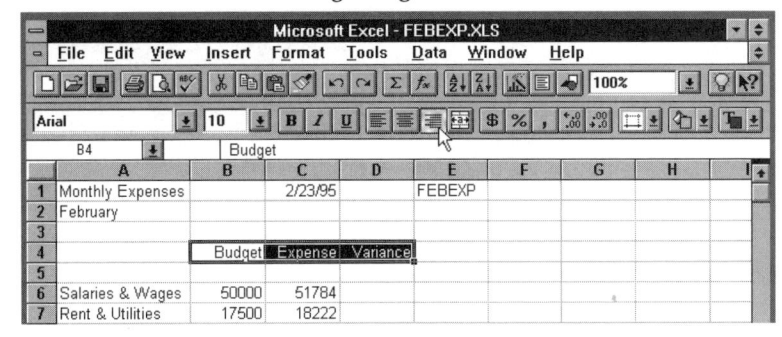

The alignment buttons in the Formatting toolbar

Button	Name	Function
	Align Left	Aligns the data at the left side of the cell.
	Center	Centers the data in the cell.
	Align Right	Aligns the data at the right side of the cell.

Procedure

1. Select the cells that contain the data you want to align.
2. Click on one of the toolbar buttons for alignment. This makes the button look as if it has been pushed in.

Notes

- To return the alignment to the default, click on the button for that alignment. Or, click again on the button you used to change the alignment (the one that looks like it has been pushed in).
- You can also align data using the Alignment tab of the dialog box that's displayed when you choose the Cells command from the Format menu. This tab presents some additional alignment options, but you're not likely to need them.

Figure 1-12   How to use the Formatting toolbar to align data

How to use toolbar buttons to format numbers

The easiest way to change the format of the numbers in a cell or a range of cells is to use the toolbar buttons shown in figure 1-13. The first three buttons apply the indicated format to the selected cells. The last two buttons change the number of decimal places in the numeric format. You can use these buttons to apply most of the number formats you'll ever need in business worksheets. If you need to apply a different format, however, you can use the Cells command in the Format menu.

When you use the first three buttons in figure 1-13 to format numbers, you are actually applying a *style* to each cell. This style includes both numeric formatting and right alignment. As a result, you can't align a cell that has been formatted with one of these styles. In chapter 3, you can learn more about the use of styles, but you shouldn't have any trouble using the Currency, Percent, and Comma styles in the meantime.

Ten cells that have been formatted with the Comma style and no decimal places

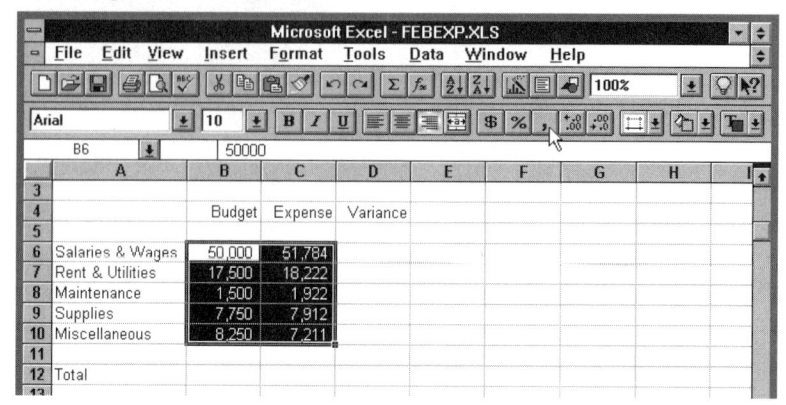

Button	Name	Function
$	Currency Style	Applies the style with two decimal places
%	Percent Style	Applies the style with no decimal places
,	Comma Style	Applies the style with two decimal places
+.0/.00	Increase Decimal	Adds one decimal place
.00/+.0	Decrease Decimal	Removes one decimal place

Procedure

1. Select the cells that contain the numbers you want to format.
2. Click on one of the style buttons to format the cells.
3. If necessary, click on one of the one of the toolbar buttons to increase or decrease the number of decimal places.

Notes

- As the button names imply, a *style* is applied to the selected range when you click on the Currency Style, Percent Style, or Comma Style button.
- When you format numbers with styles, you can't align them by clicking on the alignment buttons in the Formatting toolbar.
- You can also format numbers using the Number tab of the dialog box that's displayed when you choose the Cells command from the Format menu. This tab presents a variety of formatting options, but you're not likely to need them.

Figure 1-13   How to use the Formatting toolbar to format numbers

Exercise set 1-3

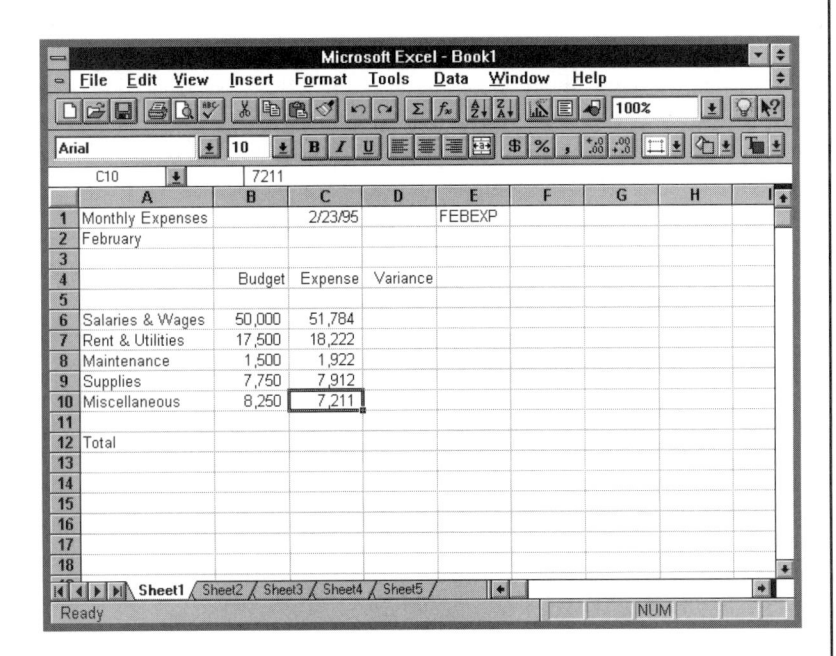

How your worksheet should look after exercise 3

1. Use the mouse or the keyboard as described in figure 1-11 to select all of the cells in the worksheet. Then, click on the Align Left button in the Formatting toolbar to align all of the entries on the left. Notice that the Align Left button now appears as if it's depressed. Click on the Align Left button again. What happens to the numbers?

2. Select columns B, C, and D, and click on the Center button to center all of the entries in those columns. Then, click on the Align Right button to align all of the entries on the right.

3. Use the mouse or the keyboard to select the range of cells that contains numbers only. Then, click on the Comma Style toolbar button to format the numbers with commas. Are all of the numbers displayed properly? Click on the Decrease Decimal button twice so that the numbers are displayed with no decimal places. Now are all of the numbers displayed as shown above?

4. With the range of numbers still selected, click on the Align Left button. Are the numbers aligned on the left? They shouldn't be because the Comma style includes right alignment.

5. Use the last technique in figure 1-11 to select all of the cells that contain text at the same time. This can be useful when you want to format several nonadjacent selections at the same time. Click anywhere in the worksheet to cancel the selections.

How to enter formulas and functions into a worksheet

When you want to perform calculations in a worksheet, you use *formulas*. To help simplify the task of creating formulas, Excel provides a set of built-in formulas, called *functions*. Functions perform a variety of operations, such as adding the values in a range and getting the average of the values in a range.

How to enter formulas into a worksheet

Figure 1-14 presents a typical procedure for entering a *formula* into a worksheet. Here, the Budget amount for Salaries & Wages in cell B6 is subtracted from the Expense amount in cell C6 to create a new value called the Variance in cell D6. When the procedure in this figure is complete, the formula is shown in the formula bar (=C6-B6) and the formatted result is shown in the cell that contains the formula (1,784).

In the procedure in figure 1-14, the mouse is used to identify the cells used in the formula, but you can also use the keyboard to identify the next cell that's used in a formula. You can even type a cell reference like C6 directly into a formula, but you're more likely to make an error that way.

Procedure

1. Click on the cell that you want to enter the formula into. Then, type an equals sign and click on the first cell to be used in the formula. Here, the formula is in cell D6 and the first value to be used is in cell C6:

	A	B	C	D	E
1	Monthly Expenses		2/23/95		FEBEXP
2	February				
3					
4		Budget	Expense	Variance	
5					
6	Salaries & Wages	50,000	51,784	=C6	
7	Rent & Utilities	17,500	18,222		
8	Maintenance	1,500	1,922		
9	Supplies	7,750	7,912		
10	Miscellaneous	8,250	7,211		
11					
12	Total				
13					

2. Type the first operator that's required. Then, click on the next cell that's required. Here, the operator is the minus sign and the next cell is cell B6:

	A	B	C	D	E
1	Monthly Expenses		2/23/95		FEBEXP
2	February				
3					
4		Budget	Expense	Variance	
5					
6	Salaries & Wages	50,000	51,784	=C6-B6	
7	Rent & Utilities	17,500	18,222		
8	Maintenance	1,500	1,922		
9	Supplies	7,750	7,912		
10	Miscellaneous	8,250	7,211		
11					
12	Total				
13					

3. Press the Enter key, and Excel calculates the result of the formula:

	A	B	C	D	E
1	Monthly Expenses		2/23/95		FEBEXP
2	February				
3					
4		Budget	Expense	Variance	
5					
6	Salaries & Wages	50,000	51,784	1,784	
7	Rent & Utilities	17,500	18,222		
8	Maintenance	1,500	1,922		
9	Supplies	7,750	7,912		
10	Miscellaneous	8,250	7,211		
11					
12	Total				
13					

Figure 1-14 How to enter a simple formula using the mouse to identify the cells used in the formula

Figure 1-15 gives all the information that you need for entering formulas into a worksheet. As you can see, a formula can consist of a series of cell references or constants that are connected by *arithmetic operators*. If there's any doubt about how the formula will be evaluated, you can add parentheses to the formula to clarify the sequence of operations. Otherwise, the formula is evaluated from left to right, one order of precedence at a time.

If you're good at math and comfortable with algebra, you shouldn't have any trouble developing the formulas that are required in your worksheets. But what if you aren't?

Because most business worksheets don't require complex formulas, you should still be able to get by. If you do the exercises in this book, you'll be introduced to the types of business formulas that you're most likely to use. As you work, you'll see that most of them require simple math, just two or three operators, and an occasional use of parentheses.

Example	Description
=C5-B5	Subtracts the value of cell B5 from the value of cell C5.
=C3+C4+C5	Adds the value of cells C3, C4, and C5.
=-D10*.065	Multiplies the negative value of cell D10 by .065.
=(C5-B5)/B5	First, subtracts the value of cell B5 from the value of cell C5; then, divides the result by the value of cell B5.
=G12^2	Raises the value of cell G12 to the second power.

General procedure

1. Start the formula by typing an equals sign (=).
2. Identify the first cell or type the first constant to be used in the formula. This can be preceded by a plus or minus sign as shown in the third example above.
3. Type an arithmetic operator, then identify the next cell or type the next constant to be used in the formula.
4. Continue in this way until the formula is complete. Then, press the Enter key.

Three ways to identify the next cell that's used in a formula

1. Use the mouse to select the cell.
2. Use the pointer-movement keys to move the cell pointer to the cell.
3. Type a direct cell reference like C5 into the formula.

The arithmetic operators you can use in a formula

Operator	Operation	Order of Precedence
+ or -	Plus or minus sign before a cell reference or constant	First
^	Exponentiation (raise to the power of)	Second
* or /	Multiplication or division	Third
+ or -	Addition or subtraction	Fourth

The sequence in which operations are performed

- This follows algebraic rules based on the order of precedence given above. The operations are done from left to right with all signs evaluated first, all exponentiation second, all multiplication and division third, and all addition and subtraction last.
- If you use parentheses, the expressions in the innermost sets of parentheses are done first followed by the expressions in subsequent sets of parentheses.

Figure 1-15 General procedures and rules for entering formulas

How to copy formulas to adjacent cells

Many worksheets contain two or more formulas that are identical except for the cells they refer to. If you look back at figure 1-14, for example, you can see that the calculations for cells D7 through D10 will be the same as for cell D6, although the cell references will be different. In a case like that, you can copy the formula from one cell to the adjacent cells using the AutoFill feature of Excel.

Figure 1-16 shows how to use the AutoFill feature to copy a formula to adjacent cells. To do that, you just drag the *fill handle* on the lower right corner of the cell that you want to copy. When you copy a formula, Excel adjusts the cell references in each formula so they refer to the appropriate cells. In figure 1-16, for example, the formula in cell D7 is =C7-B7, and the formula in cell D8 is =C8-B8.

Procedure

1. Place the cell pointer on the cell that contains the formula you want to copy. Then, place the mouse pointer over the fill handle (the lower right corner of the cell) so the pointer turns into a cross:

	A	B	C	D	E
1	Monthly Expenses		2/23/95		FEBEXP
2	February				
3					
4		Budget	Expense	Variance	
5					
6	Salaries & Wages	50,000	51,784	1,784	
7	Rent & Utilities	17,500	18,222		
8	Maintenance	1,500	1,922		
9	Supplies	7,750	7,912		
10	Miscellaneous	8,250	7,211		
11					
12	Total				
13					

D6 =C6-B6

2. Drag the fill handle across the range you want to copy the formula to:

	A	B	C	D	E
1	Monthly Expenses		2/23/95		FEBEXP
2	February				
3					
4		Budget	Expense	Variance	
5					
6	Salaries & Wages	50,000	51,784	1,784	
7	Rent & Utilities	17,500	18,222		
8	Maintenance	1,500	1,922		
9	Supplies	7,750	7,912		
10	Miscellaneous	8,250	7,211		
11					
12	Total				
13					

=C6-B6

3. Release the mouse button and the formula is copied into the range:

	A	B	C	D	E
1	Monthly Expenses		2/23/95		FEBEXP
2	February				
3					
4		Budget	Expense	Variance	
5					
6	Salaries & Wages	50,000	51,784	1,784	
7	Rent & Utilities	17,500	18,222	722	
8	Maintenance	1,500	1,922	422	
9	Supplies	7,750	7,912	162	
10	Miscellaneous	8,250	7,211	(1,039)	
11					
12	Total				
13					

D6 =C6-B6

Figure 1-16 How to use the AutoFill feature to copy formulas

How to enter functions into a worksheet

Figure 1-17 presents a typical procedure for entering a *function* into a worksheet. Here, the SUM function is entered into cell B12. This function adds the numbers in the range from cell B6 through cell B10. In other words, this function totals the numbers in the Budget column.

In figure 1-17, the mouse is used to identify the range that the function operates upon, but you can also use keyboard techniques to identify the range. You can even type the range directly into the parentheses within the function like this: b6:b10. Here again, though, you're more likely to make an error with direct entry than you are if you select the range that you want to operate upon.

Procedure

1. Click on the cell that you want to enter the function into. Then, type an equals sign, the name of the function, and a left parenthesis. Here, the function in cell B12 is SUM:

	A	B	C	D	E
1	Monthly Expenses		2/23/95		FEBEXP
2	February				
3					
4		Budget	Expense	Variance	
5					
6	Salaries & Wages	50,000	51,784	1,784	
7	Rent & Utilities	17,500	18,222	722	
8	Maintenance	1,500	1,922	422	
9	Supplies	7,750	7,912	162	
10	Miscellaneous	8,250	7,211	(1,039)	
11					
12	Total	=sum(			
13					

2. Use the mouse to identify the range you want the function to operate on. Here, the range is B6:B10:

	A	B	C	D	E
1	Monthly Expenses		2/23/95		FEBEXP
2	February				
3					
4		Budget	Expense	Variance	
5					
6	Salaries & Wages	50,000	51,784	1,784	
7	Rent & Utilities	17,500	18,222	722	
8	Maintenance	1,500	1,922	422	
9	Supplies	7,750	7,912	162	
10	Miscellaneous	8,250	7,211	(1,039)	
11					
12	Total	=sum(B6:B10			
13					

3. Press the Enter key, and Excel adds a right parenthesis and calculates the result of the function:

	A	B	C	D	E
1	Monthly Expenses		2/23/95		FEBEXP
2	February				
3					
4		Budget	Expense	Variance	
5					
6	Salaries & Wages	50,000	51,784	1,784	
7	Rent & Utilities	17,500	18,222	722	
8	Maintenance	1,500	1,922	422	
9	Supplies	7,750	7,912	162	
10	Miscellaneous	8,250	7,211	(1,039)	
11					
12	Total	85,000			
13					

Figure 1-17 How to enter a SUM function using the mouse to identify the range

Figure 1-18 gives the information that you need for entering five of the most useful *functions* into a worksheet. As you can see, each function begins with a function name like SUM. The function name is followed by a set of parentheses that may contain an *argument*. Even though the TODAY and NOW functions don't require arguments, they still require the set of parentheses. In contrast, the SUM, COUNT, and AVERAGE functions require just one argument, which is the range of cells to be summed, counted, or averaged.

Although the five functions in figure 1-18 are the ones you're most likely to use for business worksheets, Excel provides many others including statistical, financial, math, trigonometry, and engineering functions. You'll learn about some of these functions in chapter 7 along with advanced techniques for working with formulas and functions.

Additional information

✓ To find out about all of the functions that are available with Excel, you can use Excel's on-line help. To do that, choose the Search For Help On command from the Help menu and type "Worksheet functions" into the dialog box that appears. Then, click on the Show Topics button and choose a topic from those that are listed.

✓ If you use the TODAY or NOW function, you'll see that it is automatically formatted in a way that is appropriate for most worksheets. If you want to change this format, you can access the Cells command in the Format menu, then click on the Number tab and choose a new format.

Five of the most useful functions

Format	Example	Function
TODAY()	today()	Returns the current date in this form: m/d/yy.
NOW()	now()	Returns the current date and time in this form: m/d/yy h:mm
SUM(range)	sum(b5:b10)	Adds the numbers in the range.
COUNT(range)	count(b5:b10)	Counts the cells in the range that contain numbers.
AVERAGE(range)	average(b10:f10)	Calculates the average of the numbers in the range.

General procedure

1. Type the equals sign to start the formula.
2. Type the name of the function and a left parenthesis.
3. If no arguments are required, skip to step 5.
4. Identify the range for the function using one of the methods below. In the function that's displayed, the cell references for the corners of the range are separated by a colon (:).
5. Press the Enter key to complete the function. This automatically adds a right parenthesis to the function.

Three ways to identify a range

1. Use the mouse to select the range.
2. Move the cell pointer to one corner of the range. Then, hold down the Shift key while you move the pointer to the other corner of the range. When you release the Shift key, the range is added to the function.
3. Type the cell reference for one corner of the range; type a colon (:); and type the cell reference for the other corner of the range.

Notes

- If a formula consists of one function by itself, the function must be preceded by an equals sign as indicated by the procedure above.
- If a function is part of a larger formula, the equals sign is entered at the beginning of the formula and the function is entered into the formula wherever it is appropriate.

Figure 1-18   General procedures and rules for entering functions

How to use the AutoSum toolbar button

The SUM function is the most commonly used Excel function. Because of that, Excel provides a toolbar button called AutoSum that makes it easy to add SUM functions to your worksheets.

Figure 1-19 shows how easy this can be. Here, you just move the cell pointer to cell B12, click on the AutoSum button in the toolbar, and press the Enter key. In this example, you can see that Excel automatically selects the range from cell B6 through B11. Note that this range includes the empty cell above the SUM function, but there's nothing wrong with that.

If you read the notes in figure 1-19, you'll realize that the AutoSum button doesn't always select the right range for the function. That's why you should always check the selected range to make sure it's correct before you press the Enter key. If it isn't correct, you can use the mouse or keyboard to select the right range.

Procedure

1. Move the cell pointer to a cell below or to the right of the cells to be summed. Then, click on the AutoSum button, and Excel inserts the SUM function with a range argument:

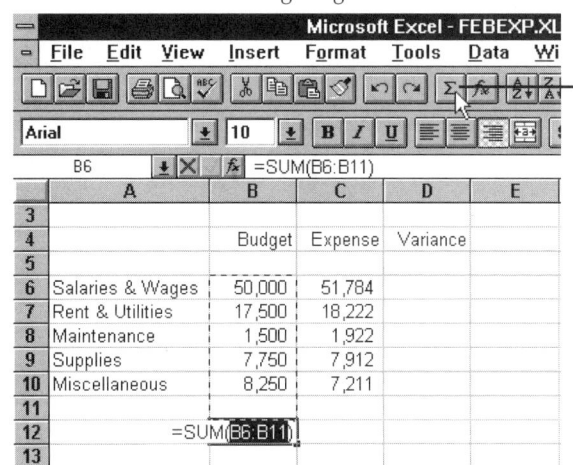

2. Press the Enter key and the result is displayed:

Notes

- If the active cell only has numbers above it, those numbers are summed by the AutoSum button. If the active cell only has numbers to its left, those numbers are summed. And if the active cell has numbers both above and to the left of it, the cells above it are summed.

- The assumed range starts with the first cell above or to the left of the active cell and continues to the first cell that is blank or doesn't contain a number.

- If you select a range and click on the AutoSum button, Excel inserts the SUM function into the first blank cell below or to the right of the range.

- If the range Excel inserts into the Sum function is incorrect, you can change it by entering or selecting a different range.

- To enter SUM functions into a range of cells, select a range below the columns of data or to the right of the rows of data you want to sum before you click on the AutoSum button.

Figure 1-19 How to use the AutoSum button

How to align and format the result of a formula or function

If the result of a formula or function is numeric and the cell hasn't been formatted yet, Excel applies the same format or style to the result cell as the cells that the formula or function refers to. In most cases, that's what you want. If you want to change the format of the cell that contains a formula or function, however, you can use the toolbar buttons that were presented in figure 1-13. You may also need to use these toolbar buttons if the cells that the formula or function refers to contain varying formats and the format Excel chooses isn't the one you want.

The alignment that Excel applies to a cell that contains a formula or function may also depend on the alignment of the cells used in the formula or function. Then, to change the alignment of the entry, you can use the buttons in the Formatting toolbar that were presented in figure 1-12. Remember, though, that the data in cells that are formatted with styles can't be aligned.

Exercise set 1-4

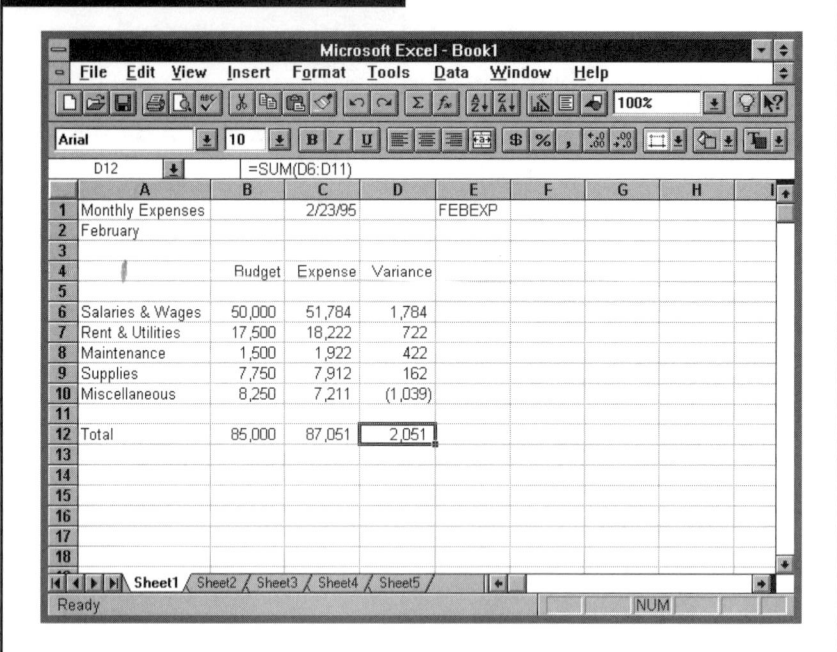

When you complete this set of exercises, your worksheet should look like the one above.

1. Use the technique illustrated in figure 1-14 to enter the formula shown in cell D6 into your worksheet. Remember to use the mouse pointer to identify the cells used in the formula instead of typing them in. How is the result of the formula formatted?

2. Use the AutoFill feature illustrated in figure 1-16 to copy the formula you entered in cell D6 to cells D7 through D10. Then, place the cell pointer on cell D10. Does the formula in the formula bar for that cell contain the correct cell references?

3. Use the technique illustrated in figure 1-17 to sum the values in the Budget column of your worksheet in cell B12. How is the result of the function formatted?

4. Use the AutoFill feature to copy the function you entered in exercise 3 into the Total row of the Expense column (cell C12).

5. Use the AutoSum button as described in figure 1-19 to sum the values in the Variance column of your worksheet in cell D12. Does Excel suggest the correct range for the function? If not, select the correct range and complete the function.

6. Select cells B12, C12, and D12, and press the Delete key to delete their contents. Then, with the cells still selected, click on the AutoSum button. What happens?

How to use the commands in the File menu

Figure 1-20 summarizes the commands in the File menu that are presented in this book. If you've used other Windows programs, you may already be familiar with many of these commands. In this chapter, you'll learn how to use all of the commands in this summary, except for the Page Setup and Print Preview commands, which are presented in chapters 3 and 4. The three commands in the File menu that aren't presented in this book go well beyond the basic functions that all Excel users need so you can easily get by without them.

Note that the first six commands in the summary in figure 1-20 apply to *workbooks*, not *worksheets*. Although the examples thus far have been for a workbook that contains just one worksheet, remember that a workbook can contain more than one worksheet. When you save a file, you save all the sheets in the workbook. And when you open a file, you retrieve all the sheets.

To the right of four of the commands in the File menu in figure 1-20, you can see the *shortcut key* for starting the command. This notation is also used in two of the other Excel menus. To start a command without pulling down the menu, just press the shortcut key. To start the Open command, for example, hold down the Ctrl key while you press the key for the letter *o*.

New...	Ctrl+N
Open...	Ctrl+O
Close	
Save	Ctrl+S
Save As...	
Save Workspace...	
Find File...	
Summary Info...	
Page Setup...	
Print Preview	
Print...	Ctrl+P
Print Report...	
1 1QEXP.XLS	
2 2QEXP.XLS	
3 3QEXP.XLS	
4 FEBEXP.XLS	
Exit	

Command	Function
New	Opens a window so you can start a new workbook.
Open	Retrieves a file from disk into a new workbook window.
Close	Closes the active workbook window.
Save	Saves the active workbook to disk. If the workbook hasn't been saved before, this works like the Save As command.
Save As	Saves the active workbook to disk after you select a drive and directory and provide a file name.
Summary Info	Lets you supply information that identifies the active workbook.
Page Setup	Lets you set options that affect the layout of the printed page (see chapters 3 and 4).
Print Preview	Displays an image of the active worksheet as it will appear when printed (see chapter 3).
Print	Prints the active worksheet or an entire workbook.
file name	Opens the file that's named. The files that are listed are the last four files you worked on.
Exit	Quits Excel.

Notes

- The shortcut key for a command is given to its right. To start the Open command, for example, you can press Ctrl+O.
- If the last four files that you used aren't listed on the File menu, this option is off on your PC. To turn it on, access the Options command in the Tools menu. Then, check the Recently Used Files List option on the General tab.

Figure 1-20   The commands of the File menu

How to print a worksheet

Figure 1-21 summarizes the use of the Print command. The notation at the top of this figure shows three ways to start this command. First, you can use the Print command in the File menu. Second, you can press Ctrl+P. Third, you can click on the Print button in the Standard toolbar. This notation is used throughout this book to show at a glance the various ways that a command can be started. Note, however, that the Print dialog box isn't displayed when you use the toolbar button.

When the Print dialog box is displayed, you can specify the number of copies that you want to print. You can also specify whether you want to print the selected worksheet, the selected cells (if you select some before you access this dialog box), or the entire workbook (if it consists of more than one worksheet). If you just want to print one copy of the current worksheet, though, the options are already set the way you want them.

If your PC is on a network so more than one printer is available to you, you can click on the Printer Setup button to display another dialog box. Then, you can select another printer for the worksheet.

When the worksheet is printed, only the range of the cells in use is printed. By default, the name on the sheet tab for the worksheet is printed at the top of the page and the page number is printed at the bottom. In chapter 3, you can learn to change these defaults. In chapter 4, you'll learn how to use the other controls in the Print dialog box.

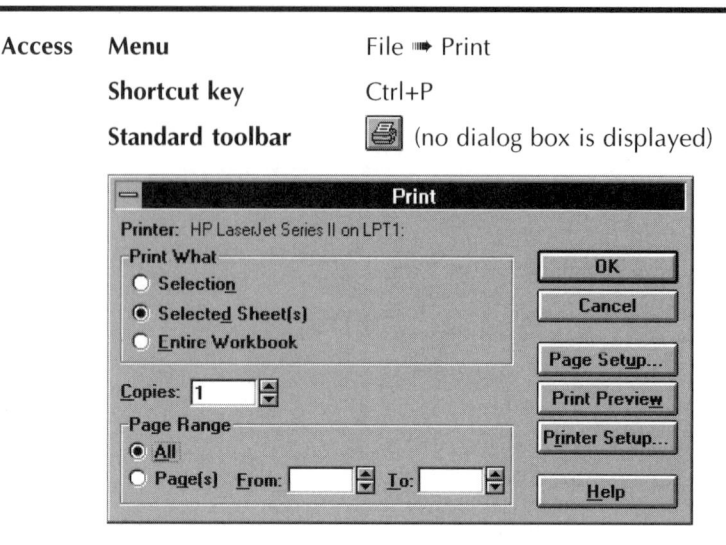

Access	Menu	File ➡ Print
	Shortcut key	Ctrl+P
	Standard toolbar	(no dialog box is displayed)

How to use the Print dialog box

- To print one copy of the active worksheet on the default printer, just click on the OK button. To print more than one copy, enter a number in the Copies box before you click on the OK button.

- A description of the printer that's going to be used is given at the top of the Print dialog box. If you want to change to another printer, click on the Printer Setup button in the Print dialog box. Then, in the Printer Setup dialog box, double-click on the printer that you want to change to.

How to use the Print toolbar button

- The Print toolbar button prints one copy of the active worksheet with the print settings that you last used. No dialog box is displayed when you start the Print command this way.

Figure 1-21   How to print a worksheet

How to create, print, and save a worksheet

How to save a workbook

When you finish a worksheet, you need to save it if you want to use it again. To do that, you use the Save or Save As command as described in figure 1-22. When you issue either of these commands from a new workbook, Excel displays the Save As dialog box, which lets you select the drive and directory for the file and supply a file name for it. If you don't supply a file name, Excel creates one for you like BOOK1.XLS, but you usually don't want that.

By default, Excel also displays the Summary Info dialog box when you save a new file. This dialog box lets you enter information that can help you identify the contents of the file. If necessary, you can change that information later by using the Summary Info command in the File menu.

Once a workbook has been saved, the Save command doesn't display the Save As dialog box. Instead, Excel saves the updated file in its previous location without displaying the Save As or Summary Info dialog boxes. So if you want to save an existing file with a different file name or in a different location, you have to use the Save As command.

Additional information

✓ You can use the General tab of the Options command in the Tools menu to turn off the Prompt for Summary Info option. Then, the Summary Info dialog box isn't displayed when you save a file. You can also use this tab to type a path for the Default File Location that's used the first time you access the Save As or Open dialog box in a work session.

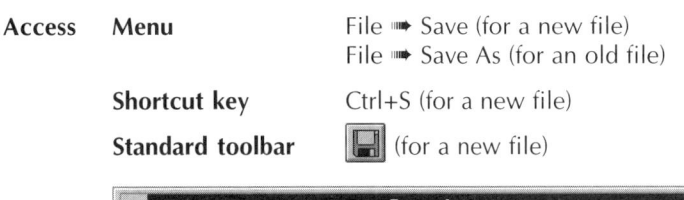

Access		
Menu		File ➡ Save (for a new file)
		File ➡ Save As (for an old file)
Shortcut key		Ctrl+S (for a new file)
Standard toolbar		💾 (for a new file)

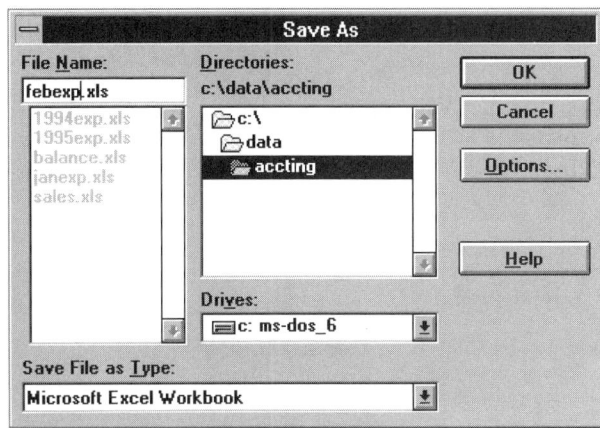

Procedure

1. Access the Save As dialog box.
2. Identify the drive and directory for the file in the Drives and Directories boxes.
3. Replace the default name in the File Name box by typing a valid file name when the default name is highlighted. If the default name isn't highlighted, you can double-click on it or press Alt+N to highlight it. If you omit the extension, XLS is used.
4. Click on the OK button. If the Summary Info option is on, this dialog box appears: 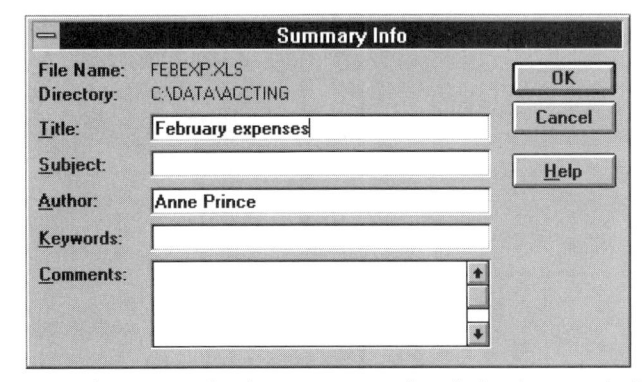
5. Type the required information into this dialog box, and click on the OK button to complete the command.

Notes

- The first time you access the Save command for a new workbook, the Save As dialog box is displayed. After that, the workbook is saved with no intervening dialog box, thus replacing the previous version of the file.
- If you have any trouble identifying the drive or directory in step 2, please refer to figure P-17 in the prerequisites chapter.

Figure 1-22 How to save a workbook

How to close a workbook

After you save a file, you can close it if you don't want to work with it any more. To do that, you issue the Close command as described in figure 1-23. Notice that if you issue this command before you save the workbook, Excel gives you an opportunity to save the workbook before it closes the workbook window.

Procedure

1. Choose the Close command from the File menu. If the workbook hasn't been saved, this dialog box appears:

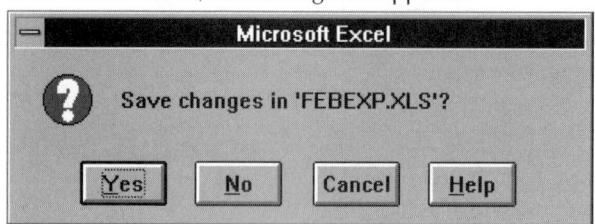

2. Click on the Yes button if you want to save the changes; click on the No button if you don't want to save the changes; and click on the Cancel button if you want to cancel the operation and return to the workbook.

Notes

- If you're closing a new workbook and you click on the Yes button to save the changes, Excel displays the Save As and Summary Info dialog boxes shown in figure 1-22. When you complete these dialog boxes, the file is saved and closed.

- If you're saving an old workbook and you click on the Yes button, the file is saved and closed without any intervening dialog boxes.

Figure 1-23   How to close a workbook

How to open a workbook

Figure 1-24 shows you how to open a workbook. Once you identify the drive and directory that the workbook is in, you simply choose the file from the list that's displayed. If the file you want to open is one of the last four files you worked on, you can also open it by choosing the file name from the bottom of the File menu.

When you *open a file*, it is retrieved from disk and displayed in a new workbook window. If you want to open more than one file at the same time, you can do that with Excel. Then, you can use the Windows menu to switch from one workbook window to another. You'll see how to do that in the next chapter.

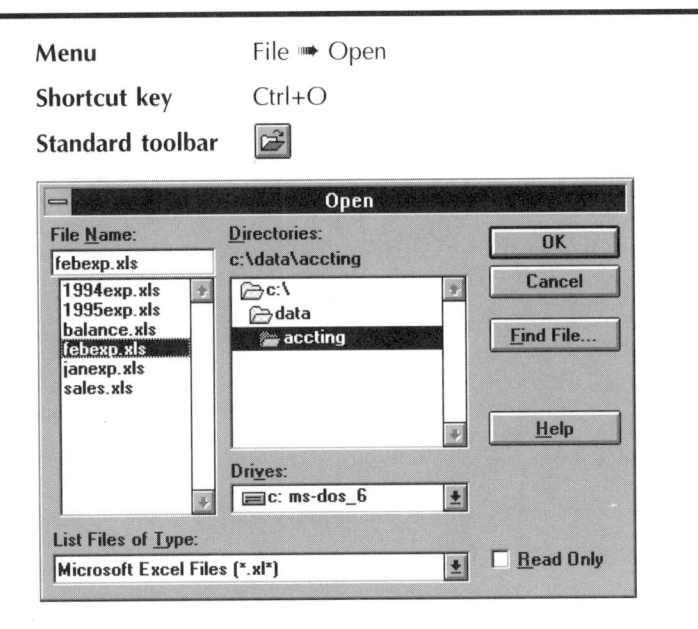

Access		
	Menu	File ➡ Open
	Shortcut key	Ctrl+O
	Standard toolbar	📂

Procedure

1. Access the Open dialog box.
2. Identify the drive and directory that contains the workbook using the Drives and Directories lists. Then, the files in that directory are displayed in the File Name list box.
3. Double-click on the name of the file you want to open, or highlight the name and click on the OK button.

Note

- If the file you want to open is one of the last four files you worked on, you can open the file by choosing the file name from the bottom of the File menu.

Figure 1-24 How to open a workbook

How to start a new workbook

When you start Excel, it displays an empty window where you can start a new workbook. Later, if you want to start another new workbook, you use the New command. You can start this command from the File menu, with its keyboard shortcut (Ctrl+N), or with the New toolbar button (it's the first one on the Standard toolbar.) Then, Excel opens up a new workbook window.

How to exit from Excel

To exit from Excel, you issue the Exit command. If you haven't saved the last changes you made to one or more of the open workbooks, a dialog box appears that gives you a chance to save the changes. Otherwise, Excel ends and you are switched to one of the other programs that's running (usually, the Program Manager).

Exercise set 1-5

1. Use the Print command or the Print button as described in figure 1-21 to print one copy of the worksheet you created in this chapter. Notice that Excel's default is to print the worksheet with a dark outline, lines between the cells, the sheet name at the top of the page, and the page number at the bottom. In chapters 3 and 4, you'll learn how to change these defaults.

2. Use the procedure in figure 1-22 to save the workbook. After you select the drive and directory, replace the default file name in the File Name box with FEBEXP. Don't use capital letters, though, and don't add an extension. Then, click on the OK button. If the Summary Info dialog box is displayed, type "February expenses" as the title and your name as the Author before clicking on the OK button to complete the command.

3. Use the Save command to save the file again. Note that no dialog box is displayed.

4. Use the procedure in figure 1-23 to close the workbook. Does a dialog box appear that asks you if you want to save the changes to the workbook?

5. Use the procedure in figure 1-24 to open the FEBEXP workbook. Do the drive and directory in the Open dialog box default to the location where you saved the workbook? Does the file name have the extension XLS?

6. Change the workbook so that it presents the monthly expenses for March as shown here:

	A	B	C	D	E	F	G	H
1	Monthly Expenses		5/1/95		MAREXP			
2	March							
3								
4			Budget	Expense	Variance			
5								
6	Salaries & Wages		50,000	51,004	1,004			
7	Rent & Utilities		17,500	17,453	(47)			
8	Maintenance		1,500	1,399	(101)			
9	Supplies		7,750	7,784	34			
10	Miscellaneous		8,250	9,374	1,124			
11								
12	Total		85,000	87,014	2,014			
13								

First, change the text in cell A2 from "February" to "March." Second, press the Delete key with the cell pointer on cell C1 to delete the date, and use the TODAY function to enter the current date in that cell. Third, change the file name in cell E1 from FEBEXP to MAREXP. Fourth, change the numbers in the Expense column (cells C6 through C10) to the ones shown above. Notice that the formulas and functions in the worksheet are recalculated each time you enter a new number.

7. Use the Save As command in the File menu to save the changed worksheet with the name MAREXP. This file should be saved in the same directory as the FEBEXP file. Next, use the Print button in the Standard toolbar to print the worksheet. Then, close the workbook.

Perspective

If you've done the exercises for this chapter, you have now entered, printed, and saved two worksheets. You've done this using the commands and techniques that the best professionals use. And you're ready to learn the editing and formatting techniques that are presented in the next two chapters.

Summary

- When you start Excel, its *application window* contains one *document*, or *workbook, window*. Within the workbook window is a *workbook*, which contains one or more *worksheets* identified by *sheet tabs*.

- Each *cell* in a worksheet is identified by a column letter and row number found in the *worksheet frame*. The *active cell* is identified by the *cell pointer*. You can use the keyboard or the mouse to move the cell pointer.

- The Standard and Formatting toolbars contain *toolbar buttons* that let you perform pre-defined functions. To start a button's function, you click on the button.

- To enter data into a cell, you move the cell pointer to the cell and type. Excel determines if the entry is *text*, a *number*, or a date or time based on the characters you type. You can also enter data into a range of cells using the range entry technique.

- If you need to change the data in a cell, you can re-enter the correct data or you can *edit* the existing data.

- You can use the mouse to change the width of a column so it accommodates the widest entry in the column or so it accommodates a specific number of characters.

- You can select a *range* of cells in a worksheet using the mouse or the keyboard.

- You can use the buttons in the Formatting toolbar to change the alignment of the data in one or more cells and to change the format of the numbers in one or more cells. You can also format numbers as you enter them when the cells have the General format.

- A *formula* performs a calculation that's based on one or more cells in a worksheet. When you enter a formula, you can use the mouse pointer or the keyboard to identify the cells that the formula refers to.

- A *function* is a pre-defined formula. The most commonly used function is the SUM function, which adds the values in a range. An easy way to enter a SUM function is to use the AutoSum button in the Standard toolbar.

- You can use the AutoFill feature to copy a formula or function to adjacent cells. When you use this feature, Excel automatically adjusts the cell references in the formulas or functions.

- You can use commands in the File menu to print, save, close, and open a workbook, start a new workbook, or exit from Excel. You can also use buttons in the Standard toolbar and shortcut keys to start some of these commands.

Chapter 2

How to edit a worksheet

When you *edit* a worksheet, you change the information it presents or how it's presented. In chapter 1, for example, you learned how to edit the contents of a cell.

In this chapter, you'll learn how to perform other editing operations such as moving and copying data and inserting and deleting rows and columns. To a large extent, how efficiently you can perform editing operations like these determines how productive you can be with Excel.

Three general skills
    How to use shortcut menus
    How to undo or repeat the last operation
    How to switch from one open workbook to another

How move, copy, or delete data
    How to move or copy data using the Cut, Copy, and Paste commands
    How to move or copy data using drag-and-drop editing
    How to copy data using the Fill commands
    How to move or copy data from one open workbook to another
    How to delete data

How to work with columns and rows
    How to adjust column widths
    How to insert or delete one or more or rows
    How to insert or delete one or more columns

Other editing skills
    How to use the AutoFill feature to generate a series
    How to sort the data in selected rows
    How to check the spelling in a worksheet
    How to search for and replace data
    How to insert or delete a range of cells

Perspective

Summary

Three general skills

Before you learn the specific skills for editing a worksheet, you should learn three general skills for editing. First, you should know how to use shortcut menus to access the editing commands. Second, you should know how to undo or repeat an operation. Third, you should know how to switch from one open workbook to another.

How to use shortcut menus

Many of the Excel commands you use most often are available from *shortcut menus*. Shortcut menus can help you work more efficiently because they're easy to access and because they're *context sensitive*. In other words, the commands in a shortcut menu change depending on what you're doing when you display the menu.

You'll use shortcut menus most often to access editing and formatting commands. Figure 2-1 shows how to do that. In this figure, the shortcut menu is for a range of cells. Although this is the shortcut menu you'll use most often, you can display other shortcut menus by clicking on other areas of a worksheet such as a row or column heading or a sheet tab. If you experiment with shortcut menus, you'll soon realize how efficient they are to use.

The shortcut menu when a range is selected

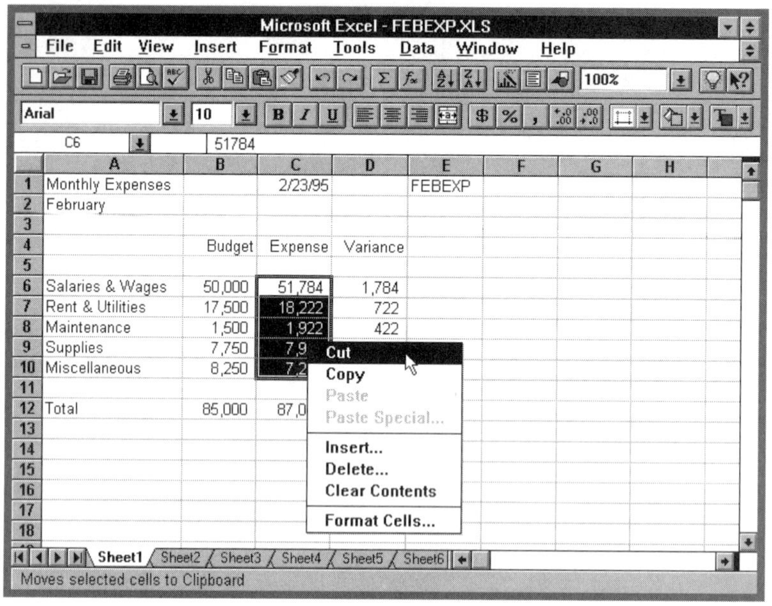

Procedure

1. Select the cell or range you want a command to affect.

2. Click the right mouse button on the selected cells to display the shortcut menu.

3. To issue a command, continue to hold the right mouse button down and drag the highlight to the command, then release the right mouse button. Or, click the left mouse button on the command after you pop up the menu.

Figure 2-1   How to use shortcut menus

How to undo or repeat the last operation

If you make a mistake while you're editing, you can easily reverse or "undo" the operation. Figure 2-2 shows three ways to do that. Note, however, that you have to undo an operation before you perform another one. That's because Excel only keeps track of the last operation you performed.

After you undo an operation, the Undo command in the Edit menu changes to Redo. Then, if you change your mind again and want to redo the operation you just undid, you can use the Redo command.

You can use the Repeat command to repeat the last editing operation. This is occasionally useful. Like the Undo command, you can only use the Repeat command to repeat the most recent operation. However, you can use the Repeat command to repeat an operation as many times as you like.

How to start the Undo and Repeat commands

	Undo	Repeat
Edit menu	Undo	Repeat
Shortcut key	Ctrl+Z	F4
Standard toolbar	[icon]	[icon]

Notes

- Not all operations can be undone. When that's the case, the words "Can't Undo" appear dimmed in the Edit menu in place of the Undo command. However, most editing and formatting operations can be undone.

- After you undo an operation, the Undo function in the Edit menu changes to Redo. Then, you can use this function to redo the operation you just undid.

- Not all operations can be repeated. When that's the case, the words "Can't Repeat" appear dimmed in the Edit menu in place of the Repeat command.

Figure 2-2 How to undo or repeat the last operation

How to switch from one open workbook to another

When you use Excel 5, you can open more than one workbook at the same time. Then, you can switch from one workbook window to another. You can also move and copy data from one workbook to another.

Figure 2-3 shows how to switch from one workbook window to another. When a workbook is open, its name is added to the bottom of the Window menu as shown in this figure. Here, three workbooks are open. Two have already been saved so their file names are listed on the Window menu. The other workbook hasn't been saved so a book number is listed for it.

To switch from one window to another, you can choose the workbook name from the Window menu. Or, you can press Ctrl+F6.

The Window menu with three open workbook windows

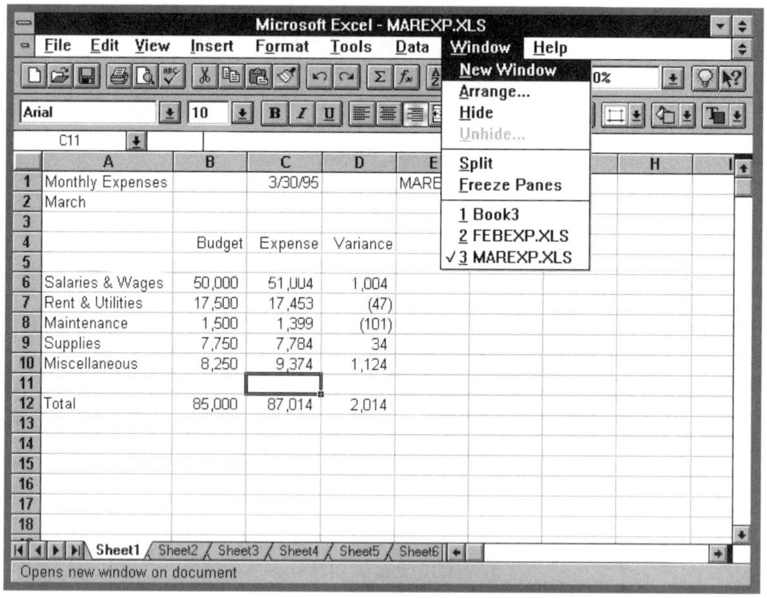

How to use the Window menu to switch to another window

Choose the name of the workbook that you want to switch to from the Window menu. The workbooks are listed by number at the bottom of the menu. If a workbook has been saved, its file name is listed. Otherwise, it is listed as Book followed by a number like Book3 in the example above.

How to use a shortcut key to switch to another window

Press Ctrl+F6 to switch to the next workbook window.

Figure 2-3   How to switch from one open workbook window to another

Exercise set 2-1

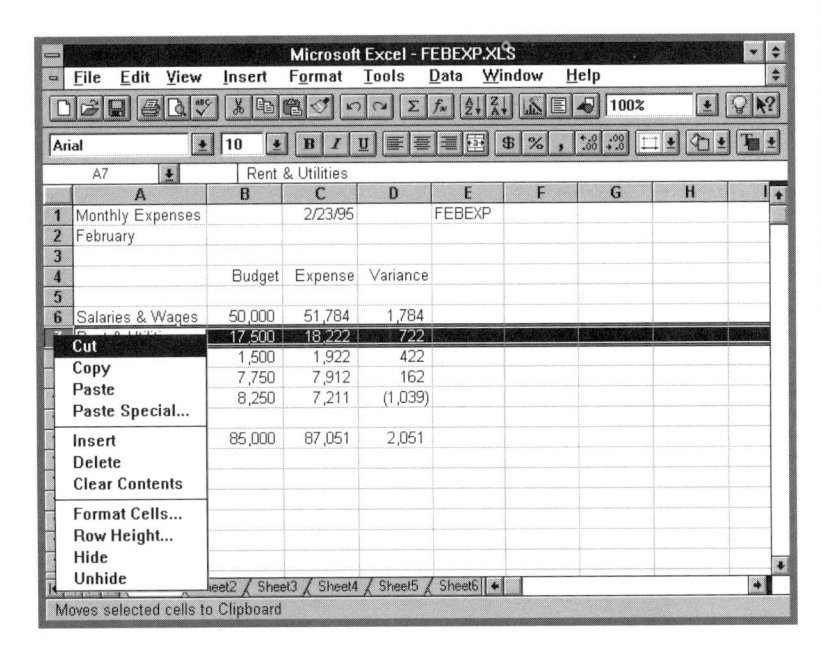

The shortcut menu that's displayed when you click on a row number in the worksheet frame

1. Open the FEBEXP workbook you created in chapter 1. Then, select any range in the worksheet and click the right mouse button on the selection to display the shortcut menu. Note the commands that are available.

2. Click the right mouse button on one of the row numbers in the worksheet frame to see what commands are included in that shortcut menu. Then, display the shortcut menus for the part of the worksheet frame that contains the column letters, for the Select All button, and for the sheet tab.

3. Edit any cell in the worksheet. Then, pull down the Edit menu and notice that the Undo command indicates that the last operation was an entry. Choose the Undo command to undo the entry operation.

4. Select the range of numbers in the Budget and Expense columns, and press the Delete key to delete them. Then, undo the deletion; redo the deletion; and undo it again.

5. Move the cell pointer to cell B4, and click on the Align Left button in the Formatting toolbar to change the alignment from right to left. Next, move the cell pointer to cell C4 and pull down the Edit menu. Notice that the Repeat command indicates that the last operation was cell formatting. Choose the Repeat command to left align the data in the active cell. Then, move the cell pointer to cell D4 and repeat the left alignment again by using the Repeat button in the toolbar or by pressing F4.

6. Open the MAREXP workbook you created in chapter 1. Two workbooks are now open. Use the Window menu to switch back to the FEBEXP workbook.

7. Press Ctrl+N to start a new workbook. Next, pull down the Window menu to see how the new workbook window is identified, and click outside the menu to close the menu. Then, press Ctrl+F6 to switch to the previous window, and press it again to see what window it switches to.

8. Close all three windows without saving the changes in any of them.

How move, copy, or delete data

When you edit a worksheet, you need to be able to move, copy, or delete the contents of cells. With Excel 5, you can do each of these functions in two or more ways.

How to move or copy data using the Cut, Copy, and Paste commands

The standard way to move and copy with any Windows program is to use the Cut, Copy, and Paste commands. This is illustrated in figure 2-4. Note that you can access these commands from the Edit or shortcut menu, with shortcut keys, or with toolbar buttons.

To start a move or a copy function, select the cells that you want to move or copy. Once that's done, you use the Cut or Copy command to place the selection on the *clipboard*. This is a temporary storage area that you don't see. Then, to copy the contents of the cells from the clipboard into the workbook, you use the Paste command.

Additional information

✓ The data on the clipboard remains there after a Paste operation so you can paste the data into more than one location. However, the data remains there only as long as the source range is marked with a shimmering border. With most other Windows programs, the data remains on the clipboard until it's replaced by another cut or copy operation.

How to start the Cut, Copy, and Paste commands

	Cut	**Copy**	**Paste**
Edit or shortcut menu	Cut	Copy	Paste
Shortcut key	Ctrl+X	Ctrl+C	Ctrl+V or Enter
Standard toolbar	✂	📋	📋

How to move the data in a range

1. Select the range of cells that you want to move:

	A	B	C	D	E
1	Monthly Expenses		2/23/95		FEBEXP
2	February				
3					
4		Budget	Expense	Variance	
5					
6	Salaries & Wages	50,000	51,784	1,784	
7	Rent & Utilities	17,500	18,222	722	

2. Cut the selected cells to the clipboard using one of the methods shown above to start the command. When the cells are cut, they remain on the screen with a shimmering border.

3. Select the cell in the upper left corner of the range where you want to move the data:

	A	B	C	D	E
1	Monthly Expenses		2/23/95		FEBEXP
2	February				
3					
4		Budget	Expense	Variance	
5					
6	Salaries & Wages	50,000	51,784	1,784	
7	Rent & Utilities	17,500	18,222	722	

4. Paste the data into the new location using one of the methods shown above to start the command. This removes the cells from their original location:

	A	B	C	D	E
1	Monthly Expenses		2/23/95		FEBEXP
2	February				
3					
4					
5		Budget	Expense	Variance	
6	Salaries & Wages	50,000	51,784	1,784	
7	Rent & Utilities	17,500	18,222	722	

How to copy the data in a range

- Use the same procedure that you use for moving data, but use the Copy command instead of the Cut command in step 2.

Figure 2-4   How to move and copy data using the Cut, Copy, and Paste commands

How to move or copy data using drag-and-drop editing

In Windows terminology, *drag-and-drop* refers to the ability to move or copy data from one location to another by dragging it with the mouse. In figure 2-5, you can see how this technique is used to move or copy a range of cells in Excel. Notice that to use this technique, the cells that contain the data you want to move or copy and the cells where you want to move or copy the data to must both be visible on the screen. Because of that, the usefulness of this technique is limited.

Additional information

- ✓ The drag-and-drop feature of Excel is activated by default. If it's not activated on your system, choose the Options command from the Tools menu, click on the Edit tab, and click on the Allow Cell Drag and Drop option.

- ✓ By default, Excel warns you if the move or copy operation will overwrite existing data. To turn this option off, access the Edit tab of the Options dialog box and click on the Alert before Overwriting Cells option.

How to move the data in a range

1. Select the cells that contain the data you want to move, then place the mouse pointer on the outline of the cells so it changes to an arrow:

	A	B	C	D	E
1	Monthly Expenses		2/23/95		FEBEXP
2	February				
3					
4		Budget	Expense	Variance	
5					
6	Salaries & Wages	50,000	51,784	1,784	
7	Rent & Utilities	17,500	18,222	722	

2. Press and hold down the left mouse button as you drag the outline of the cells to another location:

	A	B	C	D	E
1	Monthly Expenses		2/23/95		FEBEXP
2	February				
3					
4		Budget	Expense	Variance	
5					
6	Salaries & Wages	50,000	51,784	1,784	
7	Rent & Utilities	17,500	18,222	722	

3. Release the mouse button and the data is moved to its new location:

	A	B	C	D	E
1	Monthly Expenses		2/23/95		FEBEXP
2	February				
3					
4					
5		Budget	Expense	Variance	
6	Salaries & Wages	50,000	51,784	1,784	
7	Rent & Utilities	17,500	18,222	722	

How to copy the data in a range

- Use the same procedure you use for moving data, but hold down the Ctrl key as you drag the data. Notice that a plus sign (+) appears next to the arrow to indicate a copy operation.

Figure 2-5   How to move and copy data using drag-and-drop editing

How to copy data using the Fill commands

Figure 2-6 presents the procedures for using the Fill commands. Like the AutoFill feature, you can use these commands to copy formulas or other data to adjacent cells. Because the AutoFill feature is so easy to use, however, you probably won't want to use the Fill commands.

How to move or copy data from one open workbook to another

When two or more workbook windows are open, you can use the Cut, Copy, and Paste commands to move or copy data from one workbook to another. After you cut or copy the data from one workbook to the clipboard, just switch to another workbook and paste the data from the clipboard at the desired location.

How to start the Fill Right, Down, Left, and Up commands

	Right	Down	Left	Up
Edit menu, Fill submenu	Right	Down	Left	Up
Shortcut key	Ctrl+R	Ctrl+D		

How to copy data to the right

1. Select a range that includes the data you want to copy and the cells to the right where you want to copy it:

		Budget	Expense	Variance
6	Salaries & Wages	50,000	51,784	1,784
7	Rent & Utilities	17,500	18,222	722
8	Maintenance	1,500	1,922	422
9	Supplies	7,750	7,912	162
10	Miscellaneous	8,250	7,211	(1,039)
12	Total	85,000		

2. Copy the data into the range using one of the methods above to start the Fill Right command:

		Budget	Expense	Variance
6	Salaries & Wages	50,000	51,784	1,784
7	Rent & Utilities	17,500	18,222	722
8	Maintenance	1,500	1,922	422
9	Supplies	7,750	7,912	162
10	Miscellaneous	8,250	7,211	(1,039)
12	Total	85,000	87,051	2,051

How to copy data down

- Select a range that includes the data you want to copy and the cells below where you want to copy it. Then, copy the data into the range using one of the methods above to start the Fill Down command.

How to copy data to the left

- Select a range that includes the data you want to copy and the cells to the left where you want to copy it. Then, copy the data into the range using the Fill Left command in the Edit menu.

How to copy data up

- Select a range that includes the data you want to copy and the cells above where you want to copy it. Then, copy the data into the range using the Fill Up command in the Edit menu.

Figure 2-6   How to copy data to adjacent cells using the Fill commands

How to delete data

Figure 2-7 presents two ways to delete the data from a range of cells. The easiest way is to press the Delete key.

Because the Clear Contents command performs the same function as the Delete key, you probably won't use it often. However, you may want to use some of the other commands in the Clear submenu. For example, you can use the Clear Formats command to delete any formatting from the cells without deleting the contents.

The Clear submenu of the Edit menu

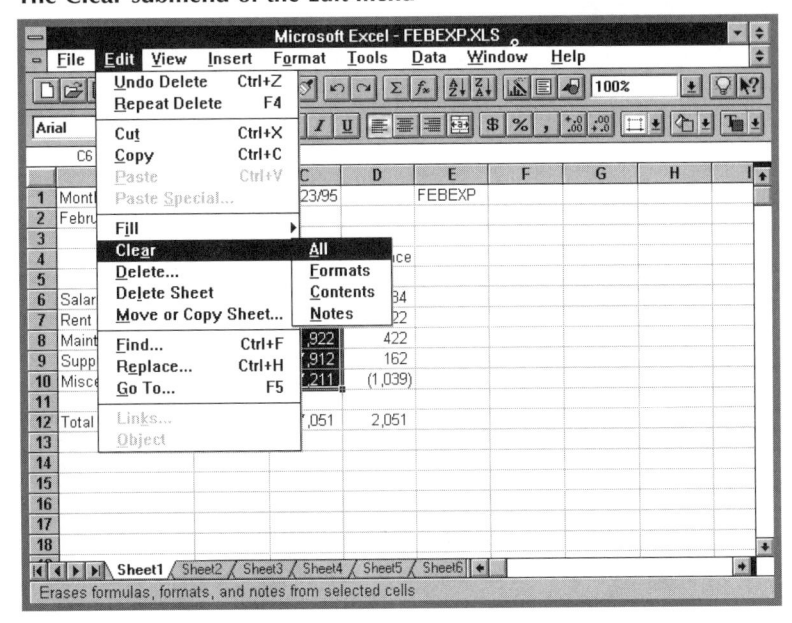

Use the Delete key

1. Select the range of cells that contains the data you want to delete.
2. Press the Delete key. That deletes the contents of the cells, but not the formatting applied to those cells.

Use the Clear Contents command

1. Select the range of cells that contains the data you want to delete.
2. Choose the Clear Contents command from the Edit menu or the shortcut menu. That too deletes the contents of the cells, but not the formatting applied to the cells.

Note

- The other commands in the Clear submenu let you delete the cell formatting (Clear Formats), the cell notes (Clear Notes), or the cell contents, formatting, and notes (Clear All).

Figure 2-7   Two ways to delete data from a range of cells

Exercise set 2-2

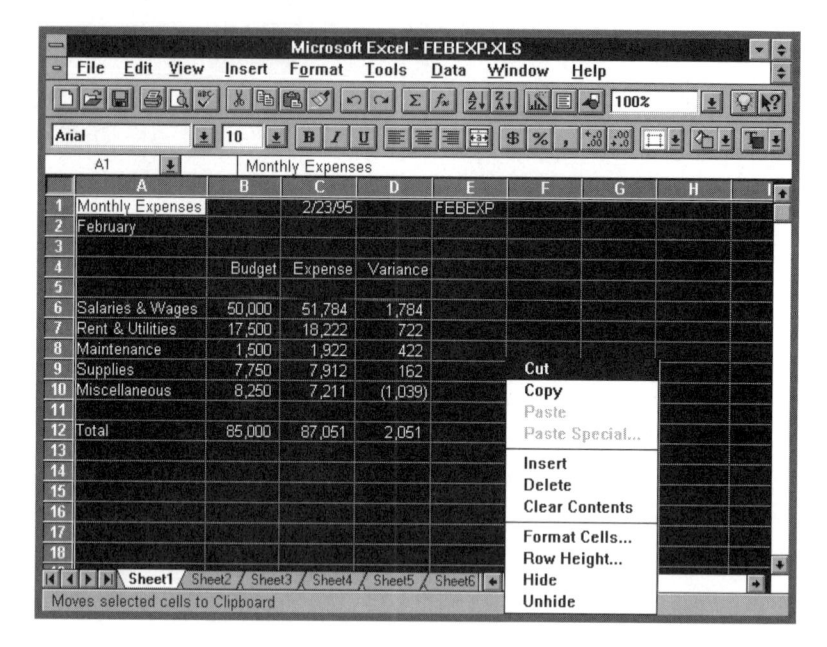

The shortcut menu that's displayed when all the cells in a worksheet are selected

1. Open the FEBEXP workbook that you created in chapter 1. Next, use the Cut and Paste procedure in figure 2-4 to move the column headings down one row. Then, use the drag-and-drop procedure in figure 2-5 to move the column headings back to row 4. Which method do you prefer?

2. Delete the totals for the Expense and Variance columns. Then, use the Fill Right command to copy the function in cell B12 two cells to the right as shown in figure 2-6. Is it easier to copy the function by dragging its fill handle?

3. Press Ctrl+N to open a second workbook window. Then, use the Copy and Paste commands to copy the FEBEXP worksheet to the new workbook window. To do that, switch to the FEBEXP window, copy the entire worksheet to the clipboard, switch to the new workbook, and paste the contents of the clipboard starting in cell A1.

4. In the new workbook window, select the cells that contain numbers. Next, issue the Clear Formats command from the Edit menu. What happens to the format and alignment of the numbers? Then, issue the Clear Contents command. What happens to the data in the selected cells?

5. Close both of the open workbooks without saving them.

How to work with columns and rows

When you edit a worksheet, you often need to perform functions on entire rows or columns. For example, you often need to change the width of two or more columns to accommodate the data they contain. You may also need to insert rows or columns into a worksheet or delete rows or columns from a worksheet.

How to adjust column widths

The easiest way to change the width of one or more columns is to use the mouse as illustrated in figure 2-8. As you can see, you can adjust the column widths so they accommodate the widest entry in each column. Or, you can adjust the widths to accommodate a specific number of characters in each column.

How to change the widths to accommodate the widest entries

1. Select the columns you want to change by dragging the mouse pointer over the column letters in the worksheet frame.

2. Place the mouse pointer on the separator line to the right of the column letter for one of the columns you selected. When the pointer is in the correct position, it will change to a double-headed arrow:

	A	B	C	D	E
1	Monthly Expenses		2/23/95		FEBEXP
2	February				
3					
4		Budget	Expense	Variance	
5					
6	Salaries & Wages	50,000	51,784	1,784	
7	Rent & Utilities	17,500	18,222	722	
8	Maintenance	1,500	1,922	422	
9	Supplies	7,750	7,912	162	
10	Miscellaneous	8,250	7,211	(1,039)	
11					
12	Total	85,000	87,051	2,051	
13					

3. Double-click the left mouse button, and the column widths are adjusted to accommodate the widest entry in each column:

	A	B	C	D	E
1	Monthly Expenses		2/23/95		FEBEXP
2	February				
3					
4		Budget	Expense	Variance	
5					
6	Salaries & Wages	50,000	51,784	1,784	
7	Rent & Utilities	17,500	18,222	722	
8	Maintenance	1,500	1,922	422	
9	Supplies	7,750	7,912	162	
10	Miscellaneous	8,250	7,211	(1,039)	
11					
12	Total	85,000	87,051	2,051	
13					

How to change the widths to a specific number of characters

1. Select the columns you want to change and position the mouse pointer so it changes to a double-headed arrow as described above.

2. Drag the double-headed arrow to the column width you want (the width in characters is displayed in the Name box).

Note

- You can change the width of a single column without selecting it first. Simply double-click on or drag the appropriate separator line.

Figure 2-8   How to adjust column widths using the mouse

Additional information

✓ You can use similar techniques to adjust the row heights. You shouldn't need to do that, though, because the row heights are automatically adjusted to the height of their contents.

Another way to change the width of one or more columns is to use the menu commands summarized in figure 2-9. However, the Column AutoFit Selection and Column Width commands perform the same adjustment functions that you can perform with the mouse. As a result, you're not likely to use them often.

If you want to change the width of one or more columns back to the default width, you can use the Column Standard Width command. It works the same way that the Column Width command works, but the column width that's displayed in its dialog box is the default: 8.43 characters.

How to change the widths to accommodate the widest entries

1. Select the columns you want to change.
2. Choose the Column AutoFit Selection command from the Format menu, and Excel adjusts the column widths to accommodate the widest entry in each column.

How to change the widths to a specific number of characters

1. Select the columns you want to change.
2. Choose the Column Width command from the Format menu or the shortcut menu so this dialog box is displayed:

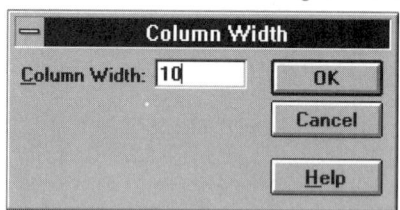

```
┌─ Column Width ─────────────┐
│ Column Width: [10]   [ OK ]│
│                  [ Cancel ]│
│                  [ Help   ]│
└────────────────────────────┘
```

3. Enter the number of characters you want the columns to accommodate and click on the OK button.

How to change the widths to the default width

1. Select the columns you want change.
2. Choose the Column Standard Width command from the Format menu, and Excel displays the Standard Width dialog box.
3. Click on OK button to return the columns to the standard width (8.43).

Notes

- You don't have to select entire columns to use these commands. Instead, you can select a range that includes at least one cell from each column that you want to change.

- When you use the Column AutoFit Selection, though, you usually should select entire columns. Otherwise, the command adjusts the column widths to the widest entries in the selected cells.

Figure 2-9 How to adjust column widths using menu commands

How to insert or delete one or more or rows

Figure 2-10 shows how to insert or delete one or more rows. Notice that you indicate the number of rows you want to insert by the number of rows you select. Also notice that when you insert rows, the new rows are inserted above the rows you select. In other words, the data in the rows you select and any rows after those rows is moved down in the worksheet to make room for the new rows.

How to start the commands for inserting or deleting rows

	Insert	Delete
Insert menu	Rows	
Edit menu		Delete
Shortcut menu	Insert	Delete
Shortcut key	Ctrl++	Ctrl+-

How to insert rows

1. Select the rows below where you want to insert new rows by dragging the mouse pointer over the row numbers in the worksheet frame. The number of rows you select will be the number of rows that are inserted:

	A	B	C	D	E
1	Monthly Expenses		2/23/95		FEBEXP
2	February				
3					
4		Budget	Expense	Variance	
5					
6	Salaries & Wages	50,000	51,784	1,784	
7	Rent & Utilities	17,500	18,222	722	
8	Maintenance	1,500	1,922	422	
9	Supplies	7,750	7,912	162	
10	Miscellaneous	8,250	7,211	(1,039)	

2. Insert the rows by using one of the methods above to start the function:

	A	B	C	D	E
1	Monthly Expenses		2/23/95		FEBEXP
2	February				
3					
4		Budget	Expense	Variance	
5					
6	Salaries & Wages	50,000	51,784	1,784	
7	Rent & Utilities	17,500	18,222	722	
8					
9					
10	Maintenance	1,500	1,922	422	

How to delete rows

- Select the rows you want to delete, and use one of the methods above to start the function.

Note

- You can also insert or delete rows by first selecting a range that contains the number of rows you want to insert or delete. Then, when you issue the Insert command from the shortcut menu or the Delete command from the Edit or shortcut menu, a dialog box is displayed that lets you specify whether you want to insert or delete the number of rows identified by the selected range or the number of columns identified by the selected range (see figure 2-17).

Figure 2-10 How to insert or delete one or more rows

How to insert or delete one or more columns

Figure 2-11 shows how to insert or delete one or more columns. Just as when you insert rows, you indicate the number of columns you want to insert by the number of columns you select. The new columns are then inserted to the left of the selected columns.

How to start the commands for inserting or deleting columns

	Insert	Delete
Insert menu	Columns	
Edit menu		Delete
Shortcut menu	Insert	Delete
Shortcut key	Ctrl++	Ctrl+-

How to insert columns

1. Select the columns to the right of where you want to insert new columns by dragging the mouse pointer over the column letters in the worksheet frame. The number of columns you select will be the number of columns that are inserted:

	A	B	C	D	E	F
1	Monthly Expenses		2/23/95		FEBEXP	
2	February					
3						
4		Budget	Expense	Variance		
5						
6	Salaries & Wages	50,000	51,784	1,784		
7	Rent & Utilities	17,500	18,222	722		
8	Maintenance	1,500	1,922	422		
9	Supplies	7,750	7,912	162		
10	Miscellaneous	8,250	7,211	(1,039)		

2. Insert the columns using one of the methods above to start the function:

	A	B	C	D	E	F	G
1	Monthly Expenses		2/23/95				FEBEXP
2	February						
3							
4		Budget	Expense			Variance	
5							
6	Salaries & Wages	50,000	51,784			1,784	
7	Rent & Utilities	17,500	18,222			722	
8	Maintenance	1,500	1,922			422	
9	Supplies	7,750	7,912			162	
10	Miscellaneous	8,250	7,211			(1,039)	

How to delete columns

- Select the columns you want to delete, and use one of the methods above to start the function.

Note

- You can also insert or delete columns by first selecting a range that contains the number of columns you want to insert or delete. Then, when you issue the Insert command from the shortcut menu or the Delete command from the Edit or shortcut menu, a dialog box is displayed that lets you specify whether you want to insert or delete the number of columns identified by the selected range or the number of rows identified by the selected range (see figure 2-17).

Figure 2-11   How to insert or delete one or more columns

Exercise set 2-3

How your FEBEXP worksheet should look after exercise 5

	A	B	C	D	E
1	Monthly Expenses		2/23/95		FEBEXP
2	February				
3					
4				Dollar	Percent
5		Budget	Expense	Variance	Variance
6	Salaries & Wages	50,000	51,784	1,784	3.6%
7	Rent & Utilities	17,500	18,222	722	4.1%
8	Maintenance	1,500	1,922	422	28.1%
9	Supplies	7,750	7,912	162	2.1%
10	Insurance	2,500	2,625	125	5.0%
11	Legal Fees	1,000	-	(1,000)	-100.0%
12	Miscellaneous	8,250	7,211	(1,039)	-12.6%
13					
14	Total	88,500	89,676	1,176	1.3%
15					

This exercise set has you edit the FEBEXP worksheet that you created in chapter 1 so it looks like the worksheet above. The steps that follow will guide you through the editing process, then give you some additional practice.

1. Open the FEBEXP workbook. Insert a row above the column headings, and enter the text in each of the required heading cells so the column headings look like those in rows 4 and 5 above. Then, right align the text in the heading cells that isn't right aligned.

2. Delete the row after the column headings.

3. Insert two rows into the worksheet for Insurance and Legal Fees; enter the text and numbers shown for these rows in columns A through C (the - in cell C11 is the default display for a zero); and copy the formula for Dollar Variance from the cell above the new rows to the new rows by dragging the fill handle. Are all the numbers formatted with the Comma style and zero decimal places? Have the totals been recalculated correctly? Move the cell pointer to one of the totals, and look in the formula bar to see whether the range for the SUM function has been adjusted to include the new rows.

4. Enter the formula for Percent Variance into cell E6. This is just the Dollar Variance amount divided by the Budget amount. After you enter the formula, use the toolbar buttons to format the cell with the Percent style and one decimal place so it reads as 3.6%.

5. Copy the formula in cell E6 to cells E7 through E14. Then, delete the entry in cell E13, which indicates a calculation error.

6. At this point, your worksheet should look like the one above. If it doesn't, make the appropriate adjustments. Then, print the worksheet, and save the file with the same name FEBEXP.

7. Delete row 13 in the worksheet. Next, use the Rows command in the Insert menu to add row 13 back. Then, move the cell pointer to cell B14 and look at the range shown in the formula bar for this SUM function. Does it include the row you just added? This shows that you often need to adjust the range of a function when you insert a row or column that's outside the original range. At the least, you need to check the range to make sure it's still correct.

8. Delete column D in the worksheet. Because the formulas in column E referred to the cells in the column you just deleted, all of the cells that contained formulas now contain error messages. Now, modify the formula in cell D6 so it calculates the percent variance without using the dollar variance that is no longer in the worksheet. To do so, you have to use parentheses to calculate the dollar variance so the formula in cell D6 should look like this:

   =(C6-B6)/B6

   Then, copy the formula from cell C6 to the cells below it, and delete the formula in cell D13. Are the percents the same as they were before you deleted column D? If they are, close the file without saving it. Otherwise, correct the formulas before closing the file.

Other editing skills

The editing skills you've learned so far are the ones you'll use with almost every worksheet you create. Although you won't use the editing skills that follow nearly as much, you should at least be aware that they're available.

How to use the AutoFill feature to generate a series

In chapter 1, you learned how to use the AutoFill feature to copy formulas to adjacent cells. But you can also use this feature to generate a series of entries as shown in figure 2-12.

In this figure, you can see that Excel can generate some series from a single entry. However, you can generate more complicated series by typing in two or more entries to identify the series. You can use this technique, for example, to enter a series of even or odd numbers.

Additional information

✓ If you frequently use a series that Excel doesn't recognize, you can create a custom AutoFill sequence. To do that, use the Custom Lists tab of the Options dialog box. For more information, click on the Help button on the Custom Lists tab.

✓ You can also use the Fill Series command in the Edit menu to generate a series that can't be done by the AutoFill feature. However, you'll probably never need to create a series that the AutoFill feature can't generate.

How to generate a series from a single entry

1. Type the first entry in the series. Then, select the entry and drag the fill handle in the lower right corner of the selection down through the cells you want to fill:

	A	B	C	D	E	F	G
1	Days	Days	Months	Months	Quarters	Dates	
2							
3	Monday	Mon	January	Jan	Q1	3/16/95	
4							
5							
6							
7							
8							
9							
10							
11							
12							
13							
14							
15							
16							

2. Release the left mouse button and Excel fills the range with the series:

	A	B	C	D	E	F	G
1	Days	Days	Months	Months	Quarters	Dates	
2							
3	Monday	Mon	January	Jan	Q1	3/16/95	
4	Tuesday	Tue	February	Feb	Q2	3/17/95	
5	Wednesday	Wed	March	Mar	Q3	3/18/95	
6	Thursday	Thu	April	Apr	Q4	3/19/95	
7	Friday	Fri	May	May	Q1	3/20/95	
8	Saturday	Sat	June	Jun	Q2	3/21/95	
9	Sunday	Sun	July	Jul	Q3	3/22/95	
10	Monday	Mon	August	Aug	Q4	3/23/95	
11	Tuesday	Tue	September	Sep	Q1	3/24/95	
12	Wednesday	Wed	October	Oct	Q2	3/25/95	
13	Thursday	Thu	November	Nov	Q3	3/26/95	
14	Friday	Fri	December	Dec	Q4	3/27/95	
15	Saturday	Sat	January	Jan	Q1	3/28/95	
16							

How to generate a series of consecutive numbers

- Enter the first number. Then, hold down the Ctrl key as you drag the fill handle of the cell.

How to generate a series from two or more entries

- If Excel doesn't recognize a series from a single entry, you can type in two or more entries to identify the series. If you type 2 and 4 in the first two cells, for example, Excel creates a series of even numbers. And if you type in 3/13/95 and 3/20/95, Excel creates a series that consists of every seventh date beginning with 3/13/95.

Figure 2-12 How to use the AutoFill feature to generate a series

How to sort the data in selected rows

Figure 2-13 presents the procedure for sorting the data in selected rows of a worksheet. Here, the range to be sorted is called the *data range*. The column you want to base the sort on is called the *primary sort key*. And if you want to sort on two or more columns, the additional columns are called the *secondary sort keys*. Note that for each sort key, you can choose ascending or descending sequence.

Additional information

✓ You can also use the Sort Ascending and Sort Descending buttons in the Standard toolbar to sort the selected rows. When you use these buttons, however, you can only sort by a single column. Since Excel uses the column that contains the active cell as the primary sort key, this limits the use of these buttons.

Access   **Menu**   Sort ➡ Data

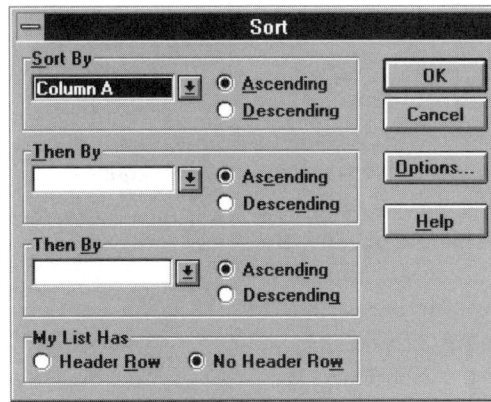

Procedure

1. Select the rows you want to sort:

	A	B	C	D	E
1	Monthly Expenses		2/23/95		FEBEXP
2	February				
3					
4		Budget	Expense	Variance	
5					
6	Salaries & Wages	50,000	51,784	1,784	
7	Rent & Utilities	17,500	18,222	722	
8	Maintenance	1,500	1,922	422	
9	Supplies	7,750	7,912	162	
10	Miscellaneous	8,250	7,211	(1,039)	
11					
12	Total	85,000	87,051	2,051	
13					

2. Access the Sort dialog box. Then, choose the column you want to use as the primary key from the drop-down list in the Sort By group, and choose the Ascending or Descending option from that group.

3. If you want to sort by more than one key, choose the column you want to use for each secondary key from the drop-down lists in the Then By groups, and choose the Ascending or Descending option from that group.

4. Click on the OK button and Excel sorts the selected rows:

	A	B	C	D	E
1	Monthly Expenses		2/23/95		FEBEXP
2	February				
3					
4		Budget	Expense	Variance	
5					
6	Maintenance	1,500	1,922	422	
7	Miscellaneous	8,250	7,211	(1,039)	
8	Rent & Utilities	17,500	18,222	722	
9	Salaries & Wages	50,000	51,784	1,784	
10	Supplies	7,750	7,912	162	
11					
12	Total	85,000	87,051	2,051	
13					

Figure 2-13   How to sort the data in selected rows

How to check the spelling in a worksheet

If the worksheet you're creating contains text, it's usually a good idea to check the spelling to make sure there aren't any errors. Figure 2-14 shows how to do that. As you can see, you have several options when Excel finds an error. You can replace the word with its correct spelling, you can skip the word without changing it, or you can add the word to the dictionary so that it's not considered an error in the future. Excel also checks for duplicate words during a spelling check so you can correct those errors as well.

Additional information

✓ Although you can add words to more than one dictionary by using the list for the Add Words To box, you shouldn't need to do that.

How to start a spelling check

Menu	Tools ➡ Spelling
Shortcut key	F7
Standard toolbar	[ABC✓]

Procedure

1. Start the spelling check.

2. Each time Excel encounters an error, it displays the Spelling dialog box so you can respond to it and correct the error:

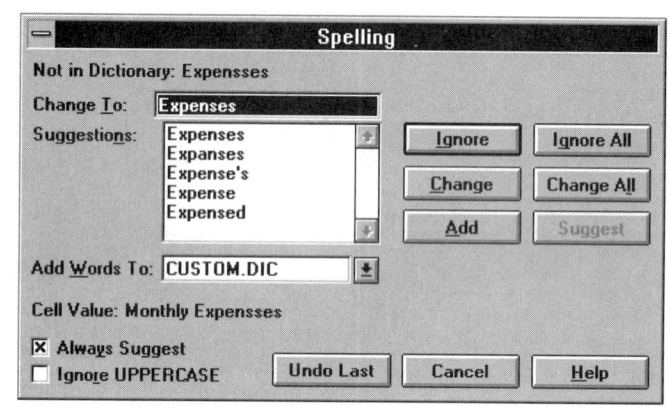

   ```
   ┌─────────────── Spelling ───────────────┐
   │ Not in Dictionary: Expensses           │
   │ Change To:  [Expenses]                 │
   │ Suggestions: Expenses    [Ignore] [Ignore All] │
   │              Expanses                  │
   │              Expense's   [Change] [Change All] │
   │              Expense                   │
   │              Expensed    [Add]    [Suggest]    │
   │ Add Words To: [CUSTOM.DIC ▼]           │
   │ Cell Value: Monthly Expensses          │
   │ [X] Always Suggest                     │
   │ [ ] Ignore UPPERCASE  [Undo Last] [Cancel] [Help] │
   └────────────────────────────────────────┘
   ```

3. When the spelling check is complete, click on the OK button in the dialog box that appears.

How to respond to the Spelling dialog box

- To replace the word, choose the new word from the Suggestions list or type the word in the Change To box. To replace that word one time only, click on the Change button. To replace all remaining occurrences of the word, click on the Change All button.

- To skip the word without changing it, click on the Ignore button. To skip all remaining occurrences of the word, click on the Ignore All button.

- To add the word to the default dictionary (CUSTOM.DIC), click on the Add button.

- Excel also checks for words that are used twice in succession during the spelling check. If it finds one, the Change and Change All buttons change to Delete and Delete All so you can delete the duplicate word.

Notes

- Excel begins the spelling check with the active cell. When it reaches the end of the worksheet, it asks if you want to continue the check at the beginning of the worksheet. If you want to limit the area that's checked, you can select a range before you start the command.

- If the Always Suggest option isn't checked, no suggestions appear in the Suggestions list so you usually want this option checked.

Figure 2-14 How to check the spelling in a worksheet

How to edit a worksheet

How to search for and replace data

The Find and Replace commands in the Edit menu let you search for text in a worksheet, and, optionally, replace it with different text. Because the find and replace commands are most useful with files that contain a lot of text, you will probably use them infrequently, if at all.

Figure 2-15 presents the procedure for using the Find command. When you use this command, you can specify several options that determine how Excel performs the search. For example, the options in the Look In list determine whether Excel looks for the text you specify in the cell values, in formulas, or in cell notes.

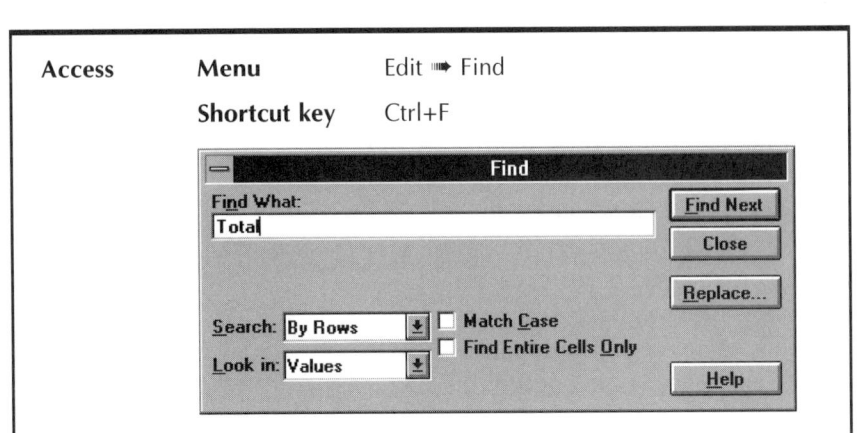

Access	Menu	Edit → Find
	Shortcut key	Ctrl+F

Find dialog box
- Find What: Total
- Search: By Rows
- Look in: Values
- Match Case
- Find Entire Cells Only
- Buttons: Find Next, Close, Replace..., Help

Procedure

1. Access the Find dialog box. Then, enter the text you want to search for in the Find What box.

2. Specify how you want Excel to search:
   - To search for text that matches the case of the text in the Find What text box, choose the Match Case option.
   - To look for cells that contain exactly what's specified in the Find What box with no additional characters, choose the Find Entire Cells Only option.
   - If necessary, you can choose an option from the Look In list to tell Excel where to look for the text. The options are Formulas, Values, and Notes. The default is Values, which is usually what you want, because it causes a search through the text, numbers, and results of formulas.
   - If necessary, you can choose an option from the Search list to specify the direction of the search. The options are By Rows and By Columns, but you usually don't need to change this.

3. To find the first occurrence of the text, click on the OK button. Then, to find the next occurrence, click on the Find Next button. Or, to start a replace operation, click on the Replace button.

Note

- If you want to limit the area that's searched, select a range before you issue the Find command.

Figure 2-15 How to search for data

Figure 2-16 presents the procedure for using the Replace command. This command is similar to the Find command except that you specify the replacement text in addition to the text you want to find. Then, each time Excel finds an occurrence of the text, you can replace it, skip it and find the next occurrence, or replace all the remaining occurrences of the text.

Since a replace operation can drastically change a worksheet in just a few seconds, there are two precautions you may want to take when you use the Replace command. First, you can save your workbook before you perform a replace operation. Then, if the replace doesn't work quite right, you can close the workbook without saving the changes. Second, you can replace the current occurrence the first couple of times instead of replacing all occurrences right away. That way, you can make sure the operation is working the way you want it to before you change the entire worksheet. Of course, you can also use the Undo command to reverse the replace operation before you perform any other operations.

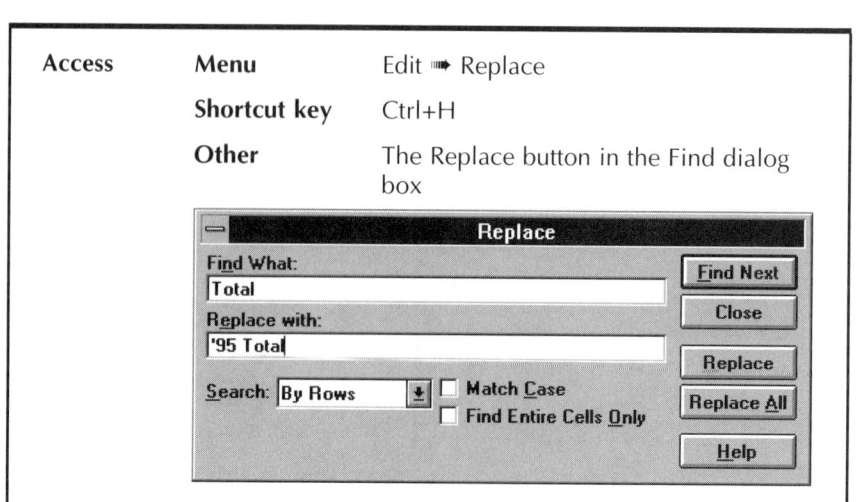

Access	Menu	Edit → Replace
	Shortcut key	Ctrl+H
	Other	The Replace button in the Find dialog box

[Replace dialog box: Find What: Total; Replace with: '95 Total; Search: By Rows; Match Case; Find Entire Cells Only; buttons: Find Next, Close, Replace, Replace All, Help]

Procedure

1. Access the Replace dialog box. Then, enter the text you want to search for in the Find What box, and enter the replacement text in the Replace With box.

2. Specify how you want Excel to search by choosing the appropriate options (see figure 2-15 for details).

3. To find the first occurrence of the text, click on the Find Next button. Then, click on the Replace button to replace the text, or click on the Find Next button to find the next occurrence of the text without replacing the current occurrence. To replace all occurrences of the text, click on the Replace All button.

Note

- If you want to limit the area that's searched, select a range before you issue the Replace command.

Figure 2-16 How to search for and replace data

How to insert or delete a range of cells

When you need to insert cells in a worksheet, you usually insert entire rows and columns. Occasionally, though, you may need to insert a range of cells. If you omit data from one or more columns, for example, you can insert blank cells so you can enter the missing data. To do that, you use the technique shown in figure 2-17. Note that when you insert a range of cells, you have to tell Excel which direction to shift the cells in the selected range: to the right or down.

Figure 2-17 also shows you how to delete a range of cells. When you delete cells, you have to tell Excel which cells you want to move into the deleted range: the cells to the right of or below the selected range.

How to insert a range of cells

Access	**Menu**	Insert ➠ Cells
	Shortcut menu	Insert
	Shortcut key	Ctrl++

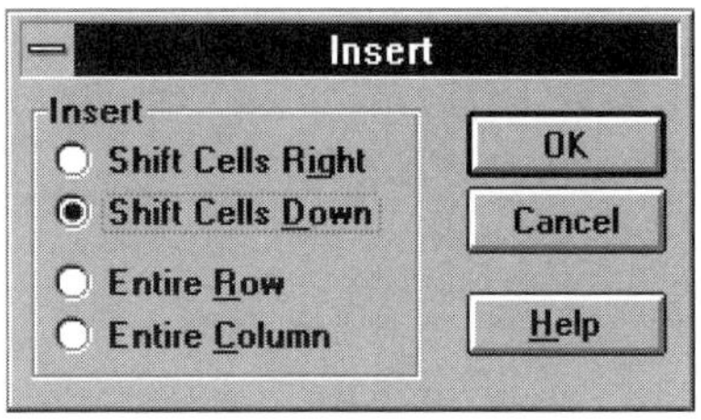

Procedure

1. Select the range where you want to insert the new cells:

1546	2938	2984	2783
1934	3940	584	1984
3584	1038	987	638
945	498	2931	2984
1258	3985	4873	1985
2396			987

2. Access the Insert dialog box, and choose the Shift Cells Right or Shift Cells Down option to indicate where you want to shift the existing data when the cells are inserted.

3. Click on the OK button, and Excel inserts the range of cells and shifts the data in the direction you specified:

1546	2938	2984	2783
1934	3940	584	1984
3584	1038	987	638
945			2984
1258	498	2931	1985
2396	3985	4873	987

How to delete a range of cells

1. Select the range of cells you want to delete, and access the Delete dialog box using one of these techniques:
   - Choose the Delete command from the Edit or shortcut menu
   - Press Ctrl+-
2. Choose the Shift Cells Up or Shift Cells Left option to indicate which cells you want to move into the deleted range.
3. Click on the OK button, and Excel deletes the cells and shifts the data from the direction you specified.

Figure 2-17 How to insert or delete a range of cells

Exercise set 2-4

How the worksheet should look after you sort the rows in exercise 3

	A	B	C	D	E	F
1	Monthly Expenses		2/23/95		FEBEXP	
2	February					
3						
4				Dollar	Percent	
5		Budget	Expense	Variance	Variance	
6	Maintenance	1,500	1,922	422	28.1%	
7	Insurance	2,500	2,625	125	5.0%	
8	Rent & Utilities	17,500	18,222	722	4.1%	
9	Salaries & Wages	50,000	51,784	1,784	3.6%	
10	Supplies	7,750	7,912	162	2.1%	
11	Miscellaneous	8,250	7,211	(1,039)	-12.6%	
12	Legal Fees	1,000	-	(1,000)	-100.0%	
13						
14	Total	88,500	89,676	1,176	1.3%	
15						

1. Open a new workbook window, and enter "January" into cell A2. Then, use the AutoFill feature as described in figure 2-12 to create a series in column A that consists of one occurrence of every month of the year.

2. Enter the number 1990 into cell B1 of the worksheet. Then, use the AutoFill feature to create a series in row 1 that consists of the years 1990 to 1995. To do that, hold down the Ctrl key as you drag the fill handle.

3. Open the expanded FEBEXP file that you updated in exercise set 2-3. Select rows 6 through 12, and use the Sort command as described in figure 2-13 to sort the rows in descending order by percent variance. Note that the drop-down list for the Sort By box gives the text that's in the first row above the selected rows. If there isn't any, it gives the column letter. When the sort is finished, the data should be in the sequence shown above.

4. Edit cell A10 so it contains this misspelling: Insurrance. Then, check the spelling in the worksheet as described in figure 2-14 and correct any errors that are encountered. When Excel displays the text "FEBEXP" as an error, click on the Ignore button.

5. Use the Find command as described in figure 2-15 to find all occurrences of "expense." How many occurrences does Excel find? Perform the find operation again, but this time check the Find Entire Cells Only option. How many occurrences does Excel find this time? Perform the find operation one more time, this time with the Match Case option checked. How many occurrences does Excel find?

6. Use the Replace command as described in figure 2-16 to replace all occurrences of the ampersand (&) with the word "and."

7. Close all workbook windows without saving the changes.

Perspective

If you've done all the exercises for this chapter, you should now realize how quickly and easily you can edit a worksheet with Excel 5. In fact, the editing features can help you make significant improvements in your productivity when you upgrade from a DOS spreadsheet program to a Windows program like Excel 5.

Summary

- If you click the right mouse button while pointing at a selected range, Excel displays a *shortcut menu* that contains the most common editing and formatting commands. You can also display shortcut menus for other areas of the worksheet.

- After you perform most operations, you can undo or repeat the operation using the Undo or Repeat command.

- If you open two or more workbook windows, you can use a shortcut key or the Window menu to switch from one open window to another.

- The Cut, Copy, and Paste commands use a temporary storage area called the *clipboard* to move and copy data. You can also use *drag-and-drop* techniques to move and copy data.

- You can use four of the Fill commands in the Edit menu to copy data to adjacent cells.

- To delete data from a range of cells, use the Delete key or the Clear Contents command in the Edit menu.

- You can use the mouse or menu commands to change the width of one or more columns. You can also use a menu command to return the column width to its default.

- You can insert or delete one or more rows or columns using menu commands.

- You can use the AutoFill feature to generate a text or number series from a single entry. To generate more complex series, you have to specify at least the first two entries in the series.

- You can use the Sort command in the Data menu to sort the data in selected rows by up to three different columns. The first column you choose is the *primary sort key*. Any other columns you choose are *secondary sort keys*. The rows you sort are the *data range*.

- You can use the Spelling command in the Tools menu or the Spelling button in the Standard toolbar to check the spelling in a worksheet.

- You can use the Find command in the Edit menu to find all occurrences of the text you specify. You can use the Replace command in the Edit menu to find all occurrences of the text and, optionally, replace it with other text.

- You can insert or delete a range of cells using menu commands. When you insert cells, cells can be shifted to the right or down to make room for the new cells. When you delete cells, cells from below or to the left can be shifted into the deleted range.

Chapter 3

How to format a worksheet

When you *format* a worksheet, you change its appearance. In chapter 1, for example, you learned how to align entries and format numbers. In this chapter, you'll learn the formatting skills that will help you create professional looking worksheets as quickly as possible.

How to change the font, font size, and font attributes
    How to change the font
    How to change the font size
    How to change the font attributes
    How to use the Font tab of the Format Cells command

How to add borders, colors, and patterns to a range
    How to add borders
    How to apply background colors and patterns
    How to use the Border and Patterns tabs of the Format Cells command
    How to use the AutoFormat command

Three more alignment skills
    How to center data across columns
    How to justify text within columns
    How to use the Alignment tab of the Format Cells command

How to format and preview the pages in a workbook
    How to change the margins
    How to change the default header and footer
    How to preview the printed worksheet

How to copy and delete formats
    How to copy and delete formats using menu commands
    How to copy formats using the Format Painter

How to create and use styles
    How to create and apply your own styles
    How to modify and delete styles
    How to copy styles from another workbook

Perspective

Summary

How to change the font, font size, and font attributes

A *font* is a set of characters including letters, numbers, and symbols, and each font has a distinctive style. The standard unit of measure for font size is a *point*, which is 1/72 of an inch.

You can tell the font and font size for a selected cell by looking in the Font and Font Size boxes at the left side of the Formatting toolbar. In figure 3-1, for example, the font is Times New Roman and its size is 10 points. The default font and font size is Arial in 10 point size.

How to change the font

Figure 3-1 shows the best way to change the font. Just select the cells and choose a font from the Font list in the Formatting toolbar. In this example, the title, subtitle, and heading cells in the first four rows are selected, and the font is being changed to Times New Roman.

Since the fonts in the list are the ones that are installed on your PC, the Font list changes from one PC to another. The three fonts that come with Windows 3.1 are Arial, Times New Roman, and Courier New, so they should be available on all Windows systems.

For most worksheets, the default font is appropriate for all cells so you don't have to change it. For special presentations, though, you may use one font for cells that have one purpose (like headings) and another font for cells that have other purposes (like data).

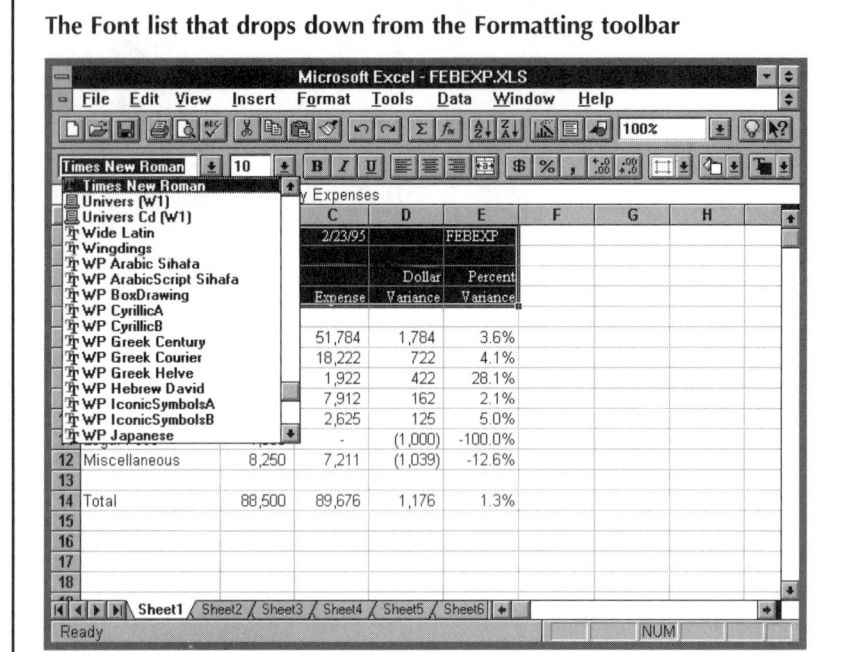

The Font list that drops down from the Formatting toolbar

How to change the font of selected cells

1. Click on the arrow to the right of the Font box to display a list of the available fonts.

2. Choose a font from the list. If necessary, scroll down the list to find the font you want.

Notes

- The small icons to the left of the font names indicate the font types. The double T icon indicates a TrueType font; the printer icon indicates a printer font. For most worksheets, you'll want to use TrueType fonts because they're displayed on the screen the way they'll look when they're printed. In contrast, printer fonts are designed for printing speed, and they don't always look the same on the screen as when they're printed.

- The fonts that are available depend on which fonts you have installed through Windows. Three fonts that come with Windows are Arial, Courier New, and Times New Roman so these should always be available.

- The default font is Arial. Since it is appropriate for most spreadsheet requirements, you shouldn't have to change it.

Figure 3-1   How to change the font

How to change the font size

Figure 3-2 shows the best way to change the font size. Just select the cells and choose a size from the Font Size list in the Formatting toolbar. In this example, the subtitle of the worksheet is being changed to 12 point size.

If you're working with a *scaleable font* like a TrueType font, you don't have to limit your choice to those in the list. If necessary, you can type the size that you want to use in the Font Size box. For fonts that aren't scaleable, though, you are limited to the sizes in the list.

The Font Size list that drops down from the Formatting toolbar

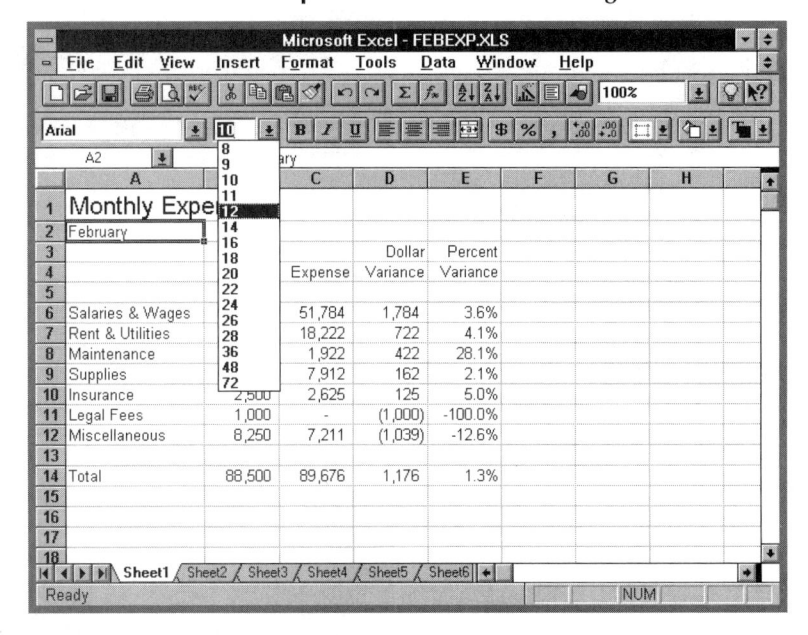

Two ways to change the font size of selected cells

- Click on the arrow to the right of the Font Size box to display a list of available font sizes. Then, choose a size from the list.

- Click in the Font Size box. Then, type in the font size you want to use and press the Enter key.

Notes

- Font size is expressed in *points* with 72 points to the vertical inch. For reading ease, a minimum font size of 10 to 12 points is recommended. Then, you can use larger sizes for titles and headings.

- The default font size is 10 points, which is appropriate for the data in most worksheets so you shouldn't have to change that.

- The sizes that are available in the font size list depend on the font. If you're using a TrueType font or another scaleable font, though, you can type any number into the Font Size box, even a fraction like 11.5.

Figure 3-2   How to change the font size

How to change the font attributes

Figure 3-3 presents the four buttons in the Formatting toolbar that you can use to change the font *attributes* of a cell: the Bold, Italic, Underline, and Font Color buttons. In this example, the bold attribute has been applied to the title, subtitle, column headings, and row headings.

If you want to apply color to the fonts used in the selected cells, you can use the Font Color palette shown in figure 3-3. After the palette drops down from the Formatting toolbar, you can drag it off the toolbar so it floats as shown in this figure. Then, you can select cells and apply colors to the fonts without having to drop the palette down each time. To apply the color that's shown on the Font Color button, though, you don't have to display the palette; you just click on the button.

A worksheet with bold titles and headings and a floating Font Color palette

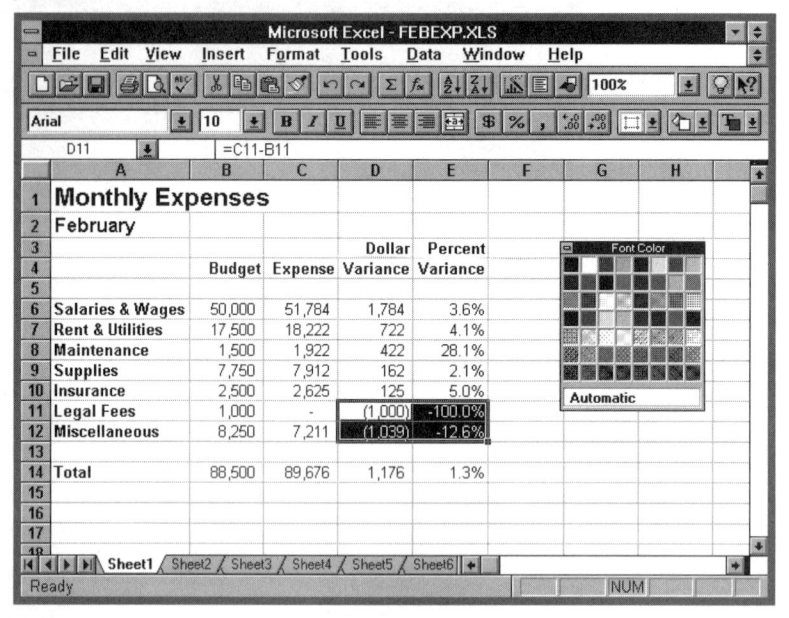

Button	Name	Shortcut key
B	Bold	Ctrl+B
I	Italic	Ctrl+I
U	Underline	Ctrl+U
	Font Color	

How to apply a font attribute to selected cells

- To apply bold, italics, or underlining, click on the toolbar button or press the shortcut key.
- To apply a font color, click on the Font Color button to apply the color that's on the button. Or, click on the arrow to the right of the Font Color button to display the Font Color palette, then click on the color you want to apply to the font.

Notes

- If you apply bold, italic, or underlining and that attribute has already been applied to the selected cells, the attribute is removed.
- To keep the Font Color palette open as shown above, drag it off the toolbar. To return it to the toolbar, click on the close box in the upper left corner.

Figure 3-3 How to change the font attributes

How to use the Font tab of the Format Cells command

Most of the time, you'll use the Formatting toolbar to change the font, font size, and font attributes of the selected cells. If necessary, though, you can also use the Font tab of the Format Cells dialog box to perform these functions. This is summarized in figure 3-4.

From the Font tab, you can access two formatting options you can't access from the Formatting toolbar. First, you can choose four different types of underlines. Second, you can apply strikethrough, superscript, and subscript effects. You can also return the font settings to their defaults by choosing the Normal Font option.

Access

Menu	Format ⇒ Cells
Shortcut menu	Format Cells
Shortcut key	Ctrl+1

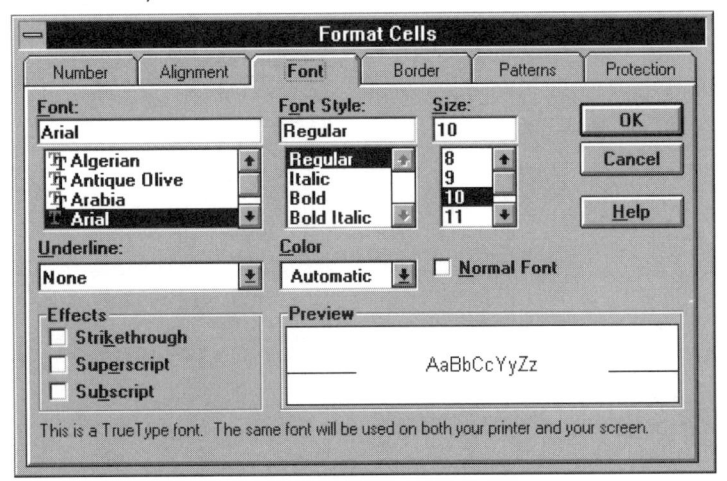

Operation

- To change the font or font size, choose an option from the Font or Size list.
- To apply an attribute or combination of attributes like bold or bold and italics, choose an option from the Font Style list.
- To apply an underline, choose an option from the Underline list.
- To change the font color, choose an option from the Color palette that's displayed when you click on the arrow to the right of the Color box.
- To apply special formats, choose an option from the Effects group.
- To restore all settings to their defaults, choose the Normal Font option.

Figure 3-4 How to use the Font tab of the Format Cells command

Exercise set 3-1

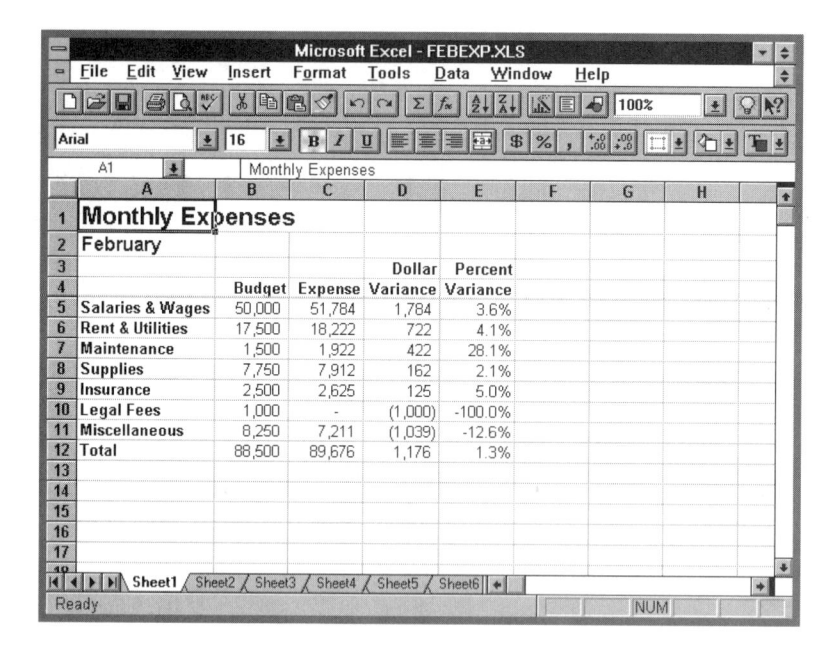

How your worksheet should look after exercise 5

1. Open the FEBEXP workbook that you created in chapter 1 and edited in chapter 2. When the cell pointer is on cell A1, what font name appears in the Font box of the Formatting toolbar and what font size appears in the Font Size box? Those are the defaults on your PC. If the defaults aren't Arial in 10 point size, select all the cells in the worksheet, change the font to Arial, and change the size to 10.

2. Delete the date in cell C1 and the file name in cell E1. Then, use the procedure in figure 3-1 to change the font for the title, subtitle, and column headings to Times New Roman. Do you like the appearance of this font better than the appearance of the Arial font? Use the Undo command to change the font back to Arial.

3. Use the Font Size list in the Formatting toolbar to change the size of the title (Monthly Expenses) to 16 points and the size of the subtitle (February) to 12 points.

4. Select all the text in the worksheet (but not the numbers and formulas) at the same time by holding down the Ctrl key as you drag the mouse over the text ranges. Then, use the Bold button in the Formatting toolbar to format these nonadjacent selections.

5. Delete row 13 and row 3 (the blank rows). Now, if your worksheet looks like the one above, save it but don't close it. Otherwise, make the necessary adjustments before saving it.

6. Use the Italic button to format all column headings with italics. Then, remove the italics by selecting the column headings and clicking on the Italic button again.

7. If you have a color monitor, use the Font Color button in the Formatting toolbar to change all negative values to red. Then, select the red cells and return the font color to black. You can do that by choosing either the black color or Automatic in the Font Color palette.

8. Select the numbers in the Budget column of the worksheet. Next, use the Format Cells command to display these cells with the strikethrough effect. Then, select these cells again, and use the Format Cells command to return these cells to normal by checking the Normal Font box.

9. Save and close the file.

How to add borders, colors, and patterns to a range

You can improve the appearance of most worksheets and make them easier to read by adding a few simple borders. For special presentations, you may also want to add background colors or patterns to some of the ranges in a worksheet.

How to add borders

Figure 3-5 shows how to use the Borders button in the Formatting toolbar to add a border to a range of cells. This button works like the Font Color button. You can click on it to apply the border shown on the button. Or, you can display the Border palette to apply a different border. If you want to add different types of borders to different ranges, you can keep this palette open by dragging it off the toolbar.

As you can see in this figure, a *border* is just a line above, below, to the right, to the left, or around a range of cells. For most worksheets, a few horizontal borders are all that you need to make the data easier to follow.

The Border palette that drops down from the Formatting toolbar

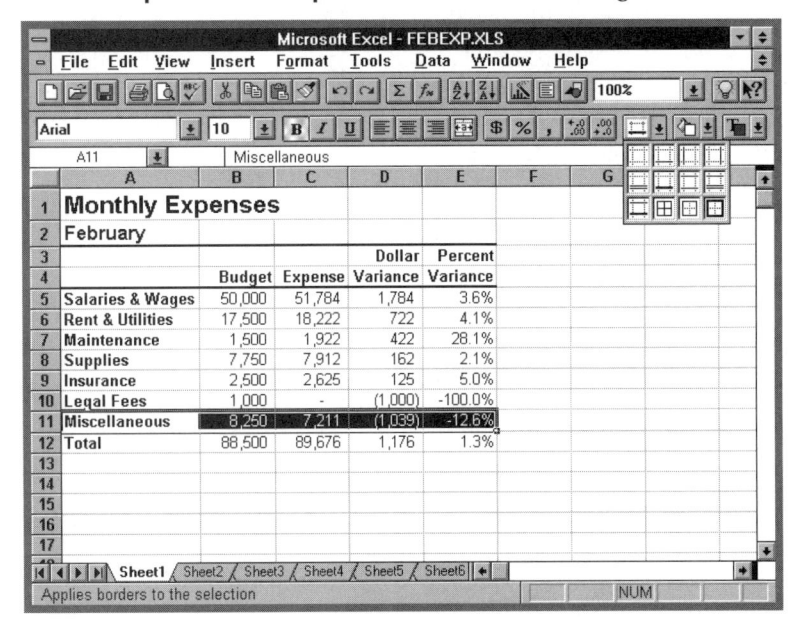

How to apply a border to selected cells

- To apply the type of border that's indicated by the picture on the Borders button, click on the button.
- To apply a border other than the one shown on the Borders button, click on the arrow on the right side of the button to drop down the Border palette, then choose a border from the palette.

Notes

- To keep the Border palette open, drag it off the toolbar. To return the palette to the toolbar, click on the close box in the upper left corner.
- To remove the border from the selected cells, click on the picture in the palette that indicates no borders.

Figure 3-5 How to add a border to a range

How to apply background colors and patterns

Figure 3-6 shows how to use the Color button to apply colors and patterns to the background of a range of cells. This button works like the Font Color and Borders buttons. You can apply the color and pattern shown on the button by clicking on the button. Or, you can choose another color and pattern from the Color palette. If you want to keep the Color palette open, you can drag it off the toolbar.

If the palette in this figure were in color, you would see that some of the colors have patterns. You would also see that several of the choices in the palette are shades of gray. When you print background colors, patterns, or grays on a black and white printer, though, the data on it becomes more difficult to read. So use these backgrounds with caution. As a general rule, you should avoid the use of backgrounds altogether unless they're clearly an improvement.

One of the most useful colors in the palette is white. When this color is applied to selected cells, the gridlines between the cells aren't displayed. You'll see how this works when you do the exercises.

The Color palette that drops down from the Formatting toolbar

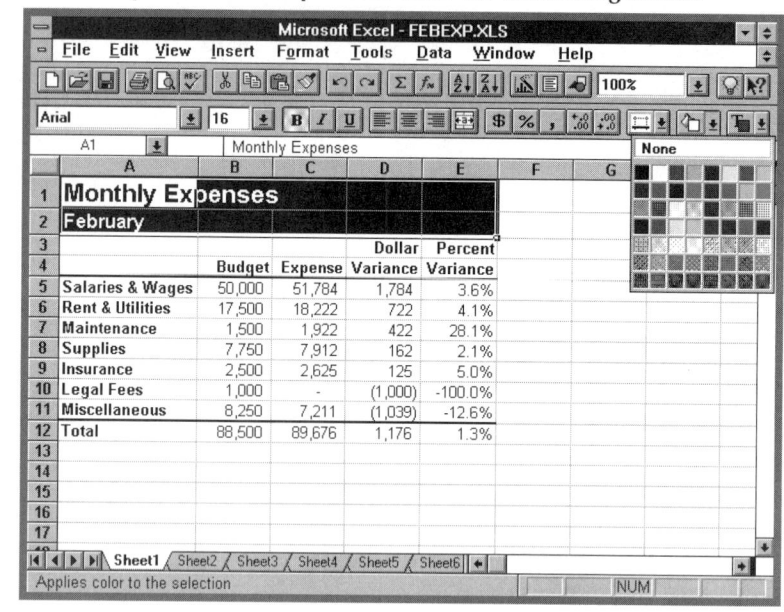

How to apply a background color to selected cells

- To apply the color that's indicated on the Color button, click on the button.
- To apply a color other than the one shown on the Color button, click on the arrow on the right side of the button to drop down the Color palette, then choose a color from the palette.

Notes

- To keep the Color palette open, drag it off the toolbar. To return the palette to the toolbar, click on the close box in the upper left corner.
- To remove the background color from the selected cells, click on None in the palette.

Figure 3-6 How to apply colors and patterns to a range

How to use the Border and Patterns tabs of the Format Cells command

Although the Borders button is easy to use, it provides a limited number of border options. If you want to add a border that's not available from this button, you can use the Border tab of the Format Cells dialog box as shown in figure 3-7. From this tab, you can choose which sides of each cell in the range will have a border; you can choose the line style for the border; and you can choose the color of the border.

If you modify a range of cells that already has a border, you might be confused to see that some of the options in the Border group are shaded. If an option is shaded, it means that only some of the cells in the range have that border. If, for example, the range of cells is outlined, that means some of the cells have a border on the left edge, some have a border on the right edge, some have a border on the top edge, some have a border on the bottom edge, and some have a mixture of borders. In that case, the Left, Right, Top, and Bottom options are shaded.

Figure 3-7 also shows how to apply colors and patterns to a range using the Patterns tab of the Format Cells dialog box. From this tab, you can choose a color or pattern from the Color palette or from the Pattern palette that pops up from the Pattern box.

Access

Menu	Format ➡ Cells
Shortcut menu	Format Cells
Shortcut key	Ctrl+1

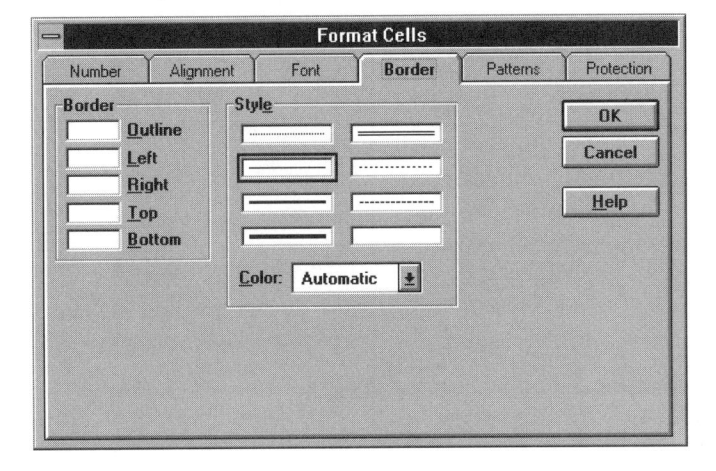

How to use the Border tab

- To add a border to a range of cells, choose the appropriate Border options: Outline, Left, Right, Top, or Bottom.
- To change the line style for a border, choose a style from the Style group after you choose the Border option. The style you choose is then used for any additional Border options you choose.
- To change the color for a border, click on the arrow to the right of the Color box, then choose a color from the color palette that's displayed. The color you choose is then used for any additional Border options you choose.

How to use the Patterns tab

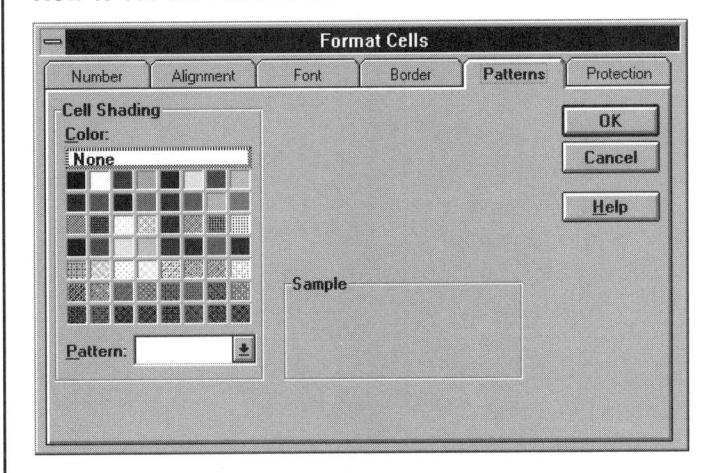

- To change the background color or pattern of a range, choose an option from the Color palette or from the Pattern palette that pops up from the Pattern box.

Figure 3-7   How to use the Border and Patterns tabs of the Format Cells command

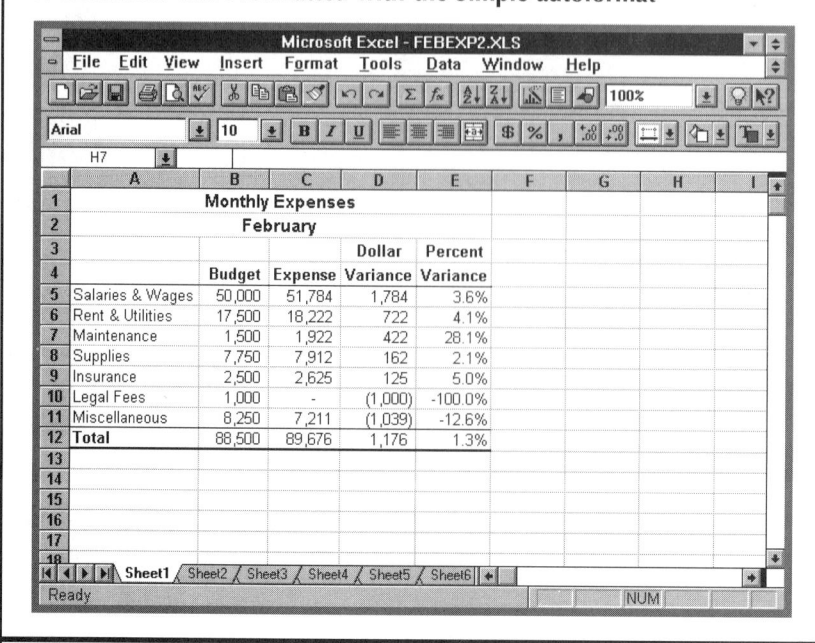

How to use the AutoFormat command

Excel comes with 16 *autoformats* that you can use to format ranges in your worksheets. To apply an autoformat, you use the AutoFormat command as illustrated in figure 3-8. All of the 16 autoformats apply borders to the selected range, and some apply colors and patterns too. In addition, some of the autoformats apply font attributes to the titles and headings, and some center the title and subtitle.

In figure 3-8, you can see the formatting that the Simple autoformat does to a worksheet that starts without font attributes or borders. This autoformat applies the bold attribute to some cells and borders to other cells. It also centers the title and subtitle. This is one of the most practical autoformats because it clearly improves the appearance and readability of the worksheet. If you experiment with the other autoformats, you'll find that many use colors and patterns that actually decrease the readability of a worksheet, especially when it's printed on a black and white printer.

Note in figure 3-8 that you can omit some of the formatting that's done by an autoformat. To do that, just click on the Options button in the AutoFormat dialog box and remove the check marks from the formats you don't want to apply. You can also use the AutoFormat command to remove the formatting from a range by choosing the None option at the top of the Table Format list.

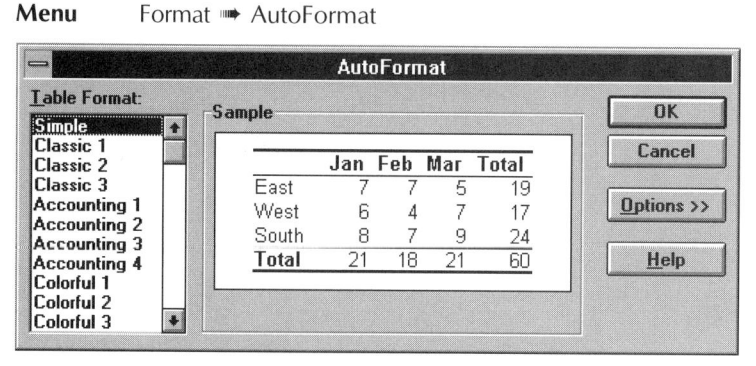

Access

Menu   Format ➡ AutoFormat

How to apply an autoformat

1. Select the range of cells you want to format, and access the AutoFormat dialog box.
2. Choose one of the formats from the Table Format list. If you don't want to apply all the formatting options for that autoformat, click on the Options button to omit some of the formatting options.
3. Click on the OK button to apply the autoformat to the selected range.

Two ways to remove an autoformat

- Undo the AutoFormat command immediately after applying it.
- Select the range that's formatted with the autoformat, access the AutoFormat dialog box, and choose the None option from the Table Format list.

A worksheet that's formatted with the Simple autoformat

Figure 3-8   How to use the AutoFormat command

Exercise set 3-2

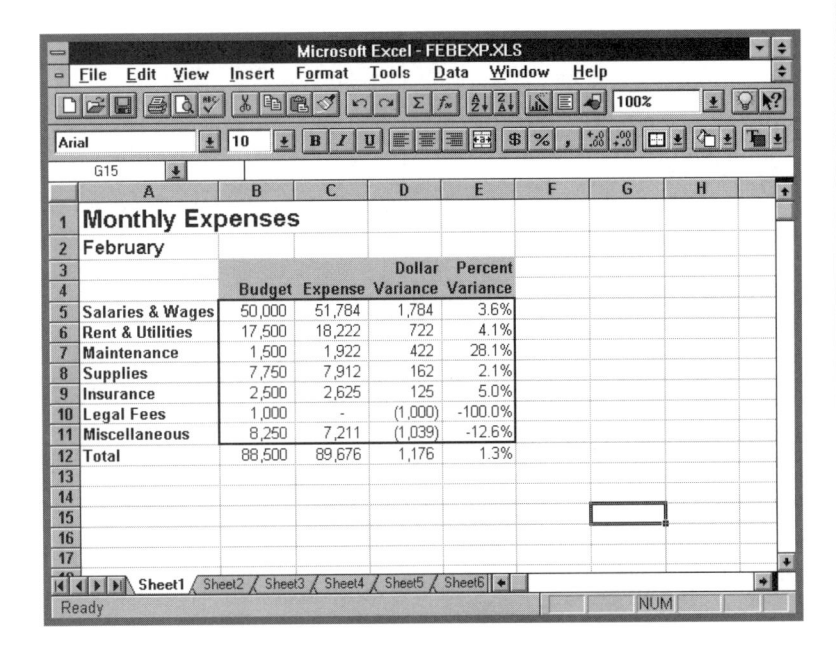

How your worksheet should look after exercise 2

1. Open the FEBEXP file. Then, use the Borders button in the Formatting toolbar to place a heavy border (lower right corner of the palette) around the numbers in the worksheet (cells B5 through E11). Does this make the worksheet easier to read and understand?

2. Use the Color button in the Formatting toolbar to change the background color of the cells that contain the column headings (cells B3 through E4) to the lightest gray that you can find in the palette. Does this make the worksheet easier to read and understand?

3. Use the Color palette to change the background color of all of the cells in the worksheet to white. Does this improve the appearance of the worksheet? Use the None option in the Color palette to remove the color from all the cells in the worksheet.

4. Select the cells in the range B5 to E11, and access the Border tab of the Format Cells dialog box. Notice that the Left, Right, Top, and Bottom boxes are shaded and the Outline box isn't. Apply a red double-line outline to the cells. (You can do that without removing the shading from the Left, Right, Top, and Bottom boxes.) This will replace the black border.

5. Select the same cells and access the Border tab again. Now, remove the left and right borders by clicking twice on the Left and Right boxes, and click on the OK button to return to the worksheet. Last, select the cells one more time and remove the red borders by clicking on the upper left button in the Border palette that drops down from the Formatting toolbar. At this point, the worksheet shouldn't have any borders, colors, or patterns.

6. Select all the cells in the worksheet, and use the Font tab of the Format Cells command to remove all font formatting (check the Normal Font option). Then, select cells A1 through E12, and use the AutoFormat command to apply the Simple autoformat. What fonts, centering, and borders does this autoformat apply? Print this worksheet so you can see how it looks in printed form.

7. Select cells A1 through E12 again, apply the 3D Effects 2 autoformat, and print the worksheet again to see how this autoformat looks when printed. Repeat this for one or more of the other autoformats. Are any of these autoformatted worksheets easier to read and understand than the one with the Simple autoformat?

8. Remove the last autoformat by selecting the cells, accessing the AutoFormat dialog box, and choosing None in the Table Format list. Then, close the workbook without saving the changes.

Three more alignment skills

In chapter 1, you learned how to use three buttons in the Formatting toolbar to align data within a cell. Now, you can learn three more alignment skills.

How to center data across columns

Figure 3-9 shows how to center data across a range of cells using the Center Across Columns button in the Formatting toolbar. Note that when you center data this way, the text is still stored in the cell where you entered it. In this example, the text is still stored in cells A1 and B1.

Procedure

1. Enter the data in the left-most column and select the cells in the columns you want the data centered across:

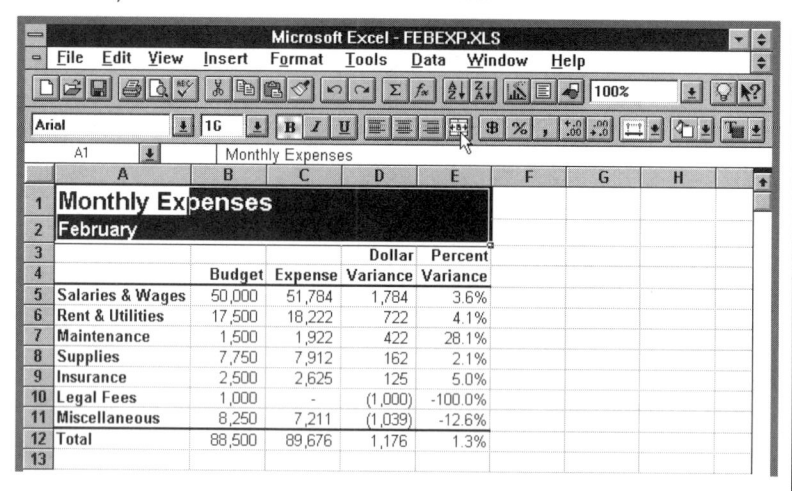

2. Click on the Center Across Columns button in the Formatting toolbar and the data is centered across the columns you highlighted:

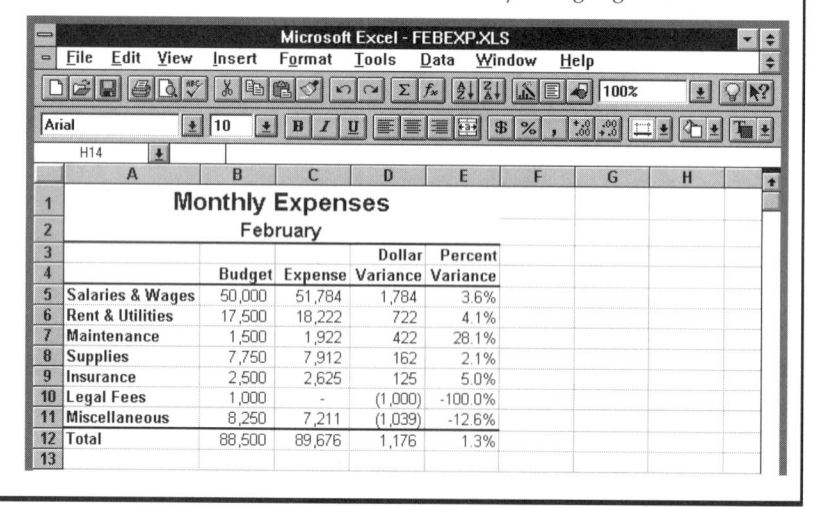

Figure 3-9   **How to center data across a range**

How to justify text within columns

Figure 3-10 shows how to justify text within a range of columns. This is useful when you want to add explanatory notes to a worksheet. To align data in this way, you first enter the text in a single cell. Then, you select the columns or cells you want to justify the text within, and select the Fill Justify command.

Procedure

1. Enter the text in a single cell. Then, select a range that includes the cell that contains the text and the columns you want to justify the text in.

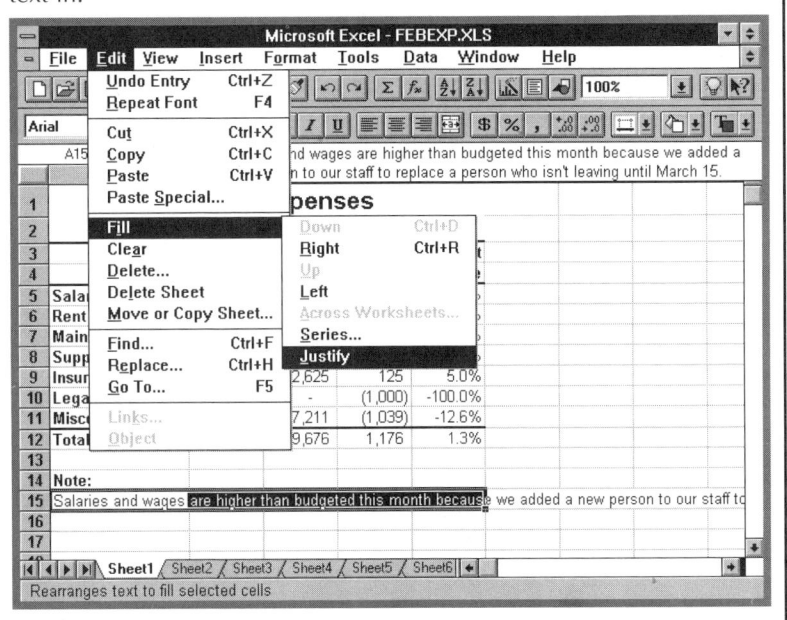

2. Issue the Fill Justify command from the Edit menu. If the selected range isn't large enough for the justified text, Excel displays a dialog box that says "Text will extend below selected range." To complete the command, click on the OK button in this dialog box.

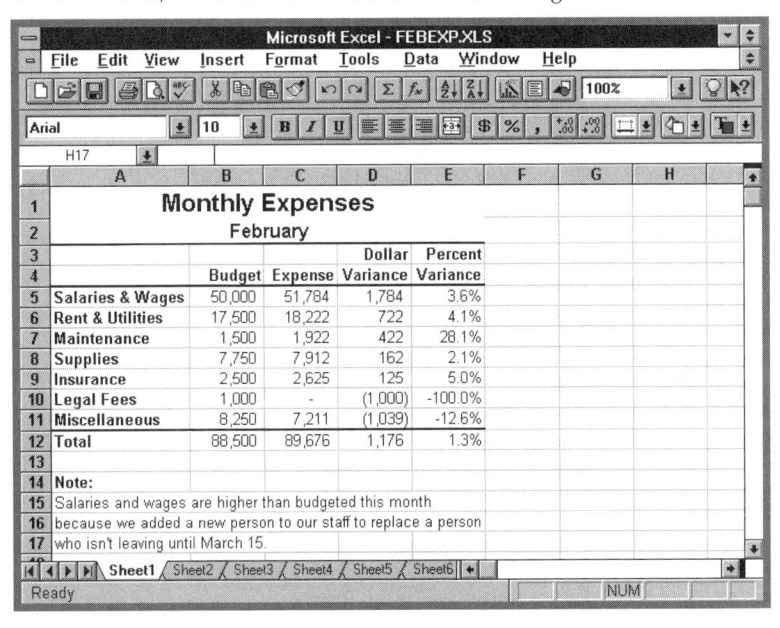

Figure 3-10 How to justify a text entry within two or more columns

How to use the Alignment tab of the Format Cells command

Figure 3-11 shows the Alignment tab of the Format Cells dialog box. If you're using narrow columns of data, one of the Orientation options can be useful for the column headings. Otherwise, you may never need this tab.

Access

Menu	Format ➡ Cells
Shortcut menu	Format Cells
Shortcut key	Ctrl+1

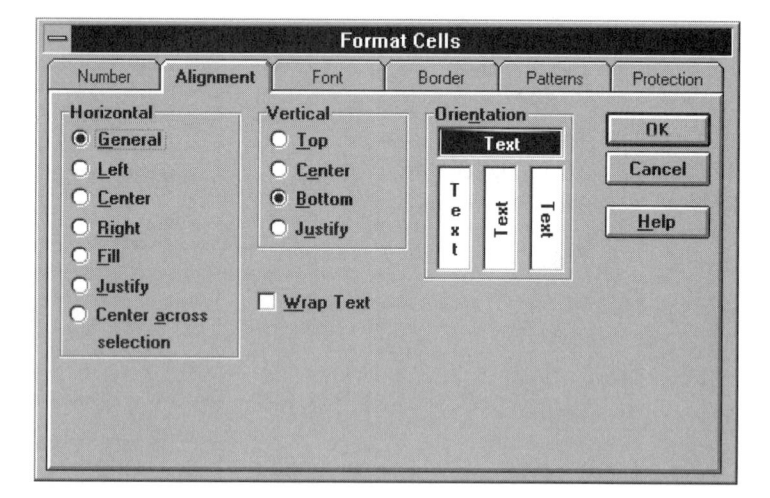

Operation

- To align the text in the selected cells horizontally, choose an option in the Horizontal group. The Fill option fills the cell by repeating the text that's in it. The Justify option arranges text that extends beyond a cell into two or more lines within the cell (similar to the Wrap Text option shown below).

- To align the data in the selected cells vertically, choose an option in the Vertical group.

- For special effects, choose an option in the Orientation group. The middle option is illustrated by the text in cells B1 through I1:

	A	B	C	D	E	F	G	H	I	J
1	Student	Test 1	Test 2	Test 3	Test 4	Test 5	Test 6	Test 7	Test 8	
2	Anne Prince	100	100	98	77	100	85	95	100	
3										

- To wrap text that overlaps the cell that it's in, check the Wrap Text box. This is illustrated by the text in cell D4:

	A	B	C	D	E
1	Monthly Expenses		2/23/95		FEBEXP
2	February				
3					
4		Budget	Expense	Dollar Variance	
5					

Figure 3-11 How to use the Alignment tab of the Format Cells command

Exercise set 3-3

	A	B	C	D	E	F
1	Monthly Expenses					
2	February					
3				Dollar	Percent	
4		Budget	Expense	Variance	Variance	
5	Salaries & Wages	50,000	51,784	1,784	3.6%	
6	Rent & Utilities	17,500	18,222	722	4.1%	
7	Maintenance	1,500	1,922	422	28.1%	
8	Supplies	7,750	7,912	162	2.1%	
9	Insurance	2,500	2,625	125	5.0%	
10	Legal Fees	1,000	-	(1,000)	-100.0%	
11	Miscellaneous	8,250	7,211	(1,039)	-12.6%	
12	Total	88,500	89,676	1,176	1.3%	
13						
14	Note:				
15	Salaries and wages expenses are higher than budgeted				
16	because we added a new person to our staff on February 16 to				
17	replace a person who isn't leaving until March 15.				
18						

How your worksheet should look after exercise 5

At this point, you should be able to format the last version of the FEBEXP worksheet so it looks like the worksheet above. If you think you can do that on your own, go to it. Otherwise, the exercises that follow guide you through the formatting.

1. Open the FEBEXP workbook. Then, use the procedure in figure 3-9 to center the title and subtitle over columns A through E.

2. Use the Border palette to add heavy bottom borders to the first five columns of rows 2, 4, 11, and 12 as shown above.

3. Use the Color palette to change the background color in the first five columns of the first two rows to white.

4. Enter and boldface the note heading in cell A14 as shown above. Next, use the procedure in figure 3-10 to add the note text to the bottom of the worksheet and to justify the note over columns A through E. Then, check the spelling to make sure you typed the text correctly.

5. Use the Color palette to change the background color in the first five columns of rows 13 through 17 to white.

6. Your worksheet should now look like the one above. If it doesn't, work with it until it does. When it does, print the worksheet. Then, save the file, but don't close it.

7. Delete row 3 of the worksheet, and edit the text in cells D3 and E3 so they contain "Dollar Variance" and "Percent Variance." Then, use the Alignment tab of the Format Cells command to turn on the Wrap Text option for these cells. This is another way to set up column headings that require two lines of text.

8. Select cells B3 and C3. Then, use the Alignment tab of the Format Cells command to apply the second vertical orientation in the Orientation group. This alignment can obviously be useful in a worksheet that has narrow columns of data. Now, close the file without saving it.

How to format and preview the pages in a workbook

You can use the Page Setup command in the File menu to change the format of the pages in a workbook. Since some of this formatting doesn't show up in the normal display of a worksheet, you can then use the Print Preview command to review the page formatting before you actually print a worksheet.

How to change the margins

Figure 3-12 shows how to use the Page Setup command to change the margins of a worksheet. Although the default margins are acceptable for most worksheets, you will frequently want to use the options in the Center on Page group to center a worksheet vertically or horizontally on the page.

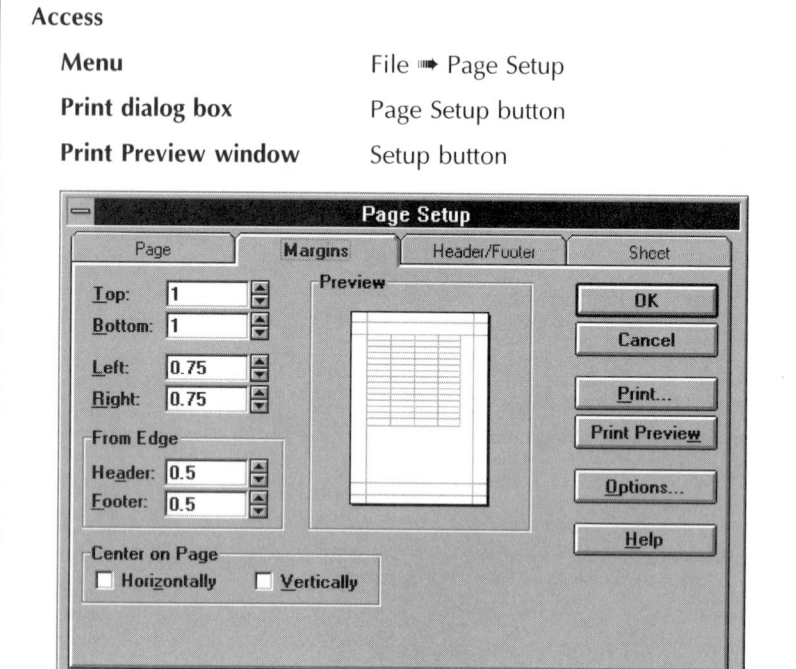

Access

Menu	File ➡ Page Setup
Print dialog box	Page Setup button
Print Preview window	Setup button

Operation

- To change the page margins, change the values in the Top, Bottom, Left, and Right boxes.
- To change the distance from the top of the paper to the header and from the bottom of the paper to the footer, change the values in the From Edge group.
- To center the worksheet horizontally or vertically on the page, check one or both boxes in the Center on Page group.

Figure 3-12   How to change the page margins

How to change the default header and footer

When you use Excel, every worksheet starts with a default *header* and *footer*. The default header gives the name of the worksheet within the workbook (Sheet1 for a one sheet workbook), and the default footer gives the page number (Page 1 for a one page worksheet). For most workbooks, however, those defaults aren't satisfactory so you'll want to change them.

Figure 3-13 shows how to change a default header or footer to one of the pre-defined headers or footers that comes with Excel. To do that, you just choose the header or footer that you want from the list that drops down from the Header or Footer text box. After you choose one, you can see the changes in the dialog box.

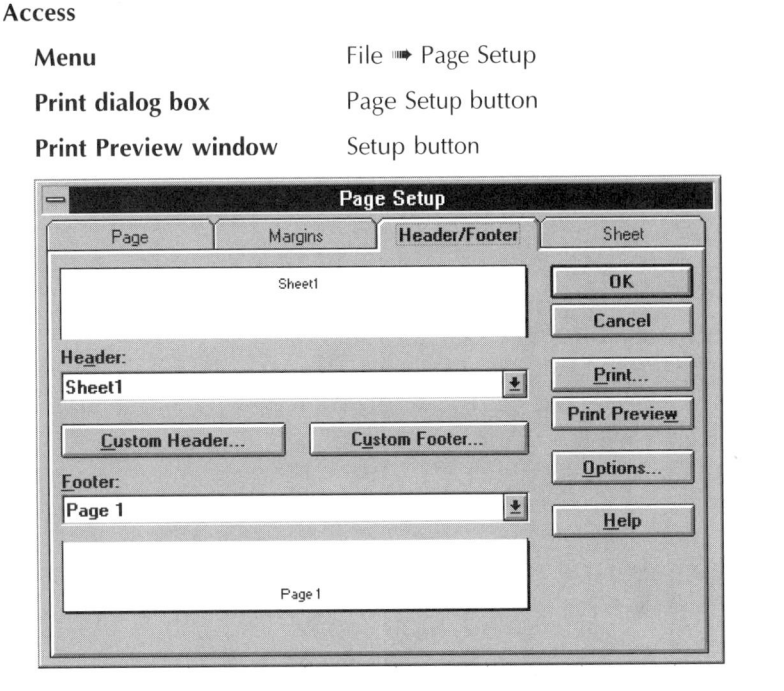

Access

Menu	File ➡ Page Setup
Print dialog box	Page Setup button
Print Preview window	Setup button

How to change the default header or footer

1. Access the Header/Footer tab of the Page Setup dialog box.

2. Click on the drop-down arrow to the right of the Header or Footer box to display a list like this one:

   ```
   Sheet1
   Anne Prince, Page 1, 11/27/93
   Prepared by Anne Prince 11/27/93, Page 1
   Mike Murach & Associates, Inc. Confidential, Sheet1
   SALESRPT.XLS
   SALESRPT.XLS, Page 1
   Sheet1
   ```

3. Choose an option from the list to change the default header or footer. Or choose None at the top of the list to remove the default header or footer from the worksheet.

Figure 3-13　How to use a pre-defined header or footer

If none of the pre-defined headers or footers is exactly what you want, you can use the procedure in figure 3-14 to create a custom header or footer. The easiest way to do that is to start with the pre-defined header or footer that's closest to what you want. In general, a header, a footer, or some combination of the two should provide the date, file name, and page number. You may also want the header and footer to provide the time, the author's name, and other text information.

The dialog box that's displayed when you click on the Custom Header button in the Header/Footer tab of the Page Setup dialog box

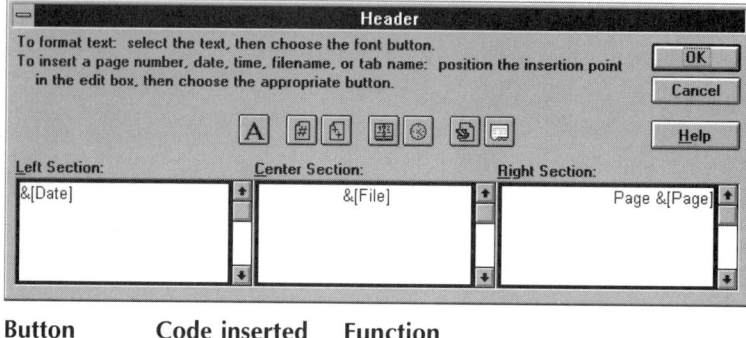

Button	Code inserted	Function
A	None	Accesses the Font dialog box so you can change the font and font attributes of the selected text in the header or footer.
#	&[Page]	Inserts the page number.
	&[Pages]	Inserts the total number of pages.
	&[Date]	Inserts the date.
	&[Time]	Inserts the time.
	&[File]	Inserts the file name.
	&[Tab]	Inserts the worksheet tab name.

Procedure

1. Choose the pre-defined header or footer you want to start from as described in figure 3-13.

2. Click on the Custom Header or Custom Footer button to display a dialog box like the one above.

3. Click in the left, center, or right boxes to move the insertion point there. Then, enter any text or click on one of the buttons in the dialog box to insert special text.

4. Click on the OK button to return to the Header/Footer tab of the Page Setup dialog box. The custom header or footer that you just created is included at the end of the Header or Footer list.

Figure 3-14 How to create a custom header or footer

How to preview the printed worksheet

Figure 3-15 shows how to preview a worksheet. Notice that you can start the preview from the File menu, the Standard toolbar, the Print dialog box, or the Page Setup dialog box. When you're sure that the worksheet is going to print the way you want it, you can start the printing by clicking on the Print button in the Print Preview toolbar.

Besides previewing, you can use the preview window to change the page margins, the margins for the header and footer, and the widths of the columns. Most of the time, though, you're better off making those adjustments from the worksheet itself.

Access		
	Menu	File ⇒ Print Preview
	Standard toolbar	
	Print dialog box	Print Preview button
	Page Setup dialog box	Print Preview button

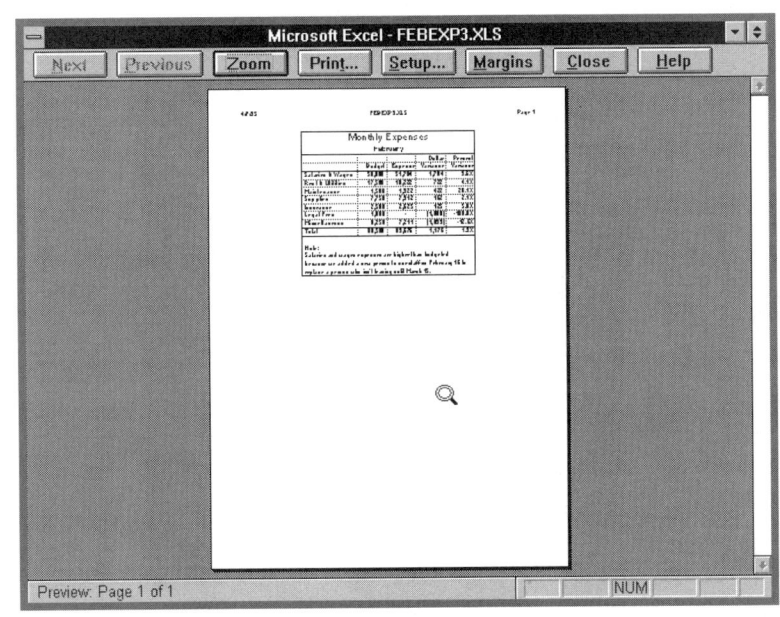

Button	Function
Next	Displays the next page.
Previous	Displays the previous page.
Zoom	Toggles between full-page and magnified view.
Print	Displays the Print dialog box.
Setup	Displays the Page Setup dialog box.
Margins	Displays handles and lines you can use to adjust the margins and column widths.
Close	Closes the Print Preview window and returns to the active workbook.
Help	Displays Help information.

Notes

- You can click on any area of a page in full-page view to magnify it. Click again to return to full-page view.
- To change a margin or column width after you click on the Margins button, place the pointer over the appropriate handle or margin line and drag it.

Figure 3-15 How to preview a worksheet

Exercise set 3-4

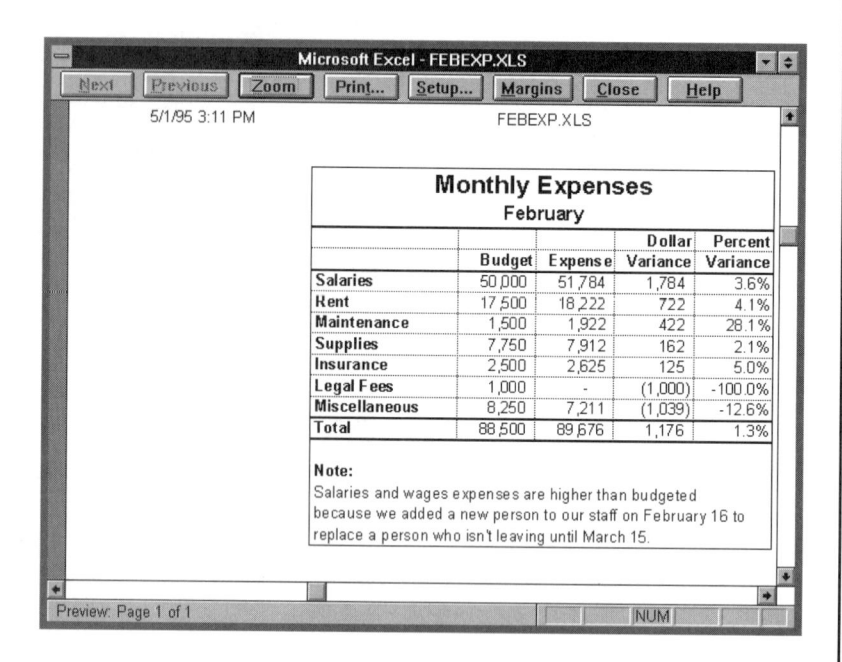

How your worksheet should look in the Print Preview window after you magnify the header in exercise 3

1. Open the FEBEXP file, access the Page Setup command, and use the Margins tab to center the page horizontally. When you return to the worksheet, can you tell that it's going to be centered when you print it?

2. Use the procedures in figures 3-13 and 3-14 to delete the default footer and add a custom header to the FEBEXP workbook. The header should consist of the date and time (left aligned), the file name (centered), and the page number (right aligned).

3. Use the Print Preview command that's summarized in figure 3-15 to preview the worksheet. Is the worksheet centered horizontally on the page? Does the header contain the correct data and is the data aligned correctly? Click the magnifying glass mouse pointer on the header to get a good look at it, and click again to return to normal magnification. If the worksheet looks the way you want it to, click on the Print button to print the worksheet. This returns you to the worksheet. Then, save the file, but don't close it.

4. Access the Print Preview command again, and click on the Margins button so you can see the handles and lines that are added to the view. Drag the top margin halfway down the page to vertically center the worksheet. Then, click on the Setup button to access the Page Setup dialog box, and look at the Margins tab to see how the top margin setting has been changed. Close the dialog box, close the print preview, and close the file without saving the margin change.

How to copy and delete formats

When you create a worksheet, you usually want ranges that contain similar data to have the same formats. If the formats are complex, you can make sure they are consistent by copying them from one range to another. To do that, you can use the methods that are presented next.

Note, however, that most Excel users don't need these extra formatting skills. So if you're satisfied with the formatting skills that you've learned to this point in the chapter, you can skip to the Perspective heading at the end of this chapter.

How to copy and delete formats using menu commands

Figure 3-16 shows how to use the Paste Special command in the Edit menu to copy formats from one range to another. Before you issue this command, you copy a cell that contains the formats you want to the clipboard. Then, when you issue the Paste Special command, you paste only the formats from the clipboard, not the data. The formats that are pasted include number formats, alignment, font, borders, colors, and patterns.

Figure 3-16 also presents the Clear Formats command. You can use this command to remove formats from selected cells. Then, the cells return to their default formats.

How to copy formats

1. Place the cell pointer on the cell that contains the formats you want to copy, and copy the cell to the clipboard.
2. Select the range where you want to copy the formats. Then, access the Paste Special command from the Edit or shortcut menu so this dialog box is displayed:

3. Choose the Formats option in the Paste group, and click on the OK button to copy the formats to the selected range.

How to delete formats

1. Select the cells that contain the formats you want to delete.
2. Choose the Clear Formats command from the Edit menu:

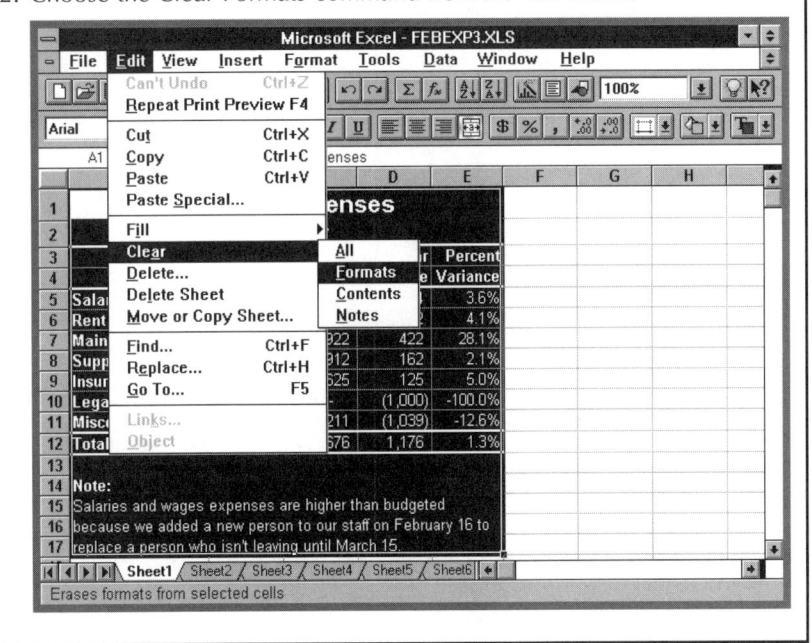

Figure 3-16 How to use menu commands to copy and delete formats

How to copy formats using the Format Painter

Figure 3-17 shows how to copy formats using the Format Painter button in the Standard toolbar. Before you click or double-click on this button, you must be sure that the cell pointer is on a cell that contains the formats you want to copy. Then, you can apply those formats to other cells just by dragging the paintbrush mouse pointer over the cells.

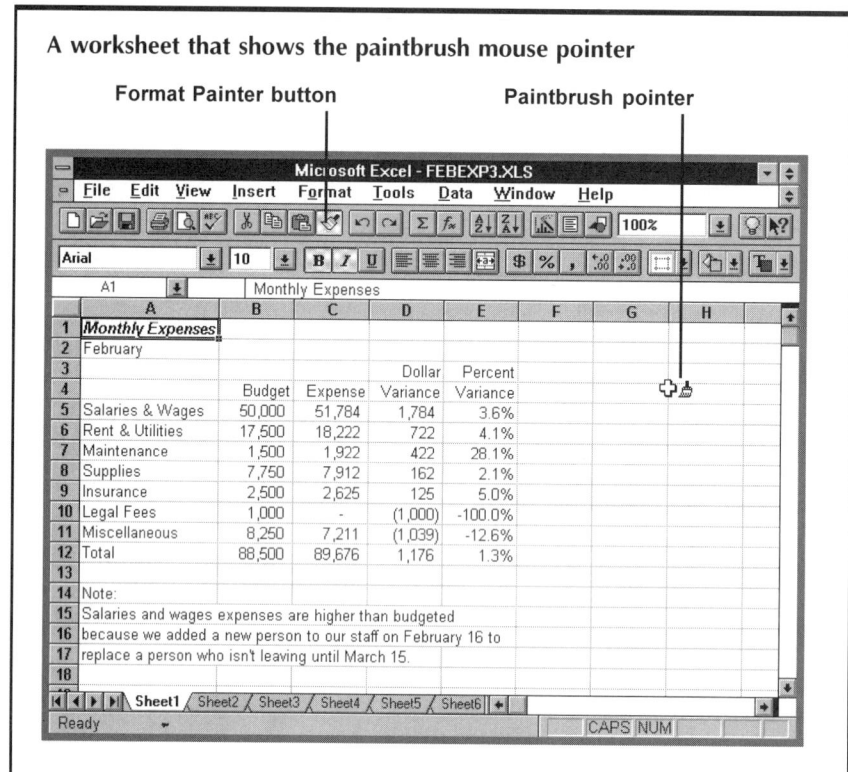

A worksheet that shows the paintbrush mouse pointer

How to copy formats to two or more selections

1. Place the cell pointer on the cell that contains the formats you want to copy to other cells.

2. Double-click on the Format Painter button in the Standard toolbar so the mouse pointer changes to the paintbrush pointer.

3. Drag the paintbrush pointer over the cells that you want to format. When you release the mouse button, the new formatting is applied to those cells. You can repeat this until you've painted all the selections.

4. To end the formatting, click on the Format Painter button again or press the Esc key.

How to copy formats to a single range

- Use the same procedure above, but single click on the Format Painter button in step 2. Then, the function ends after you format one selection so you don't have to do step 4. You probably don't need the Format Painter, though, if you're only going to format one selection.

Figure 3-17   How to use the Format Painter to copy formats

Exercise set 3-5

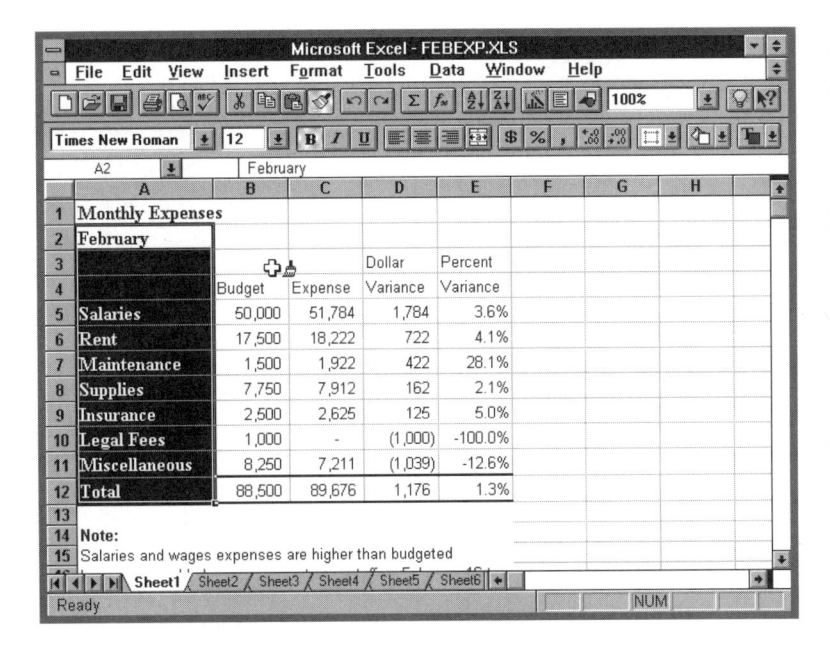

How your worksheet should look as you use the Format Painter in exercise 3

	A	B	C	D	E
1	Monthly Expenses				
2	February				
3				Dollar	Percent
4		Budget	Expense	Variance	Variance
5	Salaries	50,000	51,784	1,784	3.6%
6	Rent	17,500	18,222	722	4.1%
7	Maintenance	1,500	1,922	422	28.1%
8	Supplies	7,750	7,912	162	2.1%
9	Insurance	2,500	2,625	125	5.0%
10	Legal Fees	1,000	-	(1,000)	-100.0%
11	Miscellaneous	8,250	7,211	(1,039)	-12.6%
12	Total	88,500	89,676	1,176	1.3%
13					
14	Note:				
15	Salaries and wages expenses are higher than budgeted				

1. Open the FEBEXP file. Next, hold down the Ctrl key while you use the mouse to select all the cells that contain text (not numbers or formulas). Then, use the Clear Formats command to remove all formatting from the nonadjacent selections.

2. Change the font in cell A1 to Times New Roman in 12 point size and apply the bold attribute to it. Next, use the Copy command to copy the cell contents and formats to the clipboard. Then, use the Paste Special command that's shown in figure 3-16 to copy just the formatting from the clipboard to the subtitle, column headings, and row headings.

3. Select all the cells that contain text again, use the Clear Formats command to remove all formatting from those cells, and change the formatting for cell A1 to bold Times New Roman in 12 point size. Then, double-click on the Format Painter button, and paint the format of cell A1 onto the subtitle, column headings, and row headings. Do you prefer this method of copying formats to the use of the Paste Special command?

4. Close the file without saving it.

How to create and use styles

A *style* is a formatting combination that can be applied to a cell including number format, font, alignment, borders, and patterns. By default, all cells are formatted with the Normal style, which provides the General number format, the default font, and the default font size, but no borders or patterns.

Excel also provides five styles for formatting numbers. These include the Currency, Percent, and Comma styles that you learned to apply from the Formatting toolbar in chapter 1. They also include the Currency(0) and Comma(0) styles that format a number without any decimal places.

How to create and apply your own styles

If you want to use the same formatting combinations throughout a workbook, it sometimes makes sense to create and apply your own styles. Figure 3-18 shows how. The easiest way to create a style is to format a cell the way you want it, access the Style dialog box, and provide a style name for the formatting that's applied to the active cell.

Once you create a style, you can apply its formatting to selected cells using the second procedure in figure 3-18. Unless the formatting is complex, you can probably format more quickly without using styles. But using styles helps you make sure that the formats are applied consistently throughout a workbook.

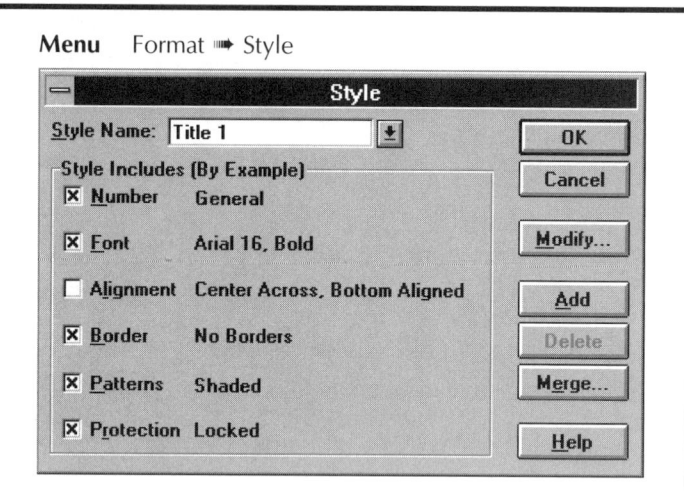

Access   **Menu**   Format ➡ Style

How to create a style

1. Place the cell pointer on the cell that contains the formats you want the style to contain.

2. Access the Style dialog box, and enter a name for the style in the Style Name box. If necessary, remove the check from any of the options in the Style Includes group that you don't want to include in the style (like the Center Across alignment option in the dialog box above). Then, click on the OK button.

How to apply a style

1. Select the cell or range you want to format with a style.

2. Access the Style dialog box, and choose a style from the Style Name list. If necessary, remove the check mark from any of the options in the Style Includes group that you don't want to apply. Then, click on the OK button.

How to modify a style

- Repeat the procedure for creating a style including the re-entry of the style name, even though it's already there. When you choose the OK button to complete the dialog box, a message is displayed that asks whether you want to redefine the style based on the selection. When you reply that you do, the style is changed and the formatting of all cells with that style is changed too.

How to delete a style

- Access the Style dialog box, and choose the style you want to delete from the Style Name list. Then, click on the Delete button. This deletes the style and returns all cells with that style to their default format.

Figure 3-18   How to create, apply, modify, and delete styles

How to modify and delete styles

The third procedure in figure 3-18 shows you how to modify a style once you've created it. And this illustrates another benefit that you get from using styles. When you change the style, the formatting in all cells that have that style applied to it is also changed. If you delete a style, the formatting for all cells with that style is returned to the Normal style.

Additional information

✓ If you choose the Modify button as you create or modify a style, the Format Cells dialog box is displayed. Then, you can use this box to change any of the formats for the style.

How to copy styles from another workbook

At this point, you can decide whether styles are a feature that you can benefit from. If you think you can, you'll want to know how to copy styles from one workbook to another. This skill is presented in figure 3-19.

When you copy styles, you actually *merge* the styles in a *source workbook* with the styles in a *destination workbook*. So if the destination workbook doesn't contain any styles or it contains styles with names that are different from those in the source workbook, the styles in the source workbook are simply copied to the destination workbook. Otherwise, you can either replace the styles in the destination workbook with the ones in the source workbook or you can cancel the entire operation.

Procedure

1. Open the workbook file that contains the styles you want to copy (the *source workbook*) and the workbook file that you want to copy the styles to (the *destination workbook*).

2. Switch to the workbook that you want to copy the styles to. Then, access the Styles dialog box as shown in figure 3-18 and click on the Merge button so this dialog box is displayed:

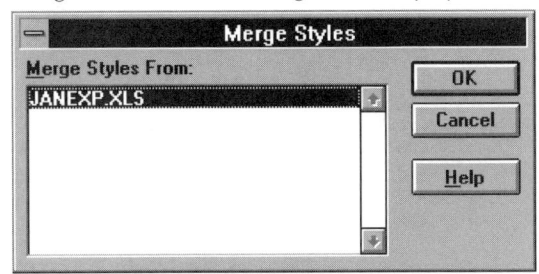

3. In the Merge Styles From box, only the names of other open workbooks are listed. Then, choose the name of the workbook that contains the styles you want to copy and click on the OK button. This adds the styles in the source workbook to the styles in the destination workbook.

Note

- If you copy styles from a source workbook that contains styles that have the same names as styles in the destination workbook, a message box appears that asks if you want to merge styles that have the same names. If you answer Yes, the styles from the source workbook replace the ones in the destination workbook. If you answer No, the operation is canceled.

Figure 3-19 How to copy styles from another workbook into the active workbook

Exercise set 3-6

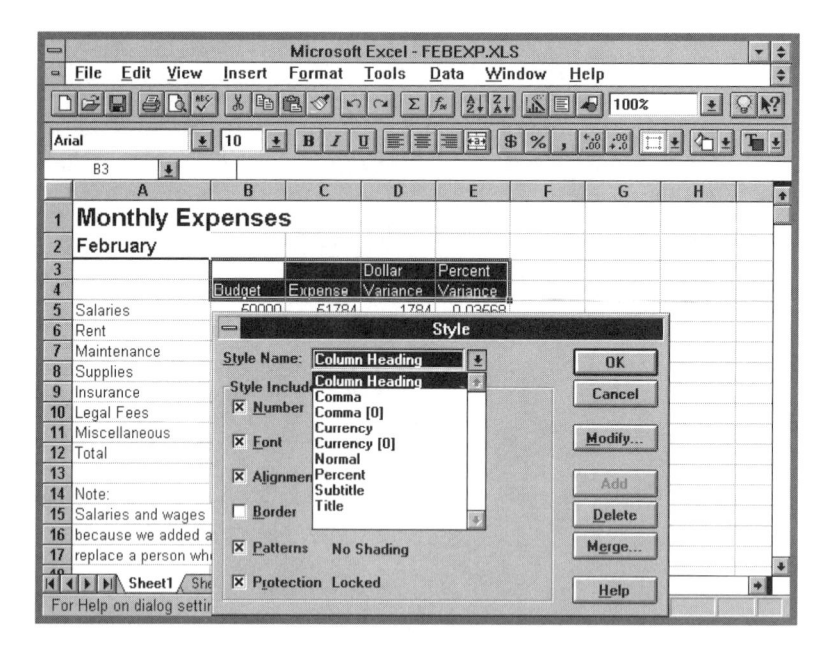

How the Style dialog box should look as you apply styles in exercise 2

1. Open the FEBEXP file. Then, use the first procedure in figure 3-18 to create three styles: one named Title with the formatting of cell A1, but not the alignment formatting; one named Subtitle with the formatting of cell A2, but not the alignment formatting; and one named Column Heading with the formatting of cell B4, but not the border formatting.

2. Select all the cells in the worksheet, and use the Clear Formats command to clear all formats. Then, format the title, subtitle, and column headings by using the second procedure in figure 3-18 to apply the styles that you just created. Also, format cells B2 through E2 with the Subtitle style because it includes the bottom border. This should give you a good idea of how styles work.

3. Add italics to the column heading in cell B4. Then, use the third procedure in figure 3-18 to modify the Column Heading style based on the new formatting for cell B4. Note that you have to retype Column Heading as the style name in the dialog box, even though it's already there. When you return to the worksheet, what has happened to the other column headings? They should be changed to italics too because their style has been changed.

4. Open the window for a new workbook (press Ctrl+N), and copy the styles from the FEBEXP workbook to the new workbook using the procedure in figure 3-19. Then, type "Report Title" in cell A1 and apply the Title style to it. This shows how you can use the same styles in more than workbook. With this as background, do you think styles are a feature that can help you work more productively?

5. Close both of the open files without saving them.

Perspective

If you've done all the exercises for this chapter, you should start to see how quickly and easily you can format your worksheets so they're attractive and easy to read. For most worksheets, you can get the results you want in a few minutes with a limited use of font sizes, font attributes, centering, and borders. And sometimes, the Simple autoformat is all that you need for effective formatting.

When in doubt, the best rule is to keep your formatting simple. If you overdo the formatting, your worksheets are likely to become less attractive and more difficult to read. And your productivity is sure to decrease.

Summary

- You can use the Formatting toolbar to change the font, font size, font attributes, and color of the data in a selected range of cells. For special effects, you can use the Font tab of the Format Cells command.

- You can use the Formatting toolbar or the Borders and Patterns tabs of the Format Cells command to add borders, colors, and patterns to a worksheet.

- You can use the AutoFormat command to apply one of 16 *autoformats* to a range within a worksheet.

- To center titles or subtitles across columns, you can use the Center Across Columns button in the Formatting toolbar. To justify text within a range of columns, you can use the Fill Justify command in the Edit menu. And for special alignment effects, you can use the Alignment tab of the Format Cells command.

- You can use the Page Setup command in the File menu to change the margins of a worksheet, center it horizontally or vertically between the margins, or change the default header or footer. Then, you can use the Print Preview command to see how a worksheet is going to look when it is printed.

- You can use the Paste Special command or the Format Painter button in the Formatting toolbar to copy formats from one cell to other ranges. To delete the formats from a range of cells, you can use the Clear Formats command in the Edit menu.

- You can use the Style command in the Format menu to create, apply, change, or delete a *style*. You can also copy styles from one workbook to another.

Chapter 4

Commands and features for working with larger worksheets

The skills that you've learned in chapters 1 through 3 can be applied to every Excel worksheet. When a worksheet becomes larger than what can be displayed in the workbook window or printed on a single sheet of paper, though, you need some additional skills. And those are the skills you'll learn in this chapter.

How to set the view so it works best for you
    How to display a worksheet in Full Screen view
    How to hide or display toolbars
    How to zoom in or out of the display
    How to view more than one area of a worksheet at the same time

How to hide and freeze columns and rows
    How to hide or reveal columns and rows using menu commands
    How to hide or reveal columns or rows using mouse techniques
    How to freeze or unfreeze one or more rows or columns
    How to use the View Manager to save and show views

How to format the pages of a multi-page worksheet
    How to change the orientation and sizing of a worksheet
    How to print titles on each page of a worksheet
    How to insert and delete page breaks

Two printing skills for multi-page worksheets
    How to print part of a worksheet
    How to cancel a print job

How to create and use names
    How to name a range of cells
    How to name several ranges at the same time
    How to move the cell pointer to a named range

Perspective

Summary

How to set the view so it works best for you

When you change the *view*, you change the way Excel and the worksheet you're working on appear on the screen. Excel provides several features for changing the view that can help you work more efficiently with larger worksheets. You can access some of these features from the View menu that's summarized in figure 4-1.

How to display a worksheet in Full Screen view

For worksheets that have more rows than can fit in the workbook window, it sometimes makes sense to hide the formula bar, status bar, and toolbars so you can see more rows. One quick way to do that is to choose the Full Screen command in the View menu. This view is illustrated in figure 4-1. Then, to return to the default view, you can either choose the Full Screen command again or click on the floating button. (That button is actually the Full View toolbar that contains but one button.)

A worksheet in Full Screen view with the View menu displayed

The commands in the View menu

Command	Function
Formula Bar	Displays or hides the formula bar.
Status Bar	Displays or hides the status bar.
Toolbars	Lets you display or hide any of the toolbars that are available with Excel.
Full Screen	Switches to or from the Full Screen view that's shown above (no formula bar, no status bar, and no toolbars). You can also switch from Full Screen view to the normal view by clicking on the single button of the Full View toolbar that's shown above.
Zoom	Lets you change the magnification of the current window, but you can do that more efficiently by using the Zoom Control list in the Standard toolbar.
View Manager	Lets you save and show views (see figure 4-10). (If the View Manager isn't listed on the View menu, it hasn't been installed on your PC.)

Figure 4-1   The commands of the View menu

How to hide or display toolbars

If you want to hide the toolbars without using Full Screen view, you can use either the shortcut menu for the toolbars or the Toolbars command in the View menu. These are illustrated in figure 4-2. You can also use either method to display toolbars. Most of the time, though, you'll want the Standard and Formatting toolbars displayed and you won't need any other toolbars, so you will rarely need to hide or display toolbars.

The shortcut menu that's displayed when you click the right mouse button on one of the toolbars

```
√ Standard
√ Formatting
  Chart
  Drawing
  Forms
  Visual Basic
  Auditing
  WorkGroup
  Microsoft
  ─────────
  Toolbars...
  Customize...
```

The Toolbars dialog box that you can access from the View menu or the shortcut menu shown above

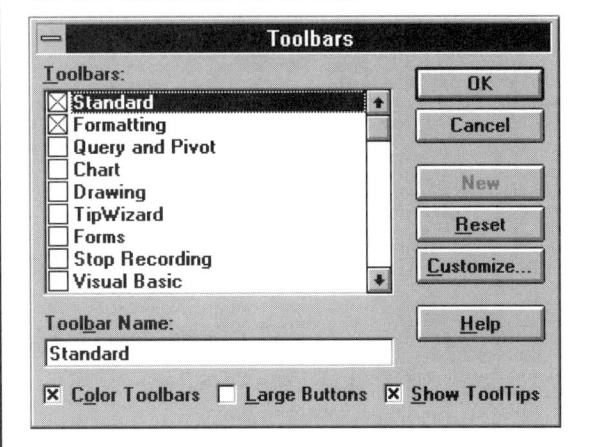

Operation

- Check a toolbar name to display the toolbar.
- Uncheck a toolbar name to remove the toolbar from the display.

Notes

- Not all of the available toolbars are included in the shortcut menu, but all are included in the Toolbars dialog box.
- The last toolbar in the Toolbars list in the Toolbars dialog box is the Full View toolbar, which is the single button shown in figure 4-1.

Figure 4-2 How to hide or display toolbars

How to zoom in or out of the display

The easiest way to change the number of rows or columns displayed in the workbook window is to use the Zoom Control list in the Standard toolbar. This list is shown in figure 4-3. As you can see, it lets you choose from several magnification settings. In this example, the setting is 75% so almost three more columns are displayed than at the 100% setting shown in figure 4-1.

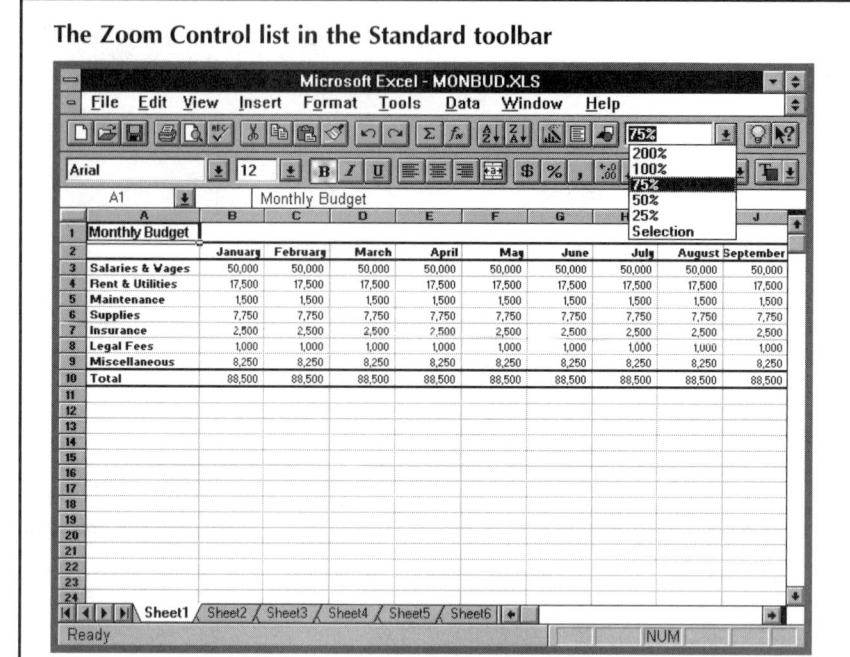

The Zoom Control list in the Standard toolbar

Operation

- Choose a percent option to display the worksheet at the indicated magnification.
- Choose the Selection option to adjust the magnification so the current selection fills the display.
- Enter a number in the Zoom Control box to set the magnification to a custom setting.

Note

- You can use the Zoom command in the View menu to perform the same functions as the Zoom Control box in the toolbar.

Figure 4-3 How to zoom in or out of the display

How to view more than one area of a worksheet at the same time

When you work with a worksheet that's too large for the workbook window, you sometimes want to look at two different areas of the worksheet at the same time. Figure 4-4 shows how you can do that. When you split a window, it's divided into *panes*. Then, you can scroll within each pane individually so a different area of the worksheet can be displayed in each pane.

When you split the window vertically, you'll notice that vertical scrolling in the two panes is automatically synchronized. That means that you'll always see the same rows in each pane. Similarly, when you split the window horizontally, horizontal scrolling is synchronized so you always see the same columns. If the screen is split both vertically and horizontally, scrolling is synchronized in two of the panes at any given time depending on which scroll bar you use.

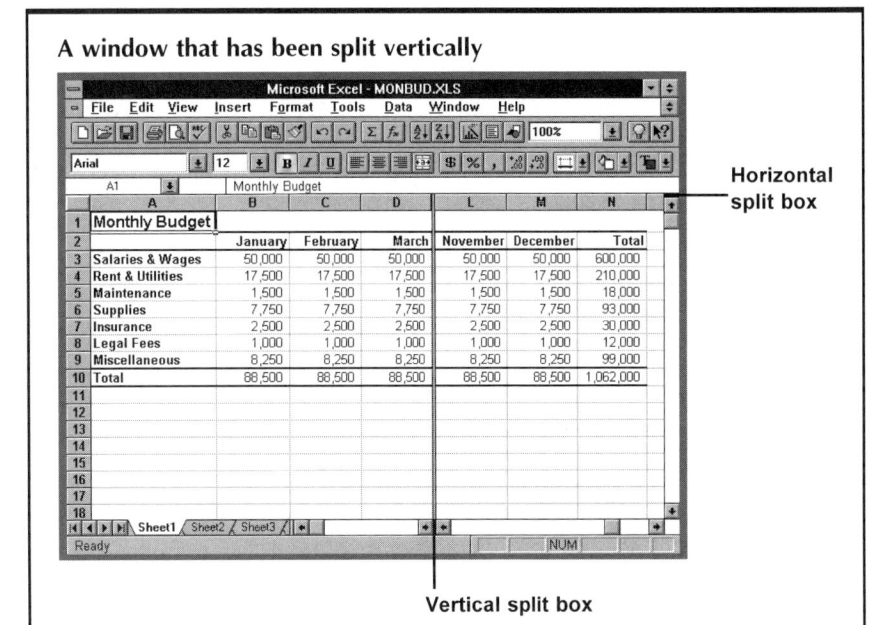

A window that has been split vertically

Horizontal split box

Vertical split box

How to split a window vertically

- Drag the vertical split box from its default position to where you want to split the window. Or, double-click on the vertical split box to split the window to the left of the active cell.

How to split a window horizontally

- Drag the horizontal split box from its default position to where you want to split the window horizontally. Or, double-click on the horizontal split box to split the window above the active cell.

How to split a window both vertically and horizontally

- Split the window both ways using the techniques above, or choose the Split command in the Window menu to split the window above and to the left of the active cell.

How to unsplit a window

- Drag a split box back to its original position, or double-click on a split box.

Notes

- Once a window is split, you can scroll each pane separately to display different areas of the worksheet.

- If any columns or rows are frozen (see figure 4-9), the split boxes aren't available. Then, to unfreeze the columns and rows and split the workbook window at the same time, you can use the Split command in the Window menu. This splits the window below the frozen rows and to the right of the frozen columns.

Figure 4-4   How to split or unsplit the workbook window

Exercise set 4-1

A worksheet named MONBUD that you create in this set of exercises

	A	B	C	D	E	F	G	N
1	Monthly Budget							
2		January	February	March	April	May	June	Total
3	Salaries & Wages	50,000	50,000	50,000	50,000	50,000	50,000	600,000
4	Rent & Utilities	17,500	17,500	17,500	17,500	17,500	17,500	210,000
5	Maintenance	1,500	1,500	1,500	1,500	1,500	1,500	18,000
6	Supplies	7,750	7,750	7,750	7,750	7,750	7,750	93,000
7	Insurance	2,500	2,500	2,500	2,500	2,500	2,500	30,000
8	Legal Fees	1,000	1,000	1,000	1,000	1,000	1,000	12,000
9	Miscellaneous	8,250	8,250	8,250	8,250	8,250	8,250	99,000
10	Total	88,500	88,500	88,500	88,500	88,500	88,500	1,062,000
11								

To do the exercises for this chapter, you need a worksheet that's too large to fit in the workbook window and too large to be printed on a single page in readable form. So this exercise set guides you through the preparation of a worksheet like the one above, including the six hidden columns between G and N.

1. Open the FEBEXP file, and save it as MONBUD. Next, delete rows 2 and 3; delete rows 11 through 15; delete columns C, D, and E; and delete the contents of cell B2. Then, change the title in cell A1 to the one shown above; change its font size to 12 points; remove its across columns centering by clicking on the Center Across Columns button in the Formatting toolbar; and change the width for column A so it's large enough for the text in cell A1. Last, apply a border like the one shown above at the bottom of cells A1 and B1. You've now got the start of the worksheet shown above.

2. Copy the cells in column B to columns C through N. The easiest way to do that is to select cells B1 through B10, then drag the fill handle of the selection to the right and release it when column N is included. This copies both the data and the borders.

3. Enter January into cell B2. Next, drag the fill handle to the right so the months of the year are filled into cells C2 through M2. Then, set the column width for columns B through N to 10.

4. Edit Total column N so it looks like the one above. To start, enter Total in cell N2. Next, delete the data in cells N3 through N9. Then, enter the SUM functions in cells N3 through N9. You can use the AutoSum button to enter the function in cell N3, then copy that function down to cells N4 through N9, but be sure to check that the ranges are correct. (When you copy the formula to cell N9, you'll lose the border below that cell, so you'll need to add it back.) The function in cell N10 ought to work without modification.

5. At this point, your worksheet should look like the one above but with the July through December columns included. If the formatting isn't quite right, adjust it. Then, save the changes to the workbook, and close it.

Exercise set 4-2

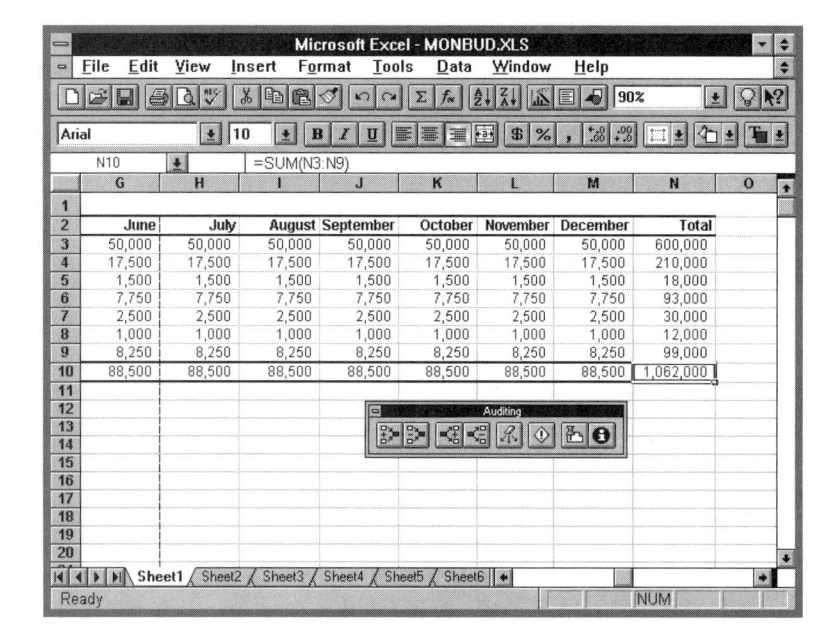

The last columns of the MONBUD workbook with the floating Auditing toolbar that you display in exercise 2

1. Open the MONBUD workbook, and note how many rows are displayed in the workbook window at 100% magnification. Then, use the Full Screen command in the View menu to remove the formula bar, the status bar, and toolbars. How many rows are displayed in the workbook window now? Is the Full Screen toolbar displayed? Return to the Normal view by clicking on the button in the Full Screen toolbar or by choosing the Full Screen command from the View menu.

2. Use the toolbar shortcut menu to display the Auditing toolbar. If it's floating, place the mouse pointer on the title bar of the toolbar and drag it to the toolbar area. When you release the mouse button, the floating toolbar takes a fixed location below the Formatting toolbar. To change it back to its floating form, drag its background back into the workbook window. You can also use these techniques to change the other toolbars to or from the floating form. Now, use the shortcut menu to hide the Auditing toolbar.

3. Use the Zoom Control list as described in figure 4-3 to change the magnification to 75%. Can you still read the data in the workbook window? Now, select columns A through D and choose the Selection option from the Zoom Control list. What's the magnification percent in the Zoom Control box? Click in the Zoom Control text box, type 70 to replace what's there, and press the Enter key. The worksheet is now displayed at a custom magnification setting. Change the magnification back to its default of 100%.

4. Move the cell pointer to column E and double-click on the vertical split box that's on the right side of the horizontal scroll bar. Notice that each pane now contains its own horizontal scroll bar, but there's only one vertical scroll bar for both windows. What happens to the rows in both panes when you scroll up and down in the worksheet? Now, use the horizontal scroll bar in the right pane to scroll to the last column in the worksheet. Does the pane on the left change? Drag the split box back to its original location or double-click on the split box to unsplit the window. Then, close the file.

How to hide and freeze columns and rows

When you don't want to display or print certain columns or rows in a worksheet, you can hide them. When you want certain columns or rows to remain on the screen no matter where you scroll, you can freeze them. Both skills come in handy when you work with a worksheet that has more columns and rows than can fit on the screen or page.

How to hide or reveal columns and rows using menu commands

As you work on a worksheet, it often makes sense to hide one or more columns or rows. If, for example, a worksheet contains one column for each month of the year, you can hide the columns for future months until you need them. Then, you can reveal or "unhide" them.

Figure 4-5 shows how to hide columns or rows using menu commands. As you can see, you simply select the columns or rows you want to hide before you issue the appropriate command. The easiest way to access the command for hiding or unhiding columns or rows is to use the shortcut menu.

When rows or columns are hidden, they are not included in the display on the screen and they are not included when you print the worksheet. However, the data in the hidden rows and columns is included in any totals or calculations that they're a part of.

How to hide one or more columns

1. Select the columns you want to hide:

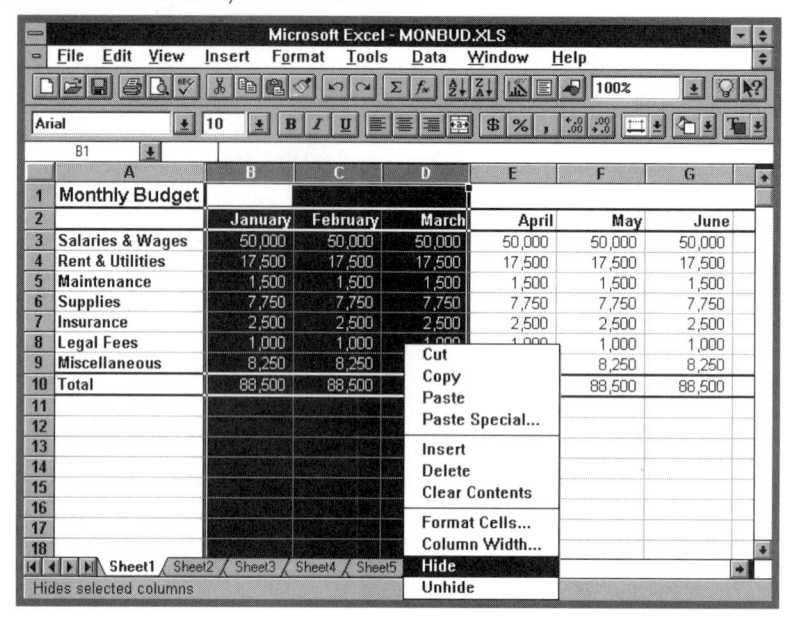

2. Choose the Hide command from the shortcut menu or the Column Hide command from the Format menu, and Excel hides the columns:

How to hide one or more rows

1. Select the rows you want to hide.

2. Choose the Hide command from the shortcut menu or the Row Hide command from the Format menu, and Excel hides the rows.

Figure 4-5   How to use commands to hide columns or rows

Figure 4-6 shows how to reveal hidden rows or columns using menu commands. To identify the columns or rows you want to reveal, you select the columns or rows on either side of the hidden columns or rows.

This works unless you have hidden column A or row 1 (usually, by accident). Then, you can use the Go To command to move the cell pointer to a cell in column A or row 1 before you issue a command to reveal that column or row. You'll learn how to use the Go To command later in this chapter.

How to reveal columns

1. Select the columns to the left and right of the hidden columns you want to reveal:

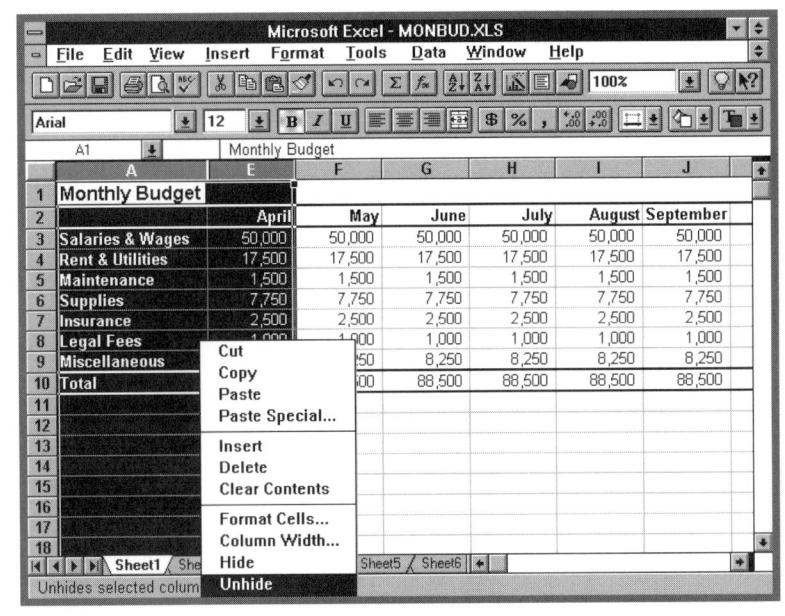

2. Choose the Unhide command from the shortcut menu or the Column Unhide command from the Format menu, and Excel reveals the columns.

How to reveal rows

1. Select the rows above and below the rows you want to reveal.

2. Choose the Unhide command from the shortcut menu or the Row Unhide command from the Format menu, and Excel reveals the rows.

Note

- To reveal column A or row 1, use the Go To command to go to a cell in that column or row before issuing the Unhide, Column Unhide, or Row Unhide command. Then, you can use the procedures above to reveal other hidden columns or rows.

Figure 4-6   **How to use commands to reveal columns or rows**

How to hide or reveal columns or rows using mouse techniques

You can also hide one or more rows or columns using the mouse techniques that are illustrated in figure 4-7. Notice that this technique is similar to the technique you learned in chapter 2 for adjusting column widths. The only difference is that you change the column width or row height to zero.

How to hide one or more columns

1. Select the columns you want to hide. Then, place the mouse pointer on the separator line in the worksheet frame to the right of one of the selected columns. When it is in the correct position, it changes to a double-headed arrow:

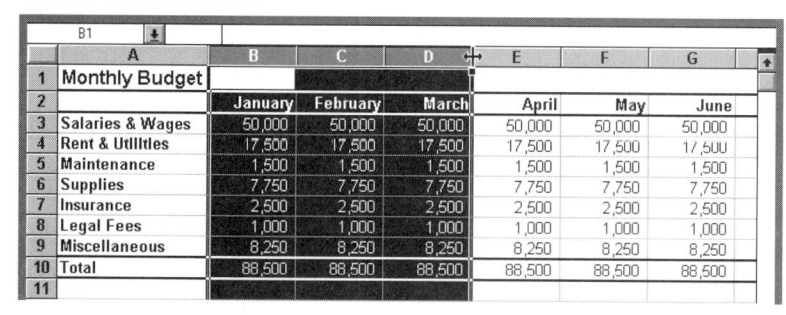

2. Drag the separator line to the left until a width of zero is displayed in the Name box:

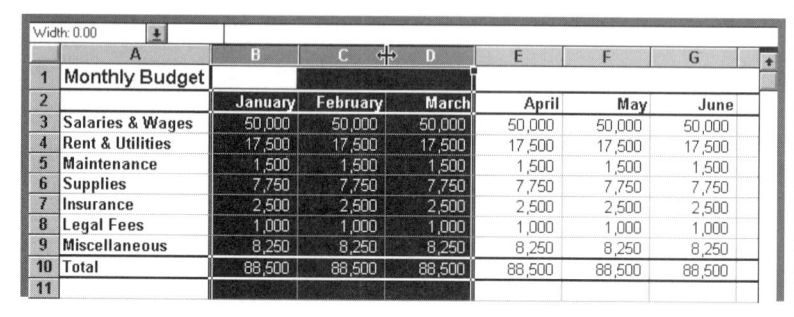

3. Release the mouse button, and the columns are hidden.

How to hide one or more rows

1. Select the rows you want to hide, and place the cell pointer on the separator line in the worksheet frame below one of those rows.
2. Drag the separator line up until a height of zero is displayed in the Name box.
3. Release the mouse button, and the rows are hidden.

Note

- You can also hide one or more columns or rows without selecting them first. To hide columns using this technique, drag a separator line to the left past the columns that you want to hide. To hide rows, drag a separator line up past the rows that you want to hide.

Figure 4-7   How to use the mouse to hide columns or rows

Figure 4-8 shows how to reveal a hidden column or row using the mouse. The trick to using this technique is positioning the mouse pointer correctly. If you position it directly over the separator line instead of slightly to the right as illustrated in the figure, the hidden column or row isn't revealed. Instead, the width of the column to the left or the height of the row above is increased. So be sure the mouse pointer looks like the one in the figure before you try to reveal a hidden column or row.

How to reveal one column at a time

1. Place the mouse pointer in the worksheet frame just to the right of the separator line where the column you want to reveal is hidden. When it is in the correct position, it turns into a double-headed arrow with a white center line:

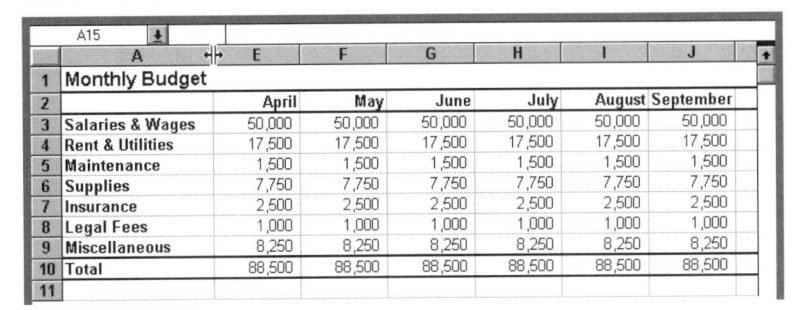

2. Drag the separator line to the right to reveal the column and set the column width:

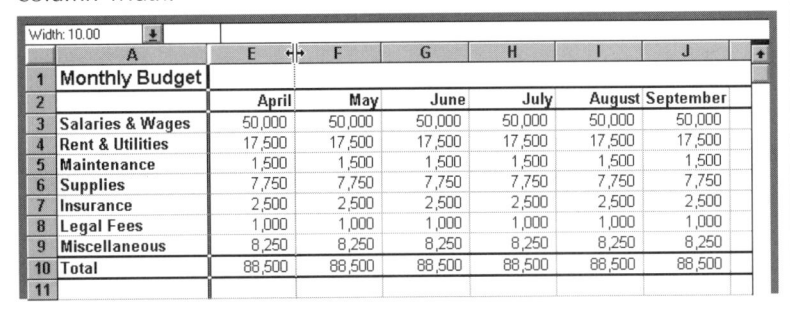

How to reveal one row at a time

1. Place the mouse pointer in the worksheet frame just below the separator line where the row you want to reveal is hidden so it turns into a double-headed arrow with a white center line.

2. Drag the separator line down to reveal the row and set the row height.

Figure 4-8 How to use the mouse to reveal one column or row at a time

How to freeze or unfreeze one or more rows or columns

When the column and row headings are scrolled off the screen, it can be difficult to remember what data each row or column contains. In that case, you can "freeze" one or more columns and rows on the screen so you can always see them. Figure 4-9 shows how this works. Notice that when columns are frozen, a black line appears to their right to indicate that they're frozen. When rows are frozen, a black line appears below them.

How to freeze columns

1. Place the cell pointer in row 1 of the column to the right of the last column you want to freeze:

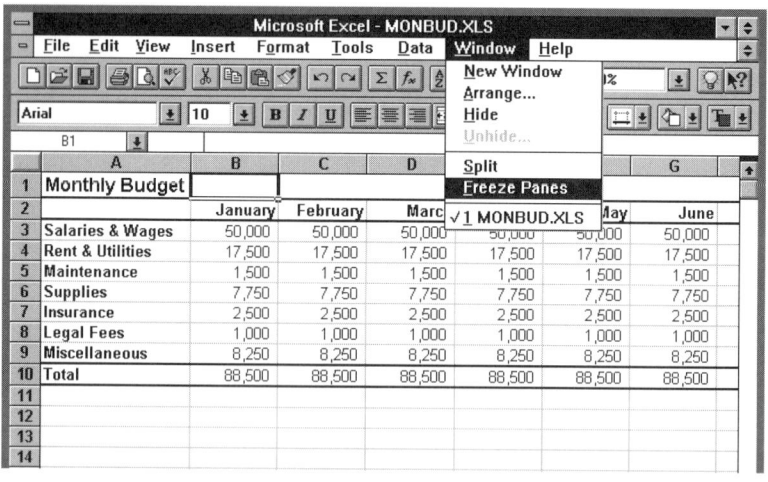

2. Choose the Freeze Panes command from the Window menu. A black line appears to the right of the frozen columns, and those columns are always displayed when you scroll:

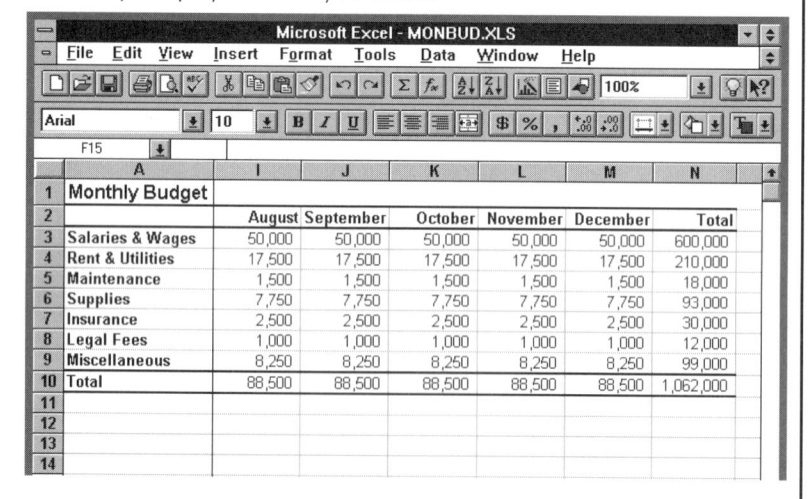

How to freeze rows

- Place the cell pointer in column A of the row below the one you want to freeze. Then, choose the Freeze Panes command from the Window menu.

How to freeze both columns and rows

- Place the cell pointer in the column to the right of the last column you want to freeze and in the row below the last one you want to freeze. Then, choose the Freeze Panes command from the Window menu.

How to unfreeze columns and rows

- Choose the Unfreeze Panes command from the Window menu. This command replaces the Freeze Panes command when columns or rows are frozen.

Figure 4-9 How to freeze or unfreeze columns and rows

Commands and features for working with larger worksheets — 127

How to use the View Manager to save and show views

When you hide columns or rows, you create a new *view* of the worksheet. Then, if you switch frequently from one view to another, you may want to save the views so you can switch between them more efficiently. To do that, you can use the View Manager as summarized in figure 4-10.

In the workbook window in figure 4-10, you can see that the columns for the first quarter of the year (January through March) and the columns for the last two quarters (July through December) are hidden. The view, then, is of the data for the second quarter of the year so it can be saved with a name like "Second quarter." To switch from one view to another, you just access the View Manager, choose the view that you want to change to, and click on the Show button.

In addition to saving hidden rows and columns in a view, Excel automatically saves other view settings such as frozen columns and rows and the zoom percentage. And if the Print Settings option is checked, the print (page setup) settings are saved with the view too. However, you're not likely to need to change these settings once you have a worksheet set up the way you want it. Because of that, the View Manager is most useful for saving different variations of hidden rows and columns.

Additional information

✓ The Print Area setting in the Sheet tab of the Page Setup dialog box (see figure 4-12) is saved with a view automatically, even if the Print Settings option isn't checked.

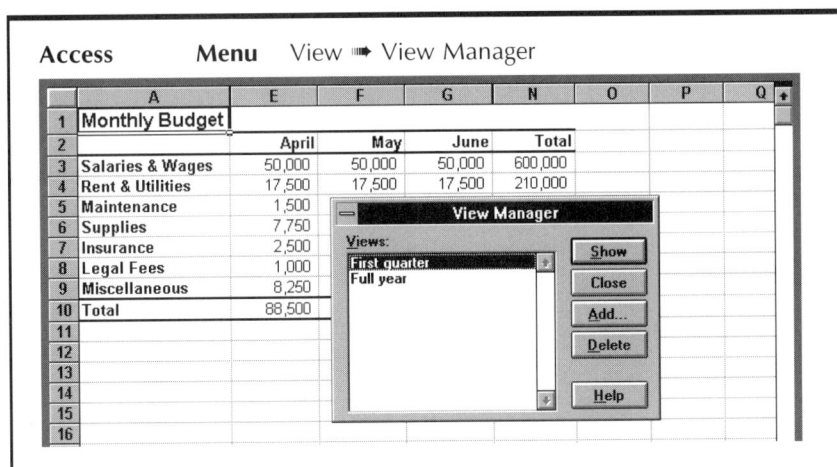

Access   Menu   View ➡ View Manager

How to save a view

1. Set the view the way you want it. The view always includes frozen columns and rows, window size and position, the zoom percentage, the active cell, and other view options you set from the Options dialog box that you access from the Tools menu. The view can also include hidden columns and rows and page setup options.

2. Access the View Manager dialog box as shown above. Then, click on the Add button so this dialog box is displayed:

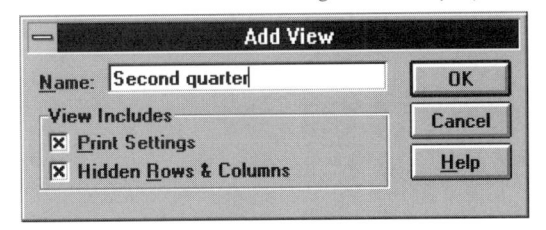

3. Enter a name for the view.

4. If you don't want to include the page setup options or the settings for hidden rows and columns, click on the Print Settings or Hidden Rows & Columns option to remove its check mark.

5. Click on the OK button to save the view and return to the worksheet.

How to show a view

- Access the View Manager dialog box, choose the view that you want displayed, and click on the Show button.

How to delete a view

- Access the View Manager dialog box, choose the view that you want to delete, and click on the Delete button.

Figure 4-10   How to use the View Manager to save and show views

Exercise set 4-3

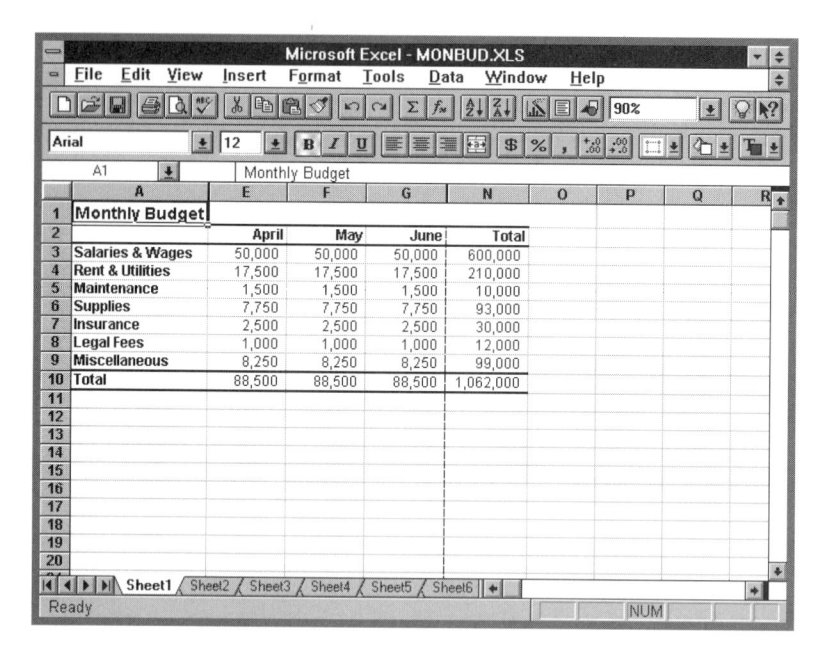

How your worksheet should look after exercise 2

1. Open the MONBUD file, and use the procedure in figure 4-5 with the shortcut menu to hide the columns for April through December. Then, scroll to the beginning of the worksheet. How can you tell that some of the columns are hidden? Do the totals in the Total column include the numbers in the hidden columns? Print the worksheet in this form to see whether the hidden columns are printed.

2. Use the procedure in figure 4-6 to reveal the hidden columns. Next, use the procedure in figure 4-7 to hide the columns for January through March and July through December.

3. Use the procedure in figure 4-8 to reveal the columns for January through March. (The column width should be 10.) Then, use the procedure in figure 4-6 to reveal the columns for July through December. Which procedure is easier to use?

4. Use the procedure in figure 4-9 to freeze column A of the worksheet. Then, scroll to the last column in the worksheet. Can you still see column A?

5. Use the procedure in figure 4-10 to add a view named "Full year" to the View Manager. Then, hide the columns for April through December, unfreeze column A, and add a view named "First quarter" to the View Manager (be sure the Hidden Rows & Columns option is on).

6. Use the View Manager to display the view for the full year. Is column A frozen? Next, use the View Manager to display the view for the first quarter. Is column A frozen?

7. Save and close the file. Then, open the file to see that the view for the first quarter is still displayed. Use the View Manager to switch to the full year view, then save and close the file.

How to format the pages of a multi-page worksheet

When you develop a worksheet that won't fit on a single page, you can use the Page Setup command to adjust the way the pages are printed. You can also insert page breaks into a worksheet so the worksheet pages are divided where you want them to be.

How to change the orientation and sizing of a worksheet

Figure 4-11 shows how to change the orientation or sizing of a worksheet. The orientation of a worksheet determines whether it's printed the normal way on the page (Portrait mode) or sideways (Landscape mode). For worksheets that are wider than they are tall, the Landscape mode can help fit a worksheet to the page.

If a worksheet doesn't quite fit on a page in either Portrait or Landscape mode, you can sometimes size the worksheet so it will fit on one page. As you can see in figure 4-11, you can scale a worksheet to a specific percent of its original size. Or, you can scale it so that it fits on a specific number of pages.

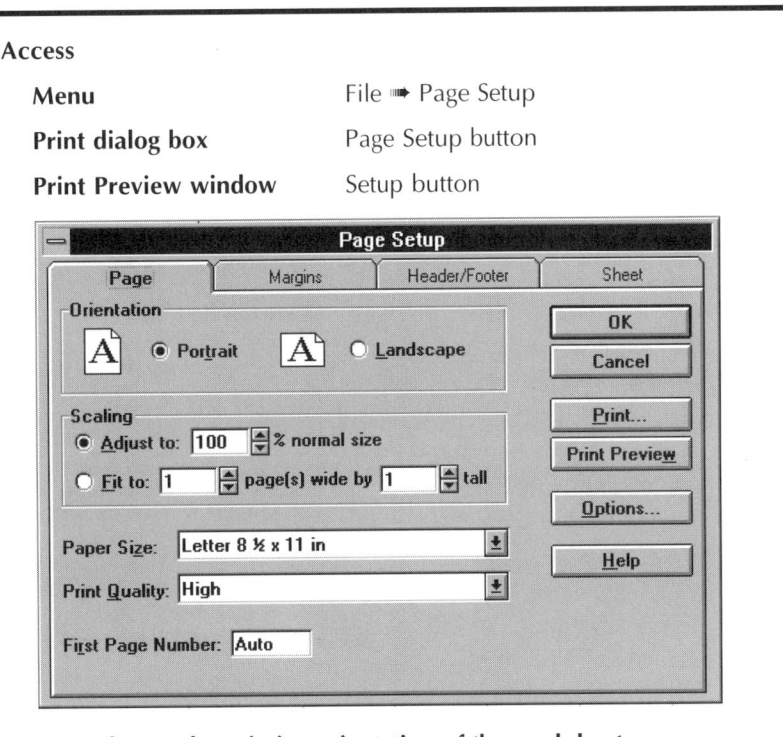

Access

Menu	File ➡ Page Setup
Print dialog box	Page Setup button
Print Preview window	Setup button

How to change the printing orientation of the worksheet

- To print the worksheet sideways on the page, choose the Landscape option in the Orientation group.

How to change the size of the printing

- To reduce or enlarge the printing of a worksheet to a percent of its original size, enter the percent in the Adjust To box in the Scaling group. This can be used to reduce the size of a worksheet so it fits on a page, but it can also be used to enlarge a worksheet for a visual presentation.

- To fit the worksheet onto one or more pages, choose the Fit to option in the Scaling group, and specify the number of pages wide and tall you want the document fitted to.

Note

- You can also change the paper size, the print quality, and the first page number by entering the appropriate options in the Paper Size, Print Quality, and First Page Number boxes. The default option for the first page number is Auto, which means that Excel will use the number of the first page you're printing in the worksheet.

Figure 4-11 How to change the orientation and sizing of a workbook

How to print titles on each page of a worksheet

When you print a worksheet that's more than one page long, you may want to repeat the column headings on each page to make the worksheet easier to read. Similarly, when you print a worksheet that's more than one page wide, you may want to repeat the row headings.

Figure 4-12 shows how to repeat rows and columns on each page of a worksheet. In this example, column A will be printed on each page of the worksheet. The first page will print the data for the first six months of the year, and the second page will print the data for the last six months of the year. Without the repetition of column A, it would be difficult to interpret the data on page 2. You'll see how this works when you do the next set of exercises.

If you look at the range reference in the Columns to Repeat at Left box in figure 4-12, you'll see dollar signs before the column letters and you won't see any row numbers. Don't let that confuse you, though. The dollar signs just indicate that the reference is absolute, and the row numbers aren't needed in this dialog box. In chapter 7, you'll learn more about absolute references.

Access		
Menu		File ➡ Page Setup
Print dialog box		Page Setup button
Print Preview window		Setup button

How to print the contents of one or more columns on each page

- Click in the Columns to Repeat at Left box to move the insertion point there. Then, select the columns in the worksheet with the mouse. In the example above, column A has been selected. If you prefer, you can type in a reference that includes at least one cell from each column you want to repeat.

How to print the contents of one or more rows on each page

- This works like the procedure above, but you click in the Rows to Repeat at Top box to move the insertion point there, and you select or enter a reference for the rows you want to repeat on each page.

Notes

- You can use the Print Area text box to identify the range that you want to print. You don't need this for most worksheets, though, because it's easier to select the range that you want to print just before you access the Print dialog box.

- The Gridlines option in the Print group is on by default. If you turn it off, the gridlines aren't printed.

- If a worksheet is more than a single page wide and tall, you can determine the order in which pages are printed by choosing an option in the Page Order group.

Figure 4-12 How to print titles on each page of a worksheet

How to insert and delete page breaks

By default, Excel inserts *automatic page breaks* when a worksheet can't be printed on a single page. Excel automatically inserts *horizontal page breaks* based on the settings for the top and bottom margins and *vertical page breaks* based on the settings for the left and right margins.

Often, though, the automatic page breaks don't occur where you want them to. In that case, you can insert *manual page breaks* as summarized in figure 4-13. This tells Excel where you want the page breaks to occur.

A worksheet with an automatic page break after column G

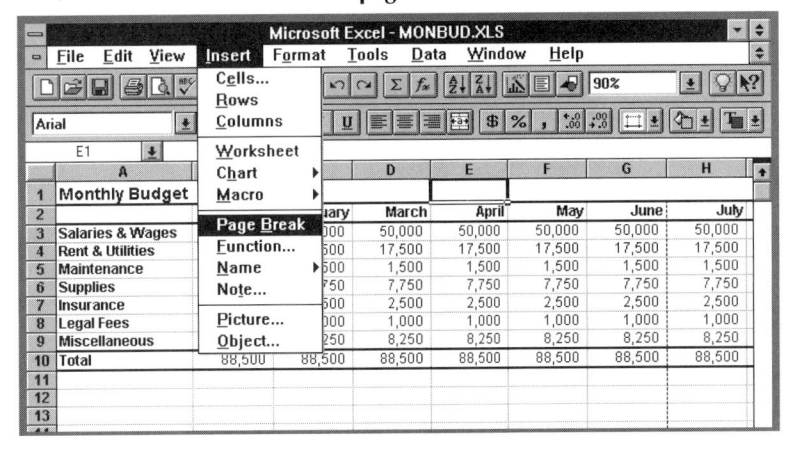

How to insert a vertical page break

- Place the cell pointer in row 1 of the column to the right of where you want to insert the page break (like cell E1 above). Then, choose the Page Break command from the Insert menu.

How to insert a horizontal page break

- Place the cell pointer in column A of the row below where you want to insert a page break. Then, choose the Page Break command from the Insert menu.

How to insert both a vertical and a horizontal page break

- Place the cell pointer in the column to the right of where you want a vertical page break and in the row below where you want a horizontal page break. Then, choose the Page Break command from the Insert menu.

How to delete a page break

- Place the cell pointer in the column to the right or in the row below the page break you want to remove, and choose the Remove Page Break command from the Insert menu.

Notes

- To display automatic page breaks, choose the Options command from the Tools menu. Then, click on the View tab and check the Automatic Page Breaks option. The next time you preview or print the worksheet, the automatic page breaks will appear in the document window.

- You can delete only the manual page breaks that you insert into a worksheet. You can't delete automatic page breaks.

- You can remove all the manual page breaks in a worksheet at once by selecting the entire worksheet and issuing the Remove Page Break command.

Figure 4-13   How to insert or delete page breaks

Exercise set 4-4

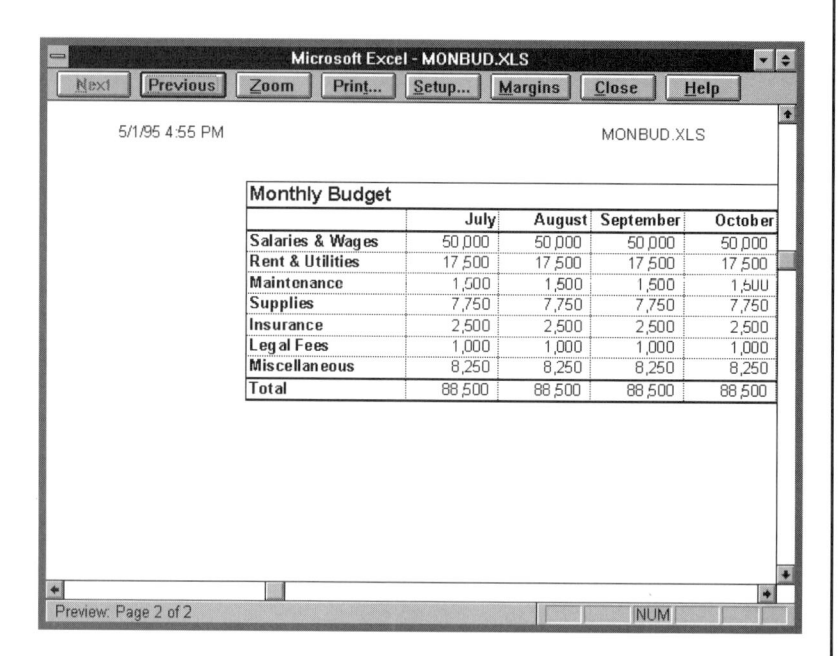

How the magnified Print Preview Window should look for the second page of the worksheet in exercise 5

```
Microsoft Excel - MONBUD.XLS
[Next] [Previous] [Zoom] [Print...] [Setup...] [Margins] [Close] [Help]

5/1/95 4:55 PM                                              MONBUD.XLS

           Monthly Budget
                          July    August  September  October
           Salaries & Wages  50,000  50,000  50,000   50,000
           Rent & Utilities  17,500  17,500  17,500   17,500
           Maintenance        1,500   1,500   1,500    1,500
           Supplies           7,750   7,750   7,750    7,750
           Insurance          2,500   2,500   2,500    2,500
           Legal Fees         1,000   1,000   1,000    1,000
           Miscellaneous      8,250   8,250   8,250    8,250
           Total             88,500  88,500  88,500   88,500

Preview: Page 2 of 2                                          NUM
```

1. Open the MONBUD file, access the Page Setup command, and click on the Page tab. Then, click on the Landscape option to change the orientation of the worksheet, and access the Print Preview window to see how the worksheet will be printed. Does the entire worksheet fit on one page?

2. Click on the Setup button to return to the Page Setup dialog box. Now, click on the Fit To option so Excel will size the worksheet so it fits on a single page, and return to the Print Preview window by clicking on the OK button in the Page Setup dialog box. Does the entire worksheet fit on the page now? Click on the Print button to print the worksheet and return to the worksheet.

3. Use the Page tab of the Page Setup command to scale the size of the worksheet to 125% of its original size. Then, print the worksheet. This shows how you can size a worksheet for visual presentations.

4. Change the sizing back to 100%. Next, use the Sheet tab of the Page Setup dialog box as described in figure 4-12 to repeat column A on each page of the worksheet. Then, click on the Print Preview button to preview the worksheet, and click on the Next button to preview page 2 of the worksheet. Is column A repeated on that page? Close the Print Preview window without printing the worksheet in this form.

5. Scroll the worksheet to the right until you see the automatic page break to the right of column J. If you don't see a page break, use the View tab as described in the first note in figure 4-13 to set the Automatic Page Breaks option on. Then, use the procedure in figure 4-13 to insert a vertical page break to the right of column G. Notice that the automatic page break disappears. Open the Print Preview window to make sure the page break works the way you want it to. Then, close the preview window, save the file, and close it.

Two printing skills for multi-page worksheets

When you work with worksheets of two or more pages, you need to know two more printing skills. First, you need to know how to print a selected range or selected pages of a worksheet. Second, you need to know how to cancel a print job.

How to print part of a worksheet

By default, Excel prints all of the active worksheet. To print anything less than the entire worksheet, you can use the Print dialog box as described in figure 4-14. From this dialog box, you can print a specific range of pages like pages 1 or 2 from a four page worksheet. Or, you can choose to print the range of cells that you select before you issue the Print command.

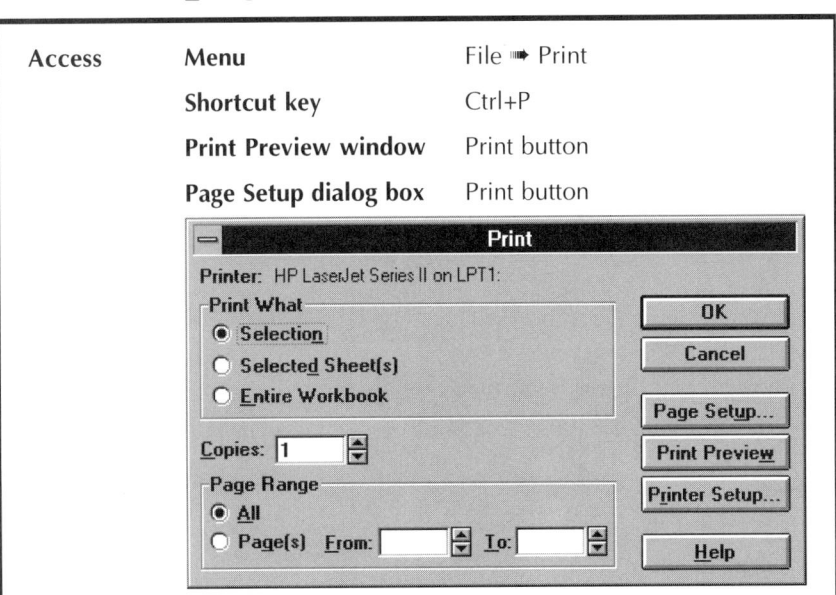

Access		
	Menu	File ➨ Print
	Shortcut key	Ctrl+P
	Print Preview window	Print button
	Page Setup dialog box	Print button

Operation

- To print a selected range, select the range before you access the Print dialog box. Then, choose the Selection option in the Print What group.
- To print a range of pages, enter the first and last page numbers in the From and To text boxes in the Page Range group. To print a single page, enter the page number in both the From and To boxes.

Notes

- If you use the Print Area box of the Sheet tab in the Page Setup dialog box to identify a print range (see figure 4-12), that range is printed when you use the Selected Sheet option. To print a different range, you need to select another range before you access the Print dialog box, then use the Selection option to print the range.
- If you start the Print command by clicking on the Print button in the Standard toolbar, the Print dialog box isn't displayed so you can't change the print options.

Figure 4-14 How to print a selected range or selected pages

How to cancel a print job

If your PC is on a network, you need to distinguish between *print jobs* that are sent to a printer that's attached to your PC (a *local printer*) and those that are sent to a *network printer*. When you send a job to a local printer, Word creates a print job for the worksheet and sends it to the Windows Print Manager where it's put into a *print queue*. This is simply a list of the jobs that are waiting to be printed. Then, you can use Excel to cancel the job before it reaches the Print Manager, and you can use the Print Manager to cancel a job once it's in the queue.

Figure 4-15 shows you how to cancel a local print job from Excel or the Print Manager. When you send a job to a network printer, though, Windows usually bypasses the Print Manager and sends the job directly to the network server. Then, the server manages the network's print queue. In this case, you can still use Excel to cancel a job before it reaches the print queue. But once in the queue, you may have little or no control over it. That depends on the network you're using and how the network is set up.

How to cancel a print job before it reaches the Print Manager or network print queue

- Click on the Cancel button in the Printing dialog box or press the Esc key:

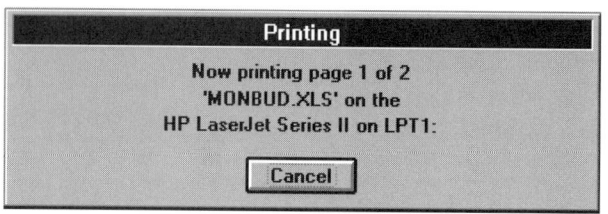

> **Printing**
> Now printing page 1 of 2
> 'MONBUD.XLS' on the
> HP LaserJet Series II on LPT1:
> [Cancel]

How to cancel a print job after it reaches the Print Manager

1. Use any standard *Windows* technique to switch from Excel to the Print Manager:

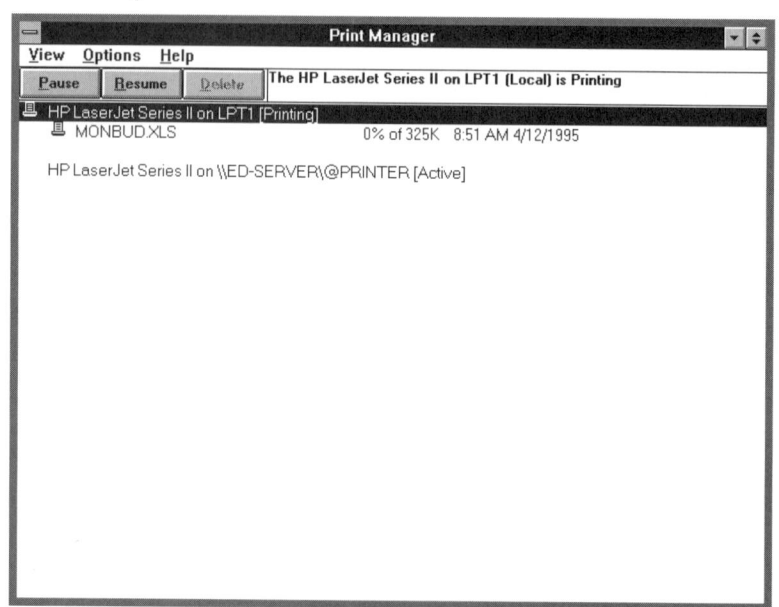

> **Print Manager**
> View Options Help
> [Pause] [Resume] [Delete] The HP LaserJet Series II on LPT1 (Local) is Printing
> HP LaserJet Series II on LPT1 [Printing]
>   MONBUD.XLS   0% of 325K   8:51 AM 4/12/1995
> HP LaserJet Series II on \\ED-SERVER\@PRINTER [Active]

2. Highlight the job you want to cancel in the Print Manager's application window and click on the Delete button (*Windows* 3.1) or press the Delete key (*Windows* 3.11).

Notes

- If you want to use Excel to cancel a print job, you need to act before Excel finishes sending it to the Print Manager or the network print queue. For a short worksheet, that doesn't give you much time.

- When you use network printers, *Windows* is usually set up so it bypasses the Print Manager and sends the job directly to the network print queue. Whether you have any control over the network print queue depends on the way your network is set up.

Figure 4-15   How to cancel a print job

Exercise set 4-5

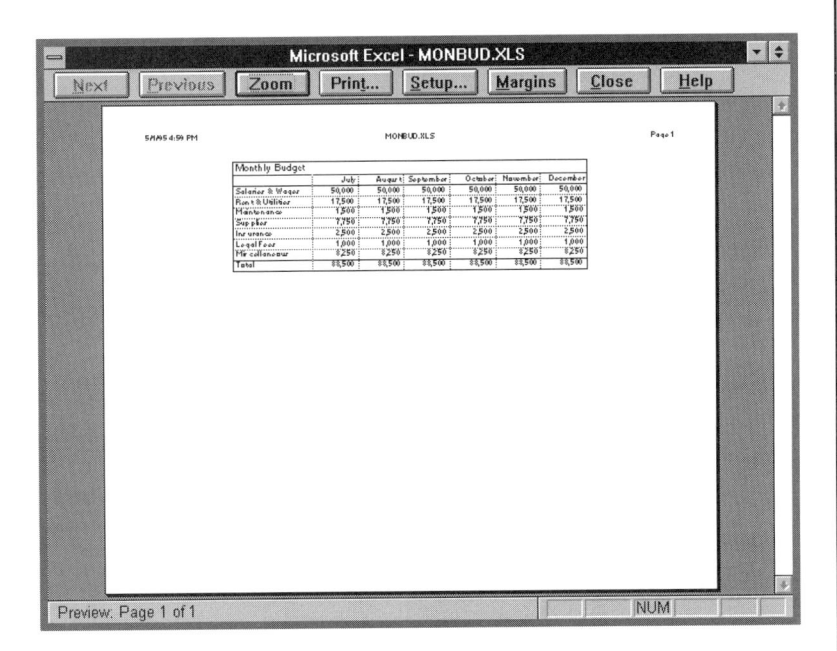

How the Print Preview window should look in exercise 2

1. Open the MONBUD file, then choose the Page Setup command from the File menu and click on the Sheet tab. Click in the Print Area box, and use the mouse to select the range for the data in the July through December columns of the worksheet. (You can move the dialog box if you need to.) Then, click on the OK button to return to the worksheet, and click on the Print Preview toolbar button to preview the printing of the worksheet. Is only the selected range going to be printed? Are the row titles in column A included with the six columns? Now, close the Print Preview window, and close the file without saving it.

2. Open the MONBUD file again, select the data in the July through December columns, access the Print dialog box using one of the methods shown in figure 4-14, and click on the Selection option. Now, click on the Print Preview button to see how these columns will be printed. Is only the selected range going to be printed? Are the row titles in column A included with the six columns?

3. Start the printing of both pages of the MONBUD worksheet, but cancel the print job as soon as it starts by clicking on the Cancel button in the Printing dialog box. (It won't take Excel long to print this worksheet, so work fast.) What portion of the worksheet is printed (if any)? Now, close the file without saving it.

How to create and use names

Because *names* are easier to remember than actual cell references, you may want to use them in large worksheets to identify one or more cells or ranges. Once you create a name, it's easy to move the cell pointer directly to the cell or range with that name. You can also use names in formulas and functions, as you'll learn in chapter 7.

How to name a range of cells

Figure 4-16 presents two procedures for naming a range of cells. The easiest way is to use the Name box. To use this technique, you just select the range and enter the name in Name box.

The Define Name command is most useful if the name you want to use for a range is entered as text in a cell that's adjacent to the range. Then, the name defaults to the text in the adjacent cell. In figure 4-16, for example, the name in the Names in Workbook box defaulted to October. You can also use the Name Define command to delete a name.

If you look at the range reference in the Refers to box of the Define Name dialog box, you'll see that it looks more complicated than the other range references you've seen thus far. That's because it starts with the sheet name (Sheet1) and a separator (!) and because each column letter and row number in the reference is preceded by a dollar sign to show that it's an absolute reference. Don't let that bother you for now, though, because you'll learn about sheet names in chapter 5 and absolute references in chapter 7.

How to use the Name box to name a range

1. Select the cells that you want to name, then click in the Name box and enter a name for the range:

2. Press the Enter key to name the range. If the name you enter already exists, Excel moves to that range instead of creating a new name.

How to use the Name Define command to name a range

1. Select the cells that you want to name and issue the Name Define command from the Insert menu, or issue the command without selecting cells:

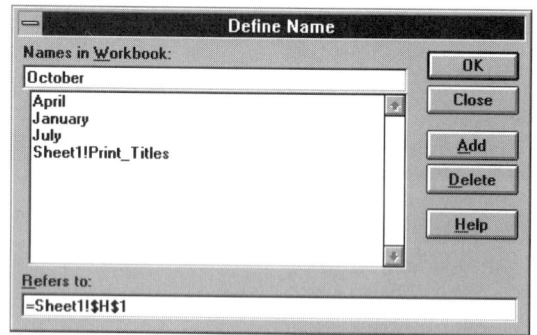

2. Enter a name in the Names in Workbook box. Then, *if you selected cells before you accessed the dialog box*, click on the OK or Add button to add the name to the list. If you click on the Add button, the dialog box remains open so you can name additional ranges. *If you didn't select cells before you accessed the dialog box*, drag the mouse pointer over the range in the Refers to box to highlight the entire range reference; use the mouse to select the range that you want to name (the new range reference replaces the old one in the Refer to box); and click on the OK or Add button to add the name to the name list.

How to delete a name

- Access the Define Name dialog box from the Insert menu. Then, highlight the name of the range you want to delete in the Names in Workbook list box, and click on the Delete button.

Rules for creating names

- The first character must be a letter, an underscore character, or a backslash; the name can't include spaces or hyphens; and the name shouldn't be a valid cell reference like D10.

Figure 4-16 How to name a range of cells

You should also notice the last name in the Define Name dialog box in figure 4-16. Excel created this name automatically when print titles were added to the worksheet. (See figure 4-12). Because the print titles apply only to the active worksheet and not to any other worksheets in the workbook, the name begins with the worksheet name.

How to name several ranges at the same time

When you use the Name box or the Name Define command, you name one range at a time. If you want to name two or more ranges at the same time, you can use the Name Create command presented in figure 4-17. Notice that to use this command, the names that you want to use for the ranges have to be in cells that are adjacent to the ranges. In figure 4-17, for example, the names of the months are above the ranges that you want those names applied to. You'll have a better idea of how this command works when you do the next exercise set.

A worksheet with six ranges selected and the Name submenu of the Insert menu pulled down

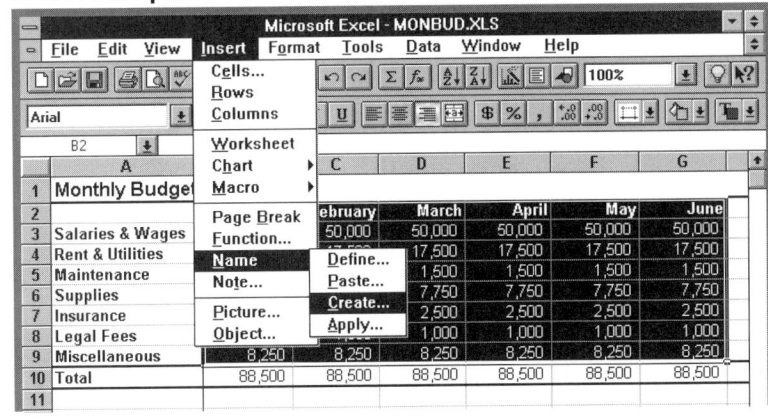

Procedure

1. Select the ranges that you want to name including cells at the top, bottom, left, or right that provide the names for the other selected cells. Then, issue the Name Create command from the Insert menu to display this dialog box:

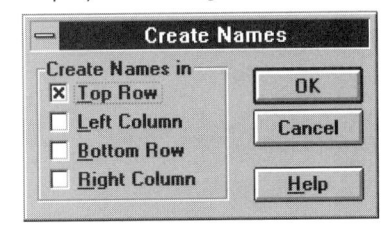

2. Check the option that indicates where the cells are that contain the names for the selected cells, and click on the OK button.

Figure 4-17   How to name several ranges at the same time

How to move the cell pointer to a named range

If you use named ranges in a worksheet, you can use the techniques in figure 4-18 to move the cell pointer to one of those ranges. If you use the list that drops down from the Name box in the formula bar, you can move to a named range by clicking on the range. This also selects the cells in the named range. If you use the Go To command to move to a named range, the result is the same, but it takes a little longer when you're using a mouse.

You can also use the Go To dialog box to move the cell pointer to any cell in a worksheet, even if it hasn't been named. To do that, just enter the cell reference in the Reference box. This is useful if you accidentally hide column A or row 1. Then, you can use the Go To command to go to cell A1, even though it's hidden, and you can use the appropriate command to unhide the column or row.

As you use the Go To command to move around a worksheet, it saves the cell references of the last four locations that you started the command from. This makes it easy for you to return to a previous location.

How to use the Name box in the formula bar

1. Click on the Name box's drop-down arrow to display a list of the names in the current workbook:

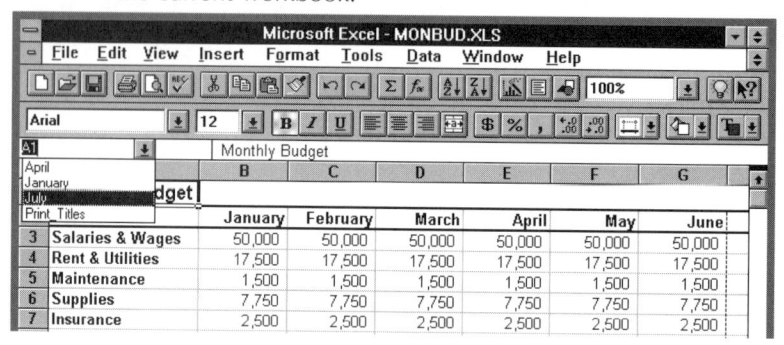

2. Click on the name you want to move the cell pointer to.

How to use the Go To command in the Edit menu

1. Access the Go To command from the Edit menu or press F5 to access it:

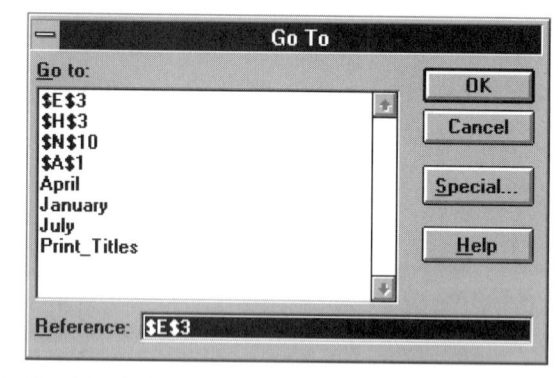

2. Double-click on a name or cell reference in the Go To list, or highlight the name or cell reference and click on the OK button.

Notes

- When you use names to move the cell pointer, the cell pointer moves to the first cell in the named range and the range is selected.
- The list in the Go To dialog box includes the cell references for the last four cells that you accessed the dialog box from.
- You can also use the Go To dialog box to move the cell pointer to a specific cell by entering its cell reference in the Reference text box.
- The Special button in the Go To dialog box provides other cell options that you can go to and select like the last cell that contains data in the worksheet or the blank cells in a worksheet.

Figure 4-18   How to move the cell pointer to a named range

Exercise set 4-6

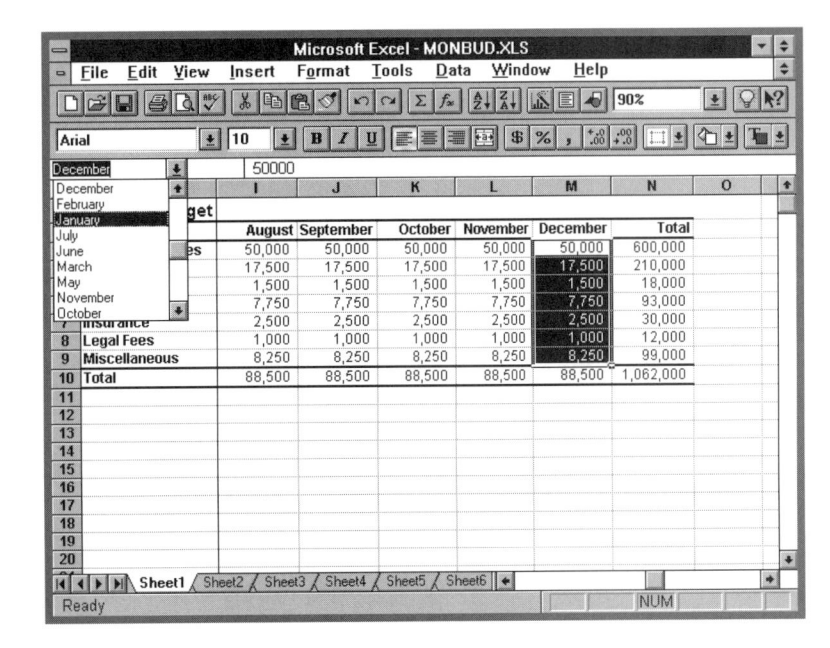

How the window should look in exercise 4 after moving to the range named December and before moving to the range named January

1. Open the MONBUD file, select cells B3 through B9, and use the Name box as described in the first procedure in figure 4-16 to give the name January to this selection. Then, select cells C3 through C9, and issue the Name Define command as described in the second procedure in figure 4-16. When the Define Name dialog box is displayed, notice that the name defaults to February since that text is in the cell above the range you selected. To give the name February to the selection and return to the worksheet, click on the OK button. Which technique was easier to use?

2. Without selecting any cells, use the second procedure in figure 4-16 to give the name March to cells D3 through D9. The trick to this is highlighting the entire range reference in the Refer To box before you select the new range so the new reference replaces the old one. If necessary, you can move the dialog box when you select the new range. When you have the correct range, click on the Add button to add the name and leave the dialog box open. Then, repeat this procedure to give the name April to cells E3 through E9, but click on the OK button to return to the worksheet.

3. Select cells F2 through M9; that includes the month names above the number ranges. Then, use the procedure in figure 4-17 to name the numbers in the May through December columns with their month names. When you complete this command, there will be names for all 12 months.

4. Use the Name box in the formula bar as described in figure 4-18 to move the cell pointer to the range named July. Then, use this technique to move to the range named December and to the range named January.

5. Issue the Go To command to display its dialog box, and double-click on the name "December" to move the cell pointer to that range. Display the Go To dialog box again, type the cell reference A1 into the Reference box, and click on the OK button to move the cell pointer to that cell. Then, display the Go To dialog box one last time, and double-click on the first cell reference in the list. Where does that take you back to? Now, save and close the file.

Perspective

You now have the skills that you need for working with large worksheets. The examples in this chapter, though, don't begin to illustrate how large some of the worksheets used in business are. Worksheets that require more than 100 rows and 50 columns aren't uncommon. And worksheets that consist of several different functional areas aren't uncommon either. In worksheets like that, hiding and freezing columns, using the View Manager, setting up the pages for effective printing, and using names to move around the worksheet become all the more important.

The larger a worksheet becomes, of course, the more difficult it is to work with. So whenever possible, you should limit the size of your worksheets by using a different worksheet for each functional area. With Excel 5, you can keep these closely related worksheets in the same workbook and switch from one to another with speed and efficiency. That's the professional way to manage large quantities of related data, and that's what you'll learn how to do in the next chapter.

Summary

- To make a worksheet easier to work with, you can change the *view*. The view is a combination of the features that are displayed and how the data is displayed. To change the view, you can hide or display the formula bar, the status bar, or any of the toolbars, and you can change the magnification percent.

- If you need to see two areas of a worksheet at the same time, you can split the workbook window into two or four *panes*.

- You can hide and unhide selected columns or rows in a worksheet using menu commands or the mouse. When columns or rows are hidden, you can't see them and they're not printed when you print the worksheet.

- You can freeze one or more columns and rows in a worksheet so those columns and rows are displayed no matter where you scroll in the worksheet.

- Excel provides a variety of features for setting up the pages of a worksheet for printing. You can use these features to change the orientation or sizing, to repeat column or row headings on each page, and to insert *manual page breaks*.

- You can use the Print dialog box to print a selected range of a worksheet or to specify a range of pages to print.

- If you send a *print job* to a *local printer* or *network printer*, you can cancel the job from Excel before it reaches the *print queue*. If you send a print job to a local printer, you can also cancel the job from the *Windows* Print Manager after it reaches the print queue.

Section 2

The commands and features that help you work like a pro

Once you know how to create, edit, and format a single worksheet, you need to learn the other commands and features that the best professionals use. So chapter 5 shows you how to work with workbooks that contain more than one worksheet. Chapter 6 shows you how to create charts from a worksheet. Chapter 7 presents advanced techniques for working with formulas and functions. And chapter 8 shows you how get the most from Excel 5 by setting defaults, protecting data, converting files, and using the Help facility.

You can read these chapters in whatever sequence you prefer. If, for example, you need to know more about some of the advanced functions that come with Excel 5, you can go from section 1 directly to chapter 7. Eventually, though, you should make a point of reading all four chapters because each one presents commands and features that you should at least be aware of.

Chapter 5

How to work with more than one worksheet at a time

When you use Excel 5.0, you can create workbooks that contain more than one worksheet. This makes sense whenever you're developing two or more closely related worksheets. That way, you can usually enter and format them more quickly than you can when they're in separate workbooks. It's also easier to develop formulas and functions that refer to the data in two or more worksheets when they're in the same workbook.

If you want to work with worksheets in two or more workbooks at the same time, you can do that too. But you rarely need to do that with Excel 5 because you can get the same results by combining the worksheets into one workbook. For those occasions when you do need to work with two or more workbooks, though, this chapter also presents those skills.

Basic skills for working with two or more worksheets in one workbook
    How to use the worksheet controls in the workbook window
    How to change the name of a worksheet
    How to move from one worksheet to another
    How to group worksheets
    How to add or delete worksheets

How to work with the data in two or more worksheets of a workbook
    How to enter, edit, and format data in more than one worksheet at the same time
    How to copy or move data from one worksheet to another
    How to enter formulas and functions that refer to other worksheets
    How to set up and print the worksheet pages

Other skills for working with two or more worksheets in one workbook
    How to move or copy worksheets
    How to hide or reveal worksheets
    How to display more than one worksheet at a time
    How to use names

How to work with worksheets from two or more workbooks
    How to open two or more workbooks and switch between them
    How to display two or more workbooks at the same time
    How to move or copy data from one workbook to another
    How to move or copy worksheets from one workbook to another

Perspective

Summary

Basic skills for working with two or more worksheets in one workbook

Figure 5-1 presents a workbook that contains four worksheets. Although you can't tell from this figure, the first three worksheets contain sales data for each month in the first quarter of the year, and the last worksheet contains the sales data for the first quarter. Before you can create and use a workbook like this, you need to learn the basic skills that follow.

How to use the worksheet controls in the workbook window

Figure 5-1 identifies the workbook window controls you can use when you're working with more than one worksheet in a single workbook. The controls you'll use most often are the *sheet tabs* that display the names of the worksheets. You can use these tabs to move from one worksheet to another or to change a worksheet's name. You'll learn how to perform these functions in just a minute.

If a workbook contains so many worksheets that Excel can't display their tabs all at once, you can use the *tab scrolling buttons* to scroll the tabs left and right. You can also increase or decrease the size of the *tab area* by dragging the *tab split box*.

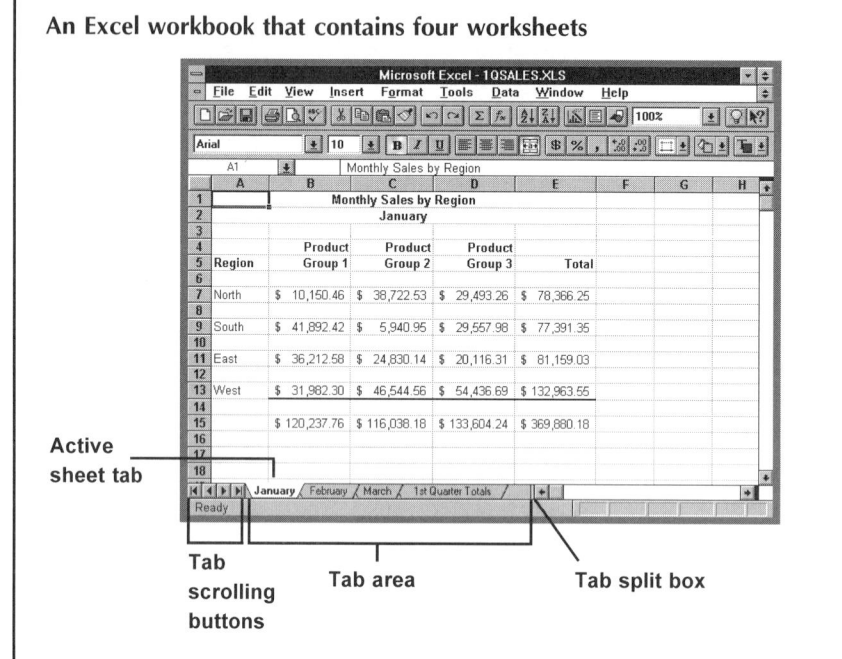

An Excel workbook that contains four worksheets

Operation

- The *sheet tabs* identify the worksheets in the workbook. To change the worksheet name, you can double-click on a tab (see figure 5-2). To move to another worksheet, you can click on a tab (see figure 5-3).

- The *tab scrolling buttons* scroll the tabs in the *tab area*. The first button scrolls to the first sheet tab, the second button scrolls to the previous sheet tab, the third button scrolls to the next sheet tab, and the last button scrolls to the last sheet tab.

- You can increase or decrease the size of the *tab area* by dragging the *tab split box*.

Figure 5-1   How to use the worksheet controls

How to change the name of a worksheet

By default, Excel names the worksheets in a workbook Sheet1, Sheet2, and so on. When you work with multiple worksheets, you'll find it helpful to change the worksheet names to indicate what's in each worksheet. If Sheet1 contains sales information for January, for example, you can change the worksheet name to January or Jan. Figure 5-2 shows how to do that.

How to move from one worksheet to another

Figure 5-3 shows how to move from one worksheet to another within a workbook. As you can see, you can use either the mouse or the keyboard. Note that when you use the mouse, you must be able to see the tab you want to move to before you can move to it. If you can't see it, you can use the tab scrolling buttons to display it as described in figure 5-1.

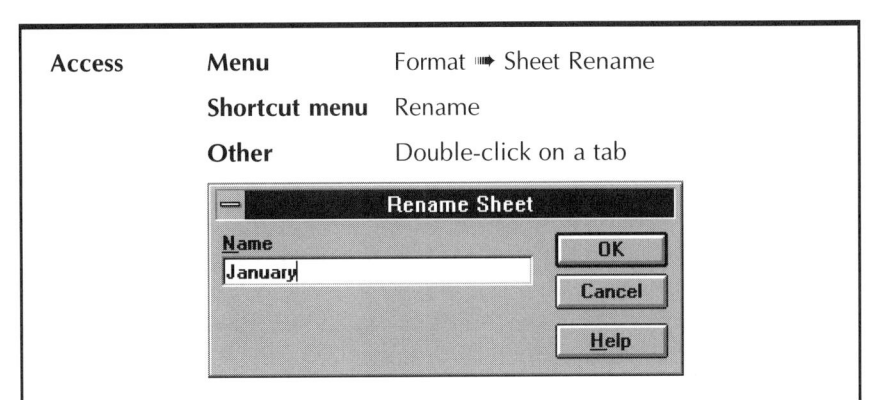

Access		
	Menu	Format ⇒ Sheet Rename
	Shortcut menu	Rename
	Other	Double-click on a tab

Rename Sheet dialog box with Name field containing "January", and OK, Cancel, Help buttons.

Procedure

1. Access the Rename Sheet dialog box using one of the methods shown above. (To display the shortcut menu for a sheet tab, click the right mouse button on it.)
2. Enter a worksheet name (it can be up to 31 characters long), and click on the OK button.

Figure 5-2   How to change the name of a worksheet

A workbook with the third worksheet displayed

	A	B	C	D	E
1		Monthly Sales by Region			
2		March			
3					
4		Product Group 1	Product Group 2	Product Group 3	
5	Region				Total
7	North	$ 21,025.43	$ 38,722.53	$ 29,493.26	$ 89,241.22
9	South	$ 41,892.42	$ 5,940.95	$ 29,557.98	$ 77,391.35
11	East	$ 36,212.58	$ 24,830.14	$ 20,116.31	$ 81,159.03
13	West	$ 31,982.30	$ 46,544.56	$ 54,436.69	$ 132,963.55
15		$ 131,112.73	$ 116,038.18	$ 133,604.24	$ 380,755.15

Tabs: January / February / March / 1st Quarter Totals

How to move to another worksheet with the mouse

- Click on the tab of the worksheet you want to move to.
- If necessary, use the tab scrolling buttons to display the tab of the sheet you want to move to.

How to move to another worksheet with the keyboard

Key	Function
Ctrl+Page-up	Moves to the previous worksheet.
Ctrl+Page-down	Moves to the next worksheet.

Figure 5-3   How to move from one worksheet to another

How to group worksheets

When you want to perform operations on two or more worksheets at the same time, you need to *group* the worksheets. Figure 5-4 shows how. As you can see, you can group both adjacent and nonadjacent worksheets.

When you group worksheets, Excel displays the word "Group" in the title bar. You can tell which worksheets are included in the group because the tabs for all the worksheets in the group are highlighted.

After you group worksheets, all the operations that you perform on one worksheet are also performed on the other worksheets in the group. That includes entering data, formatting data, and inserting and deleting rows and columns. Although this can help you work more efficiently, it also means that you have to be careful. If you forget that the worksheets are grouped when you start making modifications meant for a single worksheet, the modifications are made to the entire group. So be sure to ungroup the worksheets before you do work that's meant for just one worksheet.

A workbook with a group of three adjacent worksheets

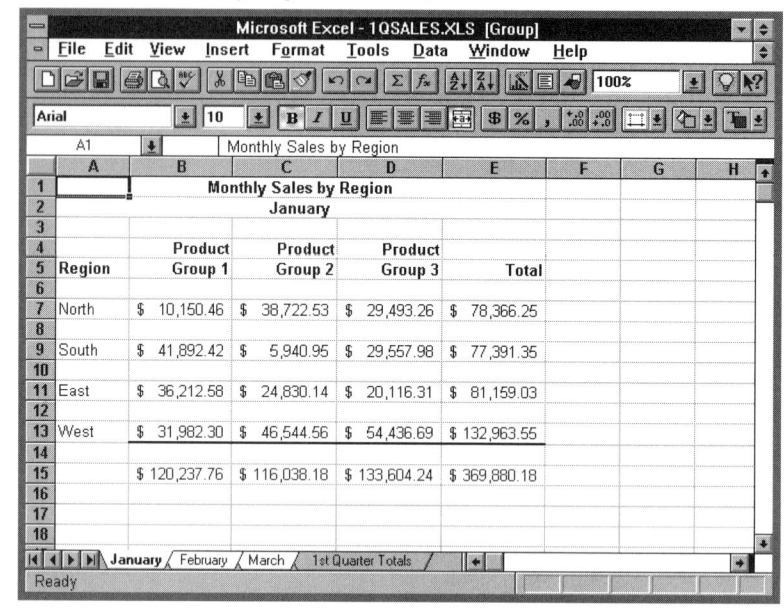

How to group adjacent worksheets

1. Click on the tab of the first worksheet you want to include in the group.
2. Hold down the Shift key and click on the tab of the last worksheet that you want to include in the group. If necessary, scroll the sheet tabs so you can see the tab of the last worksheet.

How to group nonadjacent worksheets

- Hold down the Ctrl key and click on the tab of each worksheet you want to include in the group.

How to group all the worksheets in a workbook

- Choose the Select All Sheets command from the sheet tab shortcut menu.

Two ways to ungroup worksheets

- Move to any worksheet that isn't in the group. If all of the worksheets in the workbook are included in the group, move to any one of them to ungroup them.
- Choose the Ungroup Sheets command from the sheet tab shortcut menu.

Note

- When you group worksheets, Excel displays the word "Group" to the right of the file name in the title bar and highlights all the tabs for the worksheets in the group.

Figure 5-4   How to group or ungroup worksheets

How to add or delete worksheets

By default, a workbook contains 16 worksheets, which is more than you need for most workbooks. If you change the default to a smaller number of worksheets, however, you may occasionally need to add one or more worksheets. You can also delete the worksheets you don't use, although that isn't necessary. To add or delete worksheets, you use the procedures in figure 5-5.

When you add a worksheet, Excel inserts it before, or in front of, the *active worksheet* (the one that's currently displayed in the workbook window). In figure 5-5, for example, two worksheets are inserted in front of Sheet2. Notice that even though the workbook contains only three worksheets before the new worksheets are added, the new worksheets are named Sheet17 and Sheet18. Since you normally change the worksheet names when you work with more than one worksheet, this shouldn't be a problem.

How to add worksheets

1. Group the worksheets to the right of where you want to insert the new worksheets. The number of worksheets in the group will be the number of worksheets that are inserted:

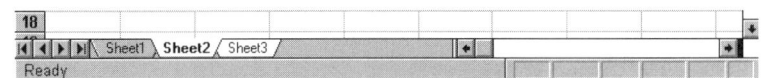

2. Choose the Worksheet command from the Insert menu to add the worksheets:

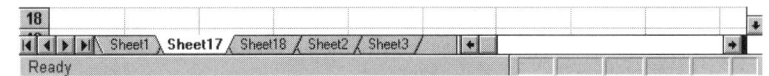

   Or, choose the Insert command from the sheet tab shortcut menu and click on the OK button in the dialog box that's displayed:

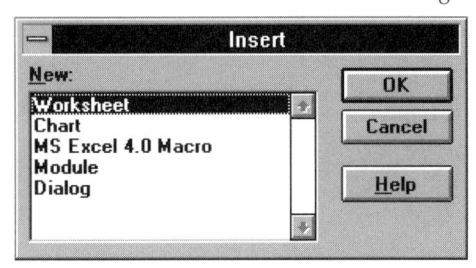

How to delete worksheets

1. Group the worksheets that you want to delete.

2. Choose the Delete Sheet command from the Edit menu or the Delete command from the shortcut menu for a sheet tab. Then, Excel displays this dialog box:

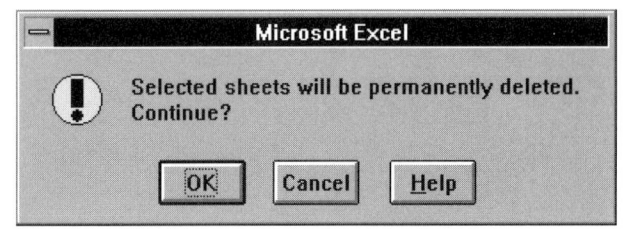

3. Click on the OK button to delete the worksheets.

Note

- By default, an Excel workbook contains 16 worksheets. To change the default, choose the Options command from the Tools menu and click on the General tab. Then, enter the number of worksheets you want each new workbook to include in the Sheets in New Workbook box.

Figure 5-5 How to add or delete worksheets

Exercise set 5-1

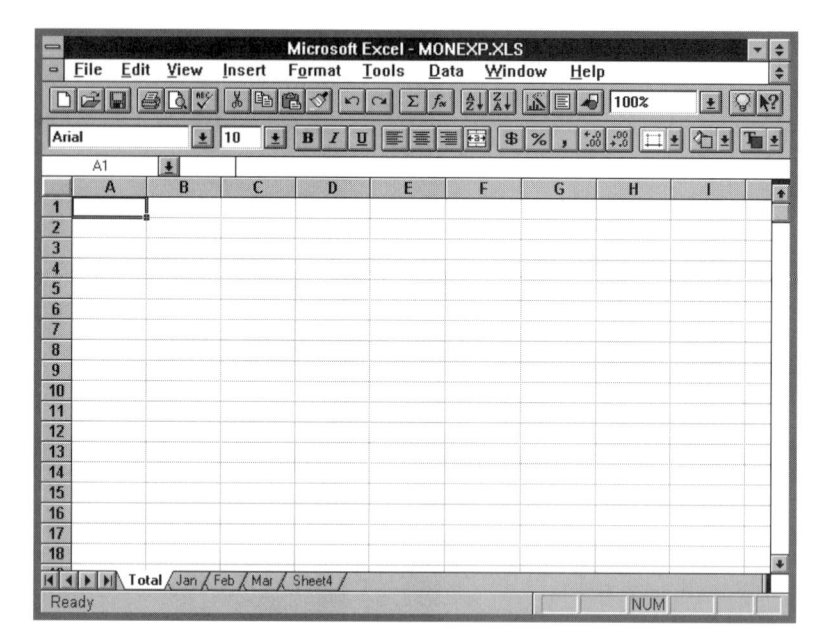

How the sheet tabs should look after exercise 6

1. Open a new workbook and use the tab scrolling buttons to display the last sheet tab in the workbook. How many worksheets are there? Click on the last sheet tab and notice how the worksheet moves to the front. (It's not as obvious that a different worksheet is displayed since there's no data in the worksheets, but you can tell from the tabs which worksheet is displayed.)

2. Place the mouse pointer over the tab split box and drag it to the right as far as you can. Notice that you can drag it so that there's no longer a horizontal scroll bar. Then, scroll back to the first worksheet in the workbook. How many sheet tabs are displayed?

3. Use the procedure in figure 5-2 to name the first three worksheets Jan, Feb, and Mar.

4. Click on the tab for the fifth worksheet. Then, hold down the Shift key, scroll the sheet tabs so the last tab is displayed, and click on the last tab. Notice that the title bar now indicates that the tabs you just selected are grouped.

5. Use the procedure in figure 5-5 to delete the worksheets you just grouped. Then, scroll the tabs so the first worksheet tab is displayed. Your workbook should now contain the three worksheets you named in exercise 3, plus a fourth one named Sheet4.

6. Use the procedure in figure 5-5 to add a worksheet in front of the worksheet named Jan. Notice the name of the new worksheet. Then, change the name to Total. The sheet tabs should now look like those above.

7. Save the workbook with the name MONEXP, and close it.

How to work with the data in two or more worksheets of a workbook

If you're creating a workbook that will contain two or more worksheets with similar information and similar formatting, you can use two different techniques to enter, edit, and format the data that's the same in each worksheet. You'll learn both of those techniques now. You'll also learn how to enter formulas and functions that refer to cells in other worksheets in the same workbook.

How to enter, edit, and format data in more than one worksheet at the same time

When you group two or more worksheets using the techniques in figure 5-4, any changes you make to one worksheet in the group affect the other worksheets in the group. If, for example, you enter data into a cell in one worksheet, the data is repeated in the same cell in the other worksheets in the group. And if you change the width of a column in one worksheet, it's changed in all the worksheets in the group. This is illustrated in figure 5-6.

You can also use these techniques to enter formulas and functions into two or more worksheets at the same time. Then, the only data you have to enter in individual worksheets is the data that changes from one worksheet to the next. Before you enter that data, though, be sure to ungroup the worksheets so the changes affect only the active worksheet.

Procedure

1. Group the worksheets you want to be affected by the operations you perform.

2. Enter, edit, and format the data in one of the worksheets in the group. As you work, all of your operations are duplicated in the other worksheets in the group:

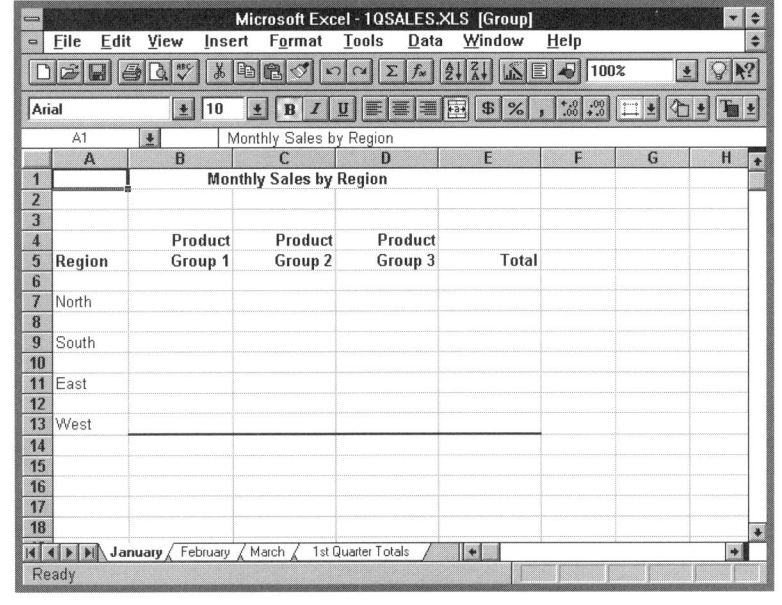

3. Ungroup the worksheets when you're ready to perform operations that apply to only one worksheet in the group. Then, when you switch to another worksheet, you can see the results of the group operations:

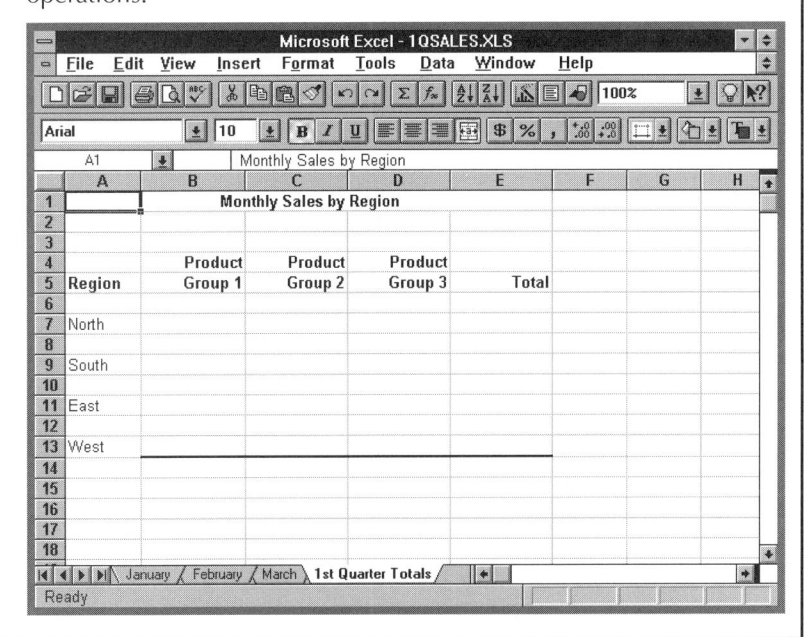

Figure 5-6   How to enter, edit, and format data in more than one worksheet at the same time

How to copy or move data from one worksheet to another

Grouping worksheets and entering, editing, and formatting the data in all of them at the same time is the easiest way to create worksheets with similar formats. Sometimes, however, you may want to create new worksheets based on an existing worksheet. To do that, you can move and copy data from the existing worksheet to the new worksheets using the techniques in figure 5-7.

Since you're already familiar with copying and moving data using the Cut, Copy, and Paste commands, you shouldn't have any trouble using those techniques. If you're moving or copying data to more than one worksheet, though, the Fill Across Worksheets command is likely to be more efficient. When you use this command, you don't identify the location where you want to paste the data. Instead, Excel copies the data in the selected cells to the same location in the other worksheets in the group. It doesn't matter whether those worksheets are before or after the worksheet with the selected cells.

How to copy data using the clipboard

1. Select the cells that contain the data you want to copy, and issue the Copy command to copy the data to the clipboard.
2. Move to the worksheet where you want to paste the data, and select the cell in the upper left corner of the range that you want to paste the data into.
3. Issue the Paste command to insert the data into the worksheet.
4. Repeat steps 2 and 3 to insert the data into additional worksheets.

How to move data using the clipboard

- Use the same procedure as above, but use the Cut command to copy the data to the clipboard. When you use the Cut command, you can only insert the data once.

How to copy data using the Fill Across Worksheets command

1. Group the worksheet that contains the data you want to copy with the worksheets you want to copy the data to.
2. Select the cell or range that contains the data you want to copy. Then, choose the Fill Across Worksheets command from the Edit menu and this dialog box appears:

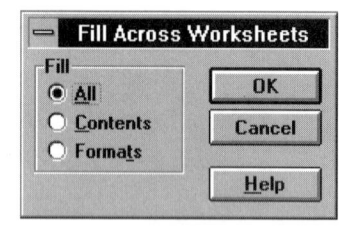

3. Choose a Fill option to copy the contents of the selected cells, the formats of the selected cells, or the contents and formats.
4. Click on the OK button to copy the data to the same location in the other worksheets in the group.

Figure 5-7   How to copy or move data from one worksheet to another

How to enter formulas and functions that refer to other worksheets

In general, the procedures for entering formulas and functions in a workbook that contains more than one worksheet are the same as the procedures for entering and editing them in a workbook that contains a single worksheet. When you have more than one worksheet in a workbook, though, a formula or function in one worksheet can include references to cells in other worksheets.

Figure 5-8 shows how to enter a formula that refers to cells in other worksheets. When you move to another worksheet and click on a cell, Excel adds the worksheet name to the cell reference in the formula like this:

`January!B7`

Here, the worksheet name is separated from the column letter and row number of the cell reference by an exclamation point. This clearly identifies the cell that's used in the formula. If you look in the formula bar after step 3 in figure 5-8, you can see that the formula includes references to cells in three different worksheets.

Procedure

1. Enter the formula up to the point where you want to enter a cell reference from another worksheet:

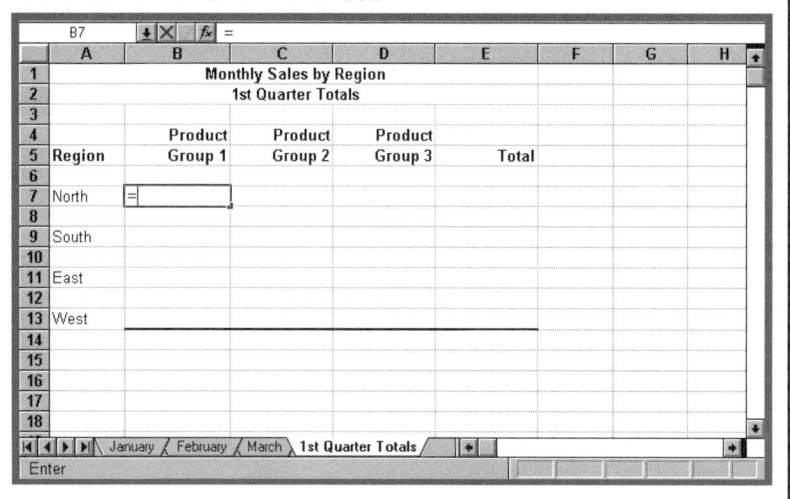

2. Move to the worksheet that contains the cell and select the cell so Excel adds the cell reference to the formula:

3. Type an operator, then move to the worksheet that contains the next cell you want to include in the formula and select the cell. Repeat this until the formula is complete. Then, press the Enter key and Excel completes the formula:

Figure 5-8   How to enter a formula that refers to cells in other worksheets

Figure 5-9 shows how to enter a function that requires a range that includes cells from two or more worksheets. A range reference like this is called a *3-D reference*. Notice that a 3-D reference always includes the same cell or cells in two or more worksheets. In figure 5-9, for example, the range consists of cell B7 in the January, February, and March worksheets.

In step 4 of figure 5-9, you can see the notation for the complete 3-D reference:

`January:March!B7`

Here, the sheet names are separated by a colon to indicate a 3-D reference. Then, these names are followed by an exclamation point that separates them from the cell reference.

Procedure

1. Enter the function up to the point where you want to insert the 3-D reference:

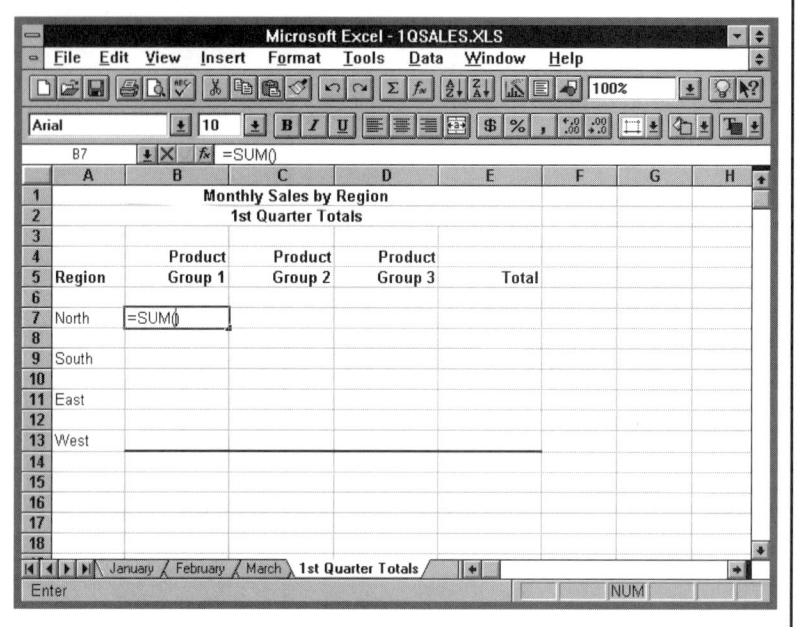

2. Move to the worksheet that contains the first cell or range in the 3-D reference, and select that cell or range. Excel then adds that cell or range to the 3-D reference:

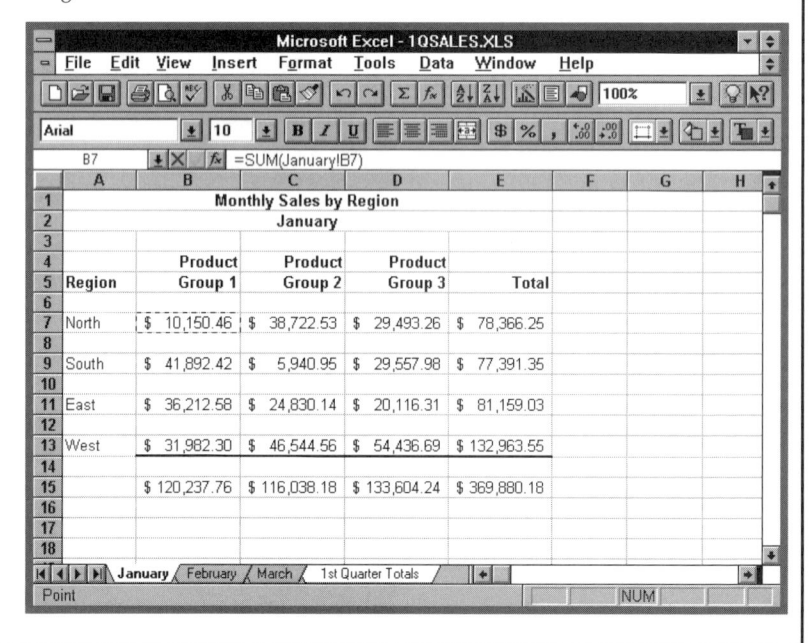

Figure 5-9   How to enter a function that contains a 3-D reference (part 1 of 2)

How to set up and print the worksheet pages

When you're working with several worksheets in a single workbook, you can use the Page Setup command in the File menu to format the pages for each worksheet separately. Then, you can print each worksheet with a different format.

Often, though, you'll want to format the pages of two or more worksheets the same way. To do that, you just group the worksheets before you use the Page Setup command.

When you access the Print dialog box for a workbook that contains more than one worksheet and the worksheets aren't grouped, the Worksheet option prints only the active worksheet. If you group two or more worksheets before you access this dialog box, though, you can use the Selected Sheet(s) option to print those worksheets. In either case, you can use the Entire Workbook option to print all of the worksheets in the workbook.

3. Press and hold the Shift key, then click on the tab for the worksheet that contains the last cell or range in the 3-D reference and Excel completes the reference:

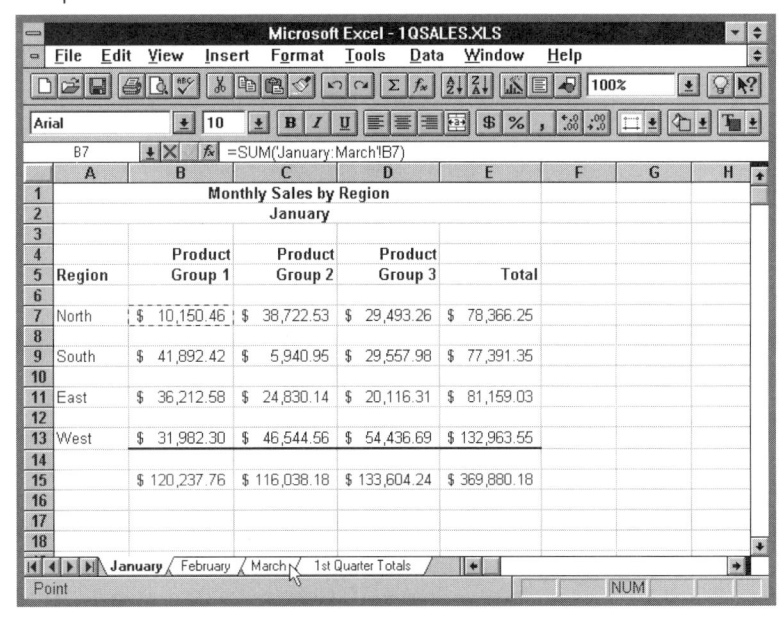

4. Press the Enter key to accept the reference and Excel completes the function:

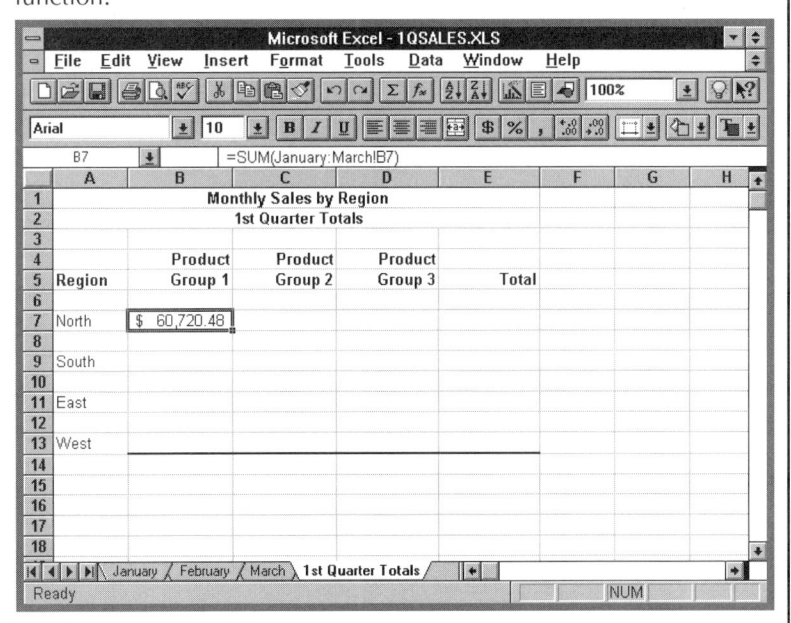

Note

- To enter a 3-D reference with the keyboard, you have to type the reference.

Figure 5-9   How to enter a function that contains a 3-D reference (part 2 of 2)

Exercise set 5-2

	A	B	C	D	E
1	Monthly Expenses				
2	January				
3		Budget	Expense	Variance	
4	Salaries & Wages	50,000	50,125	125	
5	Rent & Utilities	17,500	17,774	274	
6	Maintenance	1,500	4,459	2,959	
7	Supplies	7,750	6,217	(1,533)	
8	Miscellaneous	8,250	8,125	(125)	
9	Total	85,000	86,700	1,700	
10					

The data for the January worksheet

In this exercise set, you will enter data in the four worksheets you named Jan, Feb, Mar, and Total in exercise set 5-1. The January worksheet is shown above, and the layout for all four worksheets is the same. The only differences are the subtitles in cell A2, the expense data for the February and March worksheets, and all of the numeric data in the Total worksheet.

The expense data that you need for the February and March worksheets follows:

	February	**March**
Salaries & Wages	51,784	51,004
Rent & Utilities	18,222	17,453
Maintenance	1,922	1,399
Supplies	7,912	7,784
Miscellaneous	7,211	9,374

The numeric data in the Total worksheet should be derived from the data in the other worksheets through formulas and functions.

The quickest way to create the four worksheets is probably to group them and enter the January worksheet just as it's shown above. That establishes the basic data and formatting for all four worksheets. Then, you can ungroup the worksheets and modify the other three worksheets so they're correct too. The exercises that follow use that approach as they guide you through the creation of the four worksheets.

1. Open the MONEXP workbook that you created for exercise set 5-1, and group the first four worksheets in the workbook. Then, enter the January worksheet so it looks like the one above including all formatting, formulas, and functions. You can do this entry in any one of the four worksheets. When you're done, switch to each of the other worksheets to make sure that the January worksheet is now in the other three worksheets too.

2. Ungroup the worksheets by clicking on the tab for Sheet4. Next, switch to the February worksheet, enter February into cell A2, and enter the February expense data so it replaces the January data. The values in the Variance and Total cells should be recalculated automatically. Then, switch to the March worksheet, enter March as its subtitle, and enter the March expense data so it replaces the January data.

3. With the worksheets still ungrouped, switch to the Total worksheet, enter Total in cell A2, and delete the numbers in cells B4 through C8. Next, use the procedure in figure 5-8 to enter a formula in cell B4 that adds the contents of cell B4 in the January, February, and March worksheets. If the total is 150,000, you've done it right and the formula in the formula bar will look like this:

    `=Jan!B4+Feb!B4+Mar!B4`

    Then, copy this formula to cells B5 through B8.

4. A better way to add the data in the January, February, and March worksheets is to use a SUM function with a 3-D reference. So delete the data in cells B4 through B8 of the Total worksheet, and use the procedure in figure 5-9 to enter a function in cell B4 that sums the numbers in cell B4 in the January, February, and March worksheets. Here again, if the total is 150,000, you've done it right and the function in the formula bar will look like this:

    `=SUM(Jan:Mar!B4)`

    Then, copy this formula to cells B5 through B8, and copy the formulas in cells B4 through B8 to cells C4 through C8.

5. Review all four worksheets to make sure they're correct. If any of the worksheets aren't correct, do the required editing or formatting. Then, save and close workbook.

Exercise set 5-3

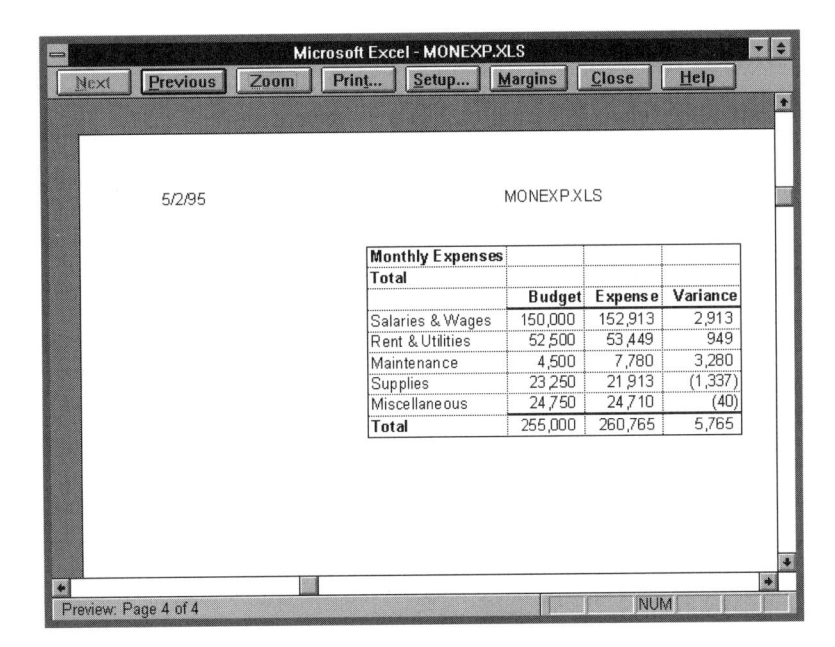

How the Print Preview window should look when you magnify the Total worksheet in exercise 2

This exercise set forces you to use some of the other techniques for creating and editing the worksheets within a workbook.

1. To see how the Fill Across Worksheets command works, open the MONEXP file; group the January and February worksheets; select the formulas in cells D4 through D8; and press the Delete key to delete them. To restore these formulas, group the January, February, and March worksheets; select cells D4 through D8 in the March worksheet; and choose the Fill Across Worksheets command from the Edit menu. This copies the formulas from the March worksheet to the other worksheets in the group. All four worksheets should now be correct again.

2. Group all four worksheets, and choose the Page Setup command from the File menu. Next, use the Margins tab to center the worksheets horizontally. And use the Header/Footer tab to delete the default footer and to add a custom header that consists of date, file name, and page number. From the Page Setup dialog box, click on the Print Preview button to preview the four worksheets and make sure the page formatting is correct. For instance, the magnified preview of the Total page should look like the one above. Then, close the preview window.

3. Ungroup the worksheets, click on the Jan sheet tab, and click on the Print Preview button in the Standard toolbar. How many of the four worksheets can you preview? Close the preview window, group the February and March worksheets, and click on the Print Preview button again. Now, how many of the worksheets can you preview?

4. Choose the Print command from the File menu so its dialog box is displayed. The Selected Sheet(s) option will print the two grouped worksheets, and the Entire Workbook option will print all four worksheets. Click on the Entire Workbook option; click on the Print Preview button to preview all four worksheets; and click on the Print button to print them.

5. Save and close the file.

Other skills for working with two or more worksheets in one workbook

The skills you've learned so far are the ones you'll use most often for working with more than one worksheet in a single workbook. But there are some other skills that you may want to use occasionally. You'll learn those skills now.

How to move or copy worksheets

Excel provides two methods for moving and copying the worksheets in a workbook. First, you can use the drag-and-drop method presented in figure 5-10. When you use this technique, you simply drag the tab for the worksheet you want to move or copy to a new location. To move or copy two or more worksheets, you group them before you drag their tabs.

How to move worksheets

1. Group the worksheets you want to move. Then, position the mouse pointer over the tab of one of the worksheets in the group and press and hold the mouse button. A small black arrowhead appears above the row of tabs marking where the worksheet will be inserted:

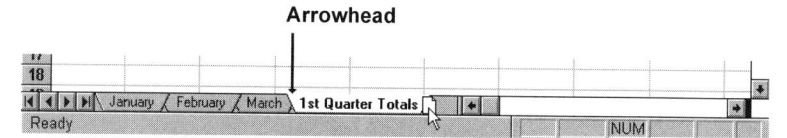

2. Drag the pointer so the arrowhead points to the location where you want to move the worksheets:

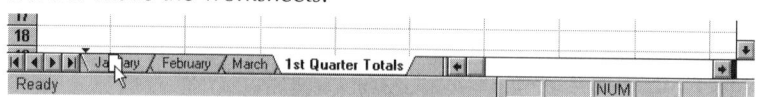

3. Release the mouse button and the worksheets are moved to the new location:

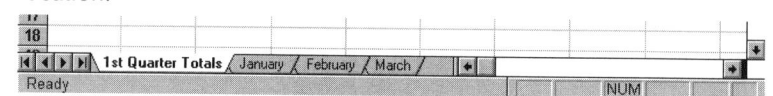

How to copy worksheets

- Use the same procedure as above, but hold down the Ctrl key as you drag the worksheets. A plus sign appears inside the worksheet pointer to indicate a copy operation.

Figure 5-10 How to move or copy worksheets using the drag-and-drop feature

Figure 5-11 presents the second method for moving or copying worksheets. When you use the Move or Copy Sheet command, Excel displays a dialog box that lets you choose the worksheet that you want to move or copy the selected worksheets in front of. Notice that you can also move or copy the worksheets to the end of the workbook by choosing the last option in the Before Sheet list.

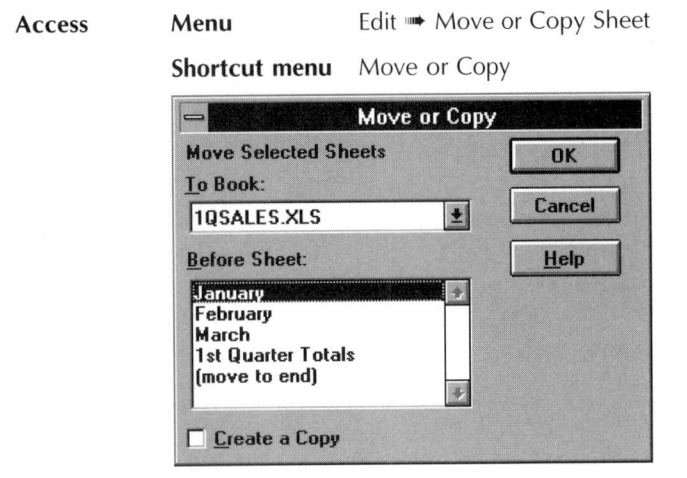

Access

Menu Edit ➡ Move or Copy Sheet

Shortcut menu Move or Copy

How to move worksheets

1. Group the worksheets you want to move.
2. Access the Move or Copy dialog box. Then, choose the worksheet in the Before Sheet list that you want to move the worksheets in front of. Or, choose the (move to end) option to move the worksheets after the last worksheet in the workbook.
3. Click on the OK button and the worksheets are moved to the new location.

How to copy worksheets

- Use the same procedure as above, but choose the Create A Copy option from the Move or Copy dialog box.

Figure 5-11 How to move or copy worksheets using the Move or Copy Sheet command

How to hide or reveal worksheets

Figure 5-12 presents the procedures for hiding and revealing worksheets. When a worksheet is hidden, it isn't included in any printing operations.

Although you probably won't need to hide worksheets often, it can be helpful if you need to move back and forth between two worksheets and you can't display the tabs for both worksheets at the same time. Then, you can hide the worksheets that are between the two worksheets you want to display so you can move easily between them.

A workbook with two worksheets (February and March) hidden

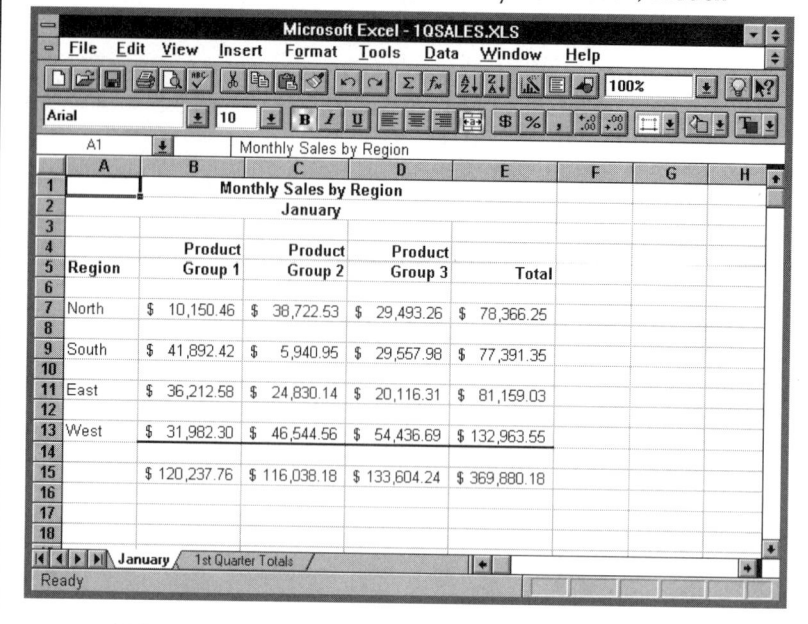

How to hide worksheets

1. Group the worksheets you want to hide.
2. Choose the Sheet Hide command from the Format menu.

How to reveal a worksheet

1. Choose the Sheet Unhide command from the Format menu to display this dialog box:

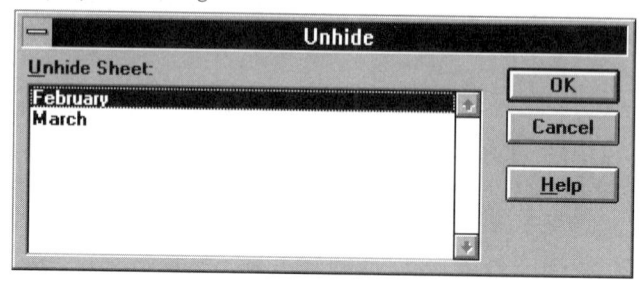

2. Double-click on the worksheet you want to reveal or highlight the worksheet and click on the OK button.

Notes

- If a workbook contains a single worksheet, you can't hide it.
- You can reveal only one worksheet at a time.

Figure 5-12   How to hide or reveal worksheets

How to display more than one worksheet at a time

Sometimes, it's easier to work with two or more worksheets if you can see more than one of them at the same time. That way, you can see how a change in one worksheet affects the others.

Figure 5-13 presents the procedure for displaying more than one worksheet at a time. To start, you have to open additional windows for the workbook. Then, you tell Excel how you want to arrange the windows on the screen so you can see all of them at the same time. Once all the windows are displayed, you can display whichever worksheet you want in each window.

In general, this works best when only two windows are displayed in either a horizontal or vertical arrangement. The more windows you have open, the less you can see in each window and the more confusing this becomes.

Additional information

✓ When you open a new window for a workbook, Excel displays the number of the window after the file name in the title bar of the window and after the file name in the Window menu.

✓ To move from one window to another, click on the window if part of it shows, press Ctrl+F6, or use the Window menu.

A workbook with two open windows in a horizontal arrangement

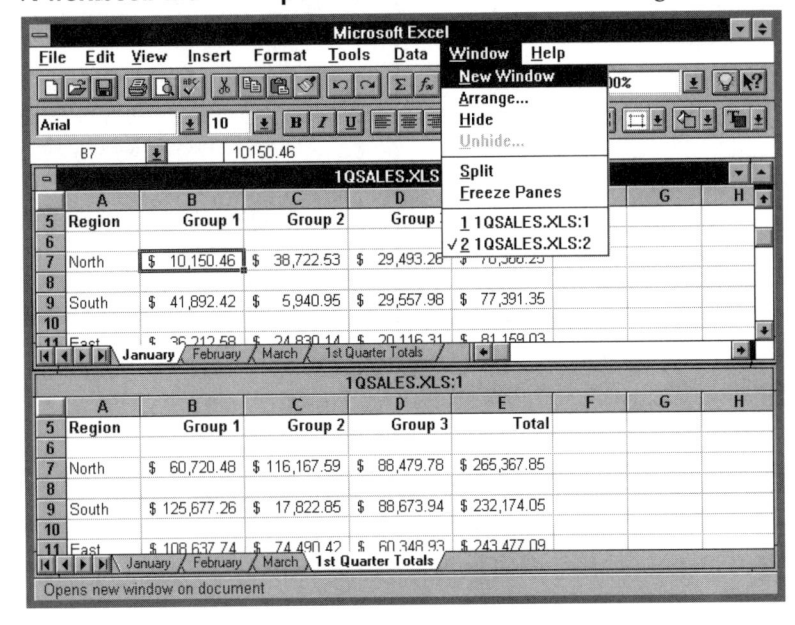

How to open another window for a workbook

- Choose the New Window command from the Window menu.

How to arrange the open windows for the active workbook

1. Choose the Arrange command from the Window menu to display this dialog box:

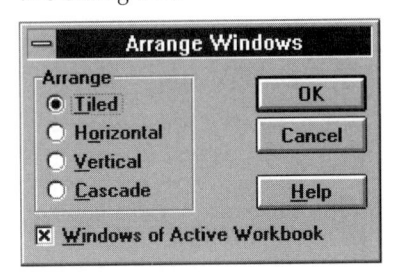

2. Choose an option from the Arrange group, and check the Windows Of Active Workbook option so the windows that contain other open workbooks (if any) aren't displayed.

3. Click on the OK button, and Excel displays the open windows for the active workbook with the active worksheet in each window.

Notes

- To change the screen back so only one worksheet is displayed, click on the maximize button in the active window.

- To close the extra windows for a workbook, you have to close the file. This closes all the windows at the same time.

Figure 5-13   How to display more than one worksheet at a time

How to use names

In chapter 4, you learned how to use names to help you move the cell pointer to named ranges in large worksheets. If you like those techniques, you can also use them in workbooks that contain more than one worksheet. For instance, you can use one name to refer to a range of cells in one worksheet and another name to refer to a range of cells in a second worksheet. Then, you can use the names to move the cell pointer from one worksheet to another.

If you want to use the same name in more than one worksheet, though, you need to include the sheet name when you define the name. For example, the name

`January!North`

refers to the range named North in the sheet named January. This type of name is only available when the active worksheet is the one included in the name, so you can't use it to move from one worksheet to another. You'll see how this works when you do the next set of exercises.

Exercise set 5-4

1. Open the MONEXP workbook, and switch to the worksheet named Total. Then, use the drag-and-drop feature described in figure 5-10 to move the worksheet after the March worksheet in the workbook. Note that the functions in the Total worksheet still work correctly.

2. Group the January, February, and March worksheets. Then, use the drag-and-drop feature to copy them before the Total worksheet. Note the sheet names for the new worksheets, and note that the 3-D references in the functions in the Total worksheet do not include the new worksheets. You could now modify the workbook so the new worksheets contain the data for April, May, and June and the Total worksheet summarizes their data too. Delete the new worksheets, though.

3. Use the procedure in figure 5-11 to repeat the copying operation that you did in exercise 2, but don't delete the new worksheets this time. Which copying method do you prefer?

4. Use the procedure in figure 5-12 to hide the new worksheets. Then, reveal the worksheets and delete them.

5. Use the procedure in figure 5-13 to open another window for the MONEXP workbook and display both windows in the vertical arrangement. Click on the Jan tab in the window on the left to display that worksheet, and click on the Feb tab in the other workbook window to display that worksheet. Next, change the window arrangement to cascade, and then to horizontal to see what those arrangements look like. To return to a one window display, click on the maximize button in the active window. Then, pull down the Window menu to see that both windows are still open even though only one is displayed.

6. Move to the January worksheet, select cells C4 through C8, and use the Name Define command in the Insert menu to name the range January. Note the reference shown in the Refers To box of the Define Name dialog box. Next, move to the February worksheet, select the same cells, and name them February. Then, use the name list in the formula bar to move to January. What happens? Use the Go To command in the Edit menu to move to February. What happens?

7. Move to the January worksheet, select cells C4 through C8, and use the Name Define command to name these cells Jan!Expense. Next, move to the February worksheet, select the same cells, and name them Feb!Expense. Then, click in cell A1 of the February worksheet, and use the Name list or the Go To command to see what names are available. When you go to Expense, what happens? Move to cell A1 in the January worksheet and go to Expense again. What happens this time? This shows that the Expense names are only active in the worksheets that they were defined for.

8. Save the workbook and close it.

How to work with worksheets from two or more workbooks

If you've been using a spreadsheet program that didn't provide for two or more worksheets in a single file, you will want to combine some of your closely related worksheets into a single workbook now that you're using Excel 5. That way, you'll be able to work with the worksheets more easily. To combine the worksheets from separate files into a single workbook, you need to learn the skills that follow.

How to open two or more workbooks and switch between them

To work with worksheets from two or more workbooks at the same time, you have to open the files that contain them. To do that, you can use one of the techniques described in figure 5-14. In the Open dialog box in this figure, three files have been highlighted. Then, when Excel performs the command, each of the files is opened in a separate workbook window.

Once the workbooks are open, you can switch from one window to another by using the Window menu or the shortcut key. You can also switch to a window by clicking on it. To do that, the windows have to be arranged so you can see part of the window you want to switch to.

Two ways to open two or more workbook files

- Issue the Open command for each workbook file you want to open. Each time you issue the Open command, Excel opens a new workbook window for the file you specify.

- If the workbook files are in the same directory, hold down the Ctrl key as you click on each file you want to open in the File Name list of the Open dialog box. Or, to highlight a range of files, click on the first file, then hold down the Shift key and click on the last file:

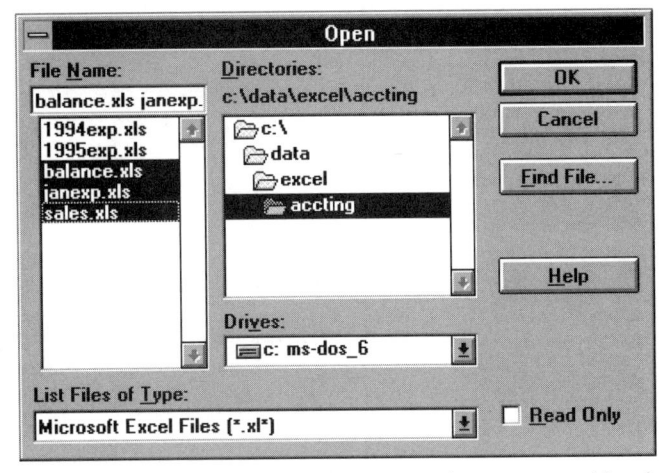

When you click on the OK button, Excel opens a workbook window for each file you highlighted.

Three ways to switch between workbooks

- Choose the workbook you want to switch to from the Window menu:

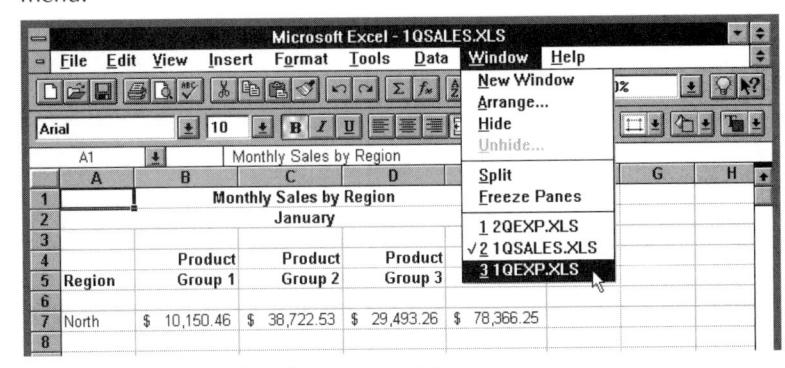

- Press Ctrl+F6 to display the next workbook.

- If the window that contains the workbook you want to switch to is visible, click anywhere on the window.

Figure 5-14 How to open and switch between two or more workbook files

How to display two or more workbooks at the same time

Figure 5-15 shows how to display all of the open workbooks at the same time. This works in much the same way that it works when you have two or more windows open for the same workbook. This time, though, you must make sure that the Windows of Active Workbook option isn't checked. Then, the windows for all of the open workbooks are displayed in the arrangement of your choice.

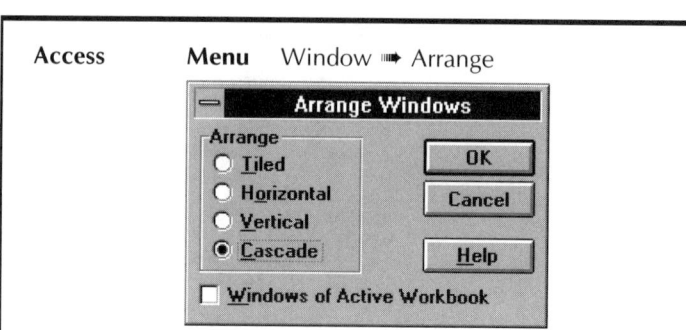

Access   Menu   Window → Arrange

Procedure

1. Open the workbook files you want to display.
2. Access the Arrange Windows dialog box, choose an Arrange option, and make sure the Windows Of Active Workbook option isn't checked.
3. Click on the OK button, and all the workbook windows are displayed.

Three workbook windows in the cascade arrangement

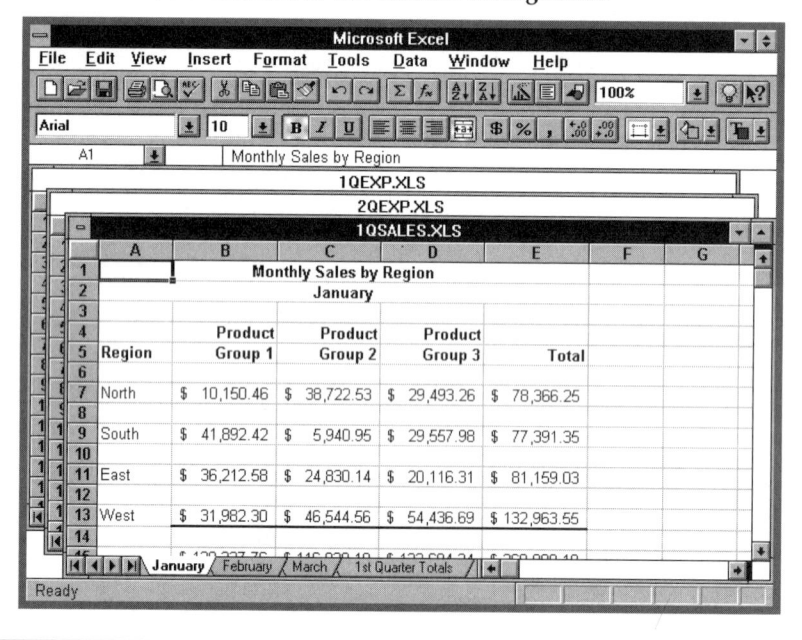

Figure 5-15   How to display two or more workbooks at the same time

How to move or copy data from one workbook to another

To move or copy data from one workbook to another, you can use the Cut, Copy, and Paste commands as summarized in the first procedure in figure 5-16. This works the same way that it does when you move or copy data from one worksheet to another within the same workbook. If you move or copy a formula without also moving or copying the cells that it refers to, though, the formula won't work in the new workbook. Instead, an error message is displayed.

The solution to this problem is to use the Paste Special command to complete the moving or copying operation as shown in the second procedure in figure 5-16. Then, the value calculated by the formula in the old workbook is pasted into the new workbook.

How to move or copy data from one open workbook to another

1. Switch to the workbook that contains the data you want to move or copy. Then, select the cells that contain the data and issue the Cut or Copy command to copy the data to the clipboard.
2. Switch to the workbook where you want to paste the data. Then, select the cell in the upper left corner of the range that you want to paste the data into, and issue the Paste command.

How to paste formulas as values in another workbook

1. Switch to the workbook that contains the formulas. Then, select the cells that contain the formulas and cut or copy them to the clipboard.
2. Switch to the workbook where you want to paste the values of the formulas. Then, place the cell pointer in the upper left corner of the range that you want to paste the values into, and choose the Paste Special command from the Edit menu to display this dialog box:

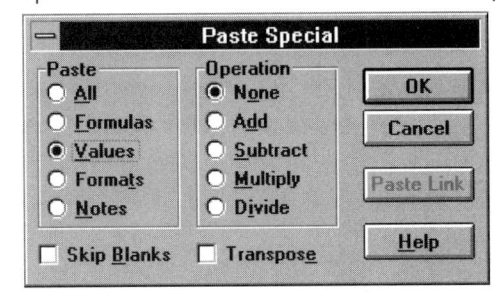

3. Choose the Values option from the Paste group and click on the OK button to paste the values (not the formulas) into the workbook.

Figure 5-16 How to move or copy data from one workbook to another

How to move or copy worksheets from one workbook to another

In addition to moving and copying data from one workbook to another, you can move and copy entire worksheets. To do that, you can use either the drag-and-drop feature or the Move or Copy Sheet command. These techniques are similar to the ones you use to move or copy worksheets within a workbook.

Figure 5-17 shows how to use the drag-and-drop feature to move or copy worksheets to another workbook. To use this feature, both workbooks must be open and the sheet tabs in both workbooks must be visible. Then, you can simply drag the worksheets from one workbook to the other.

How to move worksheets from one open workbook to another

1. Switch to the window that contains the worksheets you want to move. Group the worksheets, then press and hold the mouse button on the tab of one of the worksheets in the group. A small black arrowhead appears above the row of tabs marking where the worksheet will be inserted.

2. Drag the pointer so the arrowhead points to the location in the other workbook where you want to move the worksheets:

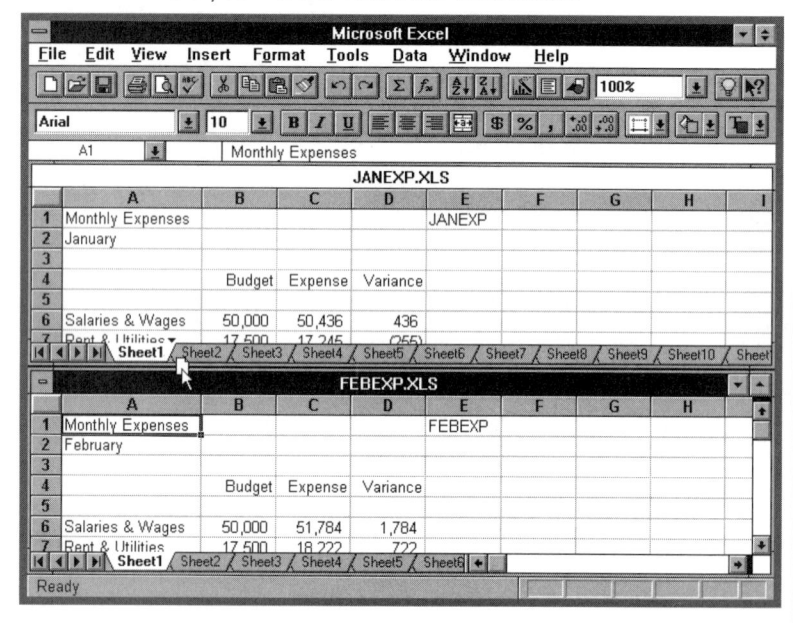

3. Release the mouse button, and the worksheets are moved to the new location.

How to copy worksheets from one workbook file to another

- Use the same procedure as above, but hold down the Ctrl key as you drag the worksheets. A plus sign appears inside the worksheet pointer to indicate a copy operation.

Note

- If the worksheets you're copying have the same names as worksheets in the workbook file you're copying them to, Excel adds a number in parentheses to the worksheet names so you can tell them apart.

Figure 5-17 How to move or copy worksheets from one workbook to another with the drag-and-drop feature

Figure 5-18 shows how to use the Move or Copy Sheet command to move or copy worksheets from one workbook to another. This works the same as it does when you move or copy worksheets within a workbook except that you choose a different workbook from the To Book list. You can also move or copy worksheets to a new workbook by choosing the New Book option from the To Book list instead of a workbook name.

Access	Menu	Edit ➡ Move or Copy Sheet
	Shortcut menu	Move or Copy

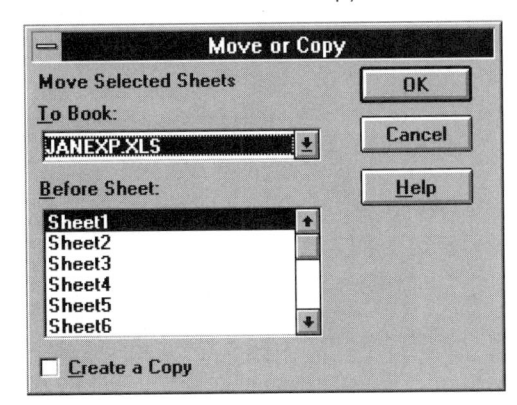

How to move worksheets from one open workbook to another

1. Switch to the workbook that contains the worksheets you want to move and group the worksheets.

2. Access the Move or Copy dialog box. Then, choose the workbook you want to move the worksheets to from the To Book list, and choose the worksheet before which you want to move the worksheets from the Before Sheet list.

3. Click on the OK button and the worksheets are moved to the new location.

How to copy worksheets from one workbook file to another

- Use the same procedure as above, but choose the Create A Copy option from the Move or Copy dialog box.

Figure 5-18 How to move or copy worksheets from one workbook to another with the Move or Copy Sheet command

Exercise set 5-5

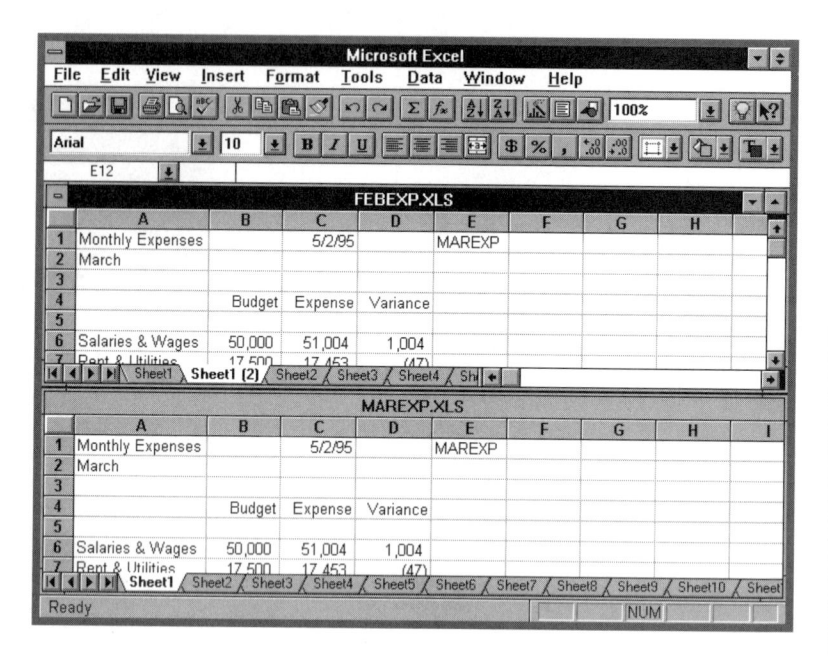

How the workbook windows should look after exercise 3

1. Open the FEBEXP and MAREXP workbooks that you created for chapter 1. (You should have modified the FEBEXP workbook so it's different from the MAREXP workbook, but don't worry about that.) If you saved the workbooks in the same directory, use the second technique in figure 5-14 to open them.

2. Use the file names at the bottom of the Window menu to switch to the workbook that's not currently displayed. Then, press Ctrl+F6 to switch back to the other workbook.

3. Use the Arrange command as described in figure 5-15 to display the workbooks in the horizontal arrangement. Then, use the drag-and-drop feature shown in figure 5-17 to copy the worksheet in the MAREXP workbook after the first worksheet in the FEBEXP workbook. Notice that the worksheet you copied is named Sheet1(2) so you can tell the worksheets apart. This shows how easy it is to combine the worksheets from two workbooks into a single workbook.

4. Use the procedure in figure 5-18 to copy the worksheet in the MAREXP workbook to the FEBEXP workbook in front of the first worksheet. This is the other method for combining worksheets from two or more workbooks. Which do you prefer? Now, close the FEBEXP workbook without saving it.

5. The active workbook should now be the MAREXP workbook. To maximize its window, click on its maximize button. Next, select cells B4 through D4, copy them to the clipboard, open a new workbook, and paste the clipboard contents starting with cell A1. Then, switch back to the MAREXP workbook, select cells B12 through D12, copy them to the clipboard, switch to the new workbook, and paste the clipboard contents starting in cell A2. What happened and why? Now, use the Paste Special command shown in figure 5-16 to paste the values, not the formulas, of the data on the clipboard starting in cell A2.

6. Close both of the open workbooks without saving the changes.

Perspective

If two or more related worksheets have the same layout, you'll almost certainly want to store them in the same workbook. Then, you can enter and edit the data that's the same in all the worksheets at the same time. And you can format all of the worksheets at the same time.

You may also want to store two or more worksheets in the same workbook if they contain related information, but don't necessarily have the same layout. For example, you may have one worksheet that shows income, one that shows expense, and a third that shows profit. Since the data in the income and expense worksheets is directly related to the data in the profit worksheet, it makes sense to store all three worksheets in the same workbook. Then, you can easily enter formulas and functions in the profit worksheet that refer to cells in the income and expense worksheets.

Summary

- You can use the *sheet tabs* at the bottom of the workbook window to switch to another worksheet or change a worksheet name. If you can't see the tab you want, you can use the *tab scrolling buttons* to scroll the tabs. You can also increase or decrease the size of the *tab area* by dragging the *tab split box*.

- By default, an Excel workbook contains 16 worksheets. However, you can add worksheets to and delete worksheets from a workbook. You can also change the default number.

- When you *group* worksheets, you can enter, edit, and format the data in more than one worksheet at a time.

- You can move or copy data from one worksheet to another using the Cut, Copy, and Paste commands or the Fill Across Worksheets command.

- When you enter a formula or function into a worksheet, you can point to cells outside the active worksheet. Then, the worksheet names are combined with the cell references so the cells are clearly identified. A reference to a range that includes cells from two or more worksheets is called a *3-D reference*.

- You can format the pages of each worksheet in a workbook separately, or you can group them and format their pages at the same time.

- As you work with the worksheets in a workbook, you can move or copy worksheets. You can hide and reveal worksheets. And you can display more than one worksheet at the same time.

- You can use a name to refer to a specific range of cells in a specific worksheet. Or, you can use the same name in more than one worksheet by including the worksheet name when you define it.

- You can open two or more workbooks at the same time and arrange them so you can see all of them at once. Then, you can move and copy entire worksheets from one workbook to another. To move and copy data from one open workbook to another, you can use the Cut, Copy, and Paste commands. To copy a formula as a value, you can use the Paste Special command.

Chapter 6

How to create charts

When you use Excel 5, you can generate a professional looking chart from the data in a worksheet in just a few minutes. By adding a chart like that to a report or visual presentation, you can often make a dramatic improvement in its effectiveness. In this chapter, you'll learn just how easy it is to create the charts you need for reports and presentations.

Basic concepts and skills for creating charts
    The types of charts you can create with Excel
    The components of a typical chart
    How to create a chart using the ChartWizard
    How to select, move, copy, size, and delete a chart
    How to select a component or subcomponent in a chart
    How to move, size, delete, or format a selected component
    How to change a chart by changing its data
    How to set up and print charts

Other skills for working with charts
    How to change the chart type, subtype, or format
    How to add or change chart and axis titles
    How to add or delete a legend
    How to add or delete gridlines
    How to use the Format command to format a chart
    How to size a chart for printing

Perspective

Summary

Basic concepts and skills for creating charts

Before you create a chart, you need to decide what type of chart you want to create. You also need to be familiar with the different components of a chart so you'll understand some of the options that are available when you create one. Once you understand these concepts and terms, it's easy to create the charts you need.

The types of charts you can create with Excel

Figure 6-1 presents eight types of charts that you can create with Excel. Although there are many others, these are the ones you'll probably find most useful. Of the eight, the *column chart* is the type you're likely to use most often.

A column chart is useful when you want to compare data elements or show the change in one or more data elements over time. A *bar chart* is similar to a column chart, but its orientation is different. The *line* and *area charts* also show the change in one or more data elements over time. However, a line chart emphasizes the time and the rate of change and an area chart emphasizes the amount of change. A *pie chart* is useful for showing how the parts compare to the whole.

Figure 6-1 also includes some *3-D charts*. Although these charts present the same information as the other charts, they tend to be more appealing visually. Unfortunately, though, 3-D charts are often more difficult to read than 2-D charts so you must use them with care.

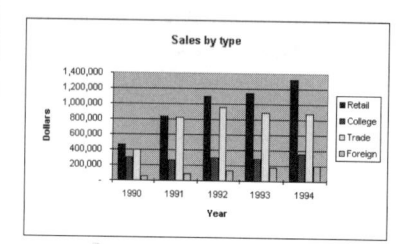

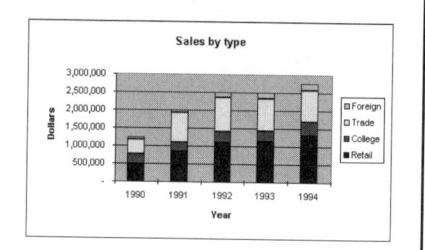

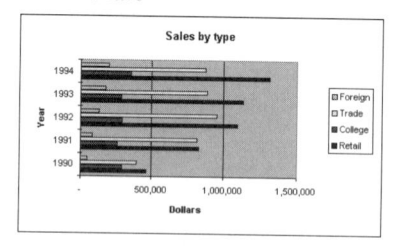

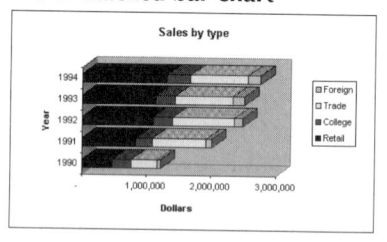

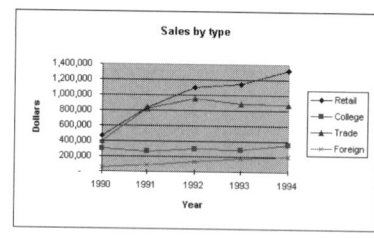

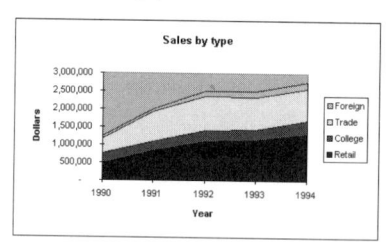

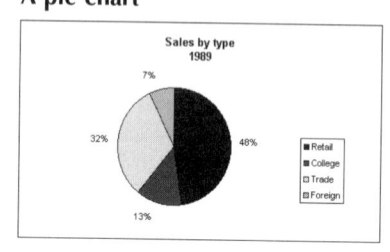

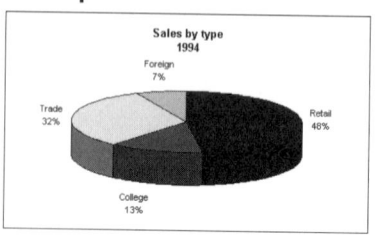

Figure 6-1   Eight of the types of charts you can create with Excel

The components of a typical chart

Figure 6-2 presents the components of a typical chart. When Excel creates a chart, it plots each *data point* in the worksheet range as a *data marker*. What the data markers look like depend on the type of chart. In figure 6-2, the data markers are represented by the columns in the column chart.

Most charts contain two axes. One axis, usually the y-axis, presents the range of values contained in the chart. The other axis, usually the x-axis, presents the different *categories* contained in the chart. In figure 6-2, the y-axis shows the range of sales in dollars, and the x-axis shows the years over which the sales are plotted.

Each category in a chart contains a data point from one or more *data series*. In figure 6-2, the data series are the different types of sales, which are identified in the *legend*. Since there are four different types of sales, each category consists of four data points, one from each data series. As described in the figure, Excel determines whether it uses the rows or the columns as the data series based on the number of rows and columns in the worksheet data that's selected for the chart. This will make more sense when you learn how to create a chart.

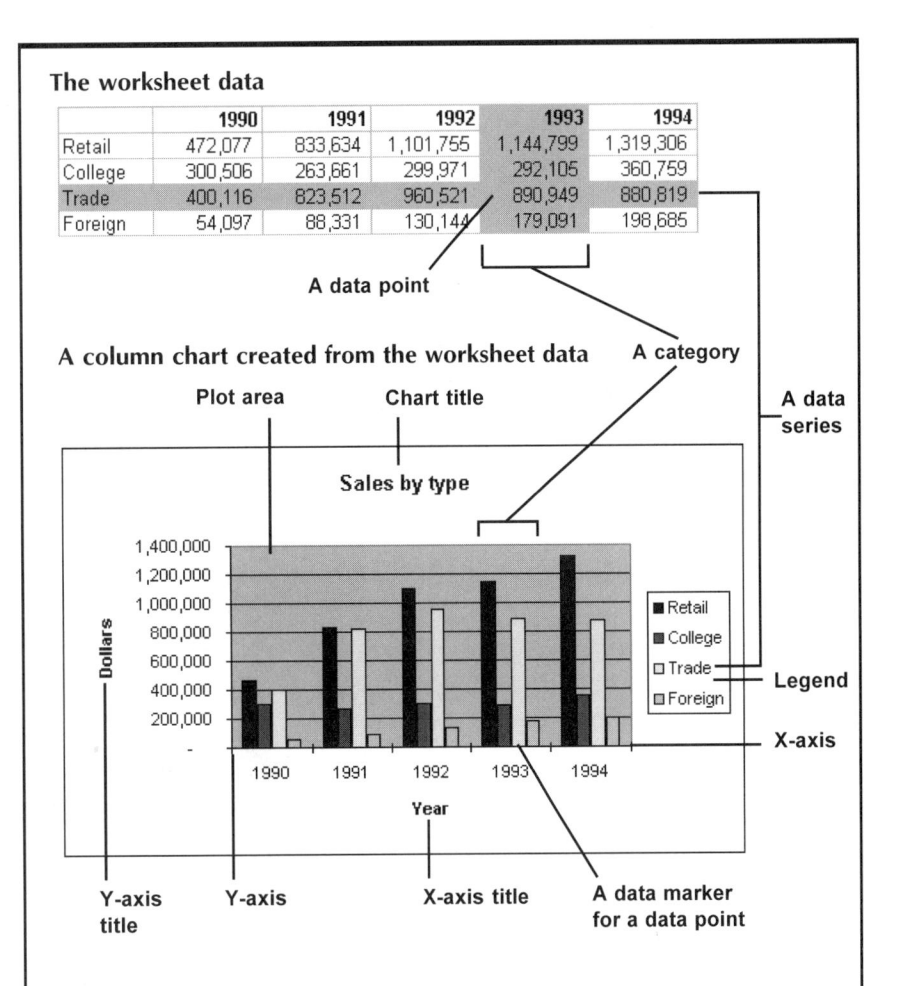

The worksheet data

	1990	1991	1992	1993	1994
Retail	472,077	833,634	1,101,755	1,144,799	1,319,306
College	300,506	263,661	299,971	292,105	360,759
Trade	400,116	823,512	960,521	890,949	880,819
Foreign	54,097	88,331	130,144	179,091	198,685

A column chart created from the worksheet data

How Excel translates worksheet data into chart data

- Each *data point* in the worksheet range is plotted as a *data marker*. Excel groups the data markers into *categories*, with each category consisting of one data marker from each *data series*.

- If the range you select for a worksheet contains fewer columns than rows, Excel's default is to chart the data in each column as a data series and to group the data in each row into a category. Otherwise, the default is to chart the data in each row as a data series and to group the data in each column into a category. You can change this default when you create a chart.

- If you include the row and column headings in the range you select for a chart, Excel automatically adds the data series descriptions to the *legend* and the category descriptions to the x-axis. Otherwise, it creates defaults for the descriptions.

- Excel determines the measurements used along the y-axis from the data in the range you select.

Figure 6-2 The components of a typical chart

How to create a chart using the ChartWizard

Figure 6-3 presents the procedures for creating a chart using the ChartWizard. As you can see, you can create either an *embedded chart*, which is stored in the same worksheet as the data it's based on, or a *chart sheet*, which is stored in a separate worksheet. Since you can perform most charting functions on either an embedded chart or a chart sheet, the type you use depends mostly on whether you want to print the chart on the same page as the data it's based on.

The critical part of creating a chart is selecting the right data. In addition to the actual numbers you want to plot in the chart, you should include any cells that identify the categories and the data series that will be represented in the chart. In figure 6-3, for example, the row that contains the years and the column that contains the types of sales are selected. If this information isn't included in the worksheet or you don't include it in the selection, Excel adds default descriptions to the chart that are of little use.

Additional information

✓ If you want to chart only some of the categories or data series in a worksheet, you can hide the rows or columns you want to exclude before you create the chart. Or, you can make nonadjacent selections that include only the data you want to chart. When you make nonadjacent selections, the ranges must form a rectangular area.

How to start the ChartWizard

Menu	Insert ➡ Chart On This Sheet (embedded chart)
	Insert ➡ Chart As New Sheet (chart sheet)
Standard toolbar	(embedded chart)

How to create an embedded chart

1. Select the range of cells for the chart including the row and column headings.
2. Start the ChartWizard using the Chart On This Sheet command or the ChartWizard button. Then, place the chart pointer where you want the upper left corner of the chart, or click and drag the mouse pointer until the chart outline is the size you want:

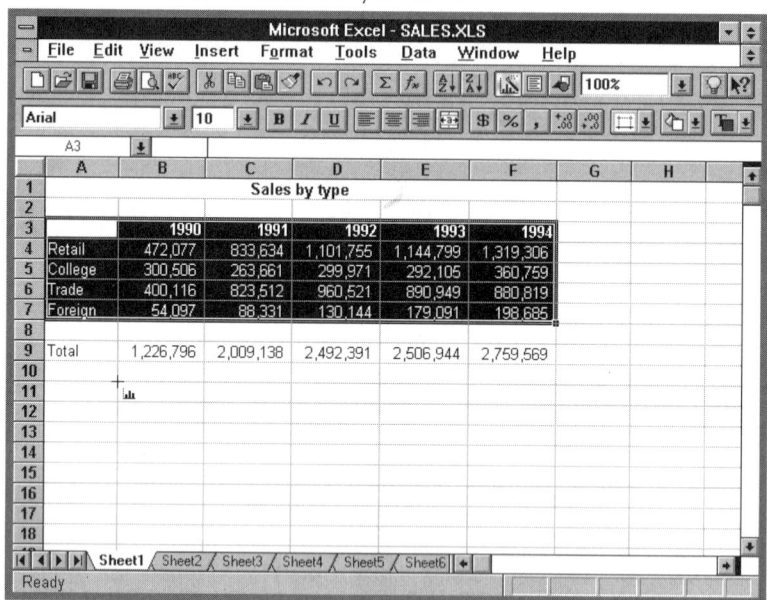

3. Release the mouse button, and this dialog box appears:

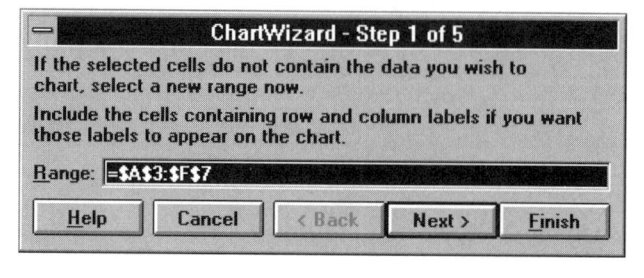

Figure 6-3 How to use the ChartWizard to create a chart (part 1 of 3)

How to create charts

Once you select the worksheet data and start the ChartWizard, the rest of the procedure is simple. As you proceed through the ChartWizard dialog boxes, you can chose the type of chart you want to create and the specific format of that chart. You can change Excel's default for the data series and for the number of rows and columns that contain the text that describes the categories and data series. You can include or exclude the legend. And you can add chart and axis titles.

If you enter the ChartWizard options carefully, the chart should be in close to final form when you're done. Often, it just needs to be sized so that all of the information fits. For example, the chart in step 8 of figure 6-3 needs to be enlarged so all of the years are displayed and so the numbers on the y-axis are displayed in smaller increments. You'll learn how to do that next.

4. Verify the range, then click on the Next button and this dialog box appears:

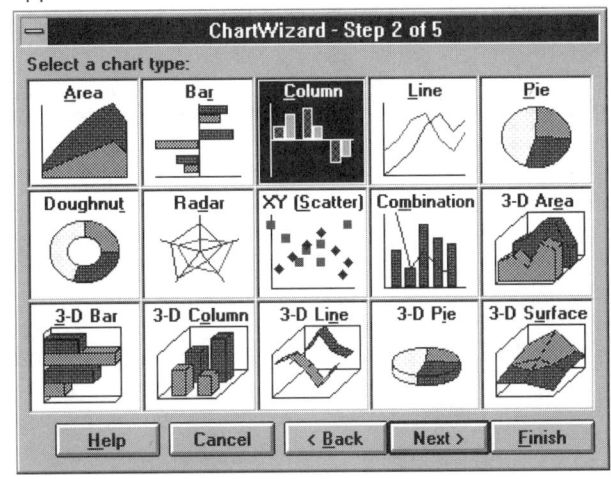

5. Choose a chart type, then click on the Next button and this dialog box appears:

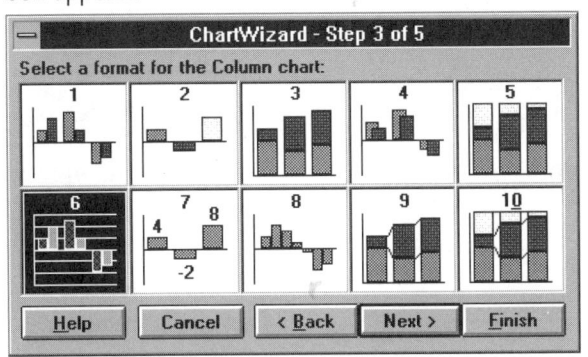

6. Choose a chart format, then click on the Next button and this dialog box appears:

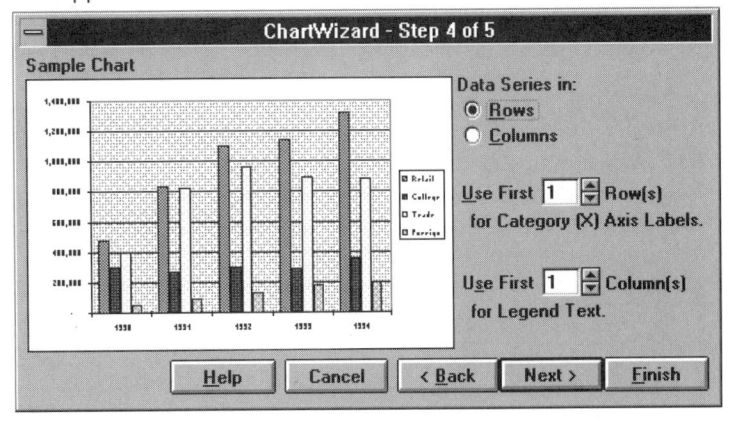

Figure 6-3 How to use the ChartWizard to create a chart (part 2 of 3)

Additional information

✓ You can create a default chart in a chart sheet by selecting the range of cells you want to include in the chart and pressing the F11 key. If Excel needs more information to complete the chart, it displays an appropriate dialog box. Then, you can modify the chart using the skills presented in this chapter.

✓ If you click on the ChartWizard button when an embedded chart is selected or a chart sheet is active, Excel displays the first ChartWizard dialog box so you can change the chart range. Then, if you click on the Next button, the fourth ChartWizard dialog box is displayed so you can change the data series or the rows and columns that are used for headings. The other ChartWizard dialog boxes aren't available for an existing chart.

7. Choose the Rows option to chart the rows as data series or the Columns option to chart the columns as data series. Make sure that the numbers in the Use First Rows and Use First Columns boxes correspond to the number of heading rows and columns you selected. Then, click on the Next button and this dialog box appears:

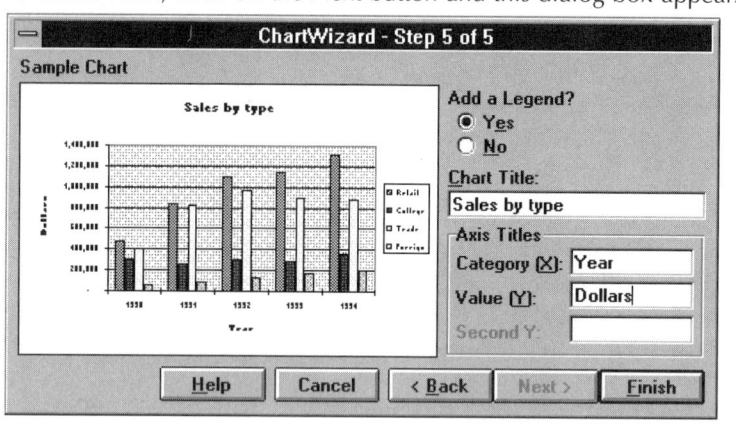

8. Choose an option to indicate whether or not you want the chart to include a legend, and enter the chart and axis titles for the chart. Then, click on the Finish button. Excel creates the chart and returns to the worksheet with the chart and the Chart toolbar displayed:

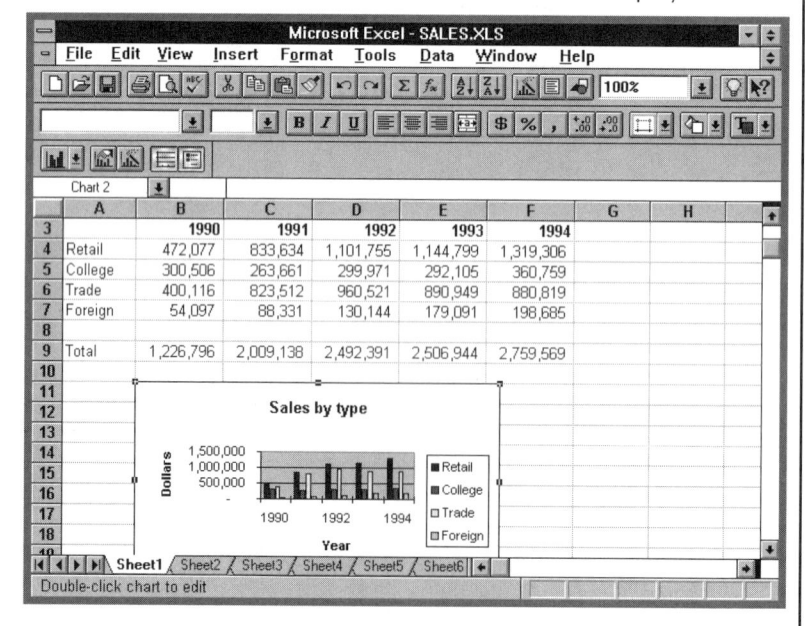

How to create a chart sheet

- Use the procedure above, but start the ChartWizard using the Chart As New Sheet command. When you complete the dialog boxes, Excel places the chart in a new worksheet.

Figure 6-3   How to use the ChartWizard to create a chart (part 3 of 3)

How to select, move, copy, size, and delete a chart

When you first create an embedded chart, it appears in the worksheet with a border and handles around it as shown in the last step in figure 6-3. The handles around a chart indicate that the chart is selected. When a chart is selected, you can move, copy, size, and delete it as described in figure 6-4. You can also use the buttons in the Chart toolbar, which appears automatically when you select a chart. You'll learn how to use this toolbar later in this chapter.

When you create a chart sheet, you usually don't need to move and size it until you print it. You'll learn how to do that later in this chapter. To delete a chart sheet, you just delete it as you would any other worksheet using the techniques presented in chapter 5.

How to select a component or subcomponent in a chart

If you want to modify a component or subcomponent within a chart, you usually start by selecting it. Figure 6-4 shows how to do that. First, you activate the chart. Then, you select a component or subcomponent by clicking on it.

Additional information

✓ When you activate an embedded chart that's too large to be displayed in the workbook window, the chart is displayed in a new window on top of the workbook window.

✓ To cancel a selection, you can select another component, press the Esc key, or click outside the chart.

The Sales chart after it has been enlarged so you can see all the categories (years) and so the y-axis scale is expanded

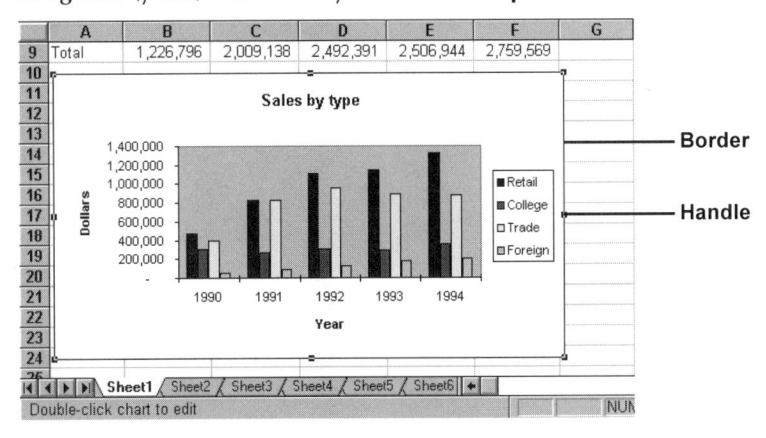

How to select, move, copy, size, and delete a chart

- To select an embedded chart, click inside its border. Then, handles appear around it and the Chart toolbar appears (see figure 6-7).

- To move an embedded chart, place the mouse pointer inside the chart border so it turns into an arrow and drag the chart. To copy an embedded chart, hold down the Ctrl key as you drag.

- To change the size of an embedded chart, place the mouse pointer over a handle so it turns into a double-headed arrow and drag the handle. When you drag a corner handle, you can hold down the Shift key to maintain the same proportion of height to width.

- To delete an embedded chart, select it, then press the Delete key or choose the Clear command from the Edit or shortcut menu. To delete a chart sheet, choose the Delete Sheet command from the Edit menu.

- Although you can select, move, and size a chart sheet too, you normally do that for printing only. See figure 6-16 for details.

How to activate a chart and select a component or subcomponent

- To activate a chart, double-click on an embedded chart or switch to a chart sheet. Then, a thick border and handles appear around an embedded chart as shown in figure 6-5. The Insert and Format menus also change as shown in figure 6-8.

- To select a component in an activated chart, click on it. Then, a border and handles appear around it as illustrated by the title in the chart in figure 6-5. If a component contains subcomponents like the legend, you can then click on a subcomponent to select it.

Figure 6-4   How to select, move, copy, size, and delete a chart and how to select its components and subcomponents

How to move, size, delete, or format a selected component

Once you select a component or subcomponent, you can use the techniques in figure 6-5 to move, size, or delete it. Note, however, that you can't move and size all types of components.

The quickest way to format a selected component or subcomponent is to use the Formatting toolbar. If, for example, you want to enlarge the title of a chart, you can select it, drop down the font list from the Formatting toolbar, and choose a larger font size. Just as easily, you can use the toolbar to change the font, font attributes, font color, or background color of the component. For most charts, this works so well that you shouldn't have to use any of the other formatting techniques.

If you're working with a pie chart, you can use the last technique in figure 6-5 to create a special type of pie chart called an *exploded pie chart*. To do that, you just drag one or more slices of the pie away from the center of the pie. You'll see how easy this is when you do exercise set 6-2.

The activated Sales chart with the title selected and the Font Size list displayed

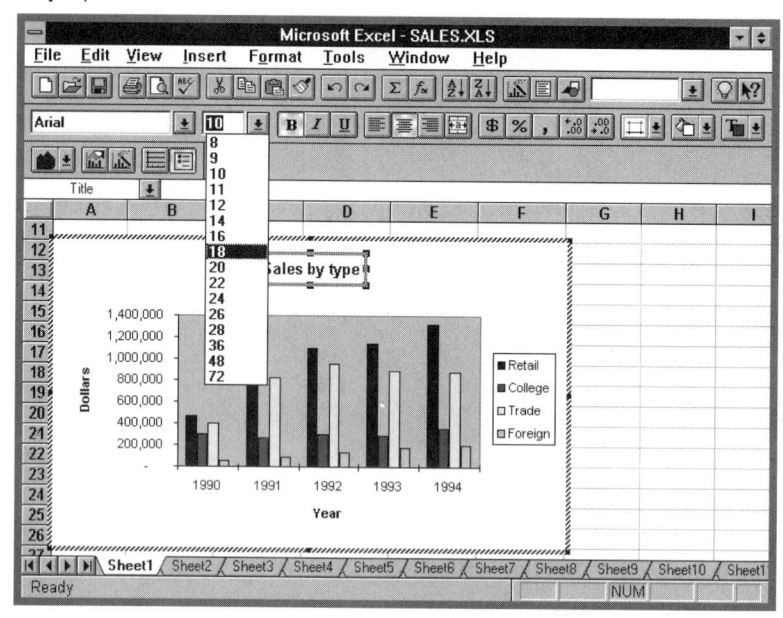

How to move, size, or delete a selected component

- To move a component, place the mouse pointer inside its border and drag. Or, for some components, drag on the border. The mouse pointer must be in the shape of an arrow to drag.

- To size a component, place the mouse pointer over a handle so it turns into a double-headed arrow and drag. You can't size all components.

- To delete a selected component or subcomponent, press the Delete key or choose the Clear command from the Edit or shortcut menu.

How to use the Formatting toolbar to format a selected component

- To format a component that contains text (like the title or legend), you can use the toolbar buttons for changing font, font size, font attribute, font color, and background color.

- To format a component that contains numbers (like the scale on the y-axis), you can also use the buttons for number styles.

- To format an area (like a plot), you can use the Color button to change the color, but you can't use the Border button.

How to create an exploded pie chart

- When you create a pie chart, you can "explode" the slices by dragging them away from the center of the pie. To explode all of the slices at one time, select the pie and drag any slice. To explode a single slice, select the slice after selecting the pie, then drag the slice.

Figure 6-5   How to move, size, delete, or format the components and subcomponents of a chart

How to change a chart by changing its data

When you create a chart, Excel maintains a link between the chart and the data that it's based on. That way, any change you make to the worksheet data is reflected in the chart as shown in figure 6-6. If you compare the worksheet data in this figure with the data in figure 6-2, you'll see that the name of the last data series was changed and the 1994 sales values were increased. This is reflected in the chart legend, the height of the data markers, and the y-axis scale.

How to set up and print charts

When you print a worksheet that includes an embedded chart, the chart is printed along with the worksheet. Then, the page setup for the worksheet applies to the chart too.

When you activate an embedded chart, though, you can print just the chart by choosing the Selected Chart option in the Print dialog box. By default, the chart is printed with a header that contains the sheet and chart name and a footer that contains the page number. To change these defaults, you can use the Page Setup command when the chart is activated. Similarly, you can change the default header and footer for a chart sheet by using the Page Setup command whenever the chart sheet is active.

By default, an activated chart in a worksheet or a chart in a chart sheet are both printed so they fill the full page. You can change that, though, by using the Page Setup command as shown in figure 6-16.

The Sales worksheet and chart after the worksheet data for 1994 and the name of the last category were changed

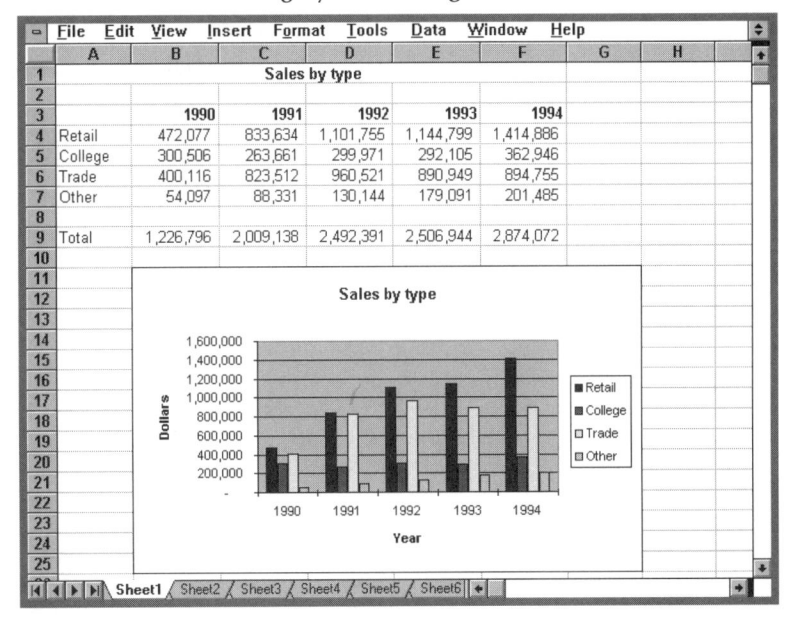

	1990	1991	1992	1993	1994
Retail	472,077	833,634	1,101,755	1,144,799	1,414,886
College	300,506	263,661	299,971	292,105	362,946
Trade	400,116	823,512	960,521	890,949	894,755
Other	54,097	88,331	130,144	179,091	201,485
Total	1,226,796	2,009,138	2,492,391	2,506,944	2,874,072

Operation

To change a chart by changing its data, just enter the new data in the worksheet that the chart is based on. The chart is immediately changed to reflect the changes in the data.

Figure 6-6 How to change a chart by changing its data

Exercise set 6-1

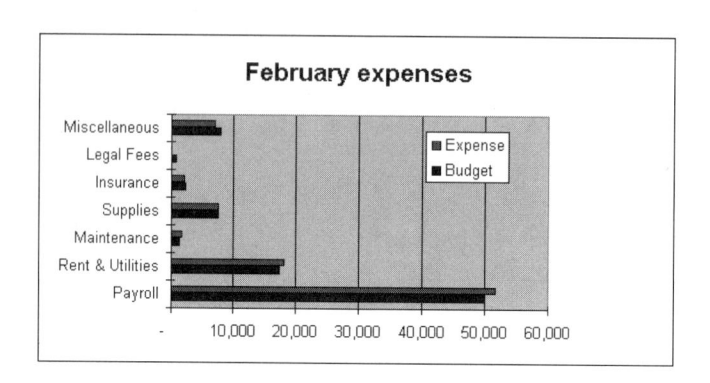

How the bar chart should look after exercise 5

1. Open the FEBEXP workbook that you modified for chapter 3. Select the range from A4 to C11, then click on the ChartWizard button in the Standard toolbar to create an embedded chart from the selected range. When the chart pointer appears, click in cell A20 so the chart will be embedded below the worksheet data. When the first ChartWizard dialog box appears, verify the range, then click on the Next button. In the second ChartWizard dialog box, choose the Bar chart type and click on the Next button. In the third dialog box, accept the default format (6) by clicking on the Next button. In the fourth dialog box, make sure that the Columns option is selected and that one row and one column is used for the headings. Then, click on the Next button. In the fifth dialog box, make sure that a legend is included. Then, enter "February expenses" for the chart title and click on the Finish button. The chart will be inserted into your worksheet, but it will not be in a very readable format. Notice that the Chart toolbar appears and the chart is selected.

2. Place the mouse pointer over the handle in the lower right corner of the chart and drag it until the values along the y-axis are in increments of 10,000 and all of the categories appear along the x-axis (the x-axis is the vertical axis in a bar chart).

3. Double-click on the chart to activate it. Then, click inside the plot area to select it. (Be sure you click on the plot area and not on a gridline, a data marker, or an axis.) Now, drag the handle on the right side of the plot area so the plot area overlaps the legend. Then, select the legend and drag inside its border to move the legend near the upper right corner of the plot area.

4. With the chart still activated, select the title and use the Font Size list in the toolbar to change the font size to 16 points. Next, select the legend and change its font size to 10 points. If necessary, enlarge the entire chart again so all the categories still appear on the x-axis.

5. Click on the x-axis or the category names to select them. Because you can't change this text, the selection isn't shown the same way that it is for the title and legend. You can still format the text, though, so change the font size to 10. Then, use the same procedure to change the font size for the values of the y-axis to 10. If necessary, enlarge the chart again to accommodate the increased font sizes. The chart should now look like the one above.

6. With the worksheet still active, access the Print dialog box. Notice that the default is to print the selected chart. Next, click on the Page Setup button and then on the Header/Footer tab to see what the default header and footer are going to be. Select "none" for the header and "none" for the footer, click on the OK button to return to the Print dialog box, and print the chart.

7. Click outside the chart to de-activate it and print the worksheet including both the data and the chart. Then, save the workbook but don't close it.

8. Change the text in cell A5 from "Salaries & Wages" to "Payroll," and change the number in cell C5 from 51,784 to 65,000. Scroll back to the chart. Are the changes you just made reflected in the chart?

9. Activate the chart again. Next, click on the title to select it, use the Font Color button or palette in the Formatting toolbar to change the font color, and use the Color button or palette to change the background color. Then, select one of the budget bars (which selects all of them), and use the Color button or palette to change the color of those bars. These are the kinds of changes that usually aren't worth taking the time to make. Now, close the workbook without saving the changes.

Exercise set 6-2

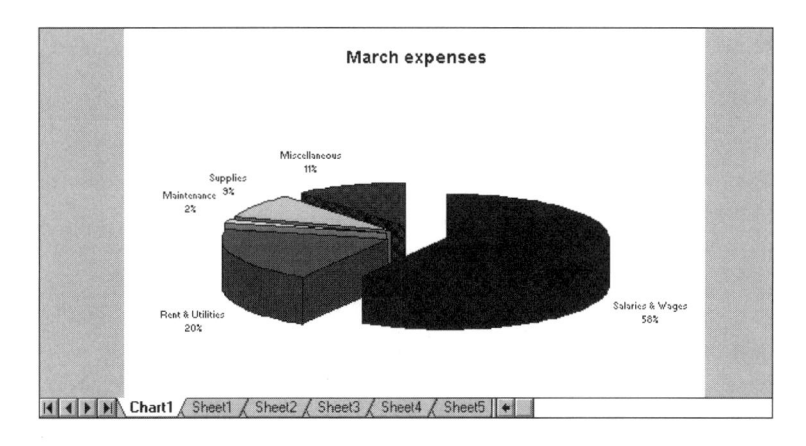

How the pie chart should look after exercise 4

To give you practice creating other types of charts, this exercise set has you create the chart sheet shown above. This chart sheet contains a pie chart that's created from the expense data in the MAREXP worksheet that you created for chapter 1. The exercises that follow guide you through the creation of this chart.

1. Open the MAREXP workbook. Notice that the data you need to create the chart above is in columns A and C. To select this data, you can make a nonadjacent selection that consists of cells A6 through A10 and C6 through C10. To do that, hold down the Ctrl key while you select the cells. The other alternative is to hide column B, then select cells A6 through C10. For this exercise, use the first method to select the cells.

2. Choose the Chart As New Sheet command from the Insert menu to start the ChartWizard. Verify the range in the first dialog box, and choose the 3-D Pie option from the second dialog box. Notice in the third dialog box that the options include the types of labels that are included in the chart and whether or not the slices of the pie are exploded. Accept the default, which will include both the category labels and percentages in the chart. Accept the defaults in the fourth dialog box. In the fifth dialog box, notice that a legend is not included in the chart. That's the default for a pie chart since it contains a single data series. Enter the chart title "March expenses" and click on the Finish button. The chart will be placed in a new worksheet named Chart1, and that worksheet will be displayed along with the Chart toolbar.

3. Click anywhere on the pie to select it. Then, place the mouse pointer over a handle on any one of the slices and drag the slice outward to "explode" the pie as illustrated in the chart above.

4. Select the title and increase its font size to 20. Then, select one of the descriptions of the pie slices and increase its font size to 12. Note that this increases the font size for all the descriptions. The chart should now look like the one above.

5. Issue the Print command to print the worksheet that contains the chart. Note the default header and footer on this chart. You can use the Page Setup command to change this header and footer just as you can for any worksheet. Now, save the workbook, but don't close it.

6. Click on the ChartWizard button in the toolbar so you can change the range that's used in the chart. When the dialog box for step 1 appears, press the Delete key to delete the range in the Range box. Then, use the mouse to select cells A6 through B10, so the budget values will be charted instead of the expense values, and click on the Finish button. This returns you to the chart sheet with the new values charted, and this shows how easy it is to change the ranges of a chart. You can also add ranges to a chart in this way. Now, close the file without saving the changes.

Other skills for working with charts

What you've learned so far in this chapter may be all you'll ever need to know about creating charts from the data in your worksheets. If you've done the exercises, you know that ChartWizard makes it easy to create the first version of a chart. After that, it's easy to format the selected components in the chart by using the Formatting toolbar.

Even so, the rest of this chapter presents some other skills that you ought to be aware of. Many of these skills help you change the features of a chart after you've created it. The alternative is often to recreate the chart from scratch, which isn't always efficient.

Most of these other commands and features are available from the Chart toolbar shown in figure 6-7 and the Insert and Format menus shown in figure 6-8. Although you won't learn how to use all of these buttons and commands in this chapter, you will learn how to use the most useful ones.

The Chart toolbar

Button	Name	Description
	Chart Type	Lets you change the type of the selected chart. See figure 6-9 for details.
	Default Chart	Changes the selected chart to the default chart format. The default format is a column chart with a legend and some basic formatting.
	ChartWizard	Starts the ChartWizard so you can modify the selected chart.
	Horizontal Gridlines	Adds or removes horizontal gridlines from the selected chart. See figure 6-14 for details.
	Legend	Adds or removes the legend from the selected chart. See figure 6-13 for details.

Note

By default, the Chart toolbar appears whenever a chart is selected or activated. If you don't want this toolbar displayed, select or activate a chart, then hide the toolbar using the shortcut menu or the Toolbar command in the View menu.

Figure 6-7 The Chart toolbar

Additional information

✓ Many of the commands in the Insert and Format menu are available from shortcut menus. To access a shortcut menu for an item, select the item and click the right mouse button on it.

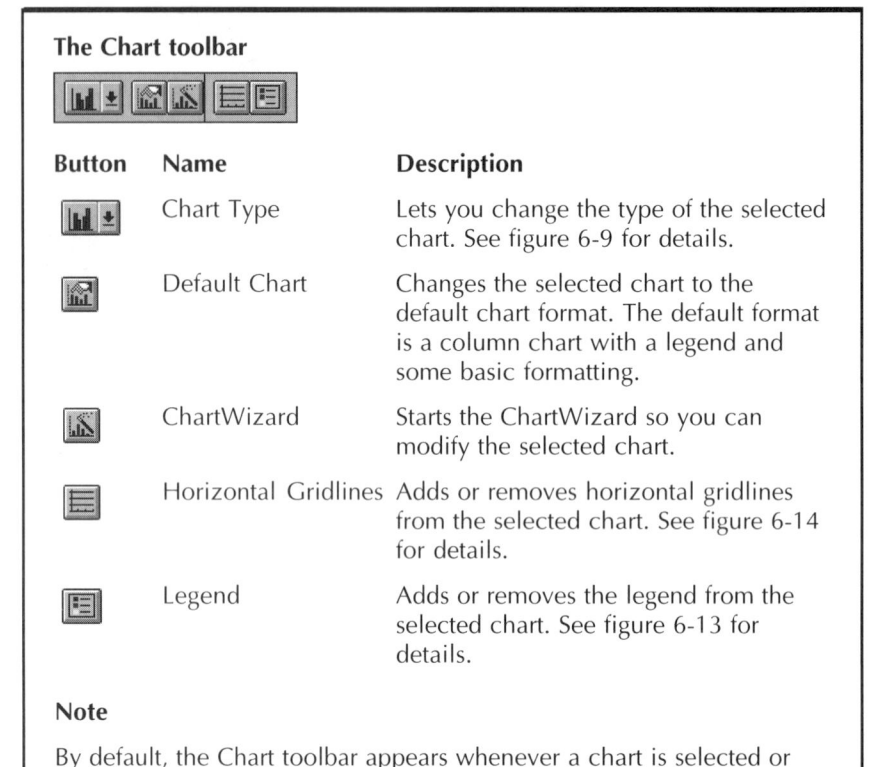

How to create charts

The Format menu

```
Selected Legend... Ctrl+1
Sheet                     ▶
Chart Type...
AutoFormat...
3-D View...
Placement                 ▶
1 Column Group...
```

The Insert menu and the Chart submenu

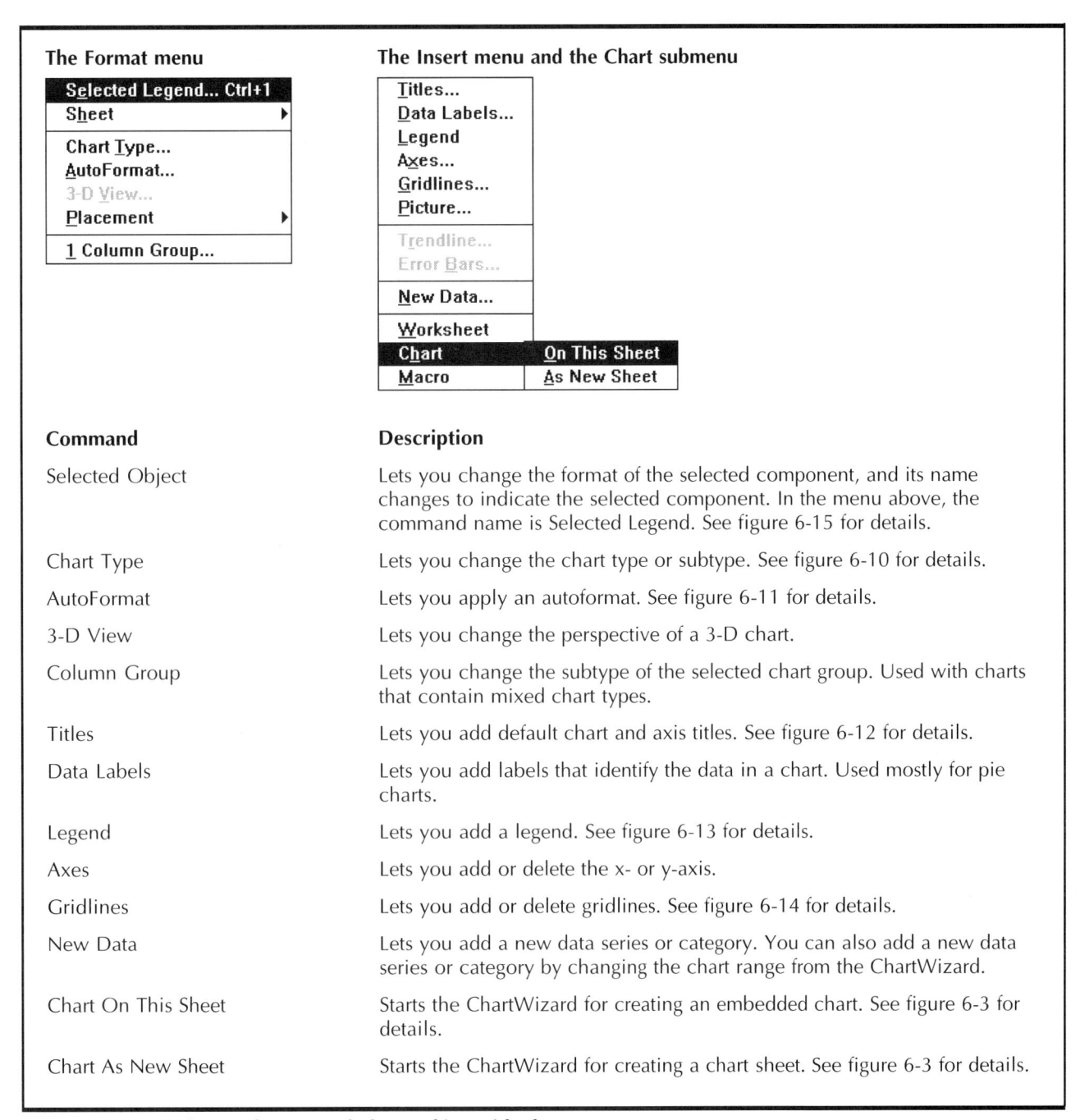

```
Titles...
Data Labels...
Legend
Axes...
Gridlines...
Picture...
Trendline...
Error Bars...
New Data...
Worksheet
Chart          │  On This Sheet
Macro          │  As New Sheet
```

Command	Description
Selected Object	Lets you change the format of the selected component, and its name changes to indicate the selected component. In the menu above, the command name is Selected Legend. See figure 6-15 for details.
Chart Type	Lets you change the chart type or subtype. See figure 6-10 for details.
AutoFormat	Lets you apply an autoformat. See figure 6-11 for details.
3-D View	Lets you change the perspective of a 3-D chart.
Column Group	Lets you change the subtype of the selected chart group. Used with charts that contain mixed chart types.
Titles	Lets you add default chart and axis titles. See figure 6-12 for details.
Data Labels	Lets you add labels that identify the data in a chart. Used mostly for pie charts.
Legend	Lets you add a legend. See figure 6-13 for details.
Axes	Lets you add or delete the x- or y-axis.
Gridlines	Lets you add or delete gridlines. See figure 6-14 for details.
New Data	Lets you add a new data series or category. You can also add a new data series or category by changing the chart range from the ChartWizard.
Chart On This Sheet	Starts the ChartWizard for creating an embedded chart. See figure 6-3 for details.
Chart As New Sheet	Starts the ChartWizard for creating a chart sheet. See figure 6-3 for details.

Figure 6-8   The Excel commands for working with charts

How to change the chart type, subtype, or format

When you create a chart using the ChartWizard, you choose a chart type and a chart format. Actually, the chart format you choose is a combination of a chart subtype and format. For example, if you choose a stacked column chart, that's a subtype of a column chart. And if you choose a chart with gridlines, the gridlines are part of the chart's format.

If you want to change only the chart type, you can use the Chart Type button in the Chart toolbar as illustrated in figure 6-9. To apply the chart type shown on the face of the button, just click on the button. To apply another chart type, pull down the Chart Type palette and click on the type you want.

The Chart Type palette that drops down from the Chart toolbar

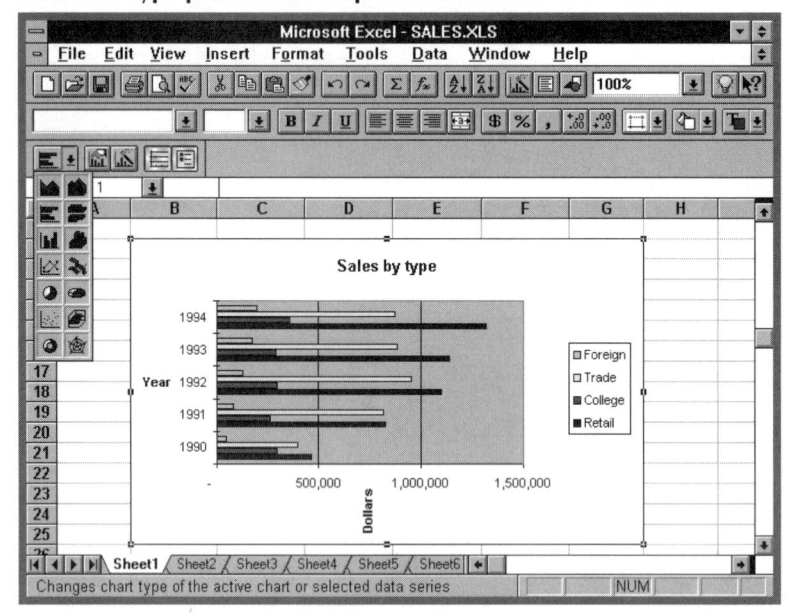

How to change the chart type of a selected chart

- To change the chart to the type indicated by the picture on the Chart Type button, click on the button.

- To change the chart to a type other than the one shown on the Chart Type button, click on the arrow on the right side of the button to drop down the Chart Type palette, then choose a type from the palette.

Note

- To keep the Chart Type palette open, drag it off the toolbar. To return the palette to the toolbar, click on its close box in the upper left corner.

Figure 6-9 How to change the chart type using the Chart Type button

If you want to change a chart's subtype as well as its type, you can use the Chart Type command presented in figure 6-10. Notice that the chart types in the Chart Type dialog box are separated into two groups: 2-D and 3-D. You can switch between the groups by choosing the appropriate option. Then, once you choose a chart type, you can display the Subtype tab of the Format Column Group dialog box to choose a chart subtype.

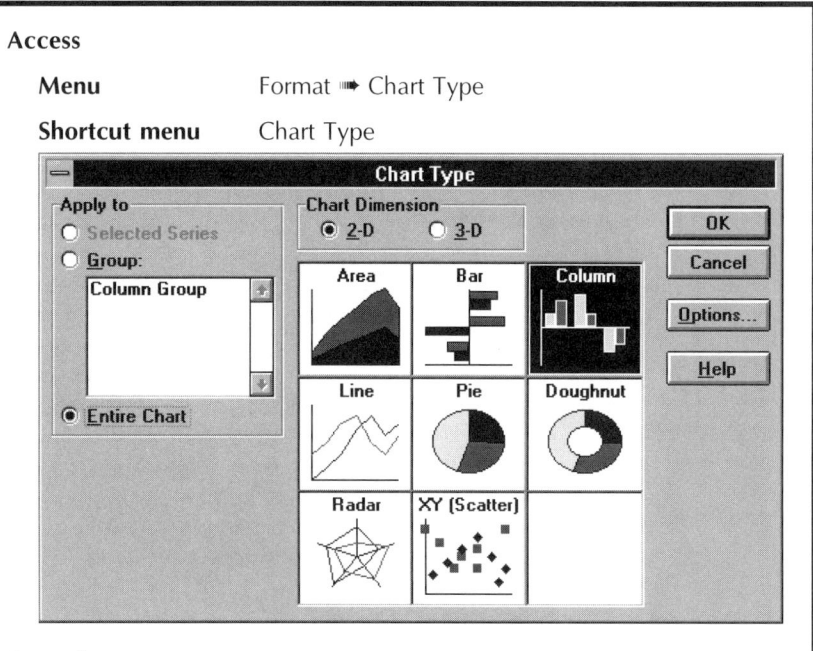

Access

Menu   Format ➠ Chart Type

Shortcut menu   Chart Type

Procedure

1. Activate the chart and access the Chart Type dialog box.

2. Choose an option from the Chart Dimension group, then choose a chart type from the available options.

3. Click on the OK button to change the chart type. Or, to change the chart subtype, click on the Options button and then on the Subtype tab to display this dialog box:

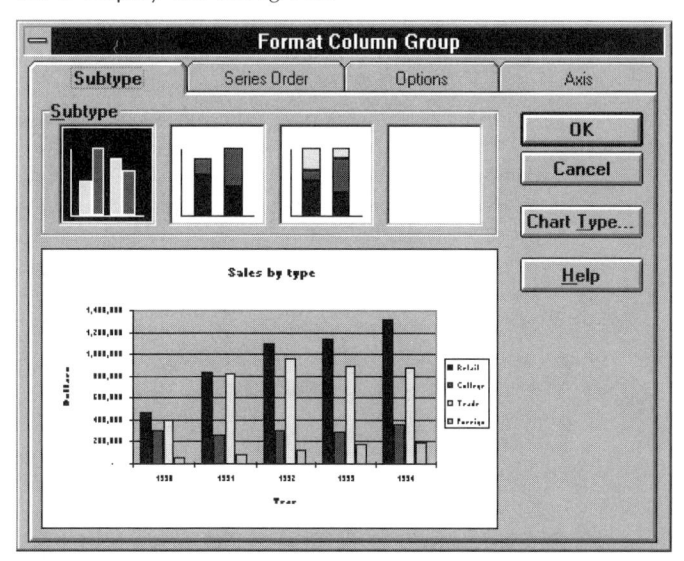

4. Choose an option from the Subtype group and click on the OK button.

Figure 6-10   How to change the chart type and subtype using the Chart Type command

If you want to change a chart's type, subtype, and format all at once, you can apply an *autoformat* to the chart. Figure 6-11 shows how to do that. Note that the chart types and formats that are available in the AutoFormat dialog box are the same as those that are available when you create a chart with the ChartWizard. So if you choose the right chart type and format when you create a chart, you won't need to use the AutoFormat feature.

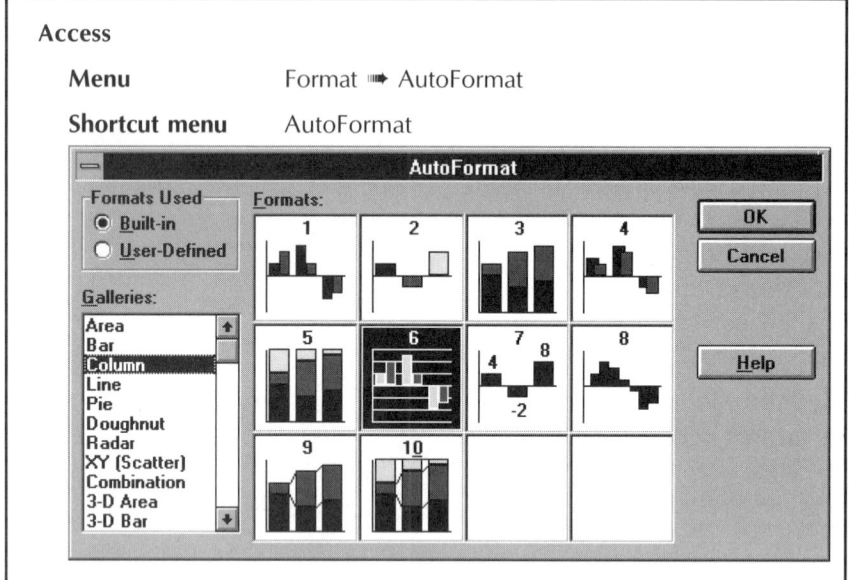

Access

Menu   Format → AutoFormat
Shortcut menu   AutoFormat

Procedure

1. Activate the chart you want to apply the autoformat to and access the AutoFormat dialog box.

2. Choose a chart type from the Galleries list, and the available formats for that chart type are displayed.

3. Click on one of the formats, then click on the OK button to apply the format to the active chart.

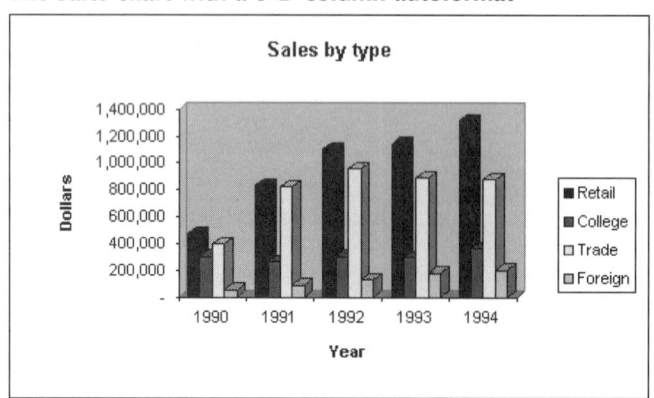

The Sales chart with a 3-D column autoformat

Note

- You can also create or apply custom autoformats by choosing the User-Defined option in the AutoFormat dialog box.

Figure 6-11   How to apply an autoformat to a chart

How to add or change chart and axis titles

Figure 6-12 presents two procedures for working with chart and axis titles. The first procedure shows how to add a chart or axis title using the Titles command. When you use this command, Excel adds default titles. For example, the default for a chart title is "Title" as shown in the figure.

After you add a default title, you can use the second procedure in figure 6-12 to change the title. You can also use this procedure to change the title that you entered when you created the chart. This procedure is particularly useful for entering titles that consist of two or more lines, since you can only enter a title on a single line from the ChartWizard.

How to add chart and axis titles

1. Activate the chart, then choose the Titles command from the Insert menu or the Insert Titles command from the shortcut menu to display this dialog box:

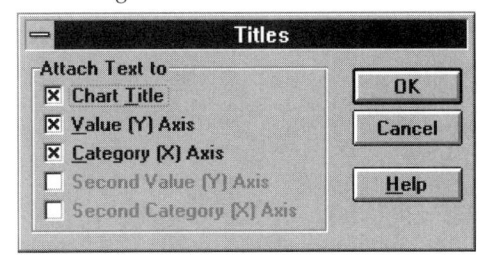

2. Choose the options for the titles you want to add. Then, click on the OK button and Excel adds default titles:

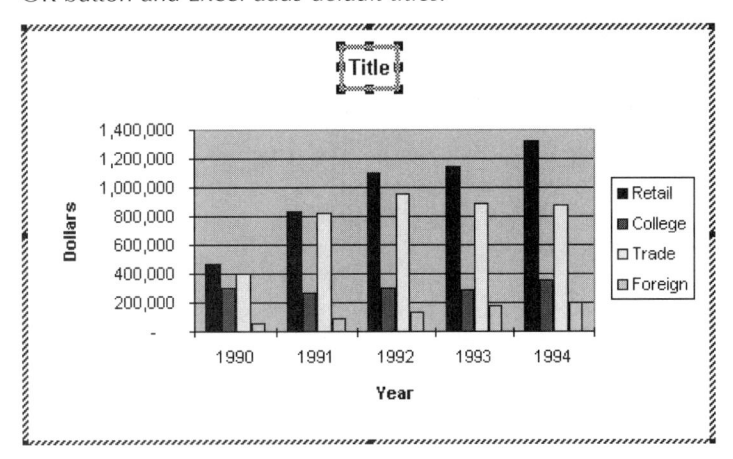

How to change chart and axis titles

1. Select the title you want to change and a border appears around it. Click inside the border and an insertion point appears. Edit the text:

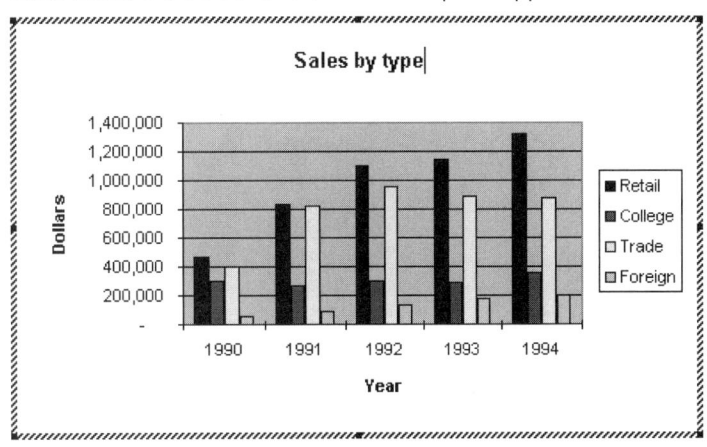

2. Click outside the title to complete the entry.

Figure 6-12 How to add or change chart and axis titles

How to add or delete a legend

Figure 6-13 shows two ways to add a legend to a chart. The easiest way is to click on the Legend button in the Chart toolbar. If you click on this button when a chart that already contains a legend is selected, the legend is deleted.

When you add a legend using either of the techniques in figure 6-13, Excel uses default descriptions for the data series unless you included the descriptions in the range you selected when you created the chart. As you can see in the chart in figure 6-13, the default descriptions aren't much use. When you create a chart, then, it's a good idea to include the cells that contain the descriptions of the data series even if you don't intend to include a legend. That way, the descriptions are available if you decide to add a legend later on.

How to issue the Legend command

Menu	Insert ➝ Legend
Chart toolbar	

Operation

- You can use either the Legend command or button to add a legend to a chart. You can also use the Legend button to delete a legend.

- If you selected the cells that describe the data series when you created the chart, Excel uses these descriptions in the legend. Otherwise, Excel uses default legend entries as shown below.

A chart with default legend entries

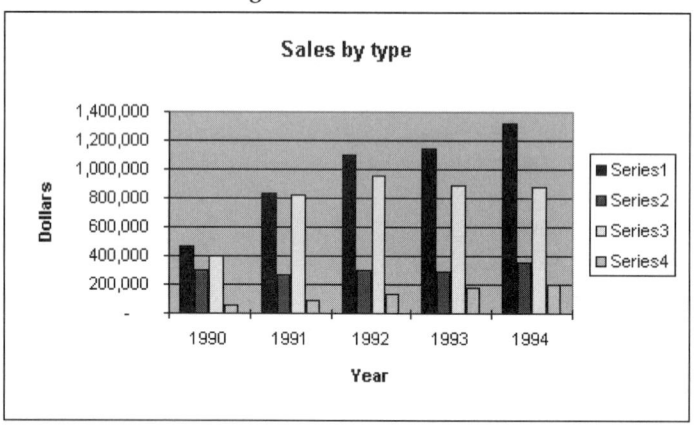

Figure 6-13   How to add or delete a legend

How to add or delete gridlines

To add gridlines to a chart, you can use one of the techniques in figure 6-14. If you need gridlines at all, the horizontal gridlines at each value on the y-axis are usually enough. The easiest way to add these gridlines is to click on the Horizontal Gridlines button in the Chart toolbar. If you want to add vertical gridlines or gridlines at more frequent intervals, you can use the Gridlines dialog box as described in the figure.

How to issue the Gridlines command

Menu	Insert → Gridlines
Shortcut menu	Insert Gridlines
Chart toolbar	🗐

Operation

- If you issue the Gridlines command from the Insert menu or the Insert Gridlines command from the shortcut menu, this dialog box appears:

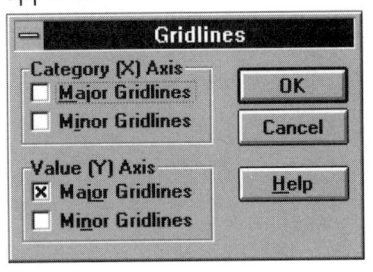

  To display gridlines between categories, choose the Major Gridlines option in the Category (X) Axis group. To display additional gridlines between the major gridlines, choose the Minor Gridlines option in that group. To display gridlines for the values on the y-axis, choose the Major Gridlines option in the Value (Y) Axis group. To display additional gridlines between the major gridlines, choose the Minor Gridlines option in that group.

- If you click on the Gridlines button, horizontal gridlines are added or deleted for the values on the y-axis.

A chart with horizontal and vertical gridlines

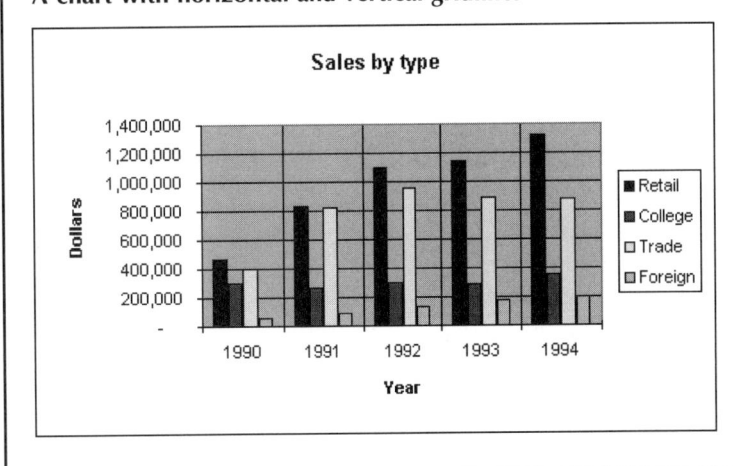

Figure 6-14 How to add or delete gridlines

How to use the Format command to format a chart

If you want to fine tune the appearance of a chart, you can use the Format Selected Object command as described in figure 6-15. This command lets you do types of formatting that can't be done with the Formatting toolbar. When you use this command, you'll notice that the actual command name changes depending on what's selected in the chart. If the legend is selected, for example, the command is Selected Legend. And if the chart title is selected, the command is Selected Chart Title.

The dialog box that's displayed when you choose this command also depends on what's selected in the chart. The first dialog box in figure 6-15 is displayed when the chart title is selected. The second one is displayed when the y-axis is selected.

The only Format dialog boxes that are likely to be confusing are the ones for the axes. These dialog boxes let you change the location of the *tick marks* on the axes (the small lines that cross the axes at given intervals) and the scales on the axis. Although you're not likely to want to change the tick marks or the scale on the x-axis, you may want to change the y-axis scale. You'll get a chance to do that in one of the exercises that follow.

How to access the Format dialog box for a selected item

Menu	Format ➠ Selected Object
Shortcut menu	Format
Shortcut key	Ctrl+1
Other	Double-click on the item you want to format

The dialog box for the Format Selected Chart Title command

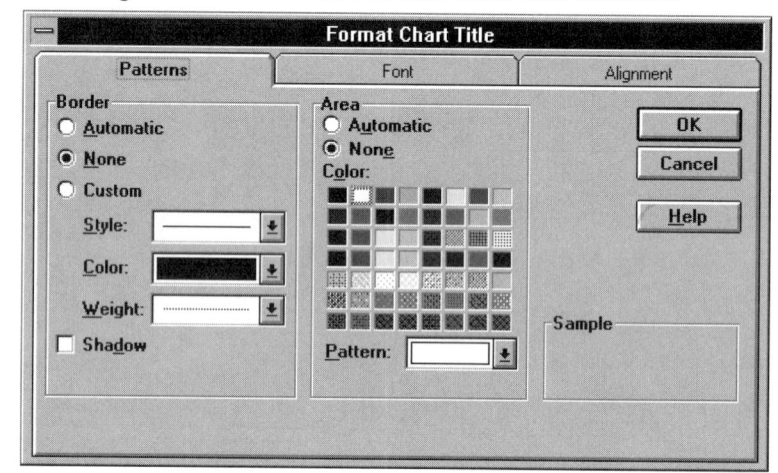

The dialog box for the Format Selected Axis command

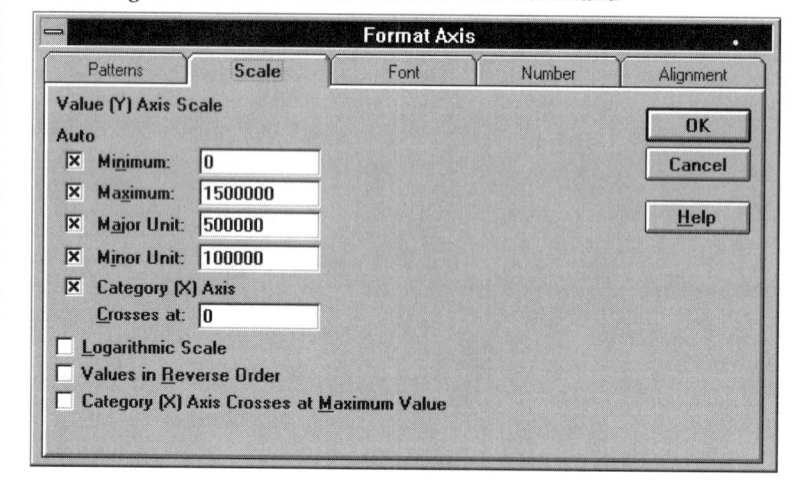

Notes

- The Selected Object command in the Format menu and the Format command in the shortcut menu change depending on the item that's selected.

- You can change the default colors used in all the charts in a workbook from the Color tab of the Options dialog box. To display this dialog box, choose the Options command from the Tools menu.

Figure 6-15 How to change the format of selected objects

How to size a chart for printing

By default, Excel prints a chart sheet or an embedded chart that has been activated so the chart fills the entire page. If you want to print a chart in a different size, though, you can use the Chart tab of the Page Setup command as described in figure 6-16.

When you use the Page Setup command, you can change the size of a chart sheet in one of two ways. First, you can size the chart to fit on the page by choosing the Scale to Fit Page option. When you do that, Excel maintains the proportions of the chart. Second, you can size and position the chart on the screen any way you like, and Excel will print the chart exactly as it appears. To do that, you choose the Custom option.

If you choose the Custom option for a chart sheet, a border with handles appears around the chart as shown in this figure. Then, you can use the borders and handles to move and size the chart just as you do an embedded chart.

Access

Menu File ➡ Page Setup

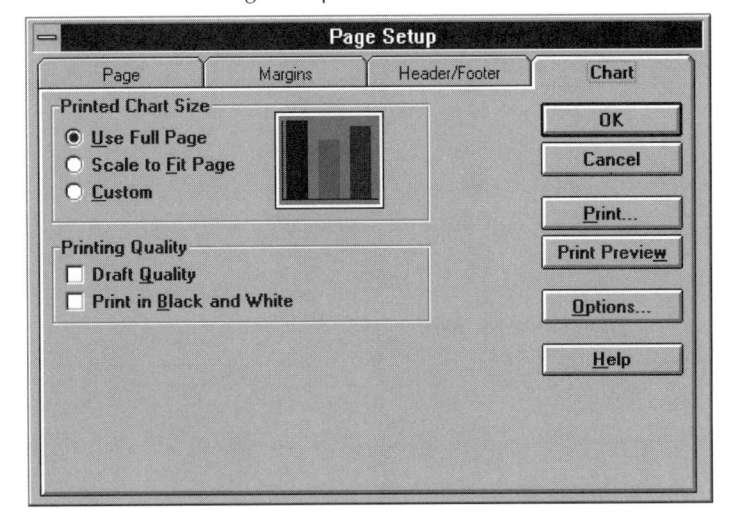

Operation

- Activate the embedded chart or chart sheet, and access the Page Setup dialog box.
- To print the chart so that it fills the entire page, choose the Use Full Page option.
- To print the chart so that it fits on the page and keeps the same proportions as on the screen, choose the Scale To Fit Page option.
- To print a chart so that it is sized and positioned as it appears on the screen, choose the Custom option. When you use this option for a chart sheet, a border appears around it that lets you move and size it:

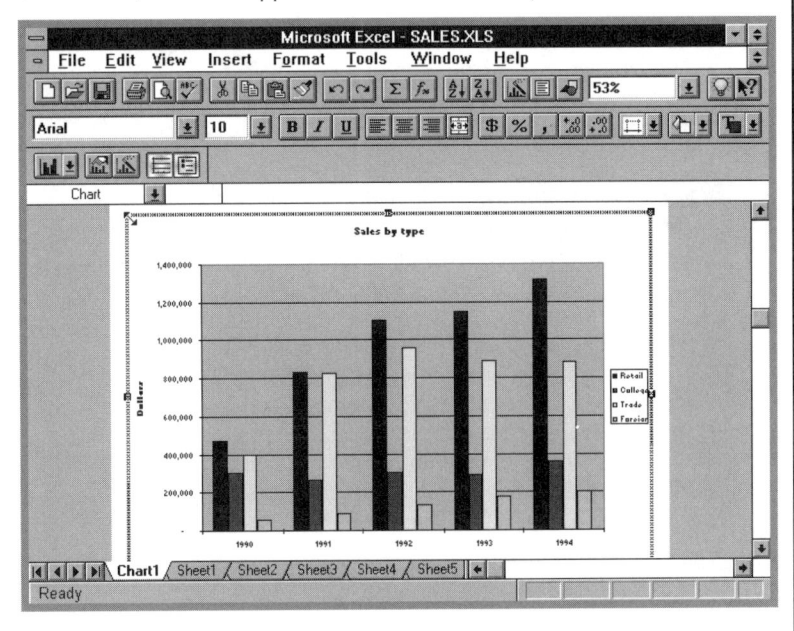

Figure 6-16 How to size a chart for printing

Exercise set 6-3

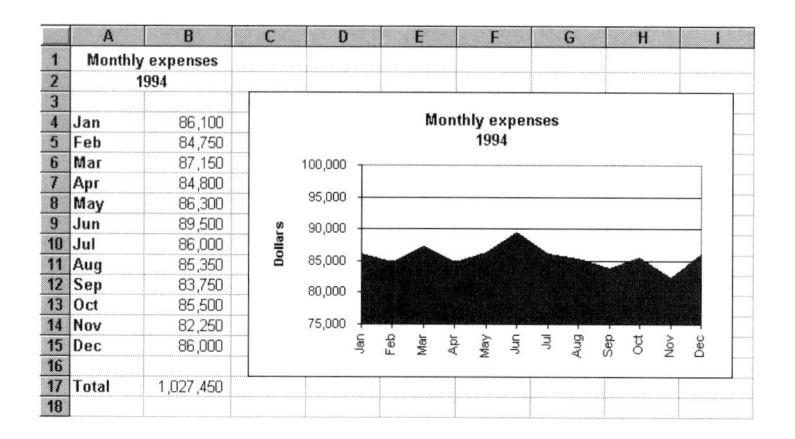

How the worksheet and area chart should look after exercise 7

	A	B
1	Monthly expenses	
2	1994	
3		
4	Jan	86,100
5	Feb	84,750
6	Mar	87,150
7	Apr	84,800
8	May	86,300
9	Jun	89,500
10	Jul	86,000
11	Aug	85,350
12	Sep	83,750
13	Oct	85,500
14	Nov	82,250
15	Dec	86,000
16		
17	Total	1,027,450

In this exercise set, you'll create the worksheet and chart shown above. As you create the chart, you'll have the chance to experiment with some of the charting commands so you can see how they work. When you're done with this exercise set, you'll have the skills to create most of the charts you'll ever need.

1. Open a new workbook window and enter the data shown in the worksheet above. Then, use the data in cells A4 through B15 and the procedure in figure 6-3 to create an embedded line chart with the default format starting in cell C3. In step 5, don't add a legend, omit the axis titles, and enter "Monthly expenses" as the chart title. Notice that there's no way to enter the year on a separate line as it appears in the chart above. You'll have to do that after you create the chart by editing the title.

2. Enlarge the chart so all the months are displayed along the x-axis and so the values on the y-axis range from 78,000 to 90,000 in increments of 2,000.

3. Use the Chart Type button as described in figure 6-9 to change the chart to a 3-D area chart (the first button in the right column of the palette). Then, activate the chart and access the Chart Type dialog box shown in figure 6-10. Click on the Options button and display the subtypes that are available for that chart type. Click on each of the options to see what happens. Then, cancel the operation. Finally, choose the AutoFormat command from the Format menu and choose the Area option from the Galleries list. Then, choose the format that contains both horizontal and vertical gridlines (4). Click on the OK button to apply the autoformat.

4. Click on the chart title to select it. Then, click inside the title and move the insertion point to the end of the title. Press the Enter key to start a new line, enter the text "1994," and complete the entry by clicking outside the title area.

5. Use the procedure in the top of figure 6-12 to add a default title to the y-axis. Then, change the title to "Dollars" as described in the bottom of figure 6-12. Notice that when you click inside the title to edit it, its orientation changes so the text is horizontal. When you accept the entry by clicking outside the title area, the text changes back to vertical orientation. (When you add the title, Excel reduces the size of the plot area to make room for the title. If the names of the months no longer fit along the x-axis, you'll need to enlarge the chart again so they fit.)

6. Use the Gridlines command as described in figure 6-14 to delete the gridlines from the chart. Then, click on the Horizontal Gridlines button in the Chart toolbar to add the horizontal gridlines back.

7. Click on the y-axis or the y-axis values to select that axis, and pull down the Format menu. Note that the first command is Selected Axis. Click in the chart to close the menu, and double-click on the y-axis or the y-axis values to start the Format Selected Axis command that way. Then, click on the Scale tab in the dialog box that appears, and change the Minimum value to 75000, the Maximum value to 100000, the Major Unit value to 5000, and the Minor Unit value to 1000. Click on the OK button and notice the change in the values on the y-axis. The chart should now look like the one shown above.

8. Select the plot area and pull down the Format menu. Notice that the first command is now Selected Plot Area. Choose that command and note the changes that you can make to the plot area from this dialog box. First, you can change or remove the border of the plot area, which you can't do from the Formatting toolbar. Second, you can select some colors and patterns that aren't available from the toolbar. For most charts, though, you shouldn't need these capabilities, so click on the cancel button to return to the chart.

9. With the chart still activated, access the Page Setup command from the File menu and click on the Chart tab. With the Use Full Page option checked, click on the Print Preview button to see how the chart will print, and click on the Setup button to return to the Page Setup dialog box. Then, check the Scale to Fit Page option, and click on the OK button to return to the Print Preview window. Note the changes to the proportions of the previewed chart, and print the chart.

10. Save the workbook with the name 1994EXP, and close the file.

Perspective

If you've done the exercises in this chapter, you now know how easy it is to create professional looking charts from the data in a worksheet. To prepare most charts, you only need a few minutes with the ChartWizard and the Formatting toolbar. Unless you have some special requirements, you don't even need the Chart toolbar and the Insert and Format menus.

If you do have special requirements, though, you should realize that Excel offers some advanced charting capabilities that haven't been mentioned in this chapter. If you want to get some idea of what they are, you can look through the dialog boxes for the charting commands in the Insert and Format menus. Most of us don't need these advanced capabilities, though, so the more time we spend experimenting with them, the less productive we are.

Summary

- You can use the ChartWizard to create a variety of charts, including *column charts*, *bar charts*, *line charts*, *area charts*, and *pie charts*. Excel provides most charts in 2-D and 3-D formats.

- Each *data point* in a worksheet is plotted as a *data marker* in a chart. Each row or column of data identifies a *category* or a *data series*. The categories are identified in the chart on one of the axes, and the data series are identified in the *legend*.

- You can use the ChartWizard to create an *embedded chart*, which is inserted into the worksheet that contains the data the chart is based on, or a *chart sheet*, which is placed in its own worksheet.

- When a chart is selected, you can move and size it. When a chart is activated, you can also move and size some of its components.

- If you change the data in the worksheet that a chart is based on, the chart is updated automatically.

- You can access many of the commands for working with charts from the Chart toolbar and the Insert and Format menus. The Chart toolbar appears automatically when you select or activate a chart, and the charting commands appear in the menus automatically when you activate a chart.

- After you create a chart, you can change its type, subtype, and format; you can add and change the chart and axis titles; you can add or delete the legend; and you can add or delete gridlines.

- You can change the format of individual chart components by using the Selected Object command in the Format menu.

- You can size a chart so that it prints on one page and keeps the same proportions as on the screen. Or, you can move and size the chart on the screen and print it exactly as it appears. By default, a chart is printed so that it fills the entire page.

Chapter 7

Advanced skills for working with formulas and functions

In chapter 1, you learned the basic skills for entering formulas and functions into a worksheet. In this chapter, you'll learn some advanced skills for creating and editing formulas and functions. You'll also learn how to audit them to make sure that they work right.

General skills for working with formulas and functions
    How to detect circular references
    How to change formulas to values
    How to use dates and times in arithmetic operations
    How to enter a name into a formula or function
    How to replace references with names

When and how to use relative, absolute, or mixed references
    How to create a relative, absolute, or mixed reference
    When to use an absolute or mixed reference

Other skills for working with functions
    An introduction to the types of functions
    How to use two typical financial functions
    How to use the Function Wizard
    How to use shortcut keys as you enter arguments

How to audit a worksheet
    How to display or print a worksheet that shows its formulas
    How to use the Go To Special command

Perspective

Summary

General skills for working with formulas and functions

This topic presents a variety of skills that you may need as you work with formulas and functions. First, you'll learn how to correct a common error, called a circular reference. Next, you'll learn how to change one or more formulas in a worksheet to values. Then, you'll learn how you can use dates and times in arithmetic operations. Finally, you'll learn how you can use names instead of references in formulas and functions.

How to detect circular references

A *circular reference* occurs when a formula refers to the cell that it's in, either directly or indirectly. A simple example of a circular reference is illustrated by the worksheet in figure 7-1. Here, the formula in cell B12 is:

    =SUM(B6:B12)

This is a circular reference because the formula in cell B12 contains a reference to cell B12.

When a circular reference occurs, Excel alerts you to the condition by displaying an error message. Then, it places the value zero in the cell that contains the circular reference and displays *Circular:* followed by the cell reference in the status bar until you correct the circular reference. If you examine the contents of the cell that contains the circular reference, you can usually determine the problem. Then, you edit the cell to remove the circular reference.

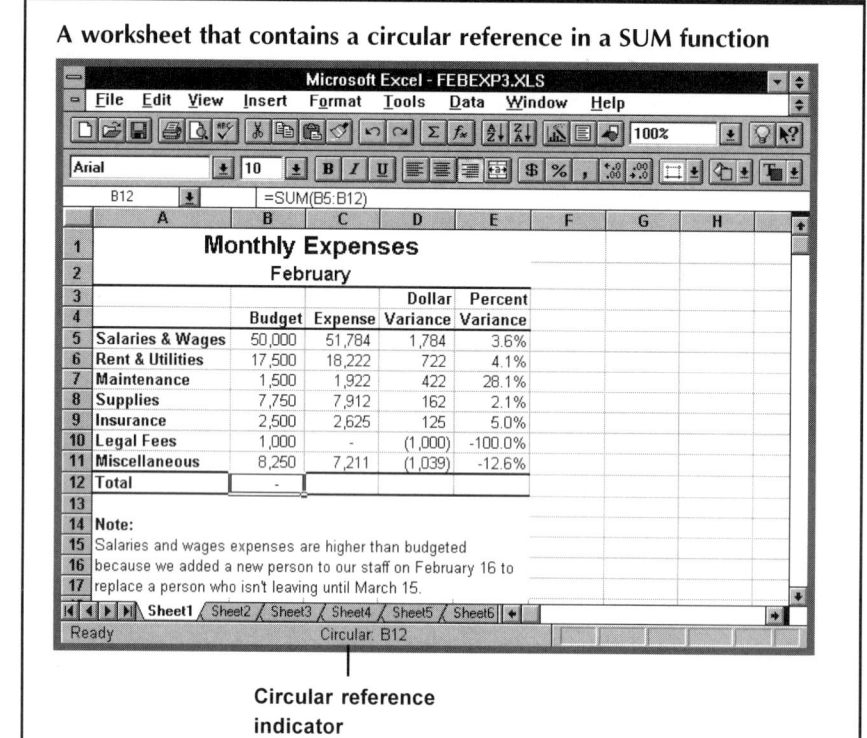

A worksheet that contains a circular reference in a SUM function

Operation

- By default, Excel displays a message when you enter a circular reference that indicates that it cannot solve the reference. When you click on the OK button, the value zero is placed in the cell and a message like the one shown above is displayed in the status bar.

- After you correct the circular reference, the message in the status bar disappears unless there's another circular reference in the worksheet. Then, Excel displays the next circular reference.

Note

- If the Iteration option in the Calculation tab of the Options dialog box is on, Excel tries to solve the circular reference instead of displaying an error message. If it's successful, the calculated value is placed in the cell and the message "Calculate" is displayed in the status bar. Because the calculated value will not be correct, you'll want to edit the cell to correct the formula and turn the Iteration option off. To turn this option off, issue the Options command from the Tools menu, then click on the Calculation tab and remove the check mark from the Iteration option.

Figure 7-1   How to detect circular references

How to change formulas to values

Occasionally, you'll want to convert the formulas in a range to their calculated values. For instance, suppose you created a worksheet that displays total sales calculated by adding values from several columns. Then, if you decide you want to delete the columns that the total sales are calculated from, you must first convert the total sales formulas to values. Otherwise, you'll lose the total sales data.

Figure 7-2 presents two methods for converting formulas to values. First, you can press the F9 (Calc) key while you're editing a cell that contains a formula. Second, you can copy a range that contains formulas to the clipboard and paste the values of the formulas back into the worksheet using the Values option of the Paste Special command. When you use this technique, you can change the formulas in two or more cells to values at the same time.

How to use the F9 (Calc) key

1. Double-click on the cell that contains the formula you want to change, or place the cell pointer on the cell and press the F2 key:

	A	B	C	D	E	F
1		Monthly Expenses				
2		February				
3				Dollar	Percent	
4		Budget	Expense	Variance	Variance	
5	Salaries & Wages	50,000	51,784	1,784	3.6%	
6	Rent & Utilities	17,500	18,222	722	4.1%	
7	Maintenance	1,500	1,922	422	28.1%	
8	Supplies	7,750	7,912	162	2.1%	
9	Insurance	2,500	2,625	125	5.0%	
10	Legal Fees	1,000	-	(1,000)	-100.0%	
11	Miscellaneous	8,250	7,211	(1,039)	-12.6%	
12	Total	88,500		=SUM(D5:D11)	1.3%	
13						

D12: =SUM(D5:D11)

2. Press the F9 (Calc) key and Excel replaces the formula with its calculated value:

	A	B	C	D	E	F
1		Monthly Expenses				
2		February				
3				Dollar	Percent	
4		Budget	Expense	Variance	Variance	
5	Salaries & Wages	50,000	51,784	1,784	3.6%	
6	Rent & Utilities	17,500	18,222	722	4.1%	
7	Maintenance	1,500	1,922	422	28.1%	
8	Supplies	7,750	7,912	162	2.1%	
9	Insurance	2,500	2,625	125	5.0%	
10	Legal Fees	1,000	-	(1,000)	-100.0%	
11	Miscellaneous	8,250	7,211	(1,039)	-12.6%	
12	Total	88,500		1176	1.3%	
13						

D12: 1176

3. Press the Enter key to accept and format the value.

How to use the Paste Special command

1. Select the range that contains the formulas and copy it to the clipboard. With the same range selected, choose the Paste Special command from the Edit or shortcut menu to display this dialog box:

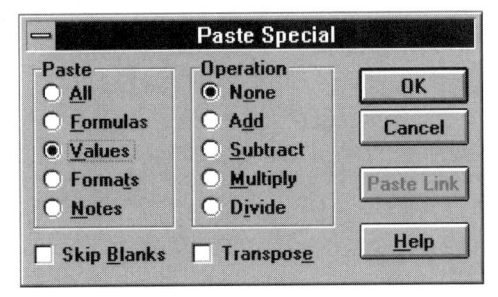

   Paste Special
   - Paste: All / Formulas / **Values** / Formats / Notes
   - Operation: **None** / Add / Subtract / Multiply / Divide
   - Skip Blanks / Transpose
   - OK / Cancel / Paste Link / Help

2. Choose the Values option in the Paste group, then click on the OK button to replace the formulas with their calculated values.

Figure 7-2   Two ways to change formulas to values

How to use dates and times in arithmetic operations

When you enter a date into a worksheet, it's displayed in one of Excel's date formats. However, the date is actually stored as a serial number that represents the number of days that have passed since January 1, 1900. That makes it easy for you to perform arithmetic operations on dates, as illustrated in figure 7-3. You can also perform arithmetic operations on times, which are stored as decimal numbers that represent the fractional portion of the day that has passed since midnight.

Figure 7-3 also shows how to enter a date or time into a formula. The easiest way is to enter the reference for the cell that contains the date or time. (Don't worry about the format of the cell reference in the formula in figure 7-3 for now. You'll learn about the different types of references later in this chapter.) You can also enter a date or time directly into a formula as described in this figure.

If you want to see the serial number or decimal number for a date or time in the worksheet, you can use the last technique in figure 7-3. Just use the Clear Formats command to return the cell that contains the date or time to the General format.

Additional information

✓ You can change the serial numbers for dates so that they represent the number of days that have passed since January 1, 1904 instead of January 1, 1900. To do that, choose the Options command from the Tools menu and click on the Calculation tab. Then, choose the 1904 Date System option.

A worksheet that uses dates to calculate the age of invoices

	A	B	C	D
1	Aged invoice report			
2	4/17/95			
3				
4	Invoice	Invoice	Age	
5	number	date	in days	
6	6274986	1/3/95	104	
7	6275217	1/18/95	89	
8	6275584	2/9/95	67	
9	6275883	2/20/95	56	
10				

C6 =$A$2-B6

How dates and times are stored

- When you enter a date into a cell, it's stored as a serial number that represents the numbers of days that have passed since January 1, 1900. For example, the serial number for 4/17/95 in the example above is 34806, and the serial number for 1/3/95 is 34702. The difference between the two is 104 as shown above.

- When you enter a time into a cell, it's stored as a decimal number that represents the fractional portion of the day that has passed since midnight. For instance, .25 represents 6:00 AM; .5 represents 12:00 noon; and .75 represents 6:00 PM.

Two ways to enter a date or time into a formula

- Enter the reference for the cell that contains the date or time using one of the standard techniques.

- Enter a date or time directly into a formula using a standard date or time format and enclose it in quotation marks. When Excel calculates the formula, it will automatically convert the date or time to a number. For example, to calculate the age of the first invoice above without using the current date in cell A2, you could enter this formula:

    ="4/17/95"-B6

How to display a date or time as a number

- To display a date as a serial number or a time as a decimal number, format the cell that contains the date or time with the General format. The easiest way to do that is by using the Clear Formats command in the Edit menu.

Figure 7-3   How to use dates and times in arithmetic operations

How to enter a name into a formula or function

If you name the ranges in a worksheet as described in chapter 4, you can use those names in formulas instead of using cell references. One way to enter a name into a formula is to type it. However, you can also use the methods shown in figure 7-4 to enter a name into a function.

The first method in figure 7-4 uses the Name box to display a list of the available names. To add a name to the formula, just click on it. The second method uses the Name Paste command to display a dialog box that shows all the available names. When you choose a name from this list, it's added to the formula.

How to use the Name box

1. Enter the formula up to the point where you want to refer to the named range. Then, click on the arrow to the right of the Name box to display a list of the available names:

2. Click on a name, and it's entered into the formula:

How to use the Name Paste command

1. Enter the formula up to the point where you want to refer to the named range. Then, press the F3 (Name) key or choose the Name Paste command from the Insert menu to display this dialog box:

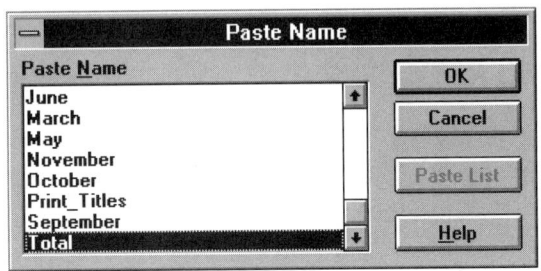

2. Choose the name from the Paste Name list, and click on the OK button to enter the name into the formula.

Figure 7-4 Two ways to enter a name into a formula

How to replace references with names

If you name the ranges in a worksheet after you enter the formulas that refer to those ranges, you may want to change the formulas so they refer to the names instead of the cell references for the ranges. To do that, you use the Name Apply command as illustrated in figure 7-5. When you use this command, the default is to apply the names to all of the formulas in the worksheet. However, if you select a range before you issue the command, the names are applied only to the selected range.

Procedure

1. Choose the Name Apply command from the Insert menu to display this dialog box:

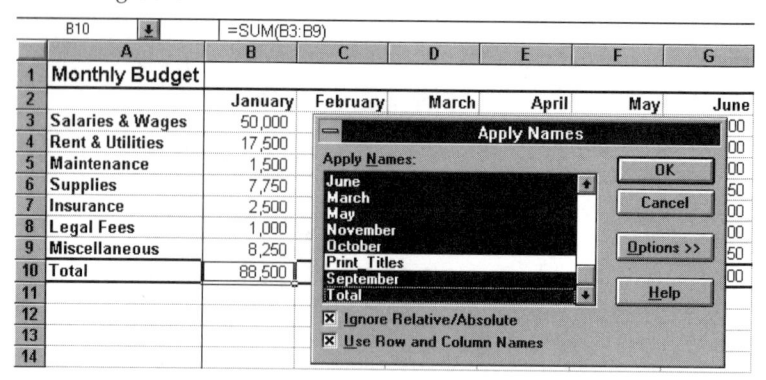

2. Click on any range names in the Apply Names list box that you don't want to use in place of references to remove the highlight from them.

3. Click on the OK button and Excel replaces all references to the named ranges with their names:

Notes

- In some cases, the names aren't highlighted when you access the Apply Names dialog box. Then, you can highlight those you want to apply by clicking on them.

- If you want to replace references with names in only part of the worksheet, select a range before you issue the Name Apply command.

- If you use the methods presented in this book, the two options in the Apply Names dialog box shouldn't affect the application of names so you can leave both options checked.

- Though you probably won't ever want to do this, you can refer to a cell by using the name of a column range that includes the cell and the name of a row range that includes the cell. If, for example, the cells in row 6 above are named Supplies, you can refer to cell D6 as March Supplies or Supplies March (a space separates the row and column names). Or, if the Use Row and Column Names option is checked when you use the Apply Names command and no other name has been given to cell D6, the row and column names are substituted for any uses of that cell reference.

Figure 7-5   How to replace references with names

Exercise set 7-1

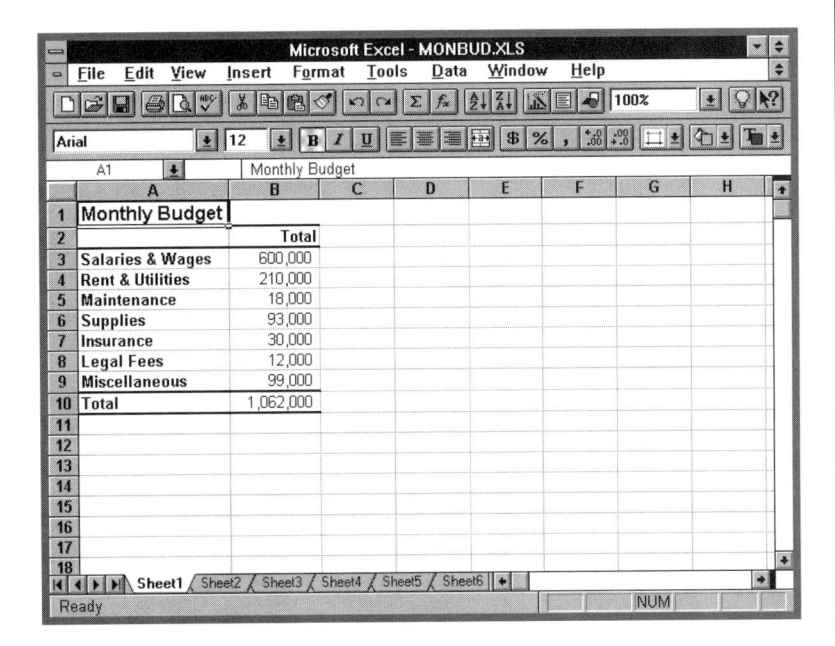

How the MONBUD worksheet should look after you convert the formulas in the Total column to values and delete columns B through M in exercise 2

1. Open the MONBUD workbook you created in chapter 4. Then, change the SUM function in cell B10 so that it includes the range from B3 to B10. Is a message displayed indicating that you've entered a circular reference? If so, click on the OK button to continue. Is the cell that contains the circular reference indicated in the status bar? If not, access the Options command from the Tools menu, click on the Calculation tab, and remove the check mark from the Iteration option. Now is the message displayed? Correct the function so that it doesn't contain a circular reference.

2. Select columns B through M and delete them. What happens to the formulas in the total column? Use the Undo command to reverse the delete operation. Then, edit cell N3 by double-clicking on the cell and pressing F9. What happens? Press the Esc key to cancel the operation. Next, select cells N3 through N9 and copy them to the clipboard. Then, use the Paste Special command to paste the values of those cells back into the cells. Now, delete columns B through M again. Are the values in the total column still there? Use the Undo command to reverse the delete operation.

3. Open a new workbook and enter the current date in cell A1 with an acceptable date format. Then, enter the date for the first day of the previous month in cell A2. Move the cell pointer to cell A3 and enter this function:

    =A1-A2

    What is the result? Select cells A1 and A2 and issue the Clear Formats command from the Edit menu to change the dates to their serial numbers. Does the value in cell A3 change? Close the new workbook without saving it.

4. Delete the contents of cell B10 in the MONBUD worksheet. Then, click on the AutoSum button to start a SUM function. Now, display the Name list and click on January to enter that name into the formula. Press the Enter key. Is the value that's displayed correct? Repeat this exercise for cell C10, but this time use the Name Paste command to enter the name February into the formula. Which technique do you like best?

5. Use the Name Apply command as described in figure 7-5 to replace the ranges in the formulas in cells C10 through M10 with their appropriate names. Move the cell pointers to each of these cells to make sure that the operation worked.

6. Close the MONBUD workbook without saving the changes.

When and how to use relative, absolute, or mixed references

Most of the references you use in formulas are *relative references*. When a formula that contains relative references is moved or copied to other cells, the relative references are adjusted accordingly. If, for example, a formula is moved two cells down, the relative references are changed so they point to cells that are two cells down too. That's usually what you want, and the formulas usually work right in their new locations.

Sometimes, however, you don't want a reference within a formula to change when the formula is copied. And sometimes you want either the row identifier or the column identifier to change when a formula is copied, but not both. In those cases, you can use absolute references or mixed references instead of relative references.

How to create a relative, absolute, or mixed reference

Figure 7-6 illustrates relative, absolute, and mixed references. As you can see, a dollar sign in a reference indicates that the following row or column identifier shouldn't change when the formula that contains the reference is copied. Because an *absolute reference* contains a dollar sign in front of both the column and row identifier, the entire reference remains unchanged when it's copied.

When you type a cell reference into a formula without using dollar signs, you create a relative reference. You also create a relative reference when you identify a cell used in a formula by pointing at it.

Reference type	Example	Meaning when copied	Sample formula
Relative	A3	Adjust both the column and row.	=A3+B3
Absolute	$C$17	Adjust neither the column nor the row.	=$C$17*.07
Mixed	B$12	Adjust the column but not the row.	=B$12*B3
	$D2	Adjust the row but not the column.	=$D2/365

Two ways to create a relative reference

- Identify a cell used in a formula by pointing to it.
- Type a cell reference into a formula without using dollar signs.

Two ways to create an absolute or mixed reference

- Type the dollar signs as you enter or edit a formula.
- Press the F4 (Absolute) key to cycle through the four reference formats as you enter or edit a formula. If the cursor is on a reference to cell B4, for example, it gets changed as follows with four repetitions of the F4 key:

    $B$4
    B$4
    $B4
    B4

Figure 7-6 How to create a relative, absolute, or mixed reference

To create an absolute or mixed reference, you can type the dollar signs where you want them. Or, you can use the F4 (Absolute) key to cycle through the four combinations for a cell reference as you enter or edit it. You'll use this technique in the next set of exercises.

When to use an absolute or mixed reference

You can use an absolute or mixed reference any time you want a reference, or part of a reference, to remain unchanged when it's copied. To illustrate, figure 7-7 presents a worksheet that uses a formula with an absolute reference. Here, the formula =$A$2-B6 is entered in cell C6. This formula subtracts the invoice date in cell B6 from the current date in cell A2 to determine the age of the invoice. Because A2 is entered as an absolute reference, it doesn't change when the formula is copied down the C column. As a result, all the dates in column B are subtracted from the date in cell A2.

The alternative is to create each formula in the C column separately. This, of course, isn't as efficient as copying one formula down the column. That's why it's worth taking the time to master the use of absolute references.

Part 1: The formula =$A$2-B6 is entered into cell C6.

	A	B	C	D
1	Aged invoice report			
2	4/17/95			
3				
4	Invoice	Invoice	Age	
5	number	date	in days	
6	6274986	1/3/95	104	
7	6275217	1/18/95		
8	6275584	2/9/95		
9	6275883	2/20/95		
10				

Part 2: When the formula in cell C6 is copied to cells C7 through C9, Excel doesn't adjust the reference to cell A2.

	A	B	C	D
1	Aged invoice report			
2	4/17/95			
3				
4	Invoice	Invoice	Age	
5	number	date	in days	
6	6274986	1/3/95	104	
7	6275217	1/18/95	89	
8	6275584	2/9/95	67	
9	6275883	2/20/95	56	
10				

Note

- If the absolute reference weren't used in the formula in cell C6, the copied formula in cell C7 would be A3-B7; the formula in cell C8 would be A4-B8; and the formula in cell C9 would be A5-B9. Of course, that wouldn't work at all.

Figure 7-7 How to use an absolute reference in a formula

In contrast, figure 7-8 presents a worksheet with a formula that uses two mixed references. This worksheet shows the effect of budget increases of four, five, and six percent over the current budget amounts.

In part 1 of this figure, you can see the formula in cell C5:

`=$B5*(1+C$4)`

When this formula is copied down to cells C6 through C11, the row identifier for cell C4 remains unchanged so it always refers to the percentages in row 4. And when this formula is copied to cells D5 through E11, the column identifier for cell B5 remains unchanged so it always refers to the dollar amounts in column B. As a result, the copied formulas work correctly in all of their new locations. In cell E11, for example, you can see that the formula has been adjusted correctly.

Because the use of mixed references tends to be confusing, you may prefer to avoid using them. In that case, you can usually get by quite well by using a few absolute references instead of one mixed reference as explained in the second note in figure 7-8. Beyond that, most worksheets don't require the use of mixed references so the problem may never come up.

Part 1: The formula =$B5*(1+C$4) is entered into cell C5.

	A	B	C	D	E	F
1	Monthly Expenses					
2	Budget Planning					
3						
4	Item	Current	4%	5%	6%	
5	Salaries & Wages	50,000	52,000			
6	Rent & Utilities	17,500				
7	Maintenance	1,500				
8	Supplies	7,750				
9	Insurance	2,500				
10	Legal Fees	1,000				
11	Miscellaneous	8,250				
12						

Part 2: When the formula is copied to cells C6 through C11 and to cells D5 through E11, the mixed references are adjusted so the formula still works correctly.

E11 =$B11*(1+E$4)

	A	B	C	D	E	F
1	Monthly Expenses					
2	Budget Planning					
3						
4	Item	Current	4%	5%	6%	
5	Salaries & Wages	50,000	52,000	52,500	53,000	
6	Rent & Utilities	17,500	18,200	18,375	18,550	
7	Maintenance	1,500	1,560	1,575	1,590	
8	Supplies	7,750	8,060	8,138	8,215	
9	Insurance	2,500	2,600	2,625	2,650	
10	Legal Fees	1,000	1,040	1,050	1,060	
11	Miscellaneous	8,250	8,580	8,663	8,745	
12						

Notes

- The formula in cell C5 could also be entered as:

    `$B5+$B5*C$4`

- If mixed references confuse you, you can enter three different formulas in cells C5, D5, and E5 using absolute references in each one to refer to cells C4, D4, and E4. For instance, the formula in cell C5 could be

    `B5*(1+$C$4)`

    and the formula in cell D5 could be

    `B5*(1+$D$4)`

    Then, you could copy the three formulas down their columns to complete the worksheet. This gets the same results that you get by using a mixed formula with only a little more effort.

Figure 7-8 **How to use mixed references in a formula**

Exercise set 7-2

	A	B	C
1	Current date:	4/18/95	
2			
3	Date	Days	
4	5/1/95	13	
5	5/8/95	20	
6	5/15/95	27	
7	5/22/95	34	
8	5/29/95	41	
9	6/5/95	48	
10	6/12/95	55	
11	6/19/95	62	
12	6/26/95	69	
13			

In this exercise set, you'll create a simple worksheet like the one above. This worksheet shows the number of days from the current date to a list of future dates. To calculate the number of days, you'll use an absolute reference. (Because you may never need to use mixed references, no exercise is included for them.)

1. Open a new workbook, enter the text shown above in cell A1, and change the column width so the text fits. Then, insert the current date in cell B1 using the TODAY function. Next, enter and format the text in cells A3 and B3 as shown above. Enter the date of the first day of the next month in cell A5, and enter the date for the eighth day of that month (7 days later) in cell A4. Now, use the AutoFill feature to continue the sequence in column A so that it includes a two month period. Your worksheet should now look similar to the one above without the numbers in column B (your dates will be different).

2. Place the cell pointer on cell B4. Then, type an equals sign to begin a formula, and click on cell A4 to add the reference for that cell to the formula. Type a minus sign, then click on cell B1. Now, press F4. What happens to the reference to cell B1? Press F4 three more times to see what happens each time. Press F4 one more time so that the reference looks like this:

    $B$1

    Press the Enter key to complete the formula.

3. Use the AutoFill feature to copy the formula in cell B4 to the rest of the cells in column B. Are the numbers in column B in increments of 7? Move the cell pointer to each of the cells in column B that contain a formula. Did the reference to cell B1 change from one cell to another? Now, close the workbook without saving it.

Other skills for working with functions

In chapter 1, you learned about five of the most useful functions. Now, you'll learn about some of the other functions that are available with Excel. You'll also learn two new techniques for entering functions.

An introduction to the types of functions

The functions that are available with Excel are divided into the eleven categories presented in figure 7-9. This figure also presents examples of the types of functions you'll find in each of the categories.

To find out more about any of the functions that are available with Excel, you can use the on-line Help information. For a complete list of the functions, choose the Search For Help On command from the Help menu. Then, search for the "worksheet functions" entry and choose the "Alphabetical List of Worksheet Functions" or the "Worksheet Functions Listed by Category" topic. To get more information about a listed item, just double-click on it.

Function category	Typical functions	Examples
Date & Time	Get the current date and time.	NOW
	Get the current date only.	TODAY
	Convert text that looks like a date to its date serial number.	DATEVALUE
Statistical	Get the average of the numbers in a range.	AVERAGE
	Count the numbers in a range.	COUNT
	Get the standard deviation of the numbers in a range.	STDEV
Financial	Calculate the periodic payment required to pay off a loan.	PMT
	Calculate the future value of a series of equal payments.	FV
Math & Trigonometry	Get the total of the numbers in a range.	SUM
	Round a number.	ROUND
	Take the square root of a number.	SQRT
	Return the integer portion of a number.	INT
	Get the sine, cosine, or tangent of an angle.	SIN, COS, TAN
Logical	Take one action if a condition is true; take another if it's false.	IF
Database & List Management	Get the average of the numbers in a field.	DAVERAGE
	Get the total of the numbers in a field.	DSUM
	Count the numbers in a field.	DCOUNT
Text	Count the characters in a text argument.	LEN
	Convert all the letters in a text argument to uppercase.	UPPER
	Get a specified number of characters from the beginning of a text argument.	LEFT
Engineering	Convert a number from one system to another.	CONVERT
	Convert a decimal number to a hexadecimal number.	DEC2HEX
	Convert a hexadecimal number to a decimal number.	HEX2DEC
Information	Return specific information about a cell, such as its contents or location.	CELL
Lookup & Reference	Count the number of columns or rows in a range.	COLUMNS ROWS
DDE & External	Connect to an external source, do a query, and return the results.	SQLREQUEST

Figure 7-9 The eleven types of functions

How to use two typical financial functions

Many of the functions that come with Excel require two or more *arguments*. When you enter these functions, you have to use its correct format or *syntax*. A function's syntax describes its arguments and their sequence. To understand how this works, you'll learn how to use two of the most commonly used financial functions.

Figure 7-10 presents the PMT function, which calculates the periodic payments required to pay off a loan. As you can see, this function has five arguments, but only the first three are required. Notice in the examples that the arguments are entered in the same sequence as prescribed by the function's syntax. Notice also that each argument is separated by a comma.

Many of the financial functions perform calculations that deal with time periods. The PMT functions in figure 7-10, for example, deal with a 5 year, or 60 month, loan period. When you specify the arguments for a function like this, you must make sure that the arguments measure time consistently. That's why both formulas in figure 7-10 divide the annual interest rate by 12 to get the monthly interest rate. And that's why the second formula multiplies the number of years in the loan by 12 to get the number of months in the loan.

Syntax
`PMT(rate,nper,pv,fv,type)`

rate	The interest rate per period.
nper	The number of payment periods.
pv	The present value of the annuity.
fv	The future value of the annuity (optional).
type	Indicates when the periodic payment is due (optional). 0 means the payment is due at the end of the period. 1 means the payment is due at the beginning of the period. 0 is the default.

A monthly payment calculated using an annual interest rate and the number of months

B4   =PMT(B2/12,B3,B1)

	A	B	C	D
1	Loan amount:	20,000		
2	Annual rate:	12.00%		
3	Months:	60		
4	Payment:	($444.89)		
5				

A monthly payment calculated using an annual interest rate and the number of years

B4   =PMT(B2/12,B3*12,B1)

	A	B	C	D
1	Loan amount:	20,000		
2	Annual rate:	12.00%		
3	Years:	5		
4	Payment:	($444.89)		
5				

Notes

- When you use an annuity function like PMT, the time units you use in the function must be consistent. To calculate monthly payments, for example, the interest rate and the number of periods must be expressed in months. If the time units in the worksheet aren't consistent, you can adjust them when you specify the arguments as shown above.

- Because the future value and type arguments aren't required for the functions above, they can be omitted.

Figure 7-10   How to use the PMT function

Both of the functions in figure 7-10 use the *ordinary annuity method* for calculating the payment amount. When you use this method to perform a financial calculation, it assumes that the payments or investments are made at the end of each period. Although this is the method that's used for most financial calculations, you may occasionally need to perform a calculation using the *annuity due method*. This method assumes that the payments or investments are made at the start of each period.

Figure 7-11 illustrates the difference between the two calculation methods. Here, the FV function is used to calculate the future value of a periodic investment. The first example in this figure uses the ordinary annuity method to calculate the future value. Since this is the default calculation method, only the three required arguments were included in the function. The second example uses the annuity due method. Here, a value of 1 was included for the fifth argument, type, to indicate that the annuity due method is to be used. Notice that an extra comma was included between the third and fifth arguments to indicate that the fourth argument was omitted.

Syntax

`FV(rate,nper,pmt,pv,type)`

rate   The interest rate per period.

nper   The number of payment periods.

pmt   The payment made each period.

pv   The present value of the annuity.

type   Indicates when the periodic payment is due (optional). 0 means the payment is due at the end of the period. 1 means the payment is due at the beginning of the period. 0 is the default.

A function that calculates the future value of an annuity paid at the end of each period (ordinary annuity calculation)

B4   =FV(B2,B3,B1)

	A	B	C
1	Periodic investment:	2,000	
2	Interest rate:	10%	
3	Term of investment:	25	
4	Future value:	($196,694)	
5			

A function that calculates the future value of an annuity paid at the beginning of each period (annuity due calculation)

B4   =FV(B2,B3,B1,,1)

	A	B	C
1	Periodic investment:	2,000	
2	Interest rate:	10%	
3	Term of investment:	25	
4	Future value:	($216,364)	
5			

Note

Because the fifth argument was required in the second example above but the fourth argument was not, an extra comma was included before the fifth argument to indicate that the fourth argument was omitted.

Figure 7-11   How to use the FV function

Advanced skills for working with formulas and functions

How to use the Function Wizard

Figure 7-12 shows how to use the Function Wizard to enter a function. This is useful when you enter a function that has more than one argument or when you can't remember the syntax of a function.

When you access the Function Wizard, it displays a dialog box that lets you choose a function. As you can see, the functions are divided into the same categories you saw in figure 7-9. In addition, the first option in the Function Category list lets you display the most recently used functions, and the second option lets you choose from all of the available functions. If you don't know the name of the function you want, you can scroll through those that are available to display a brief description of each one in the dialog box.

After you choose a function, you can display another dialog box that lets you enter that function's arguments. When you click in the box for an argument, a description of the argument is displayed. This makes it easy to use functions that you aren't familiar with. When you complete the second dialog box, the function is entered in the worksheet.

Additional information

✓ You can also use the Function Wizard to edit a function. To do that, move the cell pointer to the cell that contains the function you want to edit and access the Function Wizard. Then, a dialog box like the second one in figure 7-12 is displayed so you can change the arguments for the function.

How to access the Function Wizard

Menu	Insert → Function
Standard toolbar	*f*ₓ
Shortcut key	Shift+F3

How to enter a function in the active cell

1. Access the Function Wizard to display this dialog box:

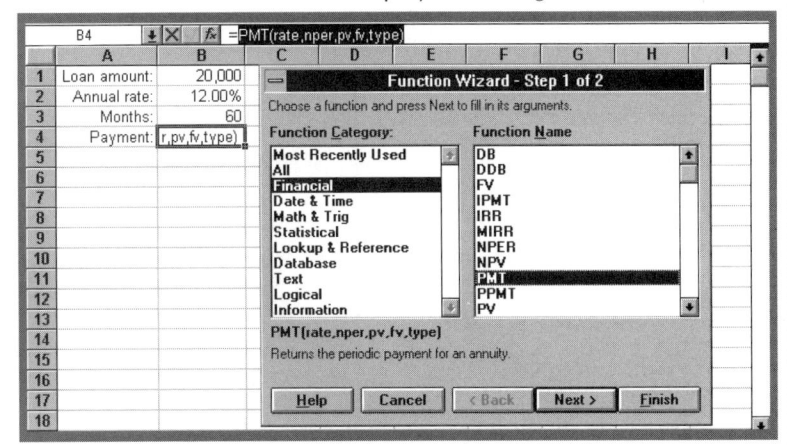

2. Choose a category from the Function Category list, and choose the function you want from the Function Name list. Then, click on the Next button to display this dialog box:

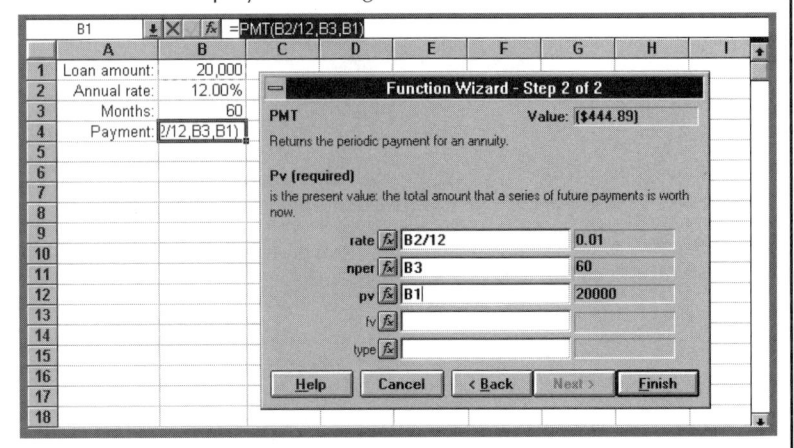

3. Enter each argument. You can identify a cell or range by selecting it in the worksheet. Click on the Finish button to insert the function into the worksheet.

Notes

- To enter a function within an argument of another function, you can click on the function button in front of the argument's text box. That starts the Function Wizard for another function.
- If you click on the Finish button from the Step 1 dialog box, the function is entered with placeholders that identify the arguments and the first placeholder is highlighted in the formula bar. Then, you can complete the function using techniques like those in figure 7-13.

Figure 7-12 How to use the Function Wizard to enter a function

How to use shortcut keys as you enter arguments

Figure 7-13 presents another technique for entering a function. To use this technique, you have to know the name of the function. Then, after you type a function name, you press Ctrl+Shift+A to insert the function's arguments in the form of placeholders. As you can see in the figure, the placeholders identify each argument. To complete the function, you replace the placeholders with the appropriate arguments and delete any commas and placeholders you don't need.

The second shortcut key in figure 7-13 provides a quicker way to access the Function Wizard if you already know the function name. After you type the name, just press Ctrl+A.

The shortcut keys that you can use after you type the function name

Key	Function
Ctrl+Shift+A	Inserts the syntax and placeholders for the function as shown below.
Ctrl+A	Accesses Step 2 of the Function Wizard for the function.

How to use placeholders as you enter a function

1. Start the formula and type the name of the function. Then, press Ctrl+Shift+A and Excel inserts placeholders for the function's arguments, along with separators and parentheses, and highlights the first argument:

	A	B	C	D	E
1	Loan amount:	20,000			
2	Annual rate:	12.00%			
3	Months:	60			
4	Payment:	=pmt(**rate**,nper,pv,fv,type)			
5					

2. Enter the first argument by identifying the cell or range in the worksheet or by typing it in. The entry replaces the highlighted placeholder:

	A	B	C	D	E
1	Loan amount:	20,000			
2	Annual rate:	12.00%			
3	Months:	60			
4	Payment:	=pmt(B2/12,nper,pv,fv,type)			
5					

3. If necessary, highlight each of the remaining placeholders and replace them with the appropriate arguments. (The easiest way to highlight a placeholder is to double-click on it.) Then, delete any placeholders and separators you don't need:

	A	B	C	D
1	Loan amount:	20,000		
2	Annual rate:	12.00%		
3	Months:	60		
4	Payment:	=pmt(B2/12,B3,B1)		
5				

4. Press the Enter key to complete the function.

Figure 7-13　How to use shortcut keys as you enter the arguments of a function

Exercise set 7-3

	A	B	C	D
1	Loan amount:	25,000		
2	Annual rate:	10.50%		
3	Months:	36		
4				
5		Ordinary	Annuity	
6		annuity	due	
7	Payment:	($812.56)	($805.51)	
8				

In this exercise set, you'll create a worksheet like the one above. This worksheet shows the monthly payment for an annuity using the ordinary annuity method and the annuity due method. To create this worksheet, you'll use the PMT function.

1. Open a new workbook and enter and format the data shown above except for the formulas in cells B7 and C7.

2. Place the cell pointer on cell B7 and access the Function Wizard using one of the techniques in figure 7-12. When the first Function Wizard dialog box appears, choose the Financial functions, then choose the PMT function and click on the Next button. With the cursor in the rate box, click on cell B2 to enter that cell reference into the argument (you can move the dialog box if you need to). Divide the cell reference by 12 to calculate the monthly interest rate. The argument should now look like this:

   B2/12

   Next, click in the nper box and click on cell B3 to enter the reference for that cell. Then, click in the pv box and click on cell B1. Click on the Finish button to complete the function.

3. Place the cell pointer on cell C7, enter "=PMT," and press Ctrl+Shift+A to enter the placeholders for the function. With the first placeholder (rate) highlighted, click on cell B2 to replace the placeholder with the cell reference for that cell. Then, divide the argument by 12 to get the monthly interest rate. Highlight the next placeholder (nper) by double-clicking on it, and click on cell B3 to replace the placeholder with that cell reference. Highlight the third placeholder (pv) and click on cell B1. Highlight the fourth placeholder (fv), and use the Delete key to delete it, but leave the comma. Then, highlight the last placeholder (type) and replace it with the number 1. Press the Enter key to complete the formula. Which technique did you like best? Now, close the workbook without saving it.

How to audit a worksheet

It's relatively easy to make a mistake as you create or modify a worksheet. That's why a high percentage of business worksheets contain one or more calculation errors. Because the worksheets look so neat and professional, though, the errors are likely to be overlooked.

When you *audit* a worksheet, you check it for accuracy. To do that, you check the values that you entered into the worksheet. But you also check the formulas to make sure they're working correctly. In this topic, you'll learn two of the easiest ways to check the formulas in a worksheet.

How to display or print a worksheet that shows its formulas

Figure 7-14 presents the procedures for displaying and printing a worksheet that shows the formulas in the worksheet instead of the values derived from the formulas. That makes it easier to check the formulas to make sure they're correct. For a small worksheet, you can usually check the formulas right on the screen. Then, you can reduce the column widths to make the worksheet easier to work with.

Larger worksheets are usually easier to audit from a printed copy that shows the formulas. When you print a worksheet this way, you'll want to include the row and column headings as described in the figure. That way, you can tell which cells the printed formulas refer to.

The FEBEXP worksheet with its formulas displayed

	A	B	C	D
1		**Monthly Expenses**		
2		February		
3				Do
4		Budget	Expense	Varia
5	Salaries & Wages	50000	51784	=C5-B5
6	Rent & Utilities	17500	18222	=C6-B6
7	Maintenance	1500	1922	=C7-B7
8	Supplies	7750	7912	=C8-B8
9	Insurance	2500	2625	=C9-B9
10	Legal Fees	1000	0	=C10-B10
11	Miscellaneous	8250	7211	=C11-B11
12	Total	=SUM(B5:B11)	=SUM(C5:C11)	=SUM(D5:D11)
13				

How to display the formulas in a worksheet

1. Choose the Options command from the Tools menu, and click on the View tab.

2. Choose the Formulas option in the Window Options group, and click on the OK button. Excel then displays the formulas rather than the results of the formulas in the worksheet. It also doubles the widths of all the columns in the worksheet.

How to print a worksheet that shows its formulas

- Access the Sheet tab of the Page Setup dialog box and check the Row and Column Headings option so that the row numbers and column letters are printed with the worksheet. If necessary, adjust the column widths and change the orientation and sizing of the worksheet so that it fits on the page the way you want. Then, print the worksheet.

Notes

- To return to normal view, remove the check mark from the Formulas option in the View tab of the Options dialog box.

- After the formulas are displayed with the doubled column widths, you may want to adjust the column widths so you can see more of the data on the screen at one time and so you can print the worksheet on fewer pages. If you plan to do that, however, you may want to save the worksheet before you display the formulas so you can revert back to the original worksheet when you're done.

Figure 7-14 How to display or print a worksheet that shows its formulas

Advanced skills for working with formulas and functions

How to use the Go To Special command

Figure 7-15 shows how to use the Go To Special command to audit a worksheet. As you can see, this command can help you identify cells with specific contents. If you choose the Formulas option, for example, Excel selects all the cells that contain formulas. Then, you can use the keystroke combinations presented in the figure to move the cell pointer within the selected range, checking the formulas as you go.

Two other options that can help you analyze the formulas in a given row or column are Row Differences and Column Differences. When you use these options, Excel compares the patterns of the formulas in the row or column with the active cell in that row or column, called the *comparison cell*. Then, Excel selects any cells in that row or column that don't match the pattern in the comparison cell. If, for example, the comparison cell in a total row contains a SUM function that sums the values in rows 4 through 10, the Row Differences option will highlight any cells in the total row that don't sum the same rows.

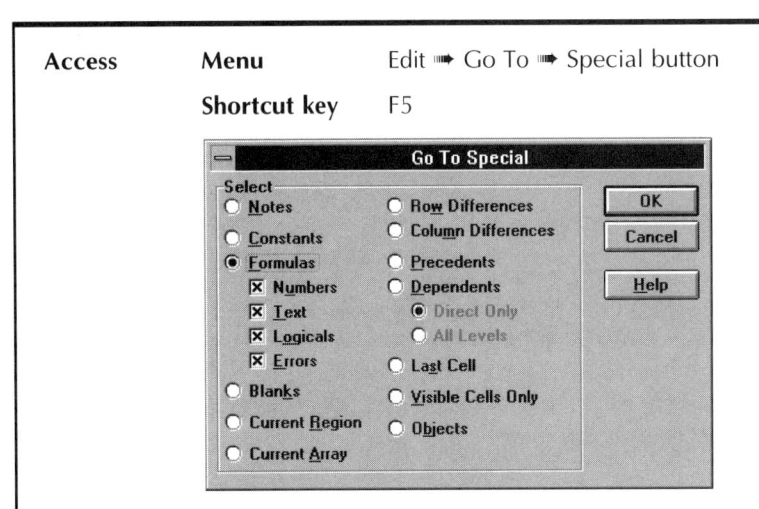

Access	Menu	Edit → Go To → Special button
	Shortcut key	F5

Go To Special dialog box

Select:
- Notes
- Constants
- ● Formulas
  - ☒ Numbers
  - ☒ Text
  - ☒ Logicals
  - ☒ Errors
- Blanks
- Current Region
- Current Array
- Row Differences
- Column Differences
- Precedents
- Dependents
  - ● Direct Only
  - ○ All Levels
- Last Cell
- Visible Cells Only
- Objects

[OK] [Cancel] [Help]

How to select the formulas in a worksheet

1. Access the Go To Special dialog box and choose the Formulas option. Then, remove the check marks from one or more of the options that are subordinate to the Formulas option if you do not want Excel to select formulas that result in numbers, text, true or false values (Logicals), or errors.

2. Click on the OK button to select the formulas. In the following example, the formulas in the FEBEXP worksheet were selected:

	A	B	C	D	E	F
1	**Monthly Expenses**					
2	February					
3				Dollar	Percent	
4		Budget	Expense	Variance	Variance	
5	Salaries & Wages	50,000	51,784	1,784	3.6%	
6	Rent & Utilities	17,500	18,222	722	4.1%	
7	Maintenance	1,500	1,922	422	28.1%	
8	Supplies	7,750	7,912	162	2.1%	
9	Insurance	2,500	2,625	125	5.0%	
10	Legal Fees	1,000	-	(1,000)	-100.0%	
11	Miscellaneous	8,250	7,211	(1,039)	-12.6%	
12	Total	88,500	89,676	1,176	1.3%	
13						

How to select cells that don't match the pattern in a row or column

1. Select the cells in a row or column you want to check, and use the techniques below to move the cell pointer to the cell that you want to compare against the other cells in the range (the *comparison cell*).

2. Access the Go To Special dialog box. If you selected the cells in a row, choose the Row Differences option to check for differences between the pattern of the formula in the comparison cell and the other cells in the row. If you selected the cells in a column, choose the Column Differences option to check for differences between the pattern of the formula in the comparison cell and the other cells in the column.

3. Click on the OK button to select the cells with different formula patterns.

Figure 7-15 How to use the Go To Special command to audit a worksheet (part 1 of 2)

You can also use the Go To Special command to identify cell precedents and dependents. A *precedent* is a cell that's referred to by a formula. A *dependent* is a cell that contains a formula that refers to other cells. The second worksheet in figure 7-15, for example, shows the precedents for the formula in cell E8. That makes it easy to tell if the formula refers to the correct cells. You can also select the precedents or dependents for a whole range of cells by selecting the range before you issue the Go To command.

For most worksheets, you can audit the cells both thoroughly and efficiently using the techniques in figures 7-14 and 7-15. As a result, you probably won't ever need the other auditing tools that Excel provides. In case you're interested, though, other auditing tools are available from the Auditing toolbar and from the Auditing submenu that you can access from the Tools menu. Now that you know what precedents and dependents are, you should be able to use these other tools with a minimum of experimentation.

How to select the cells that a formula refers to

1. Select a cell that contains a formula and access the Go To Special dialog box.
2. Choose the Precedents option. Then, choose the Direct Only option to select the cells that are referred to directly by the selected formula. Or, choose the All Levels option to select all cells that are referred to directly or indirectly by the selected formula.
3. Click on the OK button to select the precedent cells. In the following example, the cells in the FEBEXP worksheet that are referred to by the formula in cell E8 were selected:

	A	B	C	D	E	F
1	**Monthly Expenses**					
2	February					
3				Dollar	Percent	
4		Budget	Expense	Variance	Variance	
5	Salaries & Wages	50,000	51,784	1,784	3.6%	
6	Rent & Utilities	17,500	18,222	722	4.1%	
7	Maintenance	1,500	1,922	422	28.1%	
8	Supplies	7,750	7,912	162	2.1%	
9	Insurance	2,500	2,625	125	5.0%	
10	Legal Fees	1,000	-	(1,000)	-100.0%	
11	Miscellaneous	8,250	7,211	(1,039)	-12.6%	
12	Total	88,500	89,676	1,176	1.3%	
13						

How to select the formulas that refer to a cell

1. Select a cell and access the Go To Special dialog box.
2. Choose the Dependents option. Then, choose the Direct Only option to select cells with formulas that refer directly to the selected cell. Or, choose the All Levels option to select cells with formulas that refer directly or indirectly to the selected cell.
3. Click on the OK button to select the dependent cells.

How to move the cell pointer within the selected cells

- Press Enter to go down to the next cell.
- Press Shift+Enter to go up to the previous cell.
- Press Tab to go right to the next cell.
- Press Shift+Tab to go left to the previous cell.

Notes

- When you use the Row Differences or Column Differences options, you can select cells in one or more rows or columns that you want to compare. Then, the active cell identifies the row or column that contains the comparison cells.
- When you use the Precedents or Dependents options, you can select the precedents or dependents for more than one cell by selecting a range of cells before you issue the Go To command.

Figure 7-15 How to use the Go To Special command to audit a worksheet (part 2 of 2)

Exercise set 7-4

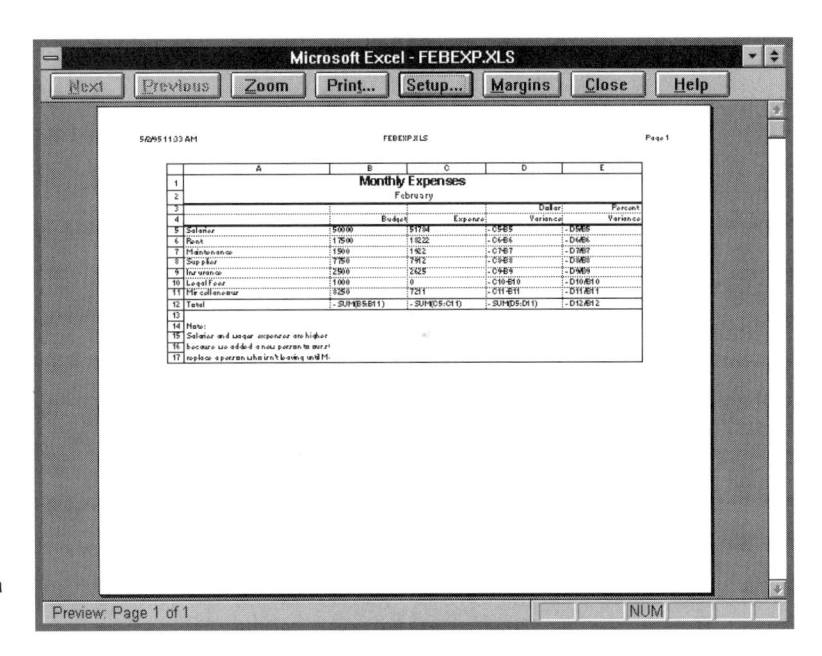

How the worksheet should look in the Print Preview window after you fit it to a single page in exercise 1

1. Open the FEBEXP workbook. Then, use the first procedure in figure 7-14 to display the formulas in the worksheet. Next, access the Sheet tab of the Page Setup dialog box and check the Row and Column Headings option. Click on the Print Preview button to preview the printed worksheet. Does the worksheet fit on the page? Click on the Setup button to return to the Page Setup dialog box and click on the Page tab. Choose the Landscape orientation option and fit the worksheet to a single page, then click on the OK button to return to the Print Preview window. Print the worksheet and use the printout to check that the formulas in the worksheet are correct. Close the workbook without saving the changes.

2. Open the FEBEXP workbook again. Then, use the Go To Special command as described in figure 7-15 to select all the cells that contain formulas. Move the cell pointer around the selected range as described in the figure to check that the formulas are correct. Do you like this better than working from the printed worksheet?

3. Move the cell pointer to cell D7 and change the formula in that cell so that it subtracts the contents of cell C7 from cell B7. Then, select the range of cells from D5 to D11 and access the Go To Special dialog box. Choose the Column Differences option and click on the OK button. This compares all the formulas in the range with the one in cell D5. Is the cell that contains the incorrect formula selected? Correct the formula.

4. Place the cell pointer on cell D12 and access the Go To Special dialog box. Choose the Precedents option and click on the OK button. Are all of the cells that are referred to directly by the formula in cell D12 selected? Move the cell pointer back to cell D12 and access the Go To Special dialog box again. Choose the Precedents option, then choose the All Levels option and click on the OK button. The range of cells from B5 to D11 should now be selected since cells D5 through D11 are referred to by cell D12, and cells B5 through C11 are referred to by cells D5 through D11.

5. Place the cell pointer on cell B5 and access the Go To Special dialog box. Choose the Dependents option and click on the OK button. Are all of the cells that contain formulas that refer directly to cell B5 selected? Move the cell pointer back to cell B5 and access the Go To Special dialog box again. Choose the Dependents option, then choose the All Levels option and click on the OK button. Cells D5, E5, and B12 should be selected since the formulas in those cells all refer directly to cell B5. Cell D12 should be selected since its formula refers to cell D5. And cell E12 should be selected since its formula refers to cell B12.

6. Close the FEBEXP workbook without saving the changes.

Perspective

With the skills presented in this chapter, you should be able to efficiently enter and edit the formulas and functions that you need for any of your worksheets. In addition, you should be able to audit your worksheets so you're confident that the formulas and functions that they contain are correct. This is a critical function that is frequently done poorly or omitted completely.

Summary

- When a formula refers to the cell that it's in, either directly or indirectly, a *circular reference* occurs. When that happens, Excel alerts you to the condition and makes it easy to identify the cell that contains the circular reference.

- If you want to delete cells in a worksheet that contain data that's used in a formula or function, you can preserve the result of the formula or function by replacing it with its calculated value.

- When you enter a date into a worksheet, it's stored as a serial number. When you enter a time into a worksheet, it's stored as a decimal number. That makes it easy to use dates and times in arithmetic operations.

- If you name cells or ranges in a worksheet, you can use those names as you enter formulas and functions. You can also replace the references in existing formulas and functions with their names.

- When you copy a formula that contains a *relative reference*, both the row and column identifier of the reference can change depending on the destination of the copied formula. When you copy a formula that contains an *absolute reference*, neither the row nor column identifier change no matter where the formula is copied. When you copy a formula that contains a *mixed reference*, either the row or the column identifier can change, but not both.

- The functions that are available with Excel are divided into eleven categories. Two of the most commonly used functions are in the Financial category. The PMT function calculates the periodic payment required to pay off a loan. And the FV function calculates the future value of a series of equal payments.

- You can use the Function Wizard to help you choose a function and to help you enter the arguments for that function. You can also use shortcut keys to help you enter the arguments of a function whose name you already know.

- The easiest way to *audit* the formulas in a worksheet is to display the formulas, then print the worksheet with its row and column headings so you can verify that they're correct. You can also audit the formulas in a worksheet using the Go To Special command. This command lets you highlight specific types of cells in a worksheet, like those that contain formulas or those that contain the *precedents* or *dependents* for another cell.

Chapter 8

How to set defaults, protect data, convert files, and use on-line Help

This chapter presents information on a variety of features. First, it shows you how to change the way Excel looks and operates by setting default options. Then, it shows you how to protect the data in individual worksheets or in an entire workbook. Next, it shows you how to convert a file that was created by another spreadsheet program to Excel 5 format. Finally, it shows you how to use the Help feature to get information about Excel. Although you may not need to use all of these features, you'll want to read about them anyway so you can decide for yourself when they might be useful.

How to set defaults
    The View defaults
    The Calculation defaults
    The Edit defaults
    The General defaults

How to protect the data in a workbook
    How to protect a worksheet from changes
    How to allow changes to selected cells in a worksheet
    How to protect a workbook from changes
    How to protect a workbook from being opened or saved

How to convert files created by other programs to Excel 5 format
    How to open a file created by another spreadsheet program
    How to save a file created by another spreadsheet program as an Excel 5 file
    How to improve the worksheets that you convert to Excel 5 format

When and how to use the Help feature
    An introduction to the commands in the Help menu
    How to get context-sensitive Help information
    How to navigate through the Help information
    How to print Help information

Perspective

Summary

How to set defaults

When you install Excel 5, the installation program sets up several values and codes that affect the way Excel works. These are called *default options*, *default settings*, or just *defaults*. For instance, one default determines whether you can use the drag-and-drop feature to move and copy cells, another determines whether the formula bar is displayed, and a third determines the size of the data that's displayed in the workbook window. Although you can use Excel without ever changing the starting defaults, you'll probably want to change some of them so Excel will work the way you want it to.

To change the Excel defaults, you use the Option command of the Tools menu. The dialog box that's displayed when you choose this command contains 10 tabs. You'll learn about four of those tabs here. You'll use the other tabs only for special situations.

The View defaults

Figure 8-1 shows the View tab of the Options dialog box and summarizes its options. As you can see, the options in this tab are divided into three groups. The options in the Show group apply to Excel and stay in effect from one work session to the next. In contrast, the options in the Objects and Window Options groups apply to the active workbook, and they are saved with the workbook. If you experiment with these options, you can quickly see how they change the view of either the workbook window or the Excel window.

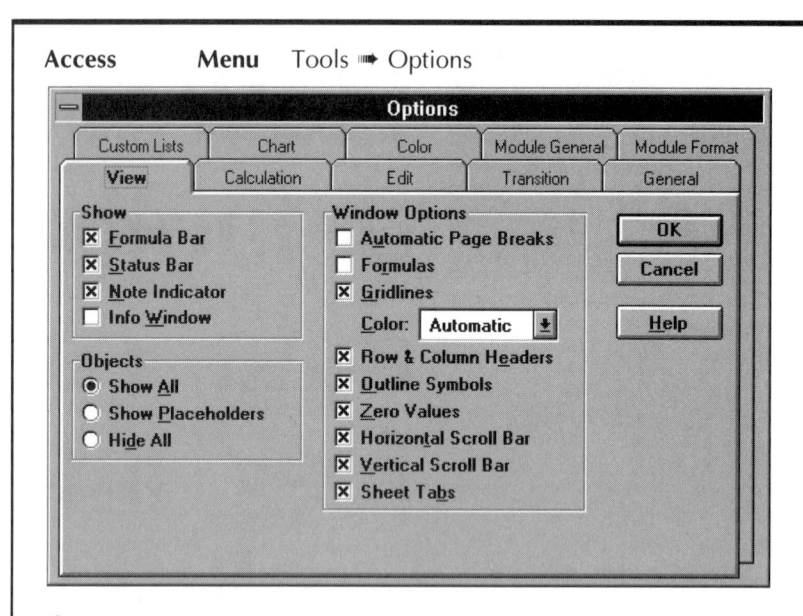

Access   Menu   Tools ➡ Options

Show group

- The options in this group apply to the application window for Excel. If an option is checked, that feature appears by default when you start Excel. The defaults stay in effect until you change them again. You can also change the Formula Bar and Status Bar defaults by using the Formula Bar and Status Bar commands in the View menu.

Objects group

- The options in this group determine how graphic objects, such as charts, are displayed. The Show All option is on by default, which means that all graphic objects are displayed. If you choose the Show Placeholders option, charts and pictures are displayed as gray rectangles, which can speed up scrolling. If you choose the Hide All option, all graphic objects are hidden. These options apply only to the active workbook. They are saved with the workbook, so they're used the next time you open it.

Window Options group

- The options in this group apply to the active workbook window and are saved with the workbook. If an option is checked, that feature appears in the workbook window.

Notes

- The Note Indicator option refers to explanatory notes that can be added to cells (not covered in this book). The Info Window option displays a window that provides information about the active cell.

- Most of the other options in the View tab are self-explanatory. For a description of the options, click on the Help button.

Figure 8-1   How to set the View defaults

The Calculation defaults

Figure 8-2 shows the Calculation tab of the Options dialog box and summarizes its options. For most workbooks, these options are set the way you want them. In particular, the Calculation option is set to Automatic, which means that formulas are recalculated whenever a cell that they depend on is changed. The only time you might want to change this option is when you're working with a worksheet so large that automatic recalculation is slowing down the operation of Excel. Then, if you change the default to Manual, you can tell Excel when you want recalculation to take place.

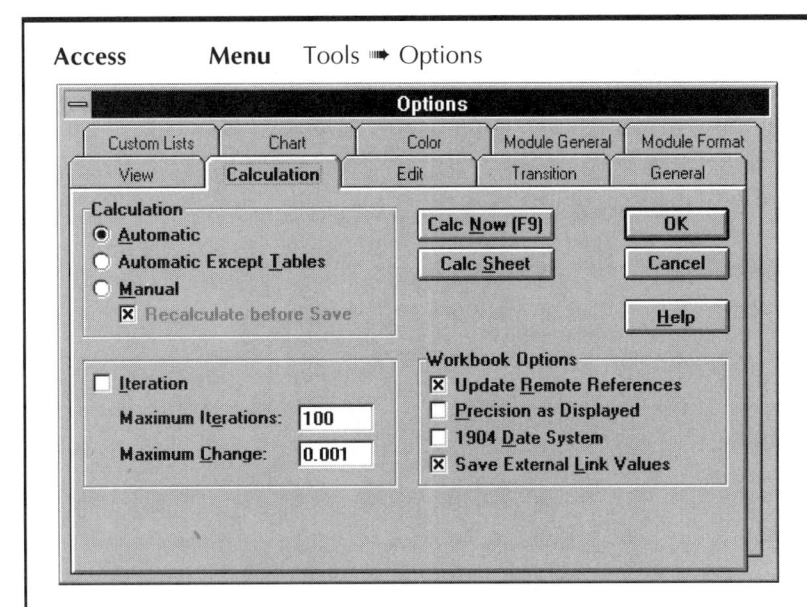

Access Menu   Tools ➡ Options

Calculation options

- The options in this group determine when the formulas in a worksheet are recalculated. The Automatic option is on by default, which means that a formula is recalculated whenever a value it depends on changes. The Automatic Except Tables option works the same way, except that data tables aren't recalculated automatically. (Data tables aren't covered in this book.)

- If you want to tell Excel when to recalcuate formulas, choose the Manual option. Then, you can recalculate all open workbooks at any time by pressing F9 or by accessing the Calculation tab and clicking on the Calc Now button. To recalculate only the active worksheet, press Shift+F9 or click on the Calc Sheet button in the Calculation tab. If the Recalculate Before Save option is checked, the workbook is always recalculated when you save it. The option you set stays in effect during the current session, but it's returned to Automatic the next time you start Excel.

Iteration options

- The options in this group limit the iterations used in a goal seeking operation or to solve formulas that contain circular references. They are effective only during the current session.

Workbook options

- The options in this group affect various aspects of workbook calculation not covered in this book. If you're converting files from a Macintosh to Excel 5, you may want to use the 1904 Date System option because that's what the Macintosh uses. Then, the date numbers start from January 2, 1904 instead of from January 1, 1900. The options in this group are saved with the active workbook.

Figure 8-2   How to set the Calculation defaults

The Edit defaults

Figure 8-3 shows the Edit tab of the Options dialog box and describes its options. The first three options are integral to the way you use Excel, so you'll want to leave them on. The fourth option, Fixed Decimal, is off by default, but you may want to use it if you need to enter a series of numbers that contain decimal digits. Then, you can enter the numbers without having to type the decimal point each time. The last two options probably won't have an effect on any of the worksheets you create.

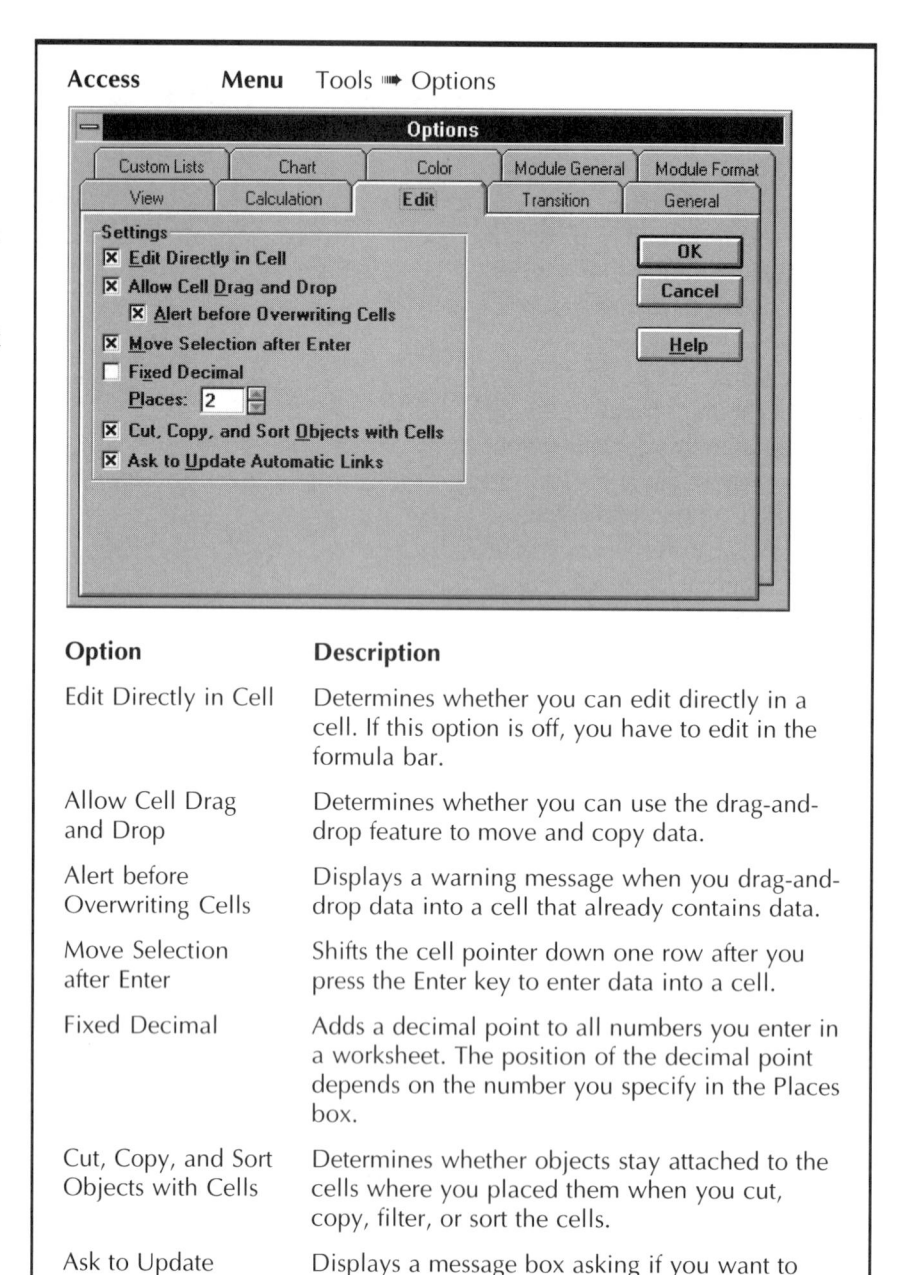

Access Menu Tools ➠ Options

Option	Description
Edit Directly in Cell	Determines whether you can edit directly in a cell. If this option is off, you have to edit in the formula bar.
Allow Cell Drag and Drop	Determines whether you can use the drag-and-drop feature to move and copy data.
Alert before Overwriting Cells	Displays a warning message when you drag-and-drop data into a cell that already contains data.
Move Selection after Enter	Shifts the cell pointer down one row after you press the Enter key to enter data into a cell.
Fixed Decimal	Adds a decimal point to all numbers you enter in a worksheet. The position of the decimal point depends on the number you specify in the Places box.
Cut, Copy, and Sort Objects with Cells	Determines whether objects stay attached to the cells where you placed them when you cut, copy, filter, or sort the cells.
Ask to Update Automatic Links	Displays a message box asking if you want to update links when you open a file that contains OLE links. (OLE links aren't covered in this book.)

Note

All of the options in this tab are saved from one Excel session to another.

Figure 8-3 How to set the Edit defaults

The General defaults

Figure 8-4 shows the General tab of the Options dialog box and describes its options. The options on this tab apply to all new workbooks. Note, however, that if you change the defaults for the font and font size, the new defaults don't go into affect until the next time you start Excel. So they don't affect the new workbooks or worksheets you create during the current session.

One option you'll probably want to change is Default File Location. This option identifies the default *working directory* Excel uses when you open or save a workbook file. When you install Excel, this default directory is C:\EXCEL, but that's not where you should save your files. Instead, you should change this directory to the one that you are currently using for most of your workbook files.

You may also want to change the Standard Font and Size defaults to the font and size you use most often. Then, you won't have to change them for each new workbook or worksheet. And you may want to change the Sheets In New Workbook option to the number of worksheets you typically store in each workbook.

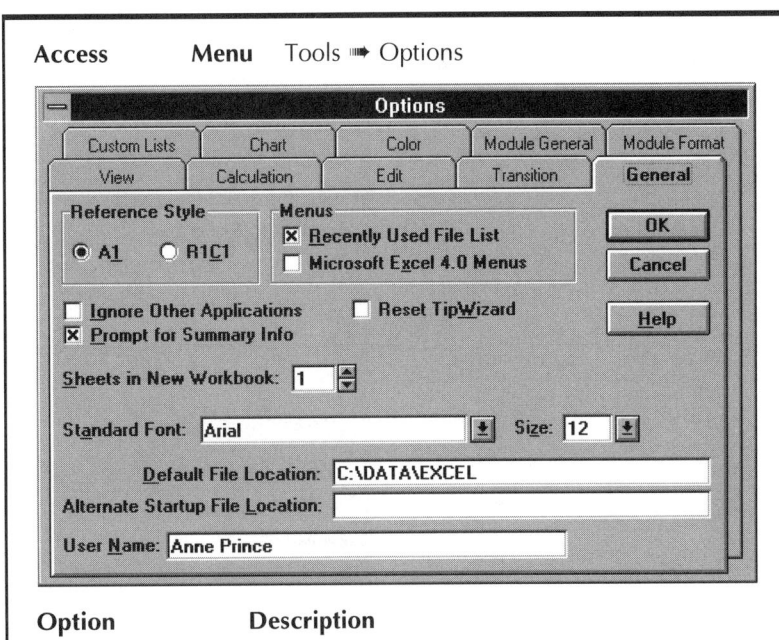

Access Menu Tools ➡ Options

Option	Description
A1/R1C1	Determines whether column headings are labeled alphabetically and row headings numerically (A1) or both are labeled numerically (R1C1). This affects the cell references in formulas and functions too.
Recently Used File List	Displays a list of the last four files used on the File menu. You can use this list to open the files.
Microsoft Excel 4.0 Menus	Replaces the Excel 5 menus with Excel 4 menus.
Ignore Other Applications	Ignores requests made from other applications using Dynamic Data Exchange.
Prompt for Summary Info	Displays the Summary Info dialog box when you save a new workbook.
Reset TipWizard	Clears the tips displayed in the TipWizard toolbar.
Sheets in New Workbook	The default number of sheets in a new workbook.
Standard Font and Size	The default font and font size for new sheets and workbooks. These options go into affect the next time you start Excel.
Default File Location	The directory Excel uses by default when you open or save a file.
Alternate Startup File Location	A directory that contains files you want opened automatically when you start Excel.
User Name	The name Excel uses in the Summary Info dialog box.

Note

All of the options in this tab of the Options dialog box are saved from one Excel session to another.

Figure 8-4 How to set the General defaults

Exercise set 8-1

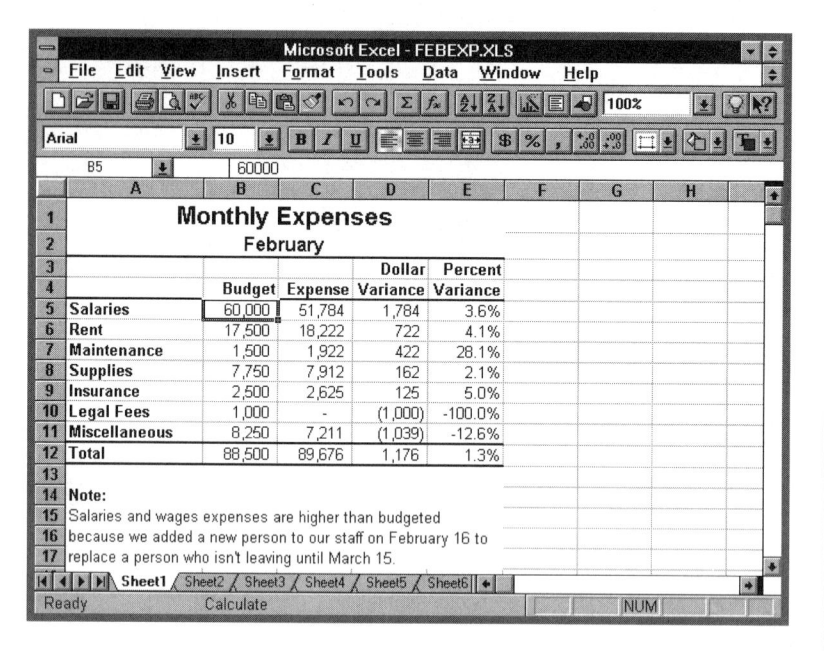

How the worksheet should look in exercise 3 before the values are recalculated

	A	B	C	D	E
1	**Monthly Expenses**				
2	February				
3				Dollar	Percent
4		Budget	Expense	Variance	Variance
5	Salaries	60,000	51,784	1,784	3.6%
6	Rent	17,500	18,222	722	4.1%
7	Maintenance	1,500	1,922	422	28.1%
8	Supplies	7,750	7,912	162	2.1%
9	Insurance	2,500	2,625	125	5.0%
10	Legal Fees	1,000	-	(1,000)	-100.0%
11	Miscellaneous	8,250	7,211	(1,039)	-12.6%
12	Total	88,500	89,676	1,176	1.3%
13					
14	Note:				
15	Salaries and wages expenses are higher than budgeted				
16	because we added a new person to our staff on February 16 to				
17	replace a person who isn't leaving until March 15.				

1. Open the FEBEXP workbook, and scroll down the worksheet so you can see the chart. Then, access the View tab of the Options dialog box, click on the Status Bar option to remove the check mark, click on the Show Placeholders option to choose that option, and click on the OK button. Has the status bar been removed from the screen? What's displayed in place of the chart? Save the file, then exit from Excel.

2. Restart Excel, and open the FEBEXP workbook. Is the status bar displayed? Is the chart displayed? Open the 1994EXP workbook you created in chapter 6. Is the chart displayed in that worksheet? Close the 1994EXP workbook. Then, use the Status Bar command in the View menu to redisplay the status bar. Access the View tab of the Options dialog box. Is the Status Bar option selected? Click on the Show All option to select it, then click on the OK button. The chart should now be displayed again. Save the file, but don't close it.

3. Access the Calculation tab of the Options dialog box, choose the Manual option, and click on the OK button. Now, change the number in cell B5 to 60,000, and notice that the status bar says "Calculate" to show that the formulas haven't been recalculated. Press the F9 key. Do the calculated values change and is the message in the status bar removed? Access the Calculation tab again, and change the option back to Automatic. Then, close the FEBEXP workbook without saving the changes.

4. Open a new workbook. Then, access the Edit tab of the Options dialog box, click on the Edit Directly in Cell option to remove the check mark, click on the Fixed Decimal option to select it, and click on the OK button. Now, enter the number 125 in cell A1. How is the value formatted? Move the cell pointer back to cell A1 and press the F2 key to edit the cell. Notice that the cursor is in the formula bar, not in the cell. Press the Esc key to cancel the edit operation. Then, double-click on cell A1. Does anything happen? Access the Edit tab of the Options dialog box, click on the Edit Directly in Cell option to select it, click on the Fixed Decimal option to remove the check mark, and click on the OK button.

5. Access the General tab of the Options dialog box, change the Sheets in New Workbook option to 5, change the Size option for the standard font to 12, and, if you haven't already done so, enter the drive and directory where your Excel workbook files are stored in the Default File Location box. What happens when you click on the OK button? To continue, click on the OK button in the dialog box that's displayed.

6. Open a new workbook. How many worksheets are in the new workbook? Access the Open dialog box. What default drive and directory are selected? Click on the Cancel button to cancel the operation. Access the General tab again and change the Size option back to 10, but leave the Sheets in New Workbook option at 5.

How to protect the data in a workbook

When you've spent many hours developing a worksheet, you don't want it to be changed by accident. In some cases, you won't even want others to look at the worksheet without authorization. In these cases, you can protect the worksheet. The type of protection you apply depends on the level of protection you need.

How to protect a worksheet from changes

Figure 8-5 shows how to use the Protect Sheet command to protect a worksheet from being changed. When you use this command, you can choose different options that specify what's protected in the worksheet. All of the options are selected by default, which is usually what you want.

You can also assign a password to a worksheet when you protect it. This prevents someone else from removing the protection for the worksheet. If you need this safeguard, be sure to use a password you'll remember. Better yet, write the password down. Without the password, you won't be able to change the worksheet either.

Access Menu Tools ⇒ Protection ⇒ Protect Sheet

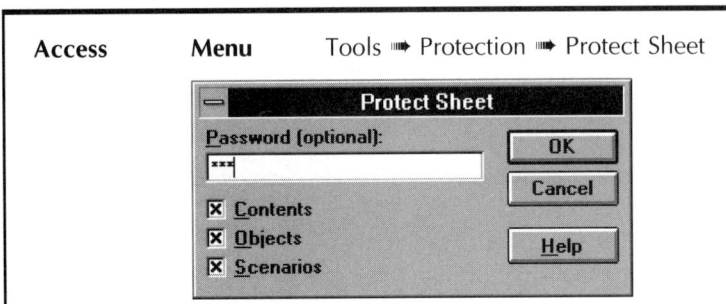

How to protect a worksheet from changes

- To prevent unauthorized users from removing sheet protection, enter a password in the Password text box. When you click on the OK button, Excel displays the Confirm Password dialog box for you to enter the password again.
- To prevent users from changing cells or chart items, choose the Contents option.
- To prevent users from changing graphic objects, choose the Objects option.
- To prevent users from changing scenarios, choose the Scenarios option.

How to remove worksheet protection

- Choose the Unprotect Worksheet command from the Protection submenu of the Tools menu. If the worksheet is password protected, a dialog box appears that asks you to enter the password. Enter the password and click on the OK button to remove the worksheet protection.

Notes

- By default, all the cells and objects in a worksheet are protected from change when you protect the worksheet. To allow changes to selected cells and objects, unlock them before you protect the worksheet using the procedure in figure 8-6.
- All passwords are case sensitive. This means that capitalization matters. For simplicity, then, you may want to enter all passwords in lowercase letters.

Figure 8-5 How to protect a worksheet from changes

How to allow changes to selected cells in a worksheet

By default, all the cells and graphic objects in a worksheet are protected when you protect the worksheet. Sometimes, however, you may want to leave some of the data unprotected. Then, you can delegate the job of keeping the worksheet up-to-date to someone else without worrying that the person will delete or change the formulas, fixed data, or objects in the worksheet.

To unprotect, or unlock, cells and graphic objects before you protect a worksheet, you use the procedures in figure 8-6. Then, after you unlock the cells and objects you want to allow changes to, you protect the worksheet so the other cells and objects can't be changed.

How to unlock cells

1. Select the cells that you want to unlock. This can be a nonadjacent selection. Then, choose the Cells command from the Format menu and click on the Protection tab to display this dialog box:

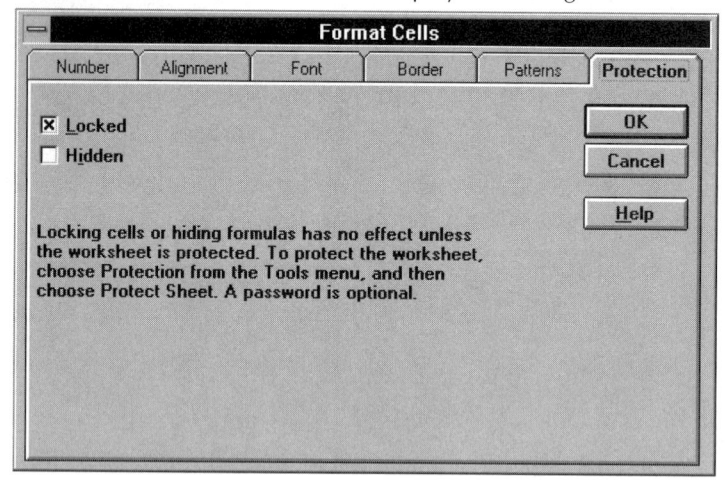

2. Click on the Locked option to remove the check mark, then click on the OK button.

How to unlock an object

- Use the procedure above, but select the object you want to protect (such as a chart) and choose the Object command from the Format menu.

How to protect the worksheet so the locked cells and objects can't be changed

- Use the Protect Sheet command presented in figure 8-5.

Note

- If a cell that contains a formula is locked and the worksheet is protected, the formula still appears in the formula bar when the cell pointer is on that cell. To hide the formula so that it doesn't appear in the formula bar, check the Hidden option in the Protection tab.

Figure 8-6   How to unlock cells or graphic objects

How to protect a workbook from changes

Although you can't change any of the information in a workbook if all of its worksheets are protected, you can change other aspects of the workbook. For example, you can display hidden worksheets and you can delete worksheets entirely. To protect against these types of changes, you can protect the workbook as described in figure 8-7.

Just as you can when you protect a worksheet, you can enter a password when you protect a workbook. Then, workbook protection can't be removed without entering the appropriate password. If you don't use a password, anyone who has access to the workbook can remove the protection and then change the workbook.

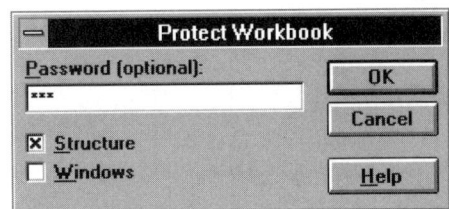

Access **Menu** Tools ➡ Protection ➡ Protect Workbook

How to protect a workbook from changes

- To prevent unauthorized users from removing workbook protection, enter a password in the Password box. When you click on the OK button, Excel displays the Confirm Password dialog box for you to enter the password again.
- To prevent users from adding, deleting, renaming, moving, hiding, or displaying sheets in the workbook, choose the Structure option.
- To prevent users from moving or resizing the workbook's windows, choose the Windows option.

How to remove workbook protection

- Choose the Unprotect Workbook command from the Protection submenu of the Tools menu. If the workbook is password protected, a dialog box appears that asks you to enter the password. Enter the password and click on the OK button to remove the workbook protection.

Note

- Protecting a workbook does not keep unauthorized users from opening it. To do that, save the workbook with a protection password (see figure 8-8).

Figure 8-7   How to protect a workbook from changes

How to protect a workbook from being opened or saved

Although protecting a workbook or worksheet can keep others from changing it, that doesn't keep them from accessing it and viewing its contents. To do that, you need to assign a *protection password* to the file as described in figure 8-8. Then, no one can open the file unless they know the password.

If you want to let other users open and work with a file but not save any changes to it, you can assign a *write reservation password* to the file. Then, when you open the file, you can supply the password so you can save any changes you make. Or, you can open the file in read-only mode without supplying the password. In read-only mode, you can view the file but you can't save any changes that you make to it.

When you assign a password, please keep in mind that there's no way to find out what it is. For a file with a write reservation password, you can get around that problem by opening the file in read-only mode and saving it to a new file without a password. For a file with a protection password, however, you can't access the file in any way without knowing the password.

How to protect a workbook file from being opened

1. Access the Save As dialog box, then click on the Options button to display this dialog box:

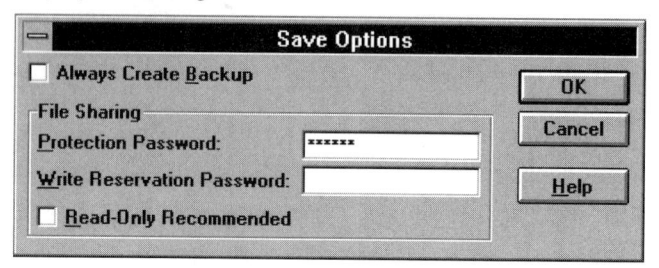

   [Save Options dialog box showing: Always Create Backup checkbox; File Sharing section with Protection Password field (filled with ******) and Write Reservation Password field; Read-Only Recommended checkbox; OK, Cancel, and Help buttons]

2. Enter a password in the Protection Password box. Then, click on the OK button and Excel displays the Confirm Password dialog box. Enter the password again and click on the OK button to return to the Save As dialog box.

3. Complete the save operation.

How to protect a workbook file from being saved

- Use the procedure above, but enter a password in the Write Reservation Password box instead of the Protection Password box.

How to open a password protected file

- Issue the Open command, enter the password, and click on the OK button. For a file with a write reservation password, you can also click on the Read Only button to open the file as read-only without entering a password.

Notes

- If you check the Read-Only Recommended option in the Save Options dialog box, Excel displays a dialog box when you open the file that recommends it be opened as a read-only file. Changes made to a read-only file can't be saved in that file. You have the option of not following the read-only recommendation.

- If you can't remember the protection password for a file, there's no way to open the file. If you can't remember the write reservation password for a file, you can still open the file as read-only. Then, you can save any changes you make to a new file.

Figure 8-8 How to protect a workbook file from being opened or saved

Exercise set 8-2

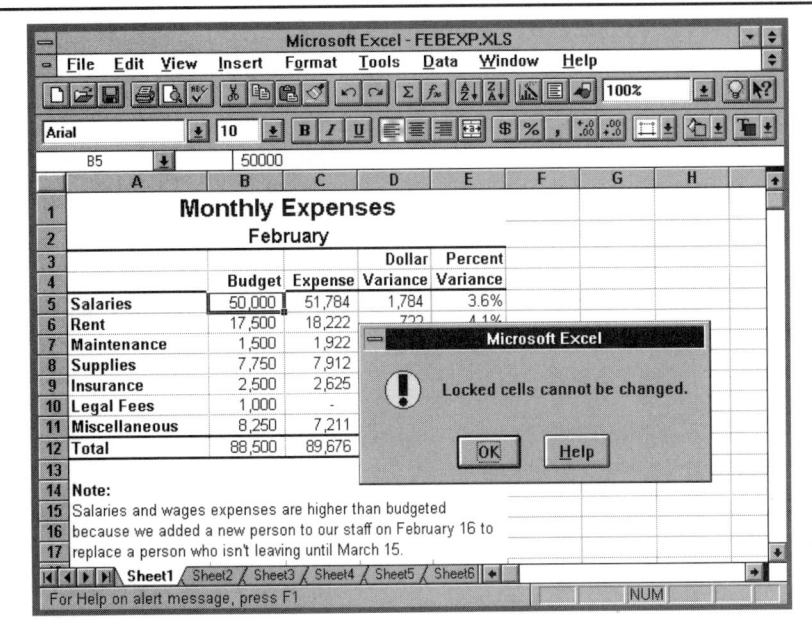

The message that should be displayed when you try to change the data in cell B5 in exercise 1

1. Open the FEBEXP workbook. Then, select cells C5 through C11, and access the Protection tab of the Format Cells dialog box shown in figure 8-6. Remove the check mark from the Locked option and click on the OK button. Next, access the Protect Sheet dialog box shown in figure 8-5 and enter a password that you're sure you'll remember. Click on the OK button, enter the password again in the next dialog box, and click on the OK button in that dialog box. If the second password you entered matches the first password, the operation is complete. Otherwise, you're asked to enter the password again until it matches. Now, try to enter the number 60,000 in cell B5. What happens. Next, enter the number 60,000 in cell C5. Do the totals in the worksheet change? Move the cell pointer to cell B12 and press the F2 key. What happens? Click on the OK button in the dialog box that's displayed. Then, choose the Unprotect Worksheet command from the Protection submenu of the Tools menu and enter the password to remove worksheet protection.

2. Access the Protect Workbook dialog box as described in figure 8-7. Enter the same password you used in the previous exercise, click on the OK button, and enter the password again. Next, pull down the Edit menu. Is the Delete Sheet command available? Pull down the Insert menu and choose the Worksheet command. What happens? Choose the Unprotect Workbook command from the Protection submenu of the Tools menu and enter the password to remove workbook protection.

3. Choose the Save As command from the File menu, and click on the Options button in the Save As dialog box. Enter the same password you used in previous exercises in the Protection Password box of the Save Options dialog box, then click on the OK button and enter the password again. Click on the OK button from the Save As dialog box, and Excel asks if you want to replace the existing file. Click on the OK button, then close the file.

4. Open the FEBEXP workbook again. When the Password dialog box is displayed, enter the password and click on the OK button. Then, access the Save As dialog box, and click on the Options button to display the Save Options dialog box. Delete the protection password, then enter the same password in the Write Reservation Password box. Click on the OK button, enter the password again, then complete the save operation and close the file.

5. Open the FEBEXP workbook. When the Password dialog box is displayed, click on the Read Only button. Change the number in cell B5 to 60,000, then issue the Save command. An error message should be displayed indicating that the file is read-only. Click on the OK button. Does the Save As dialog box appear? This shows that although you can't save changes to a read-only file, you can save the changes to another file. Click on the Cancel button to cancel the operation, then close the file.

6. Open the FEBEXP workbook one more time. When the Password dialog box appears, enter the password and click on the OK button. Then, access the Save As dialog box and click on the Options button. Delete the write reservation password and click on the OK button. Save the workbook and close it.

How to convert files created by other programs to Excel 5 format

If you're converting to Excel 5 from an earlier release of Excel or from another spreadsheet program, you'll probably want to convert your existing spreadsheet files to Excel 5 format. In most cases, the procedure for doing that is simple. You just open each file, then save it in Excel 5 format. Once you do that, you can use some of the features of Excel 5 to improve the appearance of the worksheet and to organize the worksheets so they're easier to use.

How to open a file created by another spreadsheet program

Figure 8-9 presents the procedure for opening a file that was created by another spreadsheet program. The only difference between this procedure and the one for opening an Excel 5 file is that you have to identify the type of file you want to open. Then, in most cases, the file is converted to Excel 5 format with all data and formatting intact.

As you can see in the figure, Excel provides for the most popular types of spreadsheet files. If the type of file you want to convert isn't listed, however, you may be able to convert the file to an intermediate format that Excel recognizes. For example, to convert a *Lotus 1-2-3* Release 4 file to Excel 5, you first have to convert it to *Lotus 1-2-3* Release 1 or Release 3 format. Because these Lotus formats were so popular, most programs are able to convert their files to one of those formats.

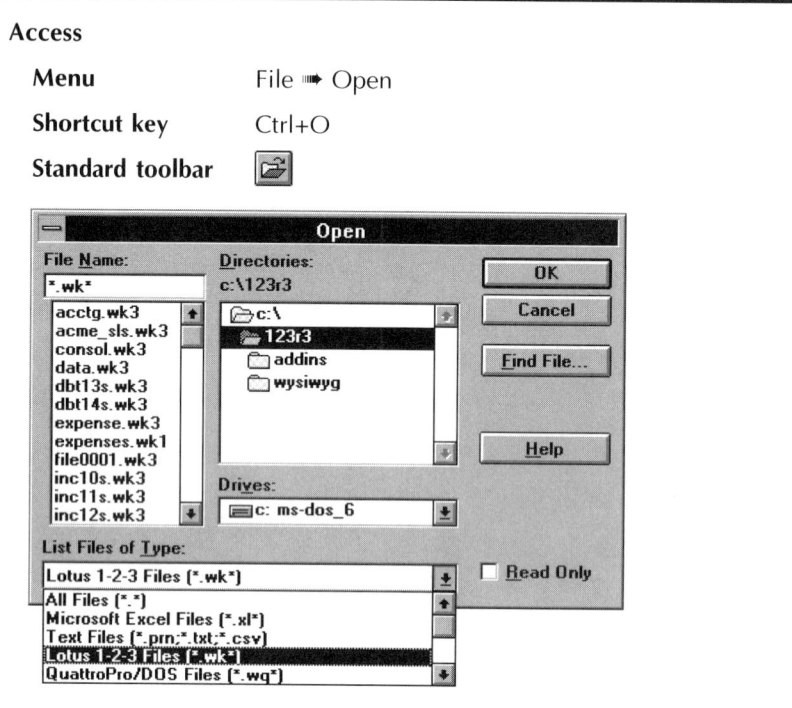

Access

Menu	File ➡ Open
Shortcut key	Ctrl+O
Standard toolbar	📂

Procedure

1. Access the Open dialog box and choose a file type from the List Files of Type drop-down list.
2. Identify the drive and directory that contains the file using the Drives and Directories boxes. Then, double-click on the file name in the File Name list or highlight the file name and click on the OK button.

Spreadsheet files you can convert to Excel 5

- Excel files prior to Excel 5 (*.xl*)
- Lotus 1-2-3 files prior to Release 4 (*.wk*)
- QuattroPro for DOS files (*.wq*)
- Multiplan files (*.*)
- Microsoft Works files (*.wks)

Notes

- When you open a file with one of the file types listed above, Excel 5 is usually able to preserve the text, numbers, formulas, and formats in the file. It can also preserve the charts in a *Lotus 1-2-3* file. It can preserve the links between the worksheets in a single *Lotus 1-2-3* file. And it can preserve the links between separate *Lotus 1-2-3* files.
- If you need to open a file created by a spreadsheet program that's not listed above, you may be able to save the file in one of the above formats using the same program that was used to create the file. To convert a *Lotus 1-2-3* Release 4 file to Excel 5, for example, you can use *Lotus 1-2-3* Release 4 to save the file in Release 3 format. Then, you can open the Release 3 file from Excel.

Figure 8-9 How to open a file created by another spreadsheet program

How to save a file created by another spreadsheet program as an Excel 5 file

Figure 8-10 presents two methods for saving a file created by another program as an Excel 5 file. Whichever method you use, the important point is that you assign the extension XLS to the file. Then, it's automatically saved in Excel 5 format.

How to improve the worksheets that you convert to Excel 5 format

In most cases, Excel is able to preserve the data, formulas, and format of a worksheet that's converted from another format. However, that doesn't mean you won't want to make any changes to the worksheets after they're converted. On the contrary, you'll want to take advantage of some of the features of Excel 5 that weren't available with the program used to create the original files.

First, you'll want to take advantage of some of the advanced formatting features of Excel 5 to improve the appearance of the worksheets. Second, and most importantly, you'll want to take advantage of the Excel 5 feature that lets you store two or more worksheets in a single workbook. Then, you can split some of the large worksheets into two or more worksheets in the same workbook. You can also combine related worksheets into a single workbook. If you do that, you'll be able to work with the worksheets more efficiently.

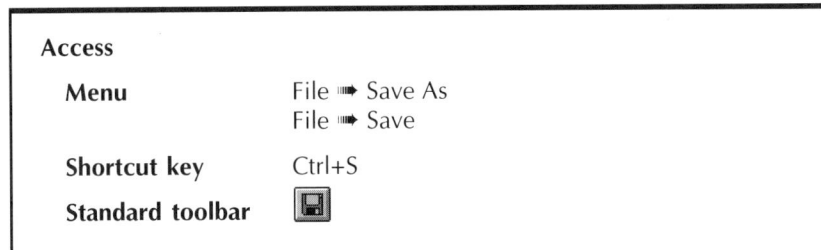

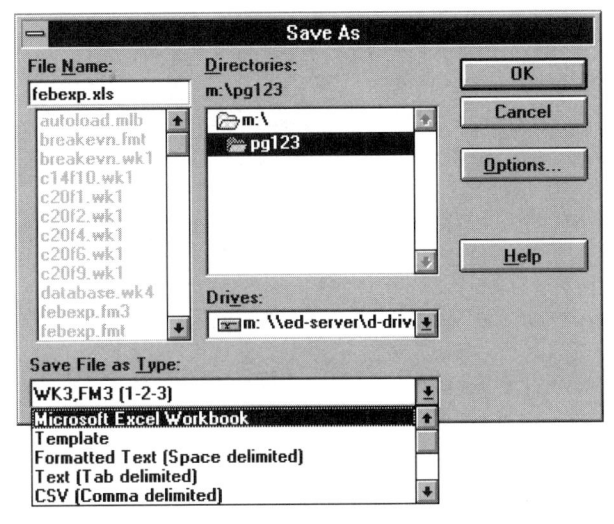

Access

Menu	File ➡ Save As
	File ➡ Save
Shortcut key	Ctrl+S
Standard toolbar	💾

Method 1

1. Access the Save As dialog box and choose the Microsoft Excel Workbook option from the Save File as Type drop-down list. The file extension for the file in the File Name text box changes to XLS.

2. Identify the drive and directory where you want to save the file using the Drives and Directories boxes, then click on the OK button to save the file with the same name.

Method 2

- Access the Save As dialog box, type the file name and extension (XLS) into the File Name text box, and click on the OK button.

Notes

- Excel displays the Save As dialog box when you try to save a converted file that hasn't yet been saved in Excel 5 format. This gives you a chance to save the file in Excel 5 format instead of the original format.

- When you try to close a converted file before you've saved it, Excel displays a dialog box that lets you know that you haven't saved it in Excel 5 format. This too gives you chance to save the file the way you want it.

Figure 8-10   How to save a file created by another spreadsheet program as an Excel 5 file

When and how to use the Help feature

If you experiment with the Help feature of Excel, you'll see that it provides a wide variety of information. In general, this information is most useful when you already know how to use a function or feature, but you just can't remember some detail. If you need to look up the syntax for the ROUND function, for example, using the Help feature is probably more efficient than using any other reference.

In contrast, the Help information is least useful when you're trying to learn the basics of Excel or how to use a new feature or function. In those cases, the Help information is likely to frustrate you. For those purposes, you need a book like this one that presents only the information you need in a logical presentation sequence.

An introduction to the commands in the Help menu

Figure 8-11 shows the Help menu and summarizes its commands. When you issue one of these commands, a window opens for the Help information. This window is actually an application window for a separate program that provides the Help information. As a result, you can minimize, maximize, restore, move, and size the window using standard techniques.

The Help menu

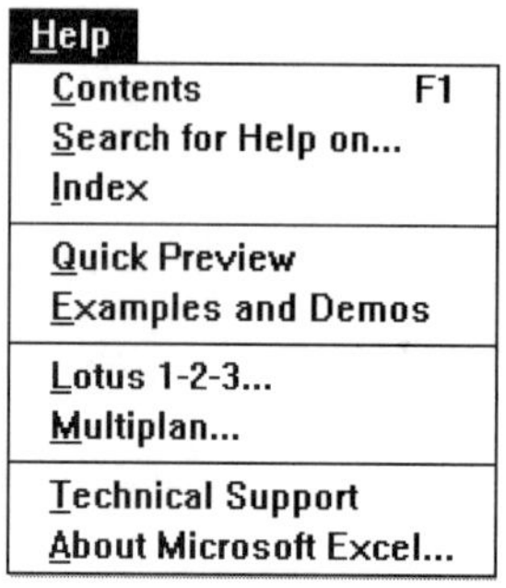

```
Help
  Contents              F1
  Search for Help on...
  Index
  Quick Preview
  Examples and Demos
  Lotus 1-2-3...
  Multiplan...
  Technical Support
  About Microsoft Excel...
```

Command	Function
Contents	Displays the table of contents for the Help information.
Search for Help on	Searches for Help information on a particular topic.
Index	Displays an alphabetical list of topics.
Quick Preview	Presents four tutorials on how to work with Excel 5.
Examples and Demos	Presents examples of and practice activities for common Excel features.
Lotus 1-2-3	Displays reference and tutorial information on Excel equivalents of *Lotus 1-2-3* features.
Multiplan	Displays reference information on Excel equivalents of *Multiplan* commands.
Technical Support	Lists answers to common technical questions and describes how to get technical support from Microsoft.
About Microsoft Excel	Displays copyright and other information about Excel.

Figure 8-11   The commands of the Help menu

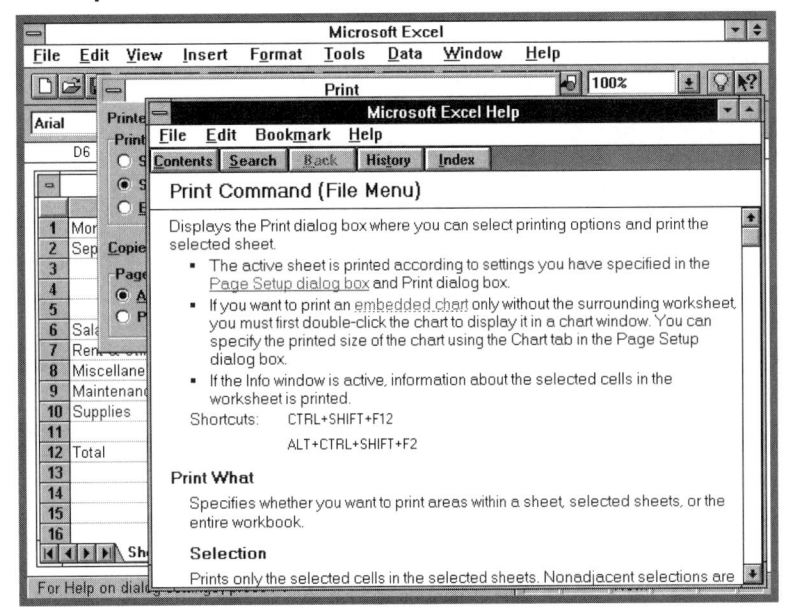

How to get context-sensitive Help information

Although you can use the Help menu to get the information that you need, using one of the techniques in figure 8-12 is usually quicker. When you use these techniques, you get *context-sensitive* information. In other words, you get information about the function you're trying to perform without having to search for it.

In figure 8-12, you can see the context-sensitive Help information for the Print command. This illustrates both the strength and weakness of the Help information that you get with Excel. The strength is that the Help window offers a large amount of information. The weakness is that the information introduces complexities (like embedded charts) that are likely to confuse and distract rather than help.

Three ways to access context-sensitive Help information

- Press the F1 key after you've started an operation.
- Click on the Help button in a dialog box.
- Click on the Help button in the Standard toolbar. Then, click on the menu command or toolbar button that you want to get information for.

The Help information for the Print command

Figure 8-12 How to get context-sensitive Help information

How to navigate through the Help information

Figure 8-13 shows the opening window for the Contents command of the Help menu. As you can see, this command displays the table of contents for Excel's Help information. To choose an entry from the table of contents, you just click on it. Then, Excel displays a list of topics for that entry so you can choose from them.

You can also use the buttons in the Help window to navigate through the Help information. The button you're most likely to use is the Search button, which you'll learn more about in a moment. In addition, you can use the Back button to return to the previous Help screen. You can use the History button to display a list of the topics you've used and to return to any of those topics. And you can use the Index button to display the index for the Help information.

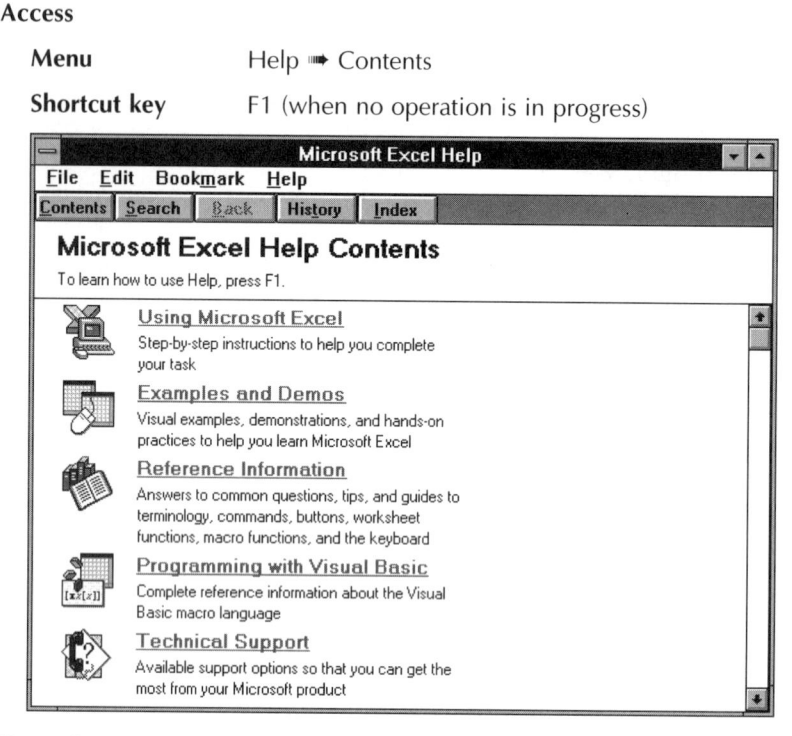

Access

Menu	Help ➔ Contents
Shortcut key	F1 (when no operation is in progress)

Operation

- To choose an entry from the table of contents, click on the entry. Then, Excel displays a list of the topics that are available for that entry. To display the information for a topic, click on it.
- To return to the first table of contents screen shown above, click on the Contents button.
- To display the Search dialog box, click on the Search button.
- To return to the previous screen, click on the Back button.
- To display a list of the topics you've used in the current Help session, click on the History button. Then, you can return to a topic by double-clicking on it in the list.
- To display the Help index, click on the Index button.

Figure 8-13 How to use the Contents command

When you click on the Search button, a dialog box like the one in figure 8-14 is displayed. However, you can also access this dialog box without going through the table of contents by using the other access methods in this figure. The easiest way is to double-click on the Help button in the Standard toolbar.

In the Search dialog box, you enter text that identifies the operation or feature you want information on. Then, Help displays a list that's based on the text you enter. When you choose an item from the list, Help displays another list that contains the topics that are available for that item. Then, you can choose a topic to display the Help information for that topic.

How to print Help information

If you want to keep a permanent copy of the information that you find through the Help feature, you have a couple of options. First, you can print a copy of the current topic by issuing the Print Topic command from the File menu of the Help application window. Second, you can copy a topic or a portion of a topic to the clipboard by issuing the Copy command from the Edit menu of the Help application window. Then, you can paste the information into a word processing program before printing it from that program.

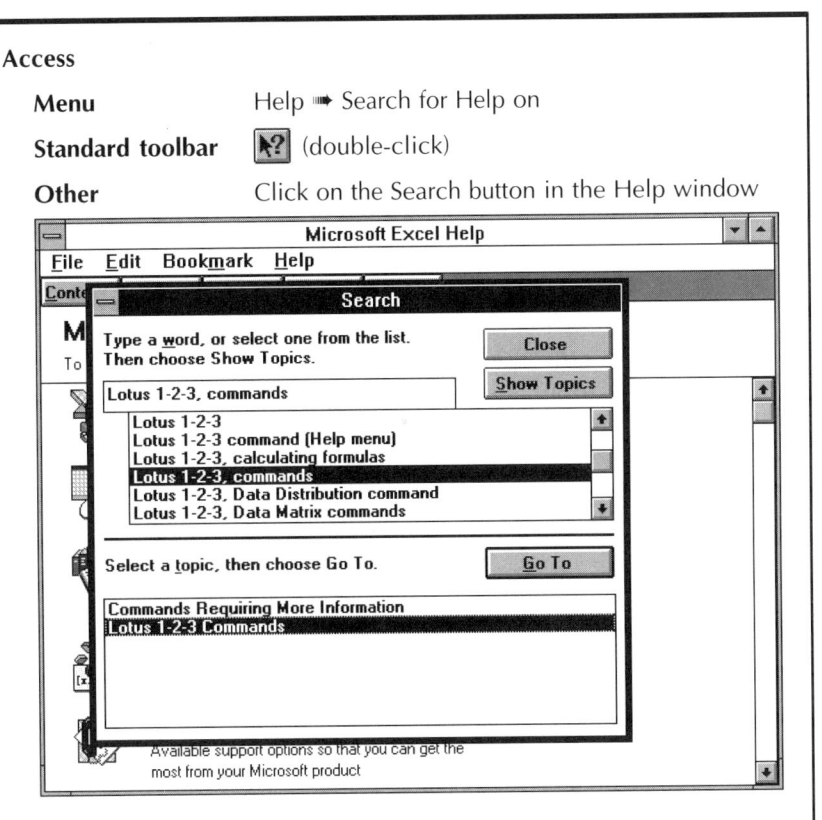

Access

Menu	Help ➡ Search for Help on
Standard toolbar	[?] (double-click)
Other	Click on the Search button in the Help window

Procedure

1. Access the Search dialog box, then enter text in the text box near the top of the dialog box to scroll the list below the text box.

2. Double-click on an item in the list or highlight an item and click on the Show Topics button. The topics for that item are displayed in the list at the bottom of the dialog box.

3. Double-click on a topic in the list or highlight a topic and click on the Go To button to display the information on that topic.

Figure 8-14   How to use the Search For Help On command

Exercise set 8-3

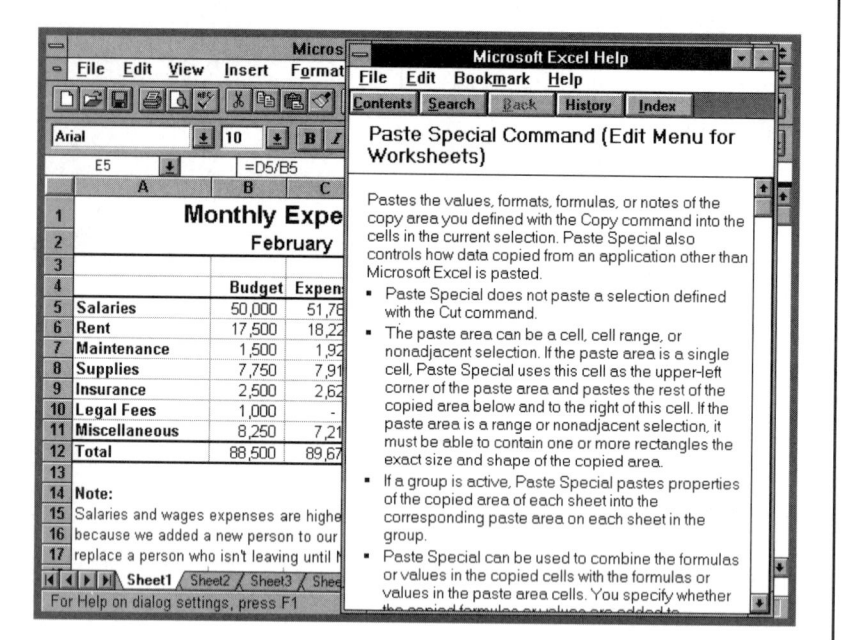

The context-sensitive Help information that should be displayed for exercise 1

1. Open the FEBEXP workbook. Select cells E5 through E11, copy them to the clipboard, and choose the Paste Special command from the Edit menu. When the dialog box appears, click on the Help button or press F1 to display context-sensitive Help information. Look for information about pasting the values instead of the formulas from the clipboard. Is this information easy to find and clearly explained?

2. Click on the Contents button to display the Help table of contents. Click on the Reference Information entry to display its subentries. Click on the Menu Commands subentry. Can you display information about a specific command this way? No, you can't, and that obviously limits the value of this navigation path.

3. Click on the Search button and enter "paste special" in the Search dialog box. With the "Paste Special command (Edit menu)" entry highlighted, click on the Show Topics button. Then, double-click on the "Paste Special Command (Edit Menu for Worksheets)" topic. Is this the same information that was displayed when you first accessed Help from the Paste Special dialog box?

4. Click on the Back button three times to return to the table of contents. Then, click on the History button to display a list of the Help topics you've accessed. Double-click on the first entry for the Paste Special command to display that Help information. Then, double-click on the control-menu box for the Help window to close that window and return to the Paste Special dialog box. Click on the Cancel button to cancel the operation.

5. Click on the Help button in the Standard toolbar, pull down the Edit menu, and click on the Paste Special command. This is another way to access Help information for a command or toolbar button. Click on the first set of highlighted words in the information that's displayed ("Paste Special Command") to return to the information that you displayed earlier. Then, pull down the File menu in the Help window. If you choose the Print Topic command, the Help information is printed. Instead, choose the Exit command to close the Help window and return to the worksheet.

6. Close the FEBEXP workbook without saving it.

Perspective

This chapter presents the last of the commands and features that you need to know to use Excel efficiently and professionally. Although Excel provides many other commands and features, most of them are either so limited that you can easily get by without them or so advanced that most Excel users in business don't need them. For a summary of the features that aren't presented in this book, please review the appendix.

Summary

- The Options command of the Tools menu lets you access tabs that you can use to change the Excel *defaults*. The View tab lets you change the defaults for options that affect the display of the Excel window or the workbook window. The Calculation and Edit tabs let you change the defaults for options that affect the operation of Excel. And the General tab lets you change the defaults for new workbooks.

- When you protect a worksheet, all of its cells and graphic objects are locked by default so they can't be changed. To allow changes to specific cells or graphic objects, unlock the cells or objects before you protect the worksheet. You can also protect the format and layout of an entire workbook. And you can assign a password to a workbook so that only someone who knows the password can open the file or so that only someone who knows the password can save changes to the file.

- You can use the Open command to open a file that was created by another spreadsheet program and convert it to Excel 5 format. Then, you can use the Save As command to save the file in Excel 5 format.

- As you perform an operation, you can get *context-sensitive* Help information by pressing F1 or clicking on the Help button in a dialog box. You can also use the Help button in the Standard toolbar and the commands in the Help menu to get Help information.

Appendix

The Excel features and commands that aren't presented in this book

If you master the features and commands that are presented in this book, you're going to be a thoroughly competent Excel user. And yet, you may be wondering what you've missed. Are there useful features and commands that you aren't aware of? Are there features and commands that could help you work even better?

To help you answer those questions, this appendix summarizes the features and commands that aren't presented in this book. Its purpose is to save you the time that it takes to search through menus, Help information, books, and manuals as you try to find out what each feature and command does. Then, if you find a feature or command in this summary that you think you need for the type of Excel work that you do, you can learn more about it.

If you're an Excel user in business, the features that you're most likely to need are the database features. To start, the Microsoft Query program lets you download data from a corporate or departmental database into Excel. Then, you can use the other database features to analyze the downloaded data. These features are so useful, in fact, that we created a mini-book called *Lists, Pivot Tables, & External Databases*. You can think of this mini-book as a final section in this book, because it uses the same presentation methods including practice exercises.

If you decide that you need some of the other features or commands and you have trouble learning how to use them on your own, we also offer a reference book called *The Essential Guide to Excel 5*. In case you have it, the summary includes references to its chapters and figures. As you can see, this book covers almost all of the Excel features and commands, including lists, pivot tables, and Microsoft Query. The notable exception is Visual Basic for creating macros, but that's a subject of its own.

Now that you've read this book, though, you should be able to master many of the minor features and commands without any manuals or books. If, for example, you want to change the number formats for some cells, try using the Number tab of the Format Cells command. Or if you want to find a misplaced file, try using the Find File command in the File menu. As long as you know what the feature or command is supposed to do, you should be able to get the results you want after a few minutes of experimentation.

As you gain confidence, you'll find that experimentation is often the quickest and best way to learn new commands and to refresh your memory about how to use other commands. Just access a command, study its dialog box, maybe click on the Help button for more information, try some options, and learn by doing. All good professionals do that for the commands that they use infrequently because no one can remember how all the commands and options work.

Database features

Feature	Description	Reference
Lists and filters	When you store information in an Excel *list*, you can think of the rows as *records* and the columns as *fields*. Then, you can use Excel to filter the records in the list based on criteria that you supply. And you can use the data form feature to maintain the records in the list.	Lists, Pivot Tables, & External Databases: Chapter 1 or Essential Guide: Chapter 14
Sorting and subtotals	You can use the Sort command to sort the records in a list as shown in figure 2-13 in this book. Then, you can use the Subtotal command in the Data menu to add subtotals to a list whenever one of the sorted fields changes.	Lists, Pivot Tables, & External Databases: Chapter 2 or Essential Guide: Chapter 15
Pivot tables	The pivot table feature is new in Excel 5. It lets you cross-tabulate and summarize the values in a selected range. Then, you can "pivot" the table to change its arrangement and recompute its summarized values.	Lists, Pivot Tables, & External Databases: Chapter 3 or Essential Guide: Chapter 16
Microsoft Query	Microsoft Query is a separate program that comes with Excel 5. It lets you download data from an external database such as an *Oracle* or an *Access* database, and it is an excellent program for downloading data from corporate or departmental databases. After you download the data, you can use the list and pivot table features to work with the data.	Lists, Pivot Tables, & External Databases: Chapter 4 or Essential Guide: Chapter 17

Other major features

Feature	Description	Reference
Advanced charting	The advanced charting features let you create mixed charts (like a column and line chart together), charts with two different y-axis scales, and a few types of charts that aren't illustrated in chapter 6 of this book.	Essential Guide: Chapter 12
Drawing	The drawing feature lets you enhance a worksheet or chart with lines, text boxes, and other graphic devices.	Essential Guide: Chapter 13
Analytical tools	The Goal Seek and Solver commands in the Tools menu are tools for iterative solutions and what-if analysis. For instance, the Goal Seek command can be used with a pro-forma worksheet model to determining break-even points, while the Solver command can be used to find values for one or more variables that solve a formula.	Essential Guide: Chapter 22
Auditing tools	Chapter 7 shows you two effective techniques for auditing a worksheet. However, Excel also provides other auditing features that can be accessed from the Auditing submenu of the Tools menu and the Auditing toolbar. These can be useful when auditing and documenting the formulas in large, complicated worksheets.	Essential Guide: Chapter 18
Scenarios	The Scenario Manager is a new feature of Excel 5 that lets you create more than one version of the same worksheet by changing some of its variables. However, a new worksheet isn't created for each version. Instead, the Manager keeps track of all versions in a single worksheet and lets you display or print the versions.	Essential Guide: Chapter 21
Recording macros	This feature lets you record the use of commands and keystrokes in a *macro*. Then, you can play the macro whenever you want to repeat the recorded commands and keystrokes.	Essential Guide: Chapter 19
Visual Basic	Visual Basic is a powerful programming language that comes with Excel. It can be used to create extensive macros. However, it is a language for programmers, not business people.	The *Visual Basic User's Guide* that comes with Excel
Object Linking & Embedding	This is actually a Windows feature that's supported by Excel 5. It lets you link an external object to a program or embed an external object in a program. It also maintains the relationship between the two so a change to the object is reflected in the program that it is embedded in or linked to.	Essential Guide: Chapter 23

Minor features

Feature	Description	Reference
Other number formats	The Number tab of the Format Cells command lets you change the number format of the selected cells. This is useful when the Currency, Percent, and Comma styles that are available from the Formatting toolbar don't suit your purposes.	Essential Guide: Figures 5-8 and 5-9
Formulas that refer to cells in other workbooks	If necessary, you can create formulas and functions that refer to cells and ranges in other workbooks. To do that, you just switch to another open workbook and select the cell or range. The reference then starts with the name of the other workbook file. This is much like referring to a cell in another worksheet within the same workbook.	Essential Guide: Figures 9-16 to 9-19
Transposing data	To transpose data from rows to columns, you can copy the data, then use the Paste Special command to paste it with the Transpose option checked. This comes in handy when you want to change the orientation of a worksheet from horizontal to vertical, or vice versa.	Essential Guide: Figure 7-17
Custom AutoFill sequences	The Custom Lists tab of the Options command in the Tools menu lets you create a custom AutoFill sequence that you can enter by dragging the Fill handle.	Essential Guide: Figure 5-16
Changing row heights	You can change row heights by using mouse techniques like the ones that you use for changing column widths. Just drag the row separator.	Essential Guide: Figures 8-5 and 8-6
Transition defaults for 1-2-3 users	You can use the Transition tab of the Options command in the Tools menu to adjust Excel so it works more like 1-2-3. We don't recommend this, though, because you only slow your progress with Excel 5 if you continue to use 1-2-3 techniques like pressing the slash key to access menus.	Essential Guide: Figure 2-33
The TextWizard	When you use Excel to open a text file, the TextWizard is automatically started. It lets you specify the points at which the text data should be divided into columns. Most programs are able to export data in 1-2-3 format as well as text format, though, and Excel 5 is able to convert 1-2-3 files automatically so you shouldn't need to work with text files.	Essential Guide: Figure 17-2
The TipWizard	This wizard monitors your work and offers suggestions in the TipWizard toolbar for how to work more efficiently. To display or hide this toolbar, click on the TipWizard button in the Standard toolbar. This can be helpful when you're new to Excel, but the best way to improve your efficiency is to master the techniques presented in this book.	Essential Guide: Figure 3-9

Miscellaneous commands

Command	Function	Reference
File ➡ Save Workspace	Saves the current arrangement of the open workbook windows on disk with a file name that has XLW as the extension. When you open the XLW file, all of the related files are opened too. This is useful if you frequently work on the same workbooks at the same time.	Essential Guide: Figure 24-1
File ➡ Find File	This command lets you find files with the name or extension that you specify on the disk drive that you specify. It also lets you copy, print, and delete any of the files that are found. For most file management, though, we recommend the use of the Windows File Manager.	Essential Guide: Figure 24-2
File ➡ Print Report	Lets you set up and print one or more *reports* for a workbook that contain customized printing specifications for one or more *sections*. Each section can identify a worksheet, a view of that worksheet, and a scenario for that worksheet. When you print a report, you print all of its sections at the same time.	Essential Guide: Figure 24-4
View ➡ Toolbars	The Toolbars dialog box lets you customize the Excel toolbars by adding or deleting buttons. It also lets you create new toolbars.	Essential Guide: Figures 20-4 to 20-7
Insert ➡ Note	Lets you attach a note to the active cell that explains the purpose of the cell or the formula that it contains. This is useful for documenting the calculations used in complex formulas within a worksheet.	Essential Guide: Figure 18-8
Insert ➡ Picture	Lets you insert a graphic object that's stored in a file created by another program into the current worksheet.	None
Tools ➡ Add-Ins	Lets you enable or disable an *add-in program* that comes with Excel like View Manager, Print Report, and Solver. Before you can use an add-in program, you need to enable it. If you don't intend to use one that's enabled, you can disable it. Then, the program isn't loaded into memory when you start Excel, which may improve operating speeds.	Essential Guide: Figure 24-9
Data ➡ Subtotals	Lets you add subtotals to a worksheet whenever the value in a sorted column changes. It can also add a grand total, and it can use functions like COUNT and AVERAGE instead of SUM.	Essential Guide: Figure 15-5
Data ➡ Tables	Lets you calculate the data in tables that are based on one or two variables. Before you can use this command, though, you have to take the time to set up the tables in the required format so you're often better off using normal worksheet commands for this purpose.	Essential Guide: Figures 24-10 and 24-11
Data ➡ Text to Columns	Lets you divide the text in a column into other columns using the TextWizard.	Essential Guide: Figure 24-12
Data ➡ Consolidate	Lets you summarize the data from two or more source areas into a destination area. The source areas can be in the same workbook or in different workbooks. Except for simple consolidations, though, it's difficult to interpret the way this command is going to work.	Essential Guide: Figure 24-13
Data ➡ Group and Outline	Displays a submenu that can be used to group and outline the levels of data in a worksheet. Then, you can use mouse techniques to hide and display data within the outline. This is yet another way to look at and rearrange the data in a worksheet.	Essential Guide: Figures 7-33 and 7-34

Index

A

About Microsoft Excel command (Help menu), 228
Absolute reference, 200, 201
Activating a chart, 175
Active application window, 10
Active cell, 32, 33
Active program, 10
Active worksheet, 147
Adding
    borders, 93, 95
    chart legend, 186
    chart titles, 185
    decimal point to numbers automatically, 218
    gridlines to a chart, 187
    worksheets, 147
Adjusting
    column width, 37, 73-74
    row height, 73
Align Left button (Formatting toolbar), 45
Align Right button (Formatting toolbar), 45
Aligning entries, 45, 54, 100
Alignment tab (Format Cells dialog box), 45, 100
Alt+Tab switching, 10
Annuity due method, 206
Application, 9
    exiting, 10, 15
    starting, 9
    switching to, 10
Application menu, 12
Application window, 2, 3
    Excel, 32
Applying
    background colors and patterns, 94, 95
    styles, 110
Applying an autoformat, 96
    to a chart, 184
Area chart, 170
Argument (function), 52, 205
Arithmetic operators, 49
Arrange command (Window menu), 159, 162
Arranging windows for a workbook, 159
Auditing a worksheet, 210-212
AutoFill feature
    copying formulas, 50
    generating a series, 78
Autoformat, 96
    applying to a chart, 184
AutoFormat command (Format menu), 96, 181, 184
Automatic page breaks, 131
Automatic recalculation, 217
AutoSum button (Standard toolbar), 53
AVERAGE function, 52
Axes command (Insert menu), 181

B

Background colors, 94, 95
Bar chart, 170
Bold button (Formatting toolbar), 90
Border tab (Format Cells dialog box), 95
Borders, 93, 95
Borders button (Formatting toolbar), 93

C

Calculation tab (Options dialog box), 217
Canceling
    commands from a dialog box, 13
    entries, 36
    print jobs, 134
Categories (chart), 171
Cell, 32
    identifying in a formula, 48, 49
Cell pointer, 32
    moving in a range, 40
    moving in a worksheet, 33
    moving to a named range, 138
    moving within selected cells, 212
Cell reference, 32
Cells
    deleting, 83
    inserting, 83
    unlocking, 222
Cells command
    Format menu, 91, 95, 100, 222
    Insert menu, 83
Center Across Columns button (Formatting toolbar), 98
Center button (Formatting toolbar), 45
Centering data across columns, 98
Changing
    chart titles, 185
    chart type and subtype, 182
    data in a chart, 177
    default directory, 219
    default number of worksheets, 147
    display in the directory window, 19
    font, 88, 91
    font attributes, 90, 91
    font size, 89, 91
    formulas to values, 195
    header and footer, 103-104
    margins, 102, 105
    name of a worksheet, 145
    orientation of a worksheet, 129
    scale on a chart axis, 188
    sizing of a worksheet, 129
    standard font and font size, 219
    tick marks on a chart axis, 188
Chart
    activating, 175
    copying, 175
    creating, 172-174
    deleting, 175
    formatting, 176
    moving, 175
    selecting, 175
    sizing for printing, 189

Chart As New Sheet command (Insert menu), 172, 181
Chart components, 171
    deleting, 176
    moving, 176
    selecting, 175
Chart On This Sheet command (Insert menu), 172, 181
Chart sheet, 172
    creating, 174
    deleting, 175
Chart subtype, 182
Chart tab (Page Setup dialog box), 189
Chart titles
    adding, 185
    changing, 185
Chart toolbar, 180
Chart Type button (Chart toolbar), 180, 182
Chart Type command (Format menu), 181, 182
Chart types, 170
    changing, 182
ChartWizard, 172-174
ChartWizard button
    Chart toolbar, 180
    Standard toolbar, 172
Check box, 13
Checking the spelling in a worksheet, 80
Circular references, 194
Clear command (Edit menu), 71, 176
Clear Formats command (Edit menu), 107
Clicking the mouse, 3
Clipboard, 68
Close command (File menu), 55, 58
Closing
    menus, 12
    workbooks, 58
Color button (Formatting toolbar), 94
Colors, 94, 95
Column AutoFit Selection command (Format menu), 74
Column chart, 170
Column Group command (Format menu), 181
Column Hide command (Format menu), 122
Column Standard Width command (Format menu), 74
Column Unhide command (Format menu), 123
Column width, 37, 73-74
Column Width command (Format menu), 74
Columns
    freezing and unfreezing, 126
    hiding, 122, 124
    revealing, 123, 125
Columns command (Insert menu), 76
Comma Style button (Formatting toolbar), 46
Command, 12, 13
Command button, 13
Comparison cell, 211
Components of a chart, 171
Contents command (Help menu), 228, 230
Context-sensitive Help information, 229
Context-sensitive menu, 64
Control menu, 4, 7, 10
Converting files to Excel 5 format, 226-227
Copy button (Formatting toolbar), 68
Copy command (Edit menu), 68, 150, 163
Copying
    charts, 175
    files, 19

Copying (continued)
    formats, 107, 108
    formulas to adjacent cells, 50
    styles from another workbook, 111
Copying data
    between workbooks, 70, 163
    between worksheets, 150
    using drag-and-drop editing, 69
    using menu commands, 68, 70
Copying worksheets
    between workbooks, 164
    within a workbook, 156-157
COUNT function, 52
Creating
    absolute references, 200
    charts, 172-174
    custom headers or footers, 104
    default charts, 174
    directories, 19
    mixed references, 200
    relative references, 200
    styles, 110
Currency format, 39
Currency Style button (Formatting toolbar), 46
Custom AutoFill sequence, 78
Cut button (Formatting toolbar), 68
Cut command (Edit menu), 68, 150, 163

D

Data
    aligning, 100
    centering across columns, 98
    copying within a worksheet, 68, 69, 70
    copying between workbooks, 70, 163
    copying between worksheets, 150
    deleting, 71
    entering, 36-42
    moving between workbooks, 70, 163
    moving between worksheets, 150
    moving within a worksheet, 68, 69
    searching for, 81
    sorting, 79
Data Labels command (Insert menu), 181
Data marker, 171
Data point, 171
Data range, 79
Data series, 171
Database & List Management functions, 204
Date & Time functions, 204
Dates
    entering into a worksheet, 41
    in arithmetic operations, 196
DDE & External functions, 204
Decimal number (time), 196
Decimal point, 218
Decrease Decimal button (Formatting toolbar), 46
Default Chart button (Chart toolbar), 180
Default file location, 57
Defaults, 216
Delete command (Edit menu), 75, 76
Delete key, 71
Delete Sheet command (Edit menu), 147, 175
Deleting
    chart components, 176

Deleting (continued)
    chart legends, 186
    chart sheets, 175
    charts, 175
    columns, 76
    data, 71
    directories, 19
    files, 19
    formats, 107
    gridlines from a chart, 187
    names, 136
    page breaks, 131
    ranges, 83
    rows, 75
    styles, 110, 111
    views, 127
    worksheets, 147
Dependents, 212
Desktop, 3
Destination workbook, 111
Detecting circular references, 194
Dialog box, 13-15
Directory, 17, 19
    selecting in a dialog box, 21
Directory pane (Directory window), 17
Directory tree, 21
Directory window (File Manager), 17
Disk drive, 17
Disk Operating System (DOS), 2
Diskette drive, 17
Displaying
    automatic page breaks, 131
    dates and times as numbers, 196
    multiple workbooks, 162
    multiple worksheets, 159
    toolbars, 117
Displaying a worksheet
    in Full Screen view, 116
    with its formulas, 210
Document window, 2, 3
    Excel, 32
DOS, 2
Double-clicking the mouse, 3
Drag-and-drop editing, 69
    moving or copying worksheets between workbooks, 164
    moving or copying worksheets within workbooks, 156
Dragging the mouse, 3
Drive, 21
Drop-down list, 13

E

Edit defaults, 218
Edit tab (Options dialog box), 218
Editing
    cell contents, 42
    data in more than one worksheet, 149
    directly in a cell, 42
    functions with the Function Wizard, 207
    in the formula bar, 42
Embedded chart, 172
Engineering functions, 204
Entering
    functions with the Function Wizard, 207
    names into a formula or function, 197

Entering (continued)
    numbers into a worksheet, 38
    text into a worksheet, 36
Entering data, 36-42
    in more than one worksheet, 149
    into a range, 40
Entering dates and times, 41
    into a formula, 196
Entering formulas, 48-49
    that refer to other worksheets, 151
Entering functions, 51-52
    that refer to other worksheets, 152
Entry area, 32
Examples and Demos command (Help menu), 228
Exit command (File menu), 15, 55, 60
Exiting
    from a program, 10, 15
    from Excel, 60
    from Windows, 7
Exploded pie chart, 176
Extending a range, 44
Extension, 18

F

File, 17
    copying, 19
    creating, 19
    moving, 19
    opening, 20-22
    renaming, 19
    retrieving from disk, 20-22
    saving, 23
    selecting in a dialog box, 22
File Manager, 17-19
File menu, 55
File name, 18
File name command (File menu), 55, 59
File protection, 224
File types, 226
Fill Across Worksheets command (Edit menu), 150
Fill Down command (Edit menu), 70
Fill handle, 50
Fill Justify command (Edit menu), 99
Fill Left command (Edit menu), 70
Fill Right command (Edit menu), 70
Fill Series command (Edit menu), 78
Fill Up command (Edit menu), 70
Financial functions, 204
Find command (Edit menu), 81
Fitting a worksheet to the page, 129
Focus, 14
Font, 88, 91, 219
Font attributes, 90, 91
Font Color button (Formatting toolbar), 90
Font list (Formatting toolbar), 88
Font size, 88, 89, 91, 219
Font Size list (Formatting toolbar), 89
Font tab (Format Cells dialog box), 91
Footer, 103-104
Format menu for a chart, 181
Format Painter, 108
Formats
    copying, 107, 108
    deleting, 107

Formatting
    data in more than one worksheet, 149
    numbers, 46
    results of formulas and functions, 54
Formatting a chart
    using the Format command, 188
    using toolbar buttons, 176
Formatting toolbar, 34
    for formatting a chart, 176
Formula bar, 32, 33
Formula Bar command (View menu), 116, 216
Formulas
    aligning results, 54
    changing to values, 163, 195
    copying to adjacent dells, 50
    displaying, 210
    entering, 48-49
    hiding, 222
    printing, 210
    selecting, 211
    that refer to other worksheets, 151
Freeze Panes command (Window menu), 126
Freezing rows and columns, 126
Full Screen command (View menu), 116
Full Screen view, 116
Full View toolbar, 116
Function, 48
    aligning results, 54, 54
    entering, 51-52
    that refer to other worksheets, 152
Function categories, 204
Function command (Insert menu), 207
Function name, 52
Function Wizard, 207
FV function, 206
F2 (Edit) key, 42
F3 (Name) key, 197
F4 (Absolute) key, 200, 201
F9 (Calc) key, 195, 217

G
General defaults, 219
General format, 38, 39, 41
General tab (Options dialog box), 219
Go To command (Edit menu), 123, 138
    for auditing a worksheet, 211
Gridlines, 130, 187
Gridlines command (Insert menu for a chart), 181, 187
Group window, 2, 3
Grouping worksheets, 146

H
Hard disk drive, 17
Header, 103-104
Header/Footer tab (Page Setup dialog box), 103
Help button
    dialog box, 229
    Standard toolbar, 229, 231
Help feature, 228-231
Help menu, 228
Hiding
    columns, 122, 123
    formulas, 222

Hiding (continued)
    rows, 122, 124
    toolbars, 117
    worksheets, 158
Horizontal Gridlines button (Chart toolbar), 180, 187
Horizontal page breaks, 131
Horizontal scroll bar, 6
Horizontal split box, 119

I
Icon, 4
Identifying
    cells in a formula, 48, 49
    ranges in a function, 51, 52
Increase Decimal button (Formatting toolbar), 46
Index command (Help menu), 228
Information functions, 204
Insert menu for a chart, 181
Inserting
    cells, 83
    columns, 76
    page breaks, 131
    rows, 75
Insertion point, 36, 42
Issuing a command, 12
    from a shortcut menu, 64
Italic button (Formatting toolbar), 90

J
Justifying text within columns, 99

L
Legend, 171, 186
Legend button (Chart toolbar), 180, 186
Legend command (Insert menu), 181, 186
Line chart, 170
List box, 13
Local printer, 134
Logical functions, 204
Lookup & Reference functions, 204
Lotus 1-2-3 command (Help menu), 228

M
Manual page breaks, 131
Manual recalculation, 217
Margins
    changing from the Margins tab, 102
    changing from the Print Preview window, 105
Margins tab (Page Setup dialog box), 102
Math & Trigonometry functions, 204
Maximizing a window, 4
Menu, 12
Menu bar, 2
    Excel, 32, 33
Merging styles, 111
Minimizing a window, 4
Mixed reference, 200, 202
Modifying styles, 110, 111
Mouse actions, 3
Move or Copy Sheet command (Edit menu), 157, 165
Moving
    between windows, 159

Moving (continued)
    between worksheets, 145
    chart components, 176
    charts, 175
    files, 19
    focus in a dialog box, 14
    windows, 5
Moving data
    between workbooks, 70, 163
    between worksheets, 150
    using drag-and-drop editing, 69
    using menu commands, 68
Moving the cell pointer, 33
    in a range, 40
    to a named range, 138
    within selected cells, 212
Moving worksheets
    between workbooks, 164
    within a workbook, 156-157
Multiplan command (Help menu), 228
Multitasking, 9

N
Name Apply command (Insert menu), 198
Name box, 32
    displaying the column width, 37
    entering a name into a formula or function, 197
    moving to a named range, 138
    naming a range, 136
Name Create command (Insert menu), 137
Name Define command (Insert menu), 136
Name Paste command (Insert menu), 197
Names, 136-138
    deleting, 136
    entering into a formula or function, 197
    replacing references, 198
    using in workbooks with multiple worksheets, 160
Naming ranges, 136, 137
Network disk drive, 17
Network printer, 134
New button (Standard toolbar), 60
New command (File menu), 55, 60
New Data command (Insert menu), 181
New Window command (Window menu), 159
Nonadjacent selections, 44
NOW function, 52
Num Lock key, 33
Number formats, 39
Number tab (Format Cells dialog box), 46
Numbers
    entering into a worksheet, 38
    formatting, 46

O
Object command (Format menu), 222
Open button (Standard toolbar), 59, 226
Open command (File menu), 20, 55, 59, 161, 224, 226
Opening
    password protected files, 224
    windows for a workbook, 159
    workbooks, 59, 161
Opening a file, 20-22
    created by another program, 226

Option button, 13
Options command (Tools menu), 216-219
Order of precedence, 49
Ordinary annuity method, 206
Orientation
    text, 100
    worksheet, 129

P
Page Break command (Insert menu), 131
Page breaks, 131
Page Setup command (File menu), 55, 102, 103, 129, 130, 153, 177, 189
Page tab (Page Setup dialog box), 129
Panes, 17, 119
Parentheses in formulas, 49
Password
    assigning to a file, 224
    assigning to a workbook, 223
    assigning to a worksheet, 221
Paste button (Formatting toolbar), 68
Paste command (Edit menu), 68, 150, 163
Paste Special command (Edit menu), 107, 163, 195
Pasting formulas as values, 163
Path, 18
Patterns, 94, 95
Patterns tab (Format Cells dialog box), 95
Percent Style button (Formatting toolbar), 46
Percentage format, 39
Pie chart, 170
    exploded, 176
Placeholders in a function, 208
PMT function, 205
Pointing with the mouse, 3
Precedents, 212
Previewing a worksheet, 105
Primary sort key, 79
Print button (Standard toolbar), 56
Print command (File menu), 55, 56, 133
Print job, 134
Print order, 130
Print orientation, 129
Print Preview command (File menu), 55, 105
Print Preview window, 105
Print queue (Print Manager), 134
Print size, 129
Printer, 56
Printer fonts, 88
Printing
    charts, 177
    formulas, 210
    gridlines, 130
    Help information, 231
    multiple worksheets, 153
    part of a worksheet, 130, 133
    titles on each page of a worksheet, 130
    worksheets, 56
Program
    exiting, 10, 15
    starting, 9
    switching to, 10
Program group, 9
Program Manager, 2-7, 9-10

Program menu, 12
Protect Sheet command (Protection submenu, Tools menu), 221, 222
Protect Workbook command (Protection submenu, Tools menu), 223
Protecting
    files from being opened or saved, 224
    workbooks, 223
    worksheets, 221
Protection password, 224
Protection tab (Format Cells dialog box), 222

Q

Quick Preview command (Help menu), 228

R

Range, 40
    identifying in a function, 51, 52
    naming, 136
    selecting, 40
Range entry, 40
Read-only mode, 224
Recalculating a worksheet, 217
Redo command (Edit menu), 65
Reducing a range, 44
References
    replacing with names, 198
    types, 200
Relative reference, 200
Remove Page Break command (Insert menu), 131
Removing
    autoformats, 96
    workbook protection, 223
    worksheet protection, 221
Renaming a file or directory, 19
Repeat command (Edit menu), 65
Replace command (Edit menu), 82
Replacing references with names, 198
Restoring a window, 4
Retrieving a file from disk, 20-22
Revealing
    columns, 123, 125
    rows, 123, 125
    worksheets, 158
Root directory, 17
Row height, 73
Row Hide command (Format menu), 122
Row Unhide command (Format menu), 123
Rows
    freezing and unfreezing, 126
    hiding, 122, 124
    revealing, 123, 125
Rows command (Insert menu), 75

S

Save As command (File menu), 23, 55, 57, 224, 227
Save button (Standard toolbar), 57, 227
Save command (File menu), 55, 57, 227
Saving
    views, 127
    workbooks, 57
Saving a file, 23
    created by another program, 227

Scale, 188
Scaleable font, 89
Scroll bar, 6
Scroll Lock key, 33
Scrolling a window, 6
Search for Help on command (Help menu), 228, 231
Searching
    for data, 81
    for Help information, 231
Secondary sort key, 79
Select All button, 44
Selected Object command (Format menu), 181, 188
Selecting
    cell dependents, 212
    cell precedents, 212
    cells that don't match a pattern, 211
    chart components, 175
    charts, 175
    directory in a dialog box, 21
    drive in a dialog box, 21
    file in a dialog box, 22
    formulas in a worksheet, 211
    printer, 56
    range, 40, 44
Serial number (date), 196
Setting defaults, 216-219
Sheet Hide command (Format menu), 158
Sheet Rename command (Format menu), 145
Sheet tab, 32, 144
Sheet tab (Page Setup dialog box), 130
Sheet Unhide command (Format menu), 158
Shell program, 2
Shortcut keys
    for applying font attributes, 90
    for entering function arguments, 208
    for moving to another worksheet, 145
    for selecting cells, 44
    for switching to another window, 66
Shortcut menu
    for a range, 64
    for toolbars, 117
Showing a view, 127
Sizing
    chart components, 176
    charts for printing, 189
    windows, 5
    worksheets, 129
Sort Ascending button (Standard toolbar), 79
Sort command (Data menu), 79
Sort Descending button (Standard toolbar), 79
Sort key, 79
Sorting data, 79
Source workbook, 111
Spelling command (Tools menu), 80
Spin box, 13
Split command (Window menu), 119
Splitting a window into panes, 119
Standard toolbar, 34
Starting
    commands from a dialog box, 13
    Windows, 2
    workbooks, 60
Starting an application
    from the File Manager, 19

Starting an application (continued)
    from the Program Manager, 9
    from Windows 95, 25
Statistical functions, 204
Status bar, 32
Status Bar command (View menu), 116, 216
Style command (Format menu), 110
Styles, 46, 110-111
Subdirectory, 17
Submenu, 12
SUM function, 52
    entering with the AutoSum button, 53
Summary Info command (File menu), 55, 57
Switch To command (Control menu), 10
Switching
    between applications, 10
    between applications in Windows 95, 26
    between tabs, 15
    between workbooks, 66, 161
Syntax (functions), 205

T
Tab, 15
Tab area, 144
Tab scrolling buttons, 144
Tab split box, 144
Task List, 10
Technical Support command (Help menu), 228
Text
    entering into a worksheet, 36
    justifying within columns, 99
Text box, 13
Text functions, 204
Text wrapping, 100
Tick marks, 188
Times
    entering into a worksheet, 41
    in arithmetic operations, 196
Title bar, 2
    Excel, 32
Titles, 130
Titles command (Insert menu), 181, 185
TODAY function, 41, 52
Toolbar buttons, 34
Toolbar shortcut menu, 117
Toolbars, 32, 33
    displaying and hiding, 117
Toolbars command (View menu), 116, 117
ToolTips, 34
Tree pane (Directory window), 17
TrueType fonts, 88, 89

U
Underline button (Formatting toolbar), 90
Undo command (Edit menu), 65
Unfreeze Panes command (Window menu), 126
Unfreezing rows and columns, 126
Ungrouping worksheets, 146
Unlocking cells and objects, 222
Unprotect Workbook command (Protection submenu, Tools menu), 223
Unprotect Worksheet command (Protection submenu, Tools menu), 221

V
Vertical page breaks, 131
Vertical scroll bar, 6
Vertical split box, 119
View, 116, 127
View defaults, 216
View Manager, 127
View Manager command (View menu), 116, 127
View menu, 116
View tab (Options dialog box), 216
Viewing multiple areas of a worksheet, 119

W
Wildcard specification, 18
Window, 2-6
    splitting into panes, 119
Window menu, 66
Windows
    exiting, 7
    starting, 2
Windows 3.0, 1
Windows 3.1, 1
Windows 95, 1, 25-26
Workbook, 32
    closing, 58
    opening, 59, 161
    saving, 57
    starting, 60
Workbook controls for working with multiple worksheets, 144
Workbook file protection, 224
Workbook name command (Window menu), 66, 161
Workbook protection, 223
Workbook window, 3, 32
Working directory, 219
Worksheet, 32
    adding, 147
    copying, 156-157, 164
    deleting, 147
    grouping, 146
    hiding, 158
    moving, 156-157, 164
    previewing, 105
    printing, 56, 153
    revealing, 158
    ungrouping, 146
Worksheet command (Insert menu), 147
Worksheet frame, 32
Worksheet name, 145
Worksheet protection, 221
Wrapping text, 100
Write reservation password, 224

X, Y, Z
X-axis, 171
Y-axis, 171
Zoom command (View menu), 116, 118
Zoom Control list (Standard toolbar), 118
Zooming the display, 118

3-D chart, 170
3-D reference, 152, 153
3-D View command (Format menu), 181

* wildcard, 18

With this NEW book, you can master the complications of Excel's list (database) features in just a couple of hours

Excel 5 for Windows:

How to work with lists, pivot tables, & external databases

by Anne Prince

Contents

- How to set up a list and use filters and forms
- How to sort and summarize the data in a list
- How to use pivot tables
- How to use Microsoft Query to import data from an external database

Every Monday, John enters the previous week's sales at his PC so he can work with the figures using Excel. He could save half an hour by downloading the numbers instead (his PC is networked to the corporate Access database where the sales are kept). But he doesn't know how.

As the Appendix in this *Pro* book points out, the Excel features you'll probably want to learn about next are the features for handling databases, or *lists*. So Anne Prince covers all you need to know in this short book.

In about two hours, you'll learn how to: create lists within Excel...use Microsoft Query, a program that comes with Excel, to import data from an external database (like an Access, dBase, or Oracle database) into an Excel list...use the sort feature, filters, and forms to organize, analyze, and update selected list data...use pivot tables to summarize list data with just a few clicks of the mouse. And all the information is presented just like it is in this *Pro* book, with plenty of examples and practice exercises.

So keep building on your professional Excel skills. To work easily with database data, get this book on Excel's list features TODAY.

4 chapters, 60 pages (49 with illustrations or exercises), **$11.95**

ISBN 0-911625-87-9

"This book includes virtually anything that anybody wants to know about this most versatile spreadsheet program....."

—Jerry Haberkost, PC Users Group of South Jersey

The Essential Guide: Excel 5 for Windows

by Anne Prince

You'll find these advanced features (see the Appendix in this *Pro* book for more details):

- More about charting
- Drawing
- The analytical tools, Goal Seek and Solver
- Auditing a worksheet
- Scenario Manager
- Using macros
- OLE

Do you want to know how to use some of the other Excel features listed in the Appendix, besides the list features? If so, this *Essential Guide* is the quick, comprehensive reference you need.

With the exception of Visual Basic (a programming tool), the *Essential Guide* covers every feature of Excel from beginning to advanced in the same practical, job-oriented way that this *Pro* book does. To make it an efficient reference, author Anne Prince has divided the content into 24 task-oriented chapters in 5 sections, with subheads that make it easy to find what you're looking for. She's also illustrated every feature, putting all the information you need in the figures. That means you can often start using a new feature without even reading the text. And you can look up forgotten details about any feature in just a moment or two.

As one customer put it: "Anne Prince has respect for her readers. The structure and content of the book prove this beyond doubt. If you use Excel 5, this book belongs in your library. Buy it!"

24 chapters, 497 pages, 295 illustrations, **$25.00**

ISBN 0-911625-79-8

Order/Comment Form

Your opinions count

If you have any comments, criticisms, or suggestions for us, I'm eager to get them. Your opinions today will affect our products of tomorrow. And if you find any errors in this book, typographical or otherwise, please point them out so we can correct them in the next printing. Thanks for your help.

Book title: *Work Like a Pro with Excel 5 for Windows*

Dear Mike:

_____
_____
_____
_____
_____
_____
_____
_____
_____
_____
_____
_____

Our Ironclad Guarantee
To our customers who order directly from us: You must be satisfied. Our books must work for you, or you can send them back for a full refund...no questions asked.

Name (& Title, if any) _____
Company (if company address) _____
Street address _____
City, State, Zip _____
Phone number (including area code) _____
Fax number (if you fax your order to us) _____

Qty	Product code and title	*Price
____	LWIN The Least You Need to Know about Windows 3.1	$20.00
____	PREX Work Like a Pro with Excel 5 for Windows	20.00
____	EXLS Excel 5: How to work with lists, pivot tables, & external databases	11.95
____	EEX5 The Essential Guide: Excel 5 for Windows	25.00
____	PRMW Work Like a Pro with Word 6 for Windows	20.00
____	MWMM Word 6: How to use the Mail Merge feature	9.95
____	MWW6 The Essential Guide: Word 6 for Windows	25.00
____	WPW6 The Essential Guide: WordPerfect 6 for Windows	25.00
____	ELW4 The Essential Guide: 1-2-3 for Windows Release 4	20.00

To order more quickly,

Call toll-free 1-800-221-5528
(Weekdays, 8 to 5 Pacific Time)
Fax: 1-209-275-9035

Mike Murach & Associates, Inc.
4697 West Jacquelyn Avenue
Fresno, California 93722-6427
(209) 275-3335

☐ Bill me for the books plus UPS shipping and handling (and sales tax within CA).

☐ Bill my company. P.O.# _____

☐ I want to **SAVE 10%** by paying in advance.
   Charge to my ____Visa ____MasterCard ____American Express:
   Card number _____
   Valid thru (mo/yr) _____
   Cardowner's signature _____

☐ I want to **SAVE 10% plus shipping and handling**. Here's my check for the books minus 10% ($_____). California residents, please add sales tax to your total. (Offer valid in U.S.)

*Prices are subject to change. Please call for current prices.

BUSINESS REPLY MAIL
FIRST-CLASS MAIL   PERMIT NO. 3063   FRESNO, CA

POSTAGE WILL BE PAID BY ADDRESSEE

Mike Murach & Associates, Inc.
4697 W JACQUELYN AVE
FRESNO CA 93722-9888

NO POSTAGE
NECESSARY
IF MAILED
IN THE
UNITED STATES